CEN

Russian Literature Since the Revolution

D0973595

Russian Literature
Since the Revolution

EDWARD J. BROWN

Collier Books

Collier-Macmillan Ltd., LONDON

Library of Congress Catalog Card Number: 69-12748

A Collier Books Original

First Edition 1963
Revised Edition 1969

The Macmillan Company
Collier-Macmillan Canada Ltd., Toronto, Ontario

Printed in the United States of America

Editor's Preface

THE REMARKABLE change in Russia's international position
since the Second World War has brought forth an unprecedented demand for information about all aspects of the land
of the Soviets. The press, radio, and television deal with
current developments, but by their very nature they can provide only casual glimpses of the factors essential to an understanding of Soviet policies and of the peculiar twists of Russian
events. Russia, moreover, is a vast, ancient, and fascinating
country, and although her cultural achievements do not go
much farther back than to the end of the eighteenth or the
beginning of the nineteenth century, there is much about
Russia that an informed person might like to know even if the
Soviets had not arrived at their present sinister prominence.

Countless elements shape the life and policies of a nation,
and the more we know about Russia's past and present, the
better are our chances to comprehend her correctly. It is a
notable and regrettable fact that until quite recently Russian
studies were largely neglected in the West. A generation ago,
interest in Russia was limited to a relatively small group of
specialists and intellectuals; today there is a widespread and
mounting demand for authoritative, dependable, and clearly
presented information on tsarist Russia and the USSR. There
are numerous books in English, some of them excellent, on the
various aspects of the Russian scene, but other aspects have
been left unexplored or call for fresh consideration.

The Russian Civilization Series of Collier Books, which
deals with both the prerevolutionary and the Soviet periods,
is designed to meet, in part, this need. Each volume is written especially for Collier Books by a specialist in his field.
The studies endeavor to maintain high levels of scholarship

5

without being too technical and to present the information in an attractive and readable style. Each volume is complete in itself and can be used independently of the others in the Series. Original works of distinction, which might formerly have been accessible to only a few, are now available to anyone who wishes to own them: the modest price of the Collier Books brings them within the reach of a wide public— with no sacrifice of scientific and literary standards.

The present volume comes from the pen of an eminent authority on Russian literature, Dr. Edward J. Brown, Professor of Russian at Brown University, Providence, Rhode Island. This distinguished and brilliantly written study presents a comprehensive and informative survey of the Russian literary scene from the inception of the Soviet regime to the present day. Simultaneously—and this is the main theme of the book —it examines, illuminates, and makes intelligible the basic and seemingly insoluble conflict between the immutable official dogma which permeates every phase of Soviet life, and that urge for untrammeled self-expression which no thinking human being can renounce without suffering grievous degradation. Dr. Brown is completely at ease in his subject. Every period in the evolution of Soviet letters, every major author, and quite a few of the less well known Russian literary figures are sharply outlined with a wealth of often unfamiliar details and a notable economy of means. The book is entirely up to date. In Chapters 11 and 12 Dr. Brown discusses with his customary insight the remarkable cases of Ehrenburg and Pasternak and elucidates what he terms the first, second, and third ("new") "thaw" of the 1950's and the early 1960's. He sees clearly the problems facing Russian authors and is both objective and understanding. He notes that a speech delivered by Khrushchev before a literary congress in 1959 and "studded with proverbial wisdom, and cheerful ignorance of all literature . . . contained a crudely dogmatic statement of the Party's demand for ideological support from the writers, and betrayed no sympathy for their recent examination of conscience." This attitude has been maintained since.

In the new Chapter 13 written for this revised edition Dr. Brown presents a detailed, vivid account of the principal literary developments of the 1960's, especially since Khrushchev's fall in October, 1964: the Fourth Congress of the Soviet Writers' Union (1967), which, unlike its predecessors, was characterized by "a dead calm at all the sessions"; the "cruel struggle" for freedom in literature; the work of authors, some of them little known, whose writings appeared abroad; the tragic case of Sinyavsky and Daniel. Curiously, in spite of the strict adherence to the principles of socialist realism, several important literary works written in the 1920's and the 1930's were permitted to appear in print in the 1960's, after a delay of two or three decades. A sympathetic and understanding critic, Dr. Brown notes nevertheless that "by comparison with the experimentation that dominates literary life in the West, Soviet prose of the sixties is conventional in form and thematically tame." Better things could be expected "should the party control loosen its hold."

In a subtle note on Russian *émigré* literature Dr. Brown comments, among other things, on Vladimir Nabokov's "essential Russianness," an observation based on an imaginative analysis of the literary style of the author of *Lolita*.

It is safe to say that those interested in Russian literature and in the working of the Soviet system, whether laymen or advanced students, will find Dr. Brown's volume exciting and rewarding.

MICHAEL T. FLORINSKY
General Editor
Russian Civilization Series

October, 1968
Vevey, Switzerland

Acknowledgments

ACKNOWLEDGMENT is made to the publishers for permission to use excerpts from the following translations: *We,* translated by Gregory Zilboorg, E. P. Dutton; *The Wayward Comrade and the Commissars,* translated by Andrew R. Mac-Andrew, Signet; "Reminiscences of Babel," translated by Patricia Blake, *Partisan Review; Chocolate,* translated by Charles Malamuth, Doubleday, Doran; *The Silent Don,* translated by Stephen Garry, A. A. Knopf; *Not by Bread Alone,* translated by Edith Bone, E. P. Dutton; *Safe Conduct,* New Directions; *Doctor Zhivago,* translated by Max Hayward, Pantheon; *The Year of Protest,* translated by McLean and Vickery, Random House. With the exceptions noted here, all of the translations from Russian in this book were made by the author, and in every case the translation has been carefully compared with the original Russian work.

Contents

Russian Literature Since the Revolution

Introduction: Literature and the Political Problem

To LINK politics and literature in speaking of contemporary Russia is a natural procedure. All forms of literature are quite frankly and directly used by the Soviet government for political purposes; the possibility of a work of art without political commitment or social involvement is not officially admitted. One cannot imagine a Soviet writer producing, for instance, the novel *Lolita,* which is the work of a Russian writer of the emigration; but if in some strange way such a novel should have come to light inside Russia, it would have been an intensely political document, a defiance of ideological requirement in the name of love, yes, even of perverted love; it would almost certainly have been intended as a ringing statement in favor of civilized literary pornography against the stifling puritanical demands of official critics. It would have become a political *cause célèbre.* And Pasternak's *Doctor Zhivago,* a novel about a "thinker, poet, and philosophical seeker," a nonpolitical novel, indeed an antipolitical novel, a novel by a poet in a poet's language, became, in the paradoxical nature of things, the most courageous political document of the last forty years. No piece of literature produced in the Soviet Union can escape involvement with politics.

The most pervasive and characteristic concern of Russian literature since the Revolution has been the paramount political problem: the fate of the individual human being in a mass society. This theme is a familiar one in the West; it is perhaps the main preoccupation of twentieth-century literature as a whole; it is our own theme. There should be no occasion for surprise if Soviet writers too, in those intervals when they have been to some extent free of official tutelage, concern themselves with the individual, with the problem of freedom

17

and responsibility, with the relationship of each separate unit of humanity to the sum total—call it the collective, the broad masses, the organization, the society, or the group. This is what Russian writers, whether Party or non-Party, pro- or anti-regime, are concerned with. The theme is recurrent and inescapable; it appears in the earliest things written on the day after the Revolution; it is the basic concern of *Doctor Zhivago* and of some of the most recent and controversial Soviet writing.

The present study is not offered as a complete and detailed history of Russian literature since the Revolution; nor is it concerned with the relationship of literature to the Soviet dictatorship. It is, rather, a search for the theme of the individual human being as developed by the finest writers of the period in their major work. It will soon become evident that Russian literature in the modern period offers a rich variety of literary situations the underlying theme of which is the tragic one of the individual person who resists the implacable pull of the "swarm life," or, as a Soviet critic would express it, "who is out of tune with history."

As we trace this theme through almost a half century of literary history it is possible to see meaningful patterns of development in what might otherwise seem an accidental miscellany of historical facts; and we may even be able to construct a working hypothesis to explain the behavior of Soviet writers and perhaps give some basis for a tentative forecast of future events. To give one example of many that might be offered: During the decade of the twenties there were in the Soviet Union a wide variety of literary schools, each with its own "theory" of literature. One faction emphasized the primary importance of intuition in the literary process; another held that the writer is psychologically conditioned by his class environment and cannot produce artistic images on demand; a third group favored factual reporting exclusively, free of ideology or invention; a fourth abjured purpose and ideology in favor of the free play of the imagination; a fifth held that literature is a craft, the tricks and devices of which can be learned by anyone, regardless of class origin or political orientation; and there were still other variations on these main ideas, of which no detailed and adequate treatment now exists. It would not be very helpful simply to list the various literary schools and painstakingly describe the tenets of each. The *meaning* of the great literary debate does not appear at all until it is shown that each group in its own way is seeking to escape the crudely utilitarian demands of the state, whose "theory of literature" threatened the existence of them all. For one of the tenets held in common by almost all the working writers of the twenties was that literature is the product of individual and free responses to the data of experience. Because such responses are autonomous and unpredictable, the state, looking upon writers with justified apprehension, sought to direct their work into useful and "good" channels. Russian writers during the Soviet period have often resisted, or nullified, or evaded this crude guidance. Alongside the official writing, which celebrates in pious numbers the new life, the new man, and the socialist future, there has always been another literature sounding a discordant note and calling in question the values of the totalitarian state. The two kinds of "Soviet literature," taken together, are a vital commentary on the dilemma which faces the writer who must live in a society and yet be to some extent free of it.

This book is intended to throw light on the nature of the dilemma and to examine the behavior of sensitive human beings who have faced it in its sharpest and most terrible form. We shall see how Russian writers have dealt with the basic political problem, and in what ways they have solved, ignored, or evaded it. We shall examine the kind of human situation those writers were drawn to portray, and we shall see how the exigencies of time and the state formed and shaped their writing.

Chapter 1 presents a concise account of Russian literary history from 1917 to the present. The intention is to provide the reader with the necessary framework for an understanding of the authors and works that will be discussed in detail throughout the book.

Chapter 1

Since 1917: A Brief History

"Soviet" Literature

BECAUSE THE TERM "Soviet literature" has no exact meaning and is charged with political connotation, it will be used sparingly in this book. In the Soviet Union the term is taken to mean all the literature produced since the Revolution, including that written in the languages of the Union republics. Excluded from the category of "truly" Soviet, however, are those writers whose work is alien to Soviet ideology, though their work may have been written and even published in the Soviet Union. Outside the Soviet Union little or no attention is paid to literature in languages other than Russian, and therefore the term "Soviet" loses much of its meaning. Non-Soviet critics, moreover, are reluctant to place under the rubric "Soviet" those writers whom the Soviets claim but who seem to be more closely bound to Western democratic habits and attitudes—Blok and Pasternak, for instance. We shall be concerned here not so much with the propagandist and Party-oriented literature, which the term "Soviet" suggests to the Western mind, nor with the voluminous literature written in the many languages of the non-Russian republics, but primarily with that Russian literature which has inherited the great tradition of Tolstoy and Dostoevsky.

The term "Soviet" suggests a break at the year 1917 in the continuing tradition of Russian literature. The break in continuity was neither abrupt nor complete, but it was real. The Bolshevik revolution brought about radical changes in the literary world, and while the transformation of the Russian writer was painful and slow, the new regime made an effort from the start to change the writer's attitude toward his work. The literature created during the nineteenth century by highly individualistic intellectuals, who were independent and often rebellious against authority, was gradually to be replaced by "Soviet literature," produced by "Soviet" intellectuals, who, finding inspiration and purpose in the collective, would be firmly tied to the aims of the state. In this historical sense the term "Soviet" as applied to certain literary phenomena has real meaning. But the regime has had only indifferent success in educating a new kind of writer, and the results of complex interaction between old tradition and new ideas were not always the expected and predicted ones.

Persistence of the Past

During the first years of the Soviet period, and especially after the liberalization signalized by Lenin's New Economic Policy (NEP), which was introduced in 1921, the Russian literary world might have appeared basically unchanged to a casual observer. It is true that many of the leading writers had emigrated; but the majority had not, and Russian literature during the twenties presented a motley spectacle in which prerevolutionary literary figures and styles still dominated the scene, often disguised in proletarian garb. The literary manner of the symbolists Bely and Remizov was imitated, perhaps unconsciously, by the young proletarian novelist Libedinsky. Proletarian poets celebrated the cosmic sweep of their revolution in poetic rhythms that suggest the work of symbolist aesthetes. The most important figures in the prewar symbolist movement, Alexander Blok and Valery Bryusov, lectured on the techniques of poetic composition in "literary studios" set up by the Proletarian Cultural and Educational Organization in 1918. The Russian Futurists, a brashly iconoclastic group before the revolution, placed their exuberant nihilism at the service of the revolutionary government. When the novel was revived in the middle twenties, its principal artificers consciously followed the paths laid down in the late nineteenth century by Gorky and the realistic school, or else, departing from realism and social content, experimented with the medium in the manner of the prewar moderns.

The persistence of the past was even more striking in the area of literary habits and attitudes. A conscious effort was made to preserve the independence and individualism of the writer and artist—to maintain, in other words, the literary profession as an activity independent of state control. The Soviet government, in the person of its Commissar for Education, Lunacharsky, discouraged the eager efforts of the Futurists and of proletarian literary groups to set up a kind of art dictatorship. As Russia recovered from war and revolution, a degree of private enterprise was readmitted in the literary field as well as in other areas of life. Cooperative and even private publishing houses were organized to satisfy a growing and heterodox demand for literature. Tales of revolutionary heroism appeared in the bookstores alongside works on religion, essays on Kantian philosophy, and translations of the novels of Edgar Wallace and Fanny Hurst. Russian writers maintained lively contacts with the European literary world, contacts which were not only cultural but commercial. Many works published during the middle twenties bear a double imprint, such as "Berlin-Petrograd," indicating that the work was published under contract to a Western publisher. Travel to Western Europe by Russian writers was frequent and to a degree informal. Ehrenburg lived alternately in Paris and Moscow, and Babel had lively and prolonged intercourse with French intellectual circles. Pilnyak made frequent journeys to the West, and Zamyatin's novel *We* was originally published, under contract, in English translation. The policy of forbearance in the literary field, effected in practice since 1921, was solemnly affirmed after a violent debate within the Party. In July, 1925, a resolution of the Central Committee was published, entitled "On the Policy of the Party in the Field of Belles-Lettres," which announced the liberal doctrine in severely dogmatic terms.

As a result of that liberal policy the years from 1921 to 1932 saw the growth of a literature in Russia which is thoroughly congenial to the taste of Western intellectuals. The astonishing variety and high quality of that literature is not generally realized. It is true that much of it reads like the testament of a few men who have survived a general disaster and are still severely shaken and suffering from emotional displacement. In their best works they treat problems that agitate Western human beings in the twentieth century, particularly the problem of sudden and catastrophic social change. In form and style the literature of the twenties is sometimes traditionally realistic but more often given to highly sophisticated formal device. Literary criticism, far from being confined to the repetition of sociological formulas, is daring and original, and the so-called Formalist school of critics, with their interest in literary structure and method, have a distinct relationship to American "New Criticism." Indeed surface appearances suggest a literary evolution in Russia along paths analogous to those traveled by other European literatures.

Fellow Travelers

Perhaps the most striking example offered by the Russian intelligentsia of their persistent attachment to individualistic attitudes was the group which called itself the Serapion Brotherhood, whose one tenet was that the group as such held no tenets in common, but that each member might have views on politics and literature that differed somewhat from those of all other members. Literature, they felt, should be created by individuals free of ideological control. Each member of the Brotherhood had his own ideology and, figuratively speaking, lived in his own cottage, which he "painted according to his own taste."

The Serapion Brotherhood was named for a character in one of E. T. A. Hoffmann's *Tales*, who believed that his personal poetic intuition provided a true vision of reality. The Brotherhood included some of the leading figures in Russian literature of the twenties, many of whom are still regarded highly in the Soviet Union. They were all in their early twenties when they published, in 1921, "manifestoes" and "platforms" which were in ironic parody of the ringing literary pronouncements delivered in all seriousness by other literary groups. Perhaps the most prominent and influential of the Serapions was Eugene Zamyatin, whose novel *We* (1920) anticipated both Huxley's *Brave New World* and Orwell's *1984*. Michael Zoshchenko was an eccentric genius who wrote short sketches in which the characters are grotesque human fauna, described and commented upon with a whimsy born of despair. Boris Pilnyak wrote a number of stories and novels which present, using the most modern devices of form and symbol, vexed scenes from the period of the Civil War. Konstantin Fedin, in *Cities and Years* and other works, deals with the problem of the intellectual at odds with himself and with his time. Venyamin Kaverin in *Artist Unknown* (1931) develops the theme of the artist's requirement of freedom. Many writers not formally connected with the Serapions were close to them in outlook. Leonid Leonov's *The Thief* (1927), a novel of sophisticated and complex structure, explores the psychology of a disillusioned revolutionary. Yury Olesha's *Envy* (1927) presents in expressionistic style the conflict between a fanciful poet and a Babbitt of the new order. Isaac Babel's highly subjective apperception of the Civil War, *Red Cavalry* (1926), transmutes scenes of blood and violence into exotic ornamental prose. Valentin Katayev's *The Embezzlers* (1927), relating the travels through Russia of a pair of absconding and inebriate officials, is an experiment in the representation of reality as refracted through an alcoholic haze.

The writers whose major work we have mentioned briefly, those who came to be known as "fellow travelers" (a name supplied for them by Trotsky), seem to have been the direct heirs of the nineteenth-century literary tradition, and their work deals precisely with the problem of the intellectual confronted with a new and alien world. The list we have given is only a partial one; other writers of a similar cast of mind and other works of those we have mentioned will be analyzed later. While their work as a whole is concerned with the aftermath of revolution and civil war, it should be stressed that they were interested in many other things. Human sexual behavior in particular concerned them, and they presented scenes of love as well as of violence with frank interest.

Proletarians

Alongside the so-called fellow travelers were the variegated groups which considered themselves "proletarian." They claimed to orient their work on the "masses" and to eschew both individualism and effete modernism. They did not form a cohesive whole but were broken up into many factions. The poets of the Smithy and the Cosmos, two organizations of proletarian writers, composed stirring hymns to the iron-willed proletarian collective, wherein no individual hero can be discerned. Alexander Serafimovich, a realist of the Gorky school, wrote a novel called *The Iron Flood* (1924), in which the focus of narrative attention is the mass movement of an army, its wives and children, and all its provisions and possessions. Dmitry Furmanov gained fame with his novel *Chapayev* (1923), which he claimed was not a novel at all but a sober record of peasant guerrilla operations under a leader whose role it was, simply, to direct the heroic mass.

Yet the collective hero did not always meet with favor among the proletarians, and even they tended to abandon sober realism in favor of stylized narrative or verbal ornament. We have already seen that the proletarian poets were in debt to the symbolists. Serafimovich at times describes the relentless march of his iron men in prose that bears more than a suggestion of Bely, and Furmanov's purely factual manner of narration is in itself a kind of literary device, employed characteristically by certain Futurist prose writers. But the rock on which proletarian unity broke was the stubborn problem of how the individual human being should be portrayed in relation to the "masses."

The earliest novel written in the proletarian milieu was Yury Libedinsky's *A Week* (1922), which sketches in sharp and cruel detail a peasant revolt against Communist rule. The violence directed at them is experienced by the reader from the viewpoint of the individual Communists themselves, each one of whom is shaken inwardly. The "masses" exist in Libedinsky's story only as a hostile element in which the individual Communists find themselves and which threatens them with destruction. The focus on individual psychology in this novel, and the absence of a healthy and heroic collective, was regarded at the time of its publication and is still regarded as a fault. Yet the proletarians continued to explore the complex experiences of the separate human beings who made up the "masses." Alexander Fadeyev's *The Nineteen* (1927) examines the varieties of individual reaction to strain in a small band of Communist guerrillas operating in the Far East. Sergey Semyonov's *Natalya Tarpova* (1927) analyzes the inner struggle of a supposedly dedicated Communist woman who falls in love with a "bourgeois." Vladimir Bakhmetev's *Crime of Martin Baimakov* (1928) is a clinical dissection of the self-doubt and guilt felt by a young man who, like Conrad's Lord Jim, fails of courage in a crisis.

Much of the work of the proletarian novelists of the twenties was concerned with psychological realism, and the problems involved in remaking the world are reflected through the prism of the individual mind. The official "Creative Platform" of the Association of Proletarian Writers urged upon its members the necessity to "show forth the complex human psyche, with all its contradictions, elements of the past and seeds of the future, both conscious and subconscious." And proletarian writers, in their exploration of the inner recesses of individual minds, found doubt, struggle, and perplexity. The romantic revolutionary poetry of the Smithy and the Cosmos and the prose of Serafimovich fell into disfavor even with proletarian writers. The work of Mikhail Sholokhov represents the best product of the proletarian milieu. In his *The Silent Don* (1928–40), no doubt the most famous of Soviet novels, Sholokhov constructed a complex and realistic panorama of the revolutionary period with its clash of ideologies and parties; but his hero, Gregor Melekhov, is an individualist who belongs to no party. From the viewpoint of official criticism, that was Gregor's tragedy: he was "divorced from the masses."

The Stalinists

Russian writers of the twenties—proletarians, fellow travelers, and others—were in the great majority concerned with exploring the strain and conflict experienced by individual human beings in adjusting to the demands of the "collective," or, in Tolstoy's phrase, the "swarm life." The literary world itself mirrored this persistent individualism in the multiplicity of distinct and separate literary groups which it proliferated. There is as yet no adequate study of this peculiarly Russian phenomenon. There is not even a catalog of the literary or-

ganizations and literary groups, and the fractions and cau-
cuses within the literary groups and ephemeral grouplets
which variegated the literary scene, consuming vast quantities
of precious paper with their creative effort and their bitter
and prolonged polemics. The groups increased and multiplied as the result of a conscious policy of the Communist
Party under the guidance of Nikolai Bukharin, a powerful
political figure of the twenties. He maintained that in the
literary field there should be no attempt to hold everyone
in a rigid mold, but that "anarchic competition" should be
encouraged and no artificial restraints should be placed upon
the competing individuals and groups. There were, of course,
some limits: any "group" openly announcing anti-Communist
views would certainly have suffered restraint; but there were
none of those.

We have already mentioned the Smithy, where poems of
iron were heated with the ardor of the Revolution, though
they were shaped with the tools of the symbolists, and the
Cosmos, whose writers cultivated a mystique of interplanetary
revolution, a mixture of science-fantasy and pseudo-religious
elation. Both of these groups issued from the Proletcult, or
Proletarian Cultural and Educational Organization, whose
raison d'être was the creation of a new proletarian literature
through the intensive training in "litstudios" of new working-
class writing cadres. The Futurists, who had been horrifying
the bourgeois since 1912 with the publication of their manifesto, "The Slap in the Face to Public Taste," had split into
Ego-Futurists and Cubo-Futurists. Under the leadership of
Mayakovsky, the Futurists formed the Left Front of Art, in
whose magazine *Lef* the Futurist poets themselves and their
avant-garde allies published some of the most original literary
work of the period. The Constructivists were a small group,
for the most part poets, related to the Futurists though at
odds with them, who stressed in their poetry the conscious
planning of literary work and the "loading" of the literary
vocabulary with the latest scientific and technical connotations. Among the groups of poets, the Imagists and Acmeists,
in their brief period, also left a distinct mark on the Soviet
literary world—Sergey Yesenin and Anna Akhmatova, both

poets of subjective experience, have always been popular in spite of official frowns.

The group called Pereval (The Divide), which we shall later treat at length, was composed for the most part of young Communists who had rejected the proletarian stereotypes and who portrayed the contemporary scene in city and village in stories of a harsh but sympathetic realism. The Russian Association of Proletarian Writers (RAPP), which presumed to speak for the Party in literary affairs, was itself split into several factions engaged in lethal politico-literary dispute.

In addition to these more important groups and organizations there were such grouplets as the Luminists, the VOKP (All-Union Organization of Peasant Writers), and the "nihil-" ists or *nichevoki,* who wrote nothing at all; and at last the Serapion Brotherhood, already mentioned, who condemned the whole idea of literary organization.

The season, as we now know, was a brief Indian summer in which flourished values that belonged, essentially, to an earlier culture. The new men who grew into authority under Stalin found that in the area of literature there was neither discipline nor purpose. They regarded with contempt writing that seemed to them "difficult" or "decadent." They evidenced a visceral suspicion of the endless and many-faceted polemic over literary themes and literary styles and over literary theory which divided even Communist writers from one another. When the first Five-Year Plan was adopted in 1928 all forces were mobilized behind it, and there is ample documentary evidence to show that no exception was made for the forces of literature. Ultimately there was to be no escape for the writer from social tasks. Party newspapers, beginning in 1929, carried editorial articles calling for a "consolidation of forces" in literature and for the application of literary talent to celebrating the achievements, real or projected, of the Plan. There appeared in *Pravda* and other papers a series of ignorant, oppressive attacks on the errors of specific "groups," and the groups, sensitive to the new situation, recanted or modified their views. Gradually the amount of variation on the literary front was greatly reduced.

After 1929, when Bukharin fell from power (Trotsky was already in exile), a new kind of organization man intruded himself on Russian intellectual life.

What manner of men were the Stalinists who dealt so rudely with the limited intellectual freedom that existed in the twenties? What motives drove them? The chief among them was Lazar Kaganovich, a member of the Politburo and an intimate of Stalin, who believed that literary men should match the achievements of labor by producing works of literature describing and celebrating great industrial projects. The poet Alexey Surkov was a passionate hater of every deviation from a political line that seemed to him true and straight, and his interest in literature was strictly secondary. Pavel Yudin was a Marxist philosopher who abjured all doubt or discussion as to the correctness of philosophical views that he found in the works of Lenin and Stalin, and who burrowed in the writings of his opponents only to find there passages which, quoted out of context, betrayed the presence or the influence of heresy. In the writings of many literary critics he found evidence of Kantian, Jungian, Bergsonian, Freudian, and of course Trotskyite infiltration, and all of this seemed to him the work of hostile forces. L. Mekhlis, secretary of the editorial board of *Pravda* in 1931 and a potent Stalinist, honored many times for his labors in peace and his heroism in war, believed that the failure of literature to reflect adequately the great issues of the day was due either to lack of planning in the literary organizations or to the excessive interest of writers in individual psychology. These men were among the leaders in the movement for a "consolidation of forces" in literature which ultimately led, in 1932, to the liquidation by Party directive of all autonomous literary organizations and the enforced membership of all Russian writers in a Union of Soviet Writers under the direct auspices of the Party. With the First Congress of Soviet Writers in 1934 the Union of Writers became a fact and the Stalinist period was launched. According to the Constitution of that Union all of its members must "accept the program of the Communist Party . . . and strive to participate in socialist construction."

The state under Stalin used writers as its instruments of education and propaganda. Many of those whose reputations had been made in the twenties and earlier conformed to the new demands and produced educational fiction on topical themes. Leonov described the building of a paper plant in the far north; Sholokhov turned out a novel on the collectivization of agriculture; Katayev devoted his considerable talents to the production of a novel about the building of a steel plant at Magnitogorsk; Zoshchenko, always an artist of paradox, wrote of a criminal's rehabilitation in the work camps of the Security Police; Pilnyak took for his topic the creation of a great dam and hydroelectric station as did Marietta Shaginyan, who urged upon her comrades the poetic power of just such themes:

Perhaps you will raise the objection that the material you are rejecting [the theme of the national economy] is not and cannot become the object of art, that "economic problems" cannot be celebrated in song or immortalized in art? You are mistaken. You are frightfully mistaken. That is a banal and stupid mistake, an unforgivable mistake. . . . The poet Blok called upon all of us to "hear the music of the Revolution." The real music is only beginning now: listen to it, comrades! Because the real music of the Revolution is socialist construction!

During the period of Stalin a number of works were written explicitly to inspire Communist ideals in the young. These works, which do not recommend themselves to the sophisticated literary taste, have circulated in the Soviet Union in millions of copies, and are widely and approvingly read by young people wherever the Soviet system reaches. Nikolai Ostrovsky's *The Making of a Hero* (1934) is the story of a poor boy who joins the underground, and overcoming obstacles of poverty, crippling wounds, and poor education, in the end realizes his ambition to carry on the fight as a writer. Boris Polevoy's *The Story of a Real Man* (1946) relates the saga of a Soviet aviator who is shot down by the Germans and though crippled by the loss of both feet, insists on returning, equipped with artificial limbs, to active air duty. Anton Makarenko's *A Teacher's Epic* (1934) describes the education of homeless and ragged delinquents in a colony for way-ward boys. Works such as these, regarded with disdain by the literary critic, have had a profound effect wherever they are read by young and unformed minds.

A number of new writers now emerged who had been formed in the Soviet schools and whose work was patterned to fit the requirements of the day. Among these were Konstantin Simonov (1915——) whose war novel *Days and Nights* (1944) described the Battle of Stalingrad; Yury Krymov (1908–1941), the author of *Tanker Derbent* (1938), a skillfully contrived study of socialist competition in the transportation industry; N. Y. Virta (1906——), a novelist and dramatist who devised the theory of "conflictless" drama; and S. P. Babayevsky (1909——), whose *Cavalier of the Gold Star* (1947) tells of the developing sense of "collective" property on the land but is lacking in verisimilitude.

Two writers of the older generation, A. N. Tolstoy and Ilya Ehrenburg, who had emigrated and lived abroad for many years, returned and remained in Russia, becoming brilliantly successful practitioners of the new literary codex, and—it can be said without exaggeration—apologists for the Stalin regime. After his return Tolstoy completed his long novel *Road to Calvary* (1920–41), which deals explicitly with the problem of the intellectual and the revolution; and in 1937 he published a novel called *Bread,* which, Soviet authorities now insist, falsified history in order to enhance the figure of Stalin as the defender of Tsaritsin in 1918. His *Peter the First* (1929–45), on the other hand, is a masterful exercise in the genre of historical fiction.

Ilya Ehrenburg's *The Extraordinary Adventures of Julio Jurenito and His Disciples* (1922), in spite of its modernistic style and its flavor of Montparnasse, contains in the germ that quality of cynical nihilism toward the values of Western bourgeois society which he himself has expressed in his career as a Soviet writer. Yet he too has faced the problem of the sensitive intellectual's alienation from the new world of massed Petyas and Anyas, and in *Out of Chaos* (1933) explores the inner tribulations of such a one. And Ehrenburg has been prominently associated with the movement for liberalization in literature which followed the death of Stalin.

Socialist Realism

The official and obligatory "style" of Soviet literature under Stalin was "socialist realism." Much intellectual effort has been spent in a quest for the meaning of this term. Its genesis is a concrete study in the operation of the Stalinist mentality. How did it come into being? In the first place, "realism" in art had in the discussions of the late twenties been equated with materialism in philosophy, and thus received official sanction as correct for Marxist writers. But what kind of "realism" should be cultivated remained a problem. Psychological realism seemed to lead into the bypath of individual psychology. "Objective" realism sometimes revealed negative and repellent aspects of Soviet life which were not regarded as "typical." Critical realism exposed the faults of society but affirmed nothing. Naturalism paid attention to biological rather than social factors in human development. The "dialectical materialist method" in realism, supported by RAPP, was both vague and doctrinaire. It was discovered in 1932—no one knows by whom, but the inspiration was attributed to Stalin—that "realism" might be qualified by the term "socialist." And since the term socialist had a generally positive connotation but no meaning at all as applied to literature, the meaning of "socialist realism" could be worked out in practice and by directive, and would be, in the end, whatever the going authority said it was. The imposition of this meaningless authoritarian term on the consciousness of Soviet writers led to monotonous uniformity in the content and form of Russian literature during the Stalin period. Very few writers escaped its noxious effect. The confirmed and incorrigible individualists, the "heretics and dreamers," either fell silent or emigrated, and the production of literature tended to become an organized and disciplined effort whose social purposes far transcended the individual human being. The literary product of those years, even when technically competent, was lacking in individuality and creativity. The deterioration increased sharply after 1946, when Andrey Zhdanov, a political leader close to Stalin, became the Party spokesman in literature. The demand for tendentious works was expressed by him and his lieutenants in crude, direct terms, and the abuse of deviant writers reached incredible extremes of harshness.

The regimentation of literature affected all writers to some extent, but there were some who, because of the nature of their work, remained relatively free of pressure. A few of these should be mentioned. Mikhail Prishvin (1873–1954), whose earliest work long antedates the Revolution, is perhaps not fully appreciated even in the Soviet Union for the variety, interest, and power of his work, and he is little known elsewhere. His works are full of knowing observation of wood, field and stream, and they contain, along with the lore of nature, poetic and philosophic reflections at times reminiscent of Thoreau. His treatment of nature is never divorced from human activities, and he records ethnographic as well as natural information. Another writer of the older generation who continued in his own characteristic vein was A. S. Grin (Grinevski) (1880–1932), a writer of fantastic tales. Long passed over by the authorities because of his romanticism, he has in recent years been accorded a growing respect for his mastery of language and storytelling art. And finally, K. G. Paustovsky (1892–1968), a writer with a variety of thematic and stylistic turns, is a lover of nature and a recorder of the transformation of nature being wrought in modern times. Each of his works, he has said, is a journey to some area of the Soviet Union.

The Thaw

Uniformity of purpose and method, or at least the appearance of such uniformity, was ruthlessly enforced throughout the era of Stalin, as is now well known. However, the thirst for variety and individuality continued to exist under the bland surface. This became clear when, after the death of Stalin, the mild relaxation of controls known as the literary thaw occasioned an eruption of articles and books revealing the existence and asserting the rights of individual human beings with their own unique and particular feelings, thoughts, and responsibilities. Among the works which appeared were Dudintsev's *Not By Bread Alone* (1956), wherein the hero is an individual who, for the sake of an idea, separates himself from the Soviet "collective," and elects to travel a "lonely, austere path." The fact that his "original idea" is a new method for the centrifugal casting of large-diameter iron drainpipes is only a detail.

Additional evidence of the persistence of life behind the monumental façade of socialist realist literature is the continued popularity of poets such as Anna Akhmatova and Boris Pasternak. Anna Akhmatova's highly personal lyrics were republished in a new edition in 1940, and she herself reappeared at the Soviet Writers' Congress in 1954. Pasternak's deepest responses to life are out of tune with the society in which he lived. No edition of his poems appeared for over twenty years; yet his work was well known to the intel- which had never been published were passed from hand to hand, copied and recopied, and widely circulated. A new edition of his poems appeared in 1965 with an introduction by Andrey Sinyavsky. His poetry expresses particular, personal emotion in a strikingly original idiom. His novel, *Doctor Zhivago* (1956), written in the Soviet Union over a period of about twenty years, is a sensitive judgment on those years. It is the judgment of a poet and philosopher whose vision of the world was singular and arbitrary to the point of strangeness; and one who, moreover, did not allow his thought, or the poetic idiom whose shape his thought took, ever to become engaged with the vulgar practices of the state.

Eugene Zamyatin, author of the brilliant anti-utopia *We*, was commissioned in 1919 to write a kind of manifesto for a newspaper to be published by a group of Petrograd intellectuals who were trying to find their place in the new world. The newspaper was to be called *Tomorrow* and, though only a single issue appeared, it exuded hope and confidence in that "tomorrow."

Yesterday [wrote Zamyatin] there was a czar and there were slaves; today there is no czar, but there are still slaves; tomorrow there will be only czars. We are marching in the name of tomorrow's free man, the czar. We have lived through the epoch of the suppression of the masses; we are now living through the epoch of the suppression of the individual in the name of the masses; but *tomorrow* will bring the liberation of the individual in the name of humanity.

What will tomorrow bring to Russian literature? There is good reason to hope for a revival in it of a high degree of individualism, and there are facts which point to such a development at the present time. Today the journals continue to feature good and useful materials produced by disciplined writers with social ends in mind. But occasionally a new note is heard: Valentin Katayev's "The Holy Well"(1966),for instance, is a symbolic fantasy. And a number of young writers who are now appearing manage to publish excellent work though for the most part they ignore social themes. We will explore these fascinating and hopeful new developments in the last chapter of this study.

Chapter 2

Mayakovsky and the Left Front of Art

The Suicide Note

No OTHER POET of the twentieth century has been accorded as much honor as Vladimir Mayakovsky. He is the object of a kind of collective worship actively supported by the Soviet state. His apartment in a quiet Moscow side street (Mayakovsky Lane) is now a museum dedicated to the life and works of the poet. The former "Triumphal Square" in Moscow has been renamed Mayakovsky Square, and the "Metro" station bearing his name, finished in baroque ornament of rust-proof steel, features the fine head of the poet in giant dimensions. On the Square itself he stands solidly on a block of granite, a bronze statue, shoulders back and coat open, afraid of nothing.

Yet the poet's biography did not yield easily to mythographic treatment. He shot himself in 1930, a deed which so shocked his young literary admirers that some of them refused to believe it. One of these reported that when he received a telegram in the provinces informing him simply, "Mayakovsky has killed himself," dated April 14, 1930, he thought it an April fool joke, and explained the date as April *first*, Old Style.[1] But it was a fact that Mayakovsky had taken his own life in Moscow, leaving the following note:

To All of You:

Don't blame anyone for my death, and please don't gossip about it. The deceased hated gossip.

Mama, sisters, comrades, forgive me. This is not a good method (I don't recommend it to others), but for me there's no other way out.

Lily, love me.

Comrade Government, my family consists of Lily Brik, mama, my sisters, and Veronica Polonsky.

If you can provide a decent life for them, thank you.

The verses I have begun give to the Briks. They'll understand them.

As they say, "The incident is closed."

> Love boat
>   Smashed on convention.
> I don't owe life a thing
>   And there's no point
> In counting over
>   Mutual hurts,
>   harms,
>   and slights.

Best of Luck!

Vladimir Mayakovsky

4/12/30

Comrades of the Proletarian Literary Organization, don't think me a coward.

Really, it couldn't be helped.

Greetings!

Tell Yermilov it's too bad he removed the slogan; we should have had it out.

V. M.

In the desk drawer I have 2000 rubles. Use them to pay my taxes. The rest can be gotten from the State Publishing House.[2]

No doubt we should honor the wish of the deceased not to gossip about his deed. We shall not, therefore, speculate about the story that he played Russian roulette and lost, a story soberly reported as fact (and supported by Ilya Ehrenburg in his memoirs[3]), although, the shot having been fired in private, there could be no evidence to confirm it. A few footnotes to this last letter may serve as an illuminating introduction to Mayakovsky.

It is a model suicide note. There is not a scintilla of self-pity or self-accusation in it; neither is there any suggestion that others—the world, the government, his friends or enemies —bear any share of blame. Neither is "life" to blame, since the suicide, having paid his own debts, refuses to count over any that may be owed to him. Lily Brik, the wife of his colleague in the Left Front of Art, Osip Brik, who may have served as the motivation for the mock-sentimental lines about a "Love boat/Smashed on convention," was a woman he had loved for most of his life. She is included in his "family," and he seems quietly confident that his "Comrade Government" will take care of her and the others. There is no anger, even, at the literary bureaucrats who called themselves proletarian writers and with whom Mayakovsky during the last years of his life had carried on a violent polemic. The "slogan" referred to was one of many agitational verses with which the auditorium was decorated during the performance of his play *The Bath* (1930), an attack on the bureaucrats and other petty forms of life which we shall examine later. This slogan, which the proletarian literary leadership insisted upon having removed, was a personal attack on one of those leaders, V. Yermilov:

It isn't easy to clean out
  the bureaucratic swarm.
There aren't enough baths
  nor is there soap enough
And these bureaucrats
  Are given aid and comfort by critics
  Like Yermilov.

The reference to his proletarian comrades recalls his entrance into RAPP, the proletarian literary organization, just two months before his suicide. He held out until then before joining the disciplined writers' collective which had the Party's support. And when he did join under pressure, the leaders received him coldly as befitted a candidate whose tongue and pen had so often lashed them. A certain Comrade Sutyrin, long since forgotten, in a speech at the meeting when

Mayakovsky became a member of RAPP, served notice on him that "egoists" and "bohemian individualists" were not needed, and that the solid ranks of proletarian literature could do without people who "overvalued themselves." The busy writers of RAPP, concerned as they were with discipline, planning, and organization, always regarded Mayakovsky as a dubious ally. He had come to them from literary bohemia, and must, they said, overcome the petit-bourgeois individualist inside himself. The capitulation to RAPP which the Party exacted from Mayakovsky was no doubt the one single event that made his suicide, in one form or another, inevitable. "It couldn't be helped, comrades," he told them in his letter.

The lines "Love boat/Smashed on convention" have been translated and interpreted in many ways. The word *byt*, which we have translated as "convention," has sometimes been rendered as "mores," or the "grind of everyday life." It is a word Mayakovsky often used in his poetry, referring to the alien element of encrusted habit and custom in which human beings live. *Byt*, which means ingrained habit, social custom, hallowed prejudice, routine and regularity, the established pattern of life, was his personal enemy. The life he lived and the poetry he wrote were an effort to overcome for himself the social routine that channels and controls the lives of most men. When, as a boy of fifteen, he joined the Social-Democrats, Bolshevik faction, and carried on propaganda among bakers and printers, he was asserting, much more than any political doctrine, his own self, Vladimir Mayakovsky. His understanding of Marx was elementary, but the ideas of Marx threatened the rigidities of Russian life, and he, Mayakovsky, found the propagation of those ideas a perfect method of self-expression on a grand scale. Marx was one weapon against *byt*, and others were soon found.

While a student of painting he met the artist David Burlyuk, who managed to stand out from his background through arrogance of manner and foppishness of dress. It was Burlyuk who discovered that Mayakovsky was a poet and encouraged him, and Mayakovsky avers that Russian Futurism was born one night in Moscow when they both left a Rachmaninoff concert in boredom and disgust:

A Most Memorable Night. Conversation. From Rachmaninoff boredom to school boredom, from school boredom to whole range of classical boredom. David had the anger of a master who had outpaced his contemporaries, I, the fervor of a Socialist aware of the inevitable doom of the old. Russian Futurism was born.[4]

The Futurist movement was for Mayakovsky an effort to create for himself a "self" that was really his own. The notion that the poet "creates himself" is embedded in Mayakovsky's life as well as his writing. He created a physical image of himself which the eye of even the tired observer could not fail to see. In his travels around Russia in the company of other Futurists he wore a yellow blouse with black stripes, a frock coat, and a top hat. Too poor for dandyism, he managed to create new sartorial concepts out of old and obvious materials:

The Yellow Blouse. Never had a suit. Had two blouses—hideous-looking affairs. A tried method was to use a tie for decoration. No money. Took a piece of yellow ribbon from my sister. Tied it round my neck. Furor. So the most conspicuous and beautiful thing about a man was his tie. Evidently if you increased the size of the tie, you increased the furor. As there is a limit to the size of a tie, I had resort to cunning. I made a tie-shirt and shirt-tie. Impression—irresistible.[5]

His poetry was a struggle against literary *byt.* The poet's word in conventional style and setting might not be heard, just as the poet himself in bourgeois dress might not be seen. Therefore the poet must *shout* his lines. His characteristic poetic line is a metrical shout. His rhythm is the rhythm of shouted remarks. Each line is short, heavily accented, self-sustaining, written "at the top of his voice." His metaphors are deliberately offensive to the conventional taste, his diction is peppered with vulgar vernacular, his rhymes are a clownish play with language and thought. Yet the total effect is one of singular beauty. Tender human feelings are expressed somehow in the phrase "sobs that leap out like prostitutes," and by "the poet's soul, deposited on the spears of houses, shred by shred." Mayakovsky's poetry is a conquest of literary convention.

The precise allusion of the lines "Love boat/Smashed on convention" is still the subject of speculation, as well as of the gossip that Mayakovsky disliked; but there can be no doubt about the general import of the line. The poet's own life was, at the time he wrote, caught in the web of new conventions and tangled by routine. Marxian ideas, once a weapon against rigidity, had been reduced to fixed formulas. Mayakovsky had discarded the mock haberdashery of Futurism for conventional jackets and properly invisible ties. He had become one of the members of the vast organization of proletarian writers, on a comradely footing with various Sutyrins and Yermilovs. He had his picture taken with Fadeyev, Surkov, and Stavsky. He was an honored employee of the state. He drew propaganda posters—three thousand of them, he said. He produced hundreds of advertisements for Soviet retail trading organizations, such as:

> Where can you buy and eat for your money
> The best and the tastiest macaroni?
> Where? Only in the Moscow Food Stores.[6]

He considered the above to be "poetry of the highest caliber." During the last year of his life, the year 1929, in addition to producing a great mass of agitational verse, he made speeches and reports almost daily in widely separated parts of the country, took part in rallies and meetings, and at the same time arranged for the presentation of his two last plays, *The Bedbug* and *The Bath*. The "love boat" of his poetry, one might conclude, had indeed been smashed.

Vladimir Mayakovsky, A Tragedy

In the Luna Park theater in St. Petersburg in December, 1913, Mayakovsky presented his verse "tragedy," *Vladimir Mayakovsky*. He played the principal part himself, and he was also the director and producer of the spectacle. The presentation was a *succès de scandale*. The audience was mocking and derisive, the reviews were for the most part contemptuous. It was another Futurist Golgotha in which the *outré* poet and irreverent innovator offered himself as a willing victim to the established literary priesthood. And they crucified him.

But there was also an appreciative audience. Not only his Futurist comrades but others who were present found the spectacle moving and were reduced to tears. The conception was simple enough. The central character was the "Poet," who, in his own person, stood on a pedestal against a backdrop which represented "a city with its spider web of streets." With him was his feminine companion—over six feet tall and broad in the shoulders—who had no lines and no business, except to stand at his side. She is perhaps an ironic counterpart to Blok's "unknown lady." The Poet on his eminence received in turn the characters in the play: "An old man with dry black cats; a man missing an eye and a leg; a man without an ear and a man without a head; a man with a long face; a man with two cardboard kisses; an average young man; three women, one with an ordinary tear, another with a little tear, a third with a huge tear; together with reporters, boys, girls, etc."

The play is about people who live in the city and who are enslaved to objects, to "things" which have no mind or heart as far as one can tell, though "they may have ears where people have eyes" or vice versa. These people are crippled, wounded, and afraid, and they bring to the Poet their suffering, their fright, and their tears. The Poet discusses these matters with them. The man with three dry old cats counsels rubbing such animals, for the sparks that these living creatures give out may run trains and light cities. God, he says, must be abandoned with all his talk of vengeance upon human beings whose poor little souls wear only worn-out sighs. The earless man tells of cripples in the city where legends of agony grow, where the chimney pots dance the "matchish," where the side streets have their sleeves rolled up for a fight, where melancholy grows like a tear on the mug of a crying dog. The Poet then discusses "god" and avers he never found a soul to insert in the wound of his lips. (Except once he thought he'd found one. It wore a blue dressing gown, and said, "Come in and sit down. I've been waiting for you. Won't you have a cup of tea?") The "Conventional Young Man," hearing all of this, is horrified at the thought of destroying the accumulated culture of the ages. Things are really not so bad, for he himself has invented a machine to cut up chops automatically, and a friend is working on a trap for bedbugs. Moreover, he has a wife, who will soon have a son and a daughter. It's terrible to talk like this, he says. They should let things be as they are and should be, for he has a sister, too, named Sonya. "But," says the Poet, "if you had been hungry as I have been, you would devour the distant skies as the sooty mugs of factories devour them." The man with the long face says, "If you had loved as I have loved you would murder love." The man without an eye and a leg announces that "on the streets, where the faces, like a burden, are all exactly the same, old-lady-time has given birth to a huge mouth-twisted rebellion! Before the mugs of crawling years, old residents of the earth have grown mute, and anger has blown up rivers on the foreheads of cities—thousand-mile-long veins. Slowly, in horror, the straight arrows of hair are raised up on the bald crown of time. And suddenly all things have shed the ragged habiliments of their worn-out names." The things themselves have rebelled, and the Poet must find new names for them. The whole of the first act is an allegory of revolution, where even objects reject their established definitions.

In the second act Mayakovsky appeared again as the Poet in a toga and wearing a laurel wreath. The crowd is ready to worship him, and comes bearing gifts. A woman brings him a tear. A second, whose son has died, brings him another tear, which would serve, she says, as a nice silver ball for his shoe buckle. There is a man with two kisses, who tells how, in women's boudoirs, "factories without smoke or smoke stacks," millions of little kisses are manufactured. The Poet gathered up all the tears in his suitcase and announced that he must abandon the laurel wreath, his happiness, and his throne, in order to carry off these tears to the farthest north, there where "in the vise of endless melancholy, with the fingers of waves, eternally, cruel ocean tears its breast. I will reach my goal, tired out, and in my last delirium will cast your tears to the dark god of storms, at the very source of beastly faiths."

Perhaps this summary gives some notion, however inadequate, of the Futurist poet and political revolutionary, Mayakovsky. He is a poet of the city, who gathers up in grotesque images the human pain that he found in the city, and who has taken that pain upon himself as a burden of suffering.[7] It may be that this image of himself is merely a poetic "persona"; but it seems more likely that Mayakovsky, a man who had suffered imprisonment and persecution, felt this role as peculiarly his own. Ensconced in the tough mail of Futurist sound and symbol, his tender soul, hypersensitive to pain in both people and animals, can hardly endure the city-monster of his own times.

The Cloud

"A Cloud in Pants" (1915), a poem about love, revolution, and God, expresses, like the tragedy, the vaulting egoism of a Mayakovsky who felt in himself the stir of genius, and who had, as Pasternak put it, made this genius of his a "prescribed theme for all time."

Mayakovsky once explained in a speech to a group of young Communists how the poem happened to get its title. The explanation is ironic and apocryphal, but it is characteristic:

"A Cloud in Pants" was first called "The Thirteenth Apostle." When I presented my work to the censor, I was asked, "What's the matter, do you want to go to jail?" I said, no, I didn't look with favor upon the idea. Then they cut out six whole pages, together with the title. That's how the problem of a title came up. They wanted to know how I could combine lyricism with coarseness, and I said, all right, if you like I'll be a madman, if you like I'll be most tender, not a man, but a cloud in pants.—Hardly anybody bought it, because the customers for verse in those days were mostly well-brought-up gentle ladies, and they couldn't buy it because of the title.[8]

Mayakovsky in these brief but inspired remarks to the assembled young Communists provides the key to his own personality and to his poetry. Harsh though they might be,

and jangled out of tune, his lines could express the most tender love, the gentlest pity, the purest sympathy. Part I of "A
Cloud" is an account of the pain caused by frustration in
love. It is a long and raucous plaint in which the poet draws
upon the linguistic reserves of the city streets and the unbridled imagery that was his alone in handling the theme of
unrequited male love: the enormous pain experienced by a
huge, sinewy clod, whose coarse bulk cries out for the soft
and feminine. The heart on fire with love gives off a smell
like roasted meat; a wild call brings the firemen to put out
the fire:

> Don't wear boots!
> Tell the firemen:
> You climb a burning heart with caresses.
> I'll take care of it!
> I'll pour barrels of tears from my eyes.
> I'll brace myself against my ribs.
> I'll jump out! Out! Out!
> Collapsed!
> But you can't jump out of your heart!

Part II suddenly drops love for the themes of poetry and
social revolution. The poet announces confidently his program of creative destruction:

> Praise me,
> I'm more than a match for the mighty.
> To everything that's been done
> I give the mark "*nihil.*"

This section contains what is no doubt the best statement of
Mayakovsky's poetic program: the source and inspiration
of his poetry is the city street with its crippled beggars, its
consumptives, its weird cacophony:

> What do I care
> if neither Homer nor Ovid
> thought of characters like us,
> sooty and pock marked.
> I know
> the sun would dim, seeing
> the gold mines in our souls!

He foresees the coming of the revolution in "the year 1916," and he, like John the Baptist, is the forerunner:

I am wherever pain is—anywhere;
on each drop of the tear stream
I have crucified myself.
Nothing must be forgiven any more!
I've burnt out of souls the place where gentleness grew.
It was harder than taking
a thousand thousand Bastilles!

And when,
his advent
with riot proclaiming,
you come out to meet your savior—
for you I
will tear out my soul;
I'll stamp on it and trample it
till it spread out!—
and I'll give it to you—a bloody banner.

The revolutionary note upon which Part II ends prepares a transition to Part III, in which the love lyric has been resolutely abandoned, the poet's song has been brought down into the streets, and he calls upon the streets to rebel against the old world. The rebellion takes place in such lines as "Come on! Let's paint Mondays and Tuesdays red with blood and make holidays out of them." The poetic outcome of the revolution is no triumph, but rather an abrupt transition, after betrayal by a sky like Judas, and a night "like the traitor Azev," to defeat and huddled despair. Part III ends on a new note of gently thoughtful melancholy, which introduces again the love theme:

I, who sang the machine and England,
maybe I am just
the thirteenth apostle
in the usual gospel.

And whenever my voice
shouts bawdily—
then, from hour to hour,
all day long
maybe Jesus Christ is sniffing
the forget-me-nots of my soul.

Part IV returns again to the theme of love, a tragic love, the love that might save a man but cannot be consummated. In the name of this unrealizable love the poem closes with a mock-blasphemous attack on heaven and on God, who hears nothing, and does not answer:

> The universe is asleep,
> its huge ear
> star-infested
> rests on a paw.

It has been pointed out by Roman Jakobson, one of the most perceptive students of Mayakovsky, that there is a regular alternation in his work between lyric themes and social or political themes. The theme of love regularly alternates with the theme of revolution in his work as a whole; and so "A Cloud in Pants," in its alternation of lyrical and political motifs, is a kind of microcosm of Mayakovsky's poetry and a guide to his life.

"The Backbone Flute"

Beauty in poems by Mayakovsky eludes translation and deceives the conventional taste; and thus Mayakovsky's wonderful song about love, which, though dedicated to Lily Brik, is probably meant for all women, has passed unnoticed outside of Russia. "The Backbone Flute" (1915) is a male lyric on the theme of love's madness and pain. The poetic figures which carry the burden of desire neither chasten nor sublimate, but present the poet's love in terms of delirium. The "her" to whom the verses are offered is a thing of hellish fantasy, invented by some heavenly E. T. A. Hoffmann; his thoughts are clots of blood issuing from the skull; he will dive down and brain himself on the pavement of Nevsky Bouvelard; God brought her up out of the hot depths of hell and gave her a human husband, and human music to set on her piano, but if one should make the sign of the cross above the quilt that covers her there would be at once a smell of scorched wool and sulphurous fumes. Even in drunken battle the words of love are not obsolete. The German speaks of Goethe's Gretchen, the Frenchman dies with a smile, remembering Traviata; but the source of his hell is no conventional literary type, she is a redhead with a painted face; when the centuries have whitened beards only she will be left—and he, rushing after her from city to city; in London fogs he will imprint on her lips the fiery kiss of street lamps; in Paris, when she wanders onto a bridge and looks down, it's him she will see pouring himself out Seine-wise, and calling to her; when she rides out on the bridle path in Sokolniki Park, he will rise over the trees, naked and expectant, a moon to torment her. But the lady's virtue is cold as monastery rock; the husband asserts his rights, and oh, that night! He tightened despair about his throat, and at his howls and laughs the smug mug of his room twisted out of shape with fright. He surrendered her; and King Albert of Belgium, all his towns surrendered, was a happy birthday boy by comparison.

Our pale paraphrase may give some notion of how Mayakovsky consciously employed near-psychopathic imagery to convey the intense force of sexual passion. Such poems do reflect Mayakovsky's own nature and his emotional experience in love, though it must be remembered that in them he is also a conscious poetic craftsman experimenting with the linguistic means for the expression of violent emotions. The complete results of his experiment we can know only if we read Russian. That experiment involved the invention of new words, and of new morphemes or "endings" for already existing words; renovation of the verbal repertory by way of new accents; the use of rhymes, sometimes conventionally correct, sometimes outrageous: for instance the writer E. T. A. Hoffmann entered "The Backbone Flute" only because the name in rapid colloquial delivery fortuitously, and humorously, rhymes with an unusual Russian verb in which the root vowel has disappeared. Thus the reader's legitimate amusement at a funny rhyme is mingled with subconscious awareness of linguistic processes. There are also occasional clichés suggesting the conventional love lyric and realistic bits of dialogue. The meter is irregular, each line a short metrical "shout" carrying a single heavy accent.

One must be wary, in the case of a literary craftsman like Mayakovsky, of searching his work for a guide to his biography. Yet there is clear evidence that Mayakovsky himself experienced the kind of irrational attack of wild emotion that his best poetry describes. Kamensky, one of his biographers, records that in Odessa once Mayakovsky fell in love with a beautiful young girl, that he "roared and stormed" and could not "cope with the great feeling." Professor Jakobson recounts how the poet acted out in a series of telegrams from Moscow to a young Russian girl in Paris a whole poem on love. His close friends have left the record of a number of incidents in which he displayed either manic elation or sudden weeping despair. Lily Brik relates that at the first reading of "The Backbone Flute" in 1915, "Volodya, upset at seeing a small group of friends instead of a packed auditorium, broke down and wept, refused to read and went off into another room." Only with difficulty was he calmed down and persuaded to return to the assembled and expectant guests and resume his reading. His chauffeur reported that a few days before his suicide, when he was returning from a rehearsal of his play *The Bath*, Mayakovsky wept:

On the day of the opening Mayakovsky was in the theater in the afternoon. And when we were returning home I noticed that something was wrong. I heard him crying and sobbing, and one could tell he was having some deep trouble. We drove past Passion Place. Vladimir was silent. I tried to question him: "Vladimir Vladimirovich, it seems you've had some trouble?" He sighed. "It's nothing," he said, but in a few seconds he added, "Don't come to the theater tonight, there won't be any performance."[9]

Ilya Ehrenburg in his reminiscences emphasizes Mayakovsky's preternatural sensitivity and insists that though he called himself an ox and claimed to have a pachyderm's hide Mayakovsky "did not even have ordinary human skin."

It is fair to say, then, that Mayakovsky's poetry reflects a highly emotional and undisciplined human personality. His emotions are experienced and expressed in a personal and individual style. The "ego" of the poet is implicit in every line and explicit in every other. He himself is the hero of his *Tragedy;* the stages in his own life are the matter of his poem "Man"; a number of the lyric poems either have the first person singular pronoun in the title or the name of the poet himself. He is totally concerned with and writes only about "I myself," the title of his autobiography. Therefore it is not surprising that in the last decade of his life, after he had helped the Bolsheviks to destroy the old society, the old culture, and the old poetry, he should have experienced some pain, bedded on eiderdown though he was, in the procrustean couch of a collective society. His suffering, outsized and hyperbolic like his poetry, reached a point at last where a bullet seemed a possible anodyne. The tragedy was not his alone, and his shot at himself spoke for others like him.

The Commune and the Left Front

But first he tried to organize and discipline himself, and that is the real meaning of the Left Front of Art, of which he was the inspiration and the leader, and of his earlier activities as editor of *Art of the Commune* and, for a brief time, arbiter of the new literary taste.

The one literary group whose members as a whole welcomed and supported the Bolshevik revolution were the Moscow Futurists, who proclaimed their readiness to celebrate it in raucous numbers. The result of this was an adventitious and short-lived alliance between Futurism and Bolshevism. The Futurists, who were installed as editors of the official journal of the Commissariat of Education, *Art of the Commune*, became the semiofficial leaders of artistic and literary life. In flamboyant pronouncements the Futurists claimed to be the original revolutionaries in art and to speak in such matters for the proletarian state. Their intransigent nihilism and their policy of a "clean sweep" for the old order of things were *at the moment* in line with official policy. The idea of radical, absolute solutions permeated the air, and so the Futurists, from their eminence as friends of the new regime, spoke of a "proletarian dictatorship" in the arts. Mayakovsky's statements of the official program, whether couched in prose or poetry, betray the strident emotional extremism that characterized both himself and the times. The poem entitled "It's Too Early to Rejoice" (1917) calls for an attack on "Pushkin, and other classic generals," and the position of the publication *Art of the Commune* was that the art of the past was of no use to the factories, the streets, and the working-class quarters of the city, and therefore should be eliminated.

Mayakovsky and his Futurist allies soon found themselves not only out of step with the proletarians whose taste in literature, if it existed at all, tended to favor the classics and to reject the sophisticated linguistic contortions of the Futurists, but sharply at odds also with the leaders of the Party-State. It is well known that Lenin regarded Mayakovsky's work with frank distaste: "Pushkin I understand and enjoy," he said, "Nekrasov I acknowledge, but Mayakovsky—excuse me. I can't understand him." The concern of Lenin and other Party leaders for preserving what they called the "cultural heritage" led them to stern disapproval of the Futurist attack on the art of the past.

The most important factor in their low estimate of Mayakovsky was the "difficulty" of his poems, and however radical the Futurists claimed to be, their message was lost not only on Lenin, but on proletarian readers who knew nothing about the "old" culture of the nineteenth century or the Futurist rebellion against that culture. As Trotsky put it: "The Futurist break with the past is, after all, a tempest in the closed-in world of the intelligentsia which grew up on Pushkin, Fet, Tiutchev, Briusov, Balmont, and Blok. . . . The Futurists have done well to push away from them. But it is not necessary to make a universal law of development out of the act of pushing away."

Mayakovsky's two most important works of the immediate revolutionary period were the long poem called "150,000,-000," and the verse drama *Mystery Bouffe*. In them he makes a conscious effort to remove his "self" into the background in favor of the "masses."

The verse play *Mystery Bouffe*, a modern variant of the medieval mystery, with added ingredients of farce and blasphemy ("bouffe") was presented in its first version in 1918 on the anniversary of the October Revolution under the directorship of Meyerhold. Difficulty was experienced in finding actors willing to perform in it. An advertisement in the Petrograd papers announced preparations for the staging of the play and called upon actors wishing to take part in it to present themselves in a certain place at a certain hour. The advertisement rang with revolutionary fervor:

Comrade Actors! You are under obligation to celebrate the great anniversary of the Revolution with a revolutionary production. You must present the play *Mystery Bouffe*, a heroic, epic, and satiric portrait of our era, written by Vladimir Mayakovsky. . . . To work, everyone! Time is precious![10]

The plot, if sensational, was very simple. After the earth has been destroyed by a flood there remain, seeking refuge at the North Pole, "seven pairs of clean" and "seven pairs of unclean." The "Clean" are various bourgeois types, such as Lloyd George, Clemenceau, and a Russian speculator; the "Unclean" are proletarians: a miner, a carpenter, a laundress, and so forth. The Unclean are deceived by the Clean, whom they throw overboard from the ark. The settings where the action takes place are various: the Universe, the Ark, hell, heaven, the cloud country, the Promised Land. The Unclean, after overthrowing the Clean, visit hell, where they deposit the latter, then a traditional heaven which they leave in disgust, and finally they return to earth and the Promised Land of the Communist Paradise.

The play is a kind of working model of the flamboyant revolutionary literature of the moment, and it succeeds in conveying the spirit of that moment, as Mayakovsky felt it. It contains the elation of victory that the Bolsheviks and their close sympathizers felt on the day after the Revolution, and it contains also an ingredient of revolutionary ethos common to the writings of Gorky and Lenin: contempt and black hatred for the "clean" world. It has a sense of the future and of historical movement. Mayakovsky speaks in it of the storming of the planets by "airships of the commune, 50 years hence"; and the "Very Ordinary Young Man" in the play speaks of a time when the "sun will perform such tricks that pineapples will yield six crops a year from pickle shoots." The play is blasphemous: Jehovah himself—the old institutionalized religion—is conquered by the Unclean, who, Prometheus-like, steal his lightnings from him and use them for "electrification." It is frankly topical and ephemeral, and it includes not only persons but phrases and ideas that were alive to the spectators of 1918 but which have only a historical interest today. Mayakovsky, in his introductory remarks to the second variant, produced in 1921, advises his posterity to introduce new topical material for each future performance —material significant for *their times*. Thus the individual ego of the author seeks to screen itself behind the mass, the Party program, and political matters of the passing moment.

The poem "150,000,000" was written in 1919 and published, after long epistolary haggling with the State Publishing House, in April, 1920. In his autobiography, *I Myself,* Mayakovsky wrote for the year 1919: "My head full of 150,000,000. Started agitational work in ROST" (State Telegraph Agency). The juxtaposition is not accidental. "150,000,-000" is frankly propagandist, just as were the cartoons and posters which he produced for ROST. And both varieties of propaganda were, in the poet's intention, anonymous. He goes on to say about the poem: "Finished 150,000,000. Published it without my name. I wanted anyone at all to add to it and improve it." But the device did not work, since the hand of Mayakovsky was clearly visible: "But no one did add to it and anyway everyone knew who wrote it. What's the difference. Publish it now under my name."

Not only was the "mass"—150,000,000 Ivans (the 1919 population of the USSR)—the hero of this poem, but the opening lines announce that the "mass" is also its author:

> 150,000,000 is the name of the creator of this poem.
> Its rhythms—bullets,
> its rhymes—fires from building to building.
> 150,000,000 speak with my lips. . . .
> Who can tell the name
> of the earth's creator—surely a genius?
> And so
> of this
> my
> poem
> no one is the author.

However, just as the poetic concepts, the characters, the rhythms and profoundly self-conscious rhyming devices employed in *Mystery Bouffe* clearly revealed the hand of the author, so in "150,000,000" the exclusive personal authorship of an intensely original individual, Mayakovsky, was immediately obvious. Considered as a literary production the poem is a sophisticated parody on the ancient folk epic, the *bylina*, a literary form developed among the more primitive peoples of the Russian empire for hundreds of years and handed down from generation to generation by word of mouth. The *bylina*, whose hyperbolized heroic figures and primitive verse system Mayakovsky imitates, was indeed an impersonal creation of the Russian "mass"; but the poem "150,000,000" is the work of a particular craftsman. There are two figures of heroic proportions in the poem: Wilson, the defender of world capitalism, and Ivan, a thoroughly Russian champion of the downtrodden. Wilson is located in Chicago, a city which stands on a single screw and is completely "electro-dynamo-mechanized." Even when a Chicagoan lifts his brow the work is done by electric power. Wilson has pistols with four cocks and a saber bent into seventy sharp blades. Ivan has only "a hand and another hand, and that one stuck in his belt." But, as in the Russian folk epic Ilya of Murom vanquishes the frightening enemy without serious difficulty, so here there is never any doubt that Wilson, "whose drawers are not drawers but a sonnet," who eats and grows fat "adding one floor after another to his belly," will succumb to the Paul Bunyan-like "Ivan." Wilson is of course no real figure but a literary symbol of evil power modeled on the Tartar enemies with whom the Russian folk heroes in the *bylina* regularly do battle. The faraway mysterious capital from which those enemies usually issued forth has become a certain "Chicago," and their devilish magic is nothing but "mechanization." Viewed as a literary production the poem is a triumph of sophistication and verbal skill; read as political commentary or propaganda it is nothing at all.

Party leaders reacted to both these works with a kind of obtuse, instinctive hostility. Lenin wrote in a note to Lunacharsky: "Aren't you ashamed of yourself for voting to publish '150,000,000' in 5000 copies? Nonsense, stupidity, double-dyed stupidity and pretentiousness! In my opinion only about one in ten such things should be published, and in editions of not more than 1500 copies—for libraries and eccentrics."[11] Trotsky, though somewhat more perceptive than Lenin, still could find no good use for Mayakovsky's agitational pieces: "How out of place and how frivolous do these primitive ballads and fairy tales sound when hurriedly adapted to Chicago mechanics and to the class struggle!"[12] In short, Mayakovsky's brave beginning as a propagandist of the new regime ended in failure. The futurist "ego" of the poet, his ever restive imagination, his instinctive iconoclasm of imagery and diction, seemed to Lenin a kind of literary "hooliganism." Such people could not be trusted. *"Mystery Bouffe,"* wrote Mayakovsky in his autobiography, "was produced three times, then lambasted. Replaced by various Macbeths."

There were other, shorter, and perhaps more successful things written in the first days of the Revolution, and Mayakovsky as an agitator and declaimer of verse was much in demand at meetings and rallies in spite of the cool reserve of the Party leaders toward his work. Physical contact with the "mass" Mayakovsky had established in his art work and through his speeches; yet something was missing. Proletarians and Party bureaucrats repeated the easy and obvious charge that he was "too much of an individualist," and he attempted to deal with this charge in a poem, "The Fifth International," which he never finished:

> The Proletcultists never speak
> of "I" or of the personality.
> They consider
> the pronoun "I"
> a kind of rascality.
> But in my opinion
> if you write petty stuff, you
> will never crawl out of your lyrical slough
> even if you substitute We for I.

Excessive individualism, unintelligibility, rowdy disrespect for fine literature, such were the shortcomings of Mayakovsky; and they threatened him with isolation from the working-class audience. Aware of this danger, he modified his literary style, did violence to his own talent, "stepped," as he himself put it, "upon the throat of his own song." At a reading of his poems in 1930 he revealed clearly the mechanics of his evolution: "One of the main difficulties in communicating with the 'workers' auditorium,' " he said, was the low standard of culture of these workers and the difficulty of communicating with them. His own things had been criticized as incomprehensible, "so the question of a clear meaning for everybody rose before me, and I started to write more for the masses."

To institutionalize and rationalize the new departure forced by circumstance, Mayakovsky and his Futurist friends organized in 1923 The Left Front of Art and began publishing the magazine *Lef.* Mayakovsky recorded and briefly characterized these events in his autobiography:

We organize "Lef." "Lef" may be defined as the encompassing of the great social theme by all the instruments of Futurism. This definition, of course, does not exhaust the question. Anyone interested should look at the issues of *Lef.* We closed ranks firmly: Brik, Kushner, Aseyev, Arvatov, Tretyakov, Rodchenko, Lavinsky. . . . One of the slogans, and one of the great achievements of *Lef,* was the de-aestheticizing of the productive arts, constructivism. Poetic supplement to the magazine: agitational pieces, and also commercial agitation: advertisements.[13]

The persons mentioned were all active figures in the Futurist movement of the Lef period. Osip Brik was Mayakovsky's publisher, his friend, and the husband of Lily; Boris Kushner was a critic and a specialist in the literary "sketch"; N. N. Aseyev was a poet follower of Mayakovsky; Sergei Tretyakov was a playwright, poet, and movie scenarist whose most famous work is the anti-imperialist propaganda play *Roar China!* (1926); Rodchenko was an artist and the author of travel sketches. Others prominent as contributors in the journal *Lef* were Victor Shklovsky, a provocative and original critic of Russian literature, and Boris Eichenbaum and Boris Tomashevsky, literary scholars and critics whose work on Pushkin and Tolstoy is a solid monument of scholarship. Futurist poets of a "dadaist" complexion, Kruchonykh for instance, occasionally contributed their suggestive verbal play. The early stories of Isaac Babel and Valentin Katayev appeared in *Lef* and *New Lef.*

Missing from the list given by Mayakovsky when he wrote those lines in 1928 is one very important name: N. F. Chuzhak-Nasimovich, the most dogmatic and articulate theoretician of Futurism in the period of Lef, and an editor of the magazines *Lef* and *New Lef*. His ascendancy is both symptomatic and illuminating. Chuzhak was a Bolshevik journalist to whom journalism seemed the highest order of creative activity under the new order of things, and his notions as to the function of literature in building life rather than "palely reflecting" it dominated the theoretical section of the magazine. The platform for *Lef*, developed under his guidance, made the following points:

It is our purpose:

1) To aid in the discovery of a Communist path for all varieties of art.

2) To re-examine the theory and practice of so-called "left" art, freeing it from individualistic distortions and developing its valuable Communist aspects.

3) To struggle with decadence and aesthetic mysticism, as well as with self-contained formalism, indifferent naturalism, and for the affirmation of tendentious realism, based on the use of the technical devices developed in all the revolutionary schools of art.

Like so much of the "manifesto" literature of the twenties this document sounds to the modern reader something like a formal prayer addressed to a God whose character and attributes have been forgotten. Yet these formulas can be translated into simple prose. Most important is the promise to "re-examine" the position taken in the recent past by the Futurists and condemned by the Party. "Individualistic distortion" refers to Mayakovsky's besetting sin of which he must purge himself. "Decadence" echoes a phrase by Lenin in his public letter on the Proletcult, in which he linked Futurists with "decadents of every stripe." To struggle against "self-contained formalism" means simply to dissociate oneself from critics such as Shklovsky and others of the formalist school who studied literature as form and device rather than as social evidence. Note, however, that the qualification "self-contained" formalism leaves the way open for any of these people to purge themselves of sin without giving up their basic heresy. The "affirmation of tendentious realism" is a retreat into the past and implies a condemnation of the "epic and heroic" style of both *Mystery Bouffe* and "150,000,000."

The "formalists" and linguistic specialists who had been close to the Futurist movement from the start continued to have a prominent place in *Lef*. A natural affinity existed between those poets who were, like Mayakovsky and Khlebnikov, laboratories of linguistic experiment themselves and scholarly specialists in the study of language. The lively interest in each other of Mayakovsky and Roman Jakobson may be explained in this way. Articles in *Lef* were heavily weighted in the direction of the *formal* or *linguistic* study of literature; evidence that the formalists were no longer "self-contained" but were now in contact with reality was provided by the lead article in one of the first numbers of *Lef*: "Lenin's Language." Formalist investigation published in *Lef* emphasized the study of specific characteristics of language as used in literature.

The magazine *Lef* was not well received, and its circulation remained small, partly, according to Mayakovsky, because of sabotage by the State Publishing House. It stopped publication in 1925 after only seven numbers, was revived as *New Lef* in 1927, and finally disappeared at the end of 1928. During the final year of *Lef* its small body of theoreticians developed in radical form the notion of the literary man as a craftsman and of literature as a craft not basically different from other socially useful occupations. The highest form of literary activity, in this paradoxical theory, and the most useful "in the epoch of socialism," was factual reporting: the writing of sketches, biographies, diaries, travel notes, and the like. The concern of the writer should be with *facts*, rather than with his own invention or fantasy. The fixation of objective fact was to be required of him, rather than the creation of artistic wholes, which tend to "destroy or disfigure the *fact*" in accordance with a subjective purpose. The activity of the craftsman-writer, moreover, should be determined by the *demand* of his client, who is, "in the epoch of socialism," the proletarian state. Since literary production is by its nature no different from other kinds of production, the writer, whatever his class origin or orientation, is simply a producer working for a client. Implicit in this theory is the tenet that the writer's ideology is not of crucial importance. Though their theories have the ring of dogma and the limits they suggest for the new "Literature of Fact" seem straitened and confining, yet it is clear that the ideas they developed would, if accepted, have had the effect of liberating the writer from the much more confining demand that he *interpret* reality in the light of dialectical materialism. To fix the writer firmly on the ground of *fact* meant to free him from the obligation to produce ideologically tendentious "artistic literature." The Marxist opponents of *Lef* did not "expose" them in this, but they left no doubt that the "factual" emphasis of the Left Front of Art would deprive the state of a useful propaganda weapon.

The alliance between formalist critics and Futurists continued in *New Lef*. Shklovsky published there a number of stimulating and highly original studies, among them his "Tolstoy's *War and Peace*, a Formal Sociological Study," and a penetrating analysis of Pushkin's *The Captain's Daughter*; Osip Brik's "The Rout of Fadeyev," a shrewd attack on the proletarian writers as poor epigones of nineteenth-century realism, appeared in 1928; Mayakovsky's irreverent letter in verse to Gorky was published in No. 1; Boris Kushner's travel sketches of Western Europe, one of the finest things in the "sketch" genre, were published in an early number of *New Lef*. In general, the material published was interesting and original, even when its purpose was agitational. In an article entitled "For Innovation," Osip Brik wrote that since Soviet literature ought to have something new to contribute to world literature, the experimenters should not be hampered in their laboratory work by the requirement that the work be intelligible to millions of new readers: "It is a mistake," he said, "to demand that every cultural work be multiplied and distributed in the hundreds of thousands."

New Lef was published for a select few in an edition of 1500 for each number. It received no warm reception either in the government offices or among the "reading mass." Even its agitational and propaganda emphasis was suspect, since those functions were carried out in its pages by iconoclastic literary critics such as Victor Shklovsky and Futurist artists indifferent to conventional standards of taste. As a result of pressures which have never been wholly explained, Mayakovsky resigned from the editorship of *New Lef* in July, 1928, after No. 7 of the magazine had been issued.[14] He explained later that "tiny literary fractionlets had outlived themselves, and instead of organizing groups literary men should transfer their activities to mass organizations carrying on agitational work: newspapers, 'agitprops,' commissions, etc. . . ." In 1929 Mayakovsky and those comrades who had together with him abandoned *Lef* formed a new organization which they called REF, the Revolutionary Front of Art. At a public meeting in October of that year he explained that the new organization was needed to carry on the struggle with "apolitical tendencies." From this must follow rejection of the theory of the "bare fact" and the demand for tendentiousness and ideas in art.

The Bedbug and *The Bath*

The plays written by Mayakovsky in 1928 and 1929 constitute a two-part dramatic satire directed against old enemies of his, whom we have already met under the generic name *byt,* and who appear now in the form of *bourgeoisis vulgaris,* a species closely allied with *bedbugus normalis,* and "the Soviet bureaucrat." Both plays are satiric utopias in the sense that they purport to foresee a future in which the world will be purified of such specimens. *The Bedbug* is a two-part drama in which the action of the first part takes place in the year 1928 and of the second part fifty years later in a well-ordered Communist state of the future. The principal character is one Prisypkin, a successful Soviet "promoted worker," for whom proletarian blood, callused palms, and the trade-union card have become symbols of privilege and power. As the play opens he has jilted his working-class girl friend for a beauty shop operator and manicurist, Elzevir Renaissance, and is shopping in a huge department store in preparation for the wedding. Various salesmen are promoting their wares—buttons, dolls, whetstones, lampshades, glue, perfumes, brassieres and the like—in jingles reminiscent of Mayakovsky's own commercial poetry. Prisypkin, with bourgeois persistence, acquires a variety of such wares, announcing that his house must be filled with such things "like a horn of plenty." The scene shifts to the wedding party, where the drunken guests set fire to the house, destroying all the inmates. Fifty years later the bridegroom Prisypkin together with a companion, a bedbug, are found, by workmen excavating for a new structure, perfectly preserved in a block of ice and are brought to life again by scientists of the "Bureau for the Resurrection of the Dead."

Prisypkin's resurrection, while a scientific success, is not an unmixed blessing to the inhabitants of the future, for the man is found to contain the petit-bourgeois infection of love, along with a fondness for strong drink and sentimental songs. He infects others with that ancient disease called love, "a state in which a person's sexual energy, instead of being rationally distributed over the whole of his life, was compressed into a single week and concentrated in one hectic process. This made him commit the most absurd and impossible acts."

The authorities in the State of the future place Prisypkin, the revived bourgeois, in a cage and display him for the education and edification of the citizens. Those men of utopia have forgotten a way of life that called for the use of poison (vodka), the disorderly consumption of tobacco in the form of cigarettes, the use of foul language, the strumming of guitars, and idle talk about one's "heart strings." But when the director of the zoo where Prisypkin is kept lets him out to see the spectators and to address a few words to them in order to prove that he has mastered human speech, Prisypkin, suddenly looking out at the theater audience, is overjoyed at seeing people like himself:

Citizens! Brothers! My own people! Darlings! How did you get here? So many of you! When were you unfrozen? Why am I alone in the cage? Darlings, friends, come and join me! Why should I alone suffer? Citizens!

This speech has been interpreted as a veiled attack on the Soviet police state, but it is nothing of the sort. Prisypkin's apostrophe to the Soviet audience of 1928 is reminiscent of a very similar scene in Gogol's *Inspector General,* when the dishonest and foolish mayor turns to the audience to ask them whether they aren't laughing at themselves rather than at him. You all have a bit of Prisypkin in you, Mayakovsky is saying in this scene, you are all attached to vulgar bourgeois values. Like Prisypkin you smoke, drink, and use intemperate language. Like him you want your houses to be "horns of plenty," chocked with buttons, brassieres, and bathos, and like him you have debased the humanitarian ideas of the revolution to the pursuit of comfort and power. Worst of all, you still preserve the infections of individualism and sexual love.

Mayakovsky's satire in *The Bedbug* is directed at himself as well as at his contemporaries. We have already noted that the ditties recited by department store salesmen in the first scene are a parody of his own verse written for the Moscow Food Stores. Mayakovsky's most accomplished work is a poetic expression of that "disease of the brain" known as sexual love. It has been pointed out that Mayakovsky, in satirizing Prisypkin's yearning for "roses" and "visions," may be lecturing himself: "Only books on horticulture have anything about roses, and visions are mentioned only in the medical books, in the section on dreaming."[15] And the ugly caricature of a "bourgeoisified" proletarian Prisypkin in search of conventional marital bliss may be that alter ego of the poet himself, with whom he disputed in the poem "About That":

> Have you greased your way
>   into that caste of theirs?
> Will you kiss?
>   Feed yourself?
>   Grow Fat?
> Do you intend
>   Yourself
> To dig yourself into their way of life
> And practice that family happiness of theirs?

The Bedbug is, therefore, a complex satiric system. The Soviet philistine symbolized by Prisypkin is the normal Soviet man of the late twenties who has deserted the "trenches" of revolution for the sake of middle-class happiness. He is also Mayakovsky himself, the unreconstructed poet of his own all-important self, who has not quite succeeded in choking off the love lyric. With his barbarous ways, Prisypkin seems no better than an animal to the citizens of the rationalized world of the future; but that world itself is presented in satiric images by the Mayakovsky who is himself part Prisypkin: the world-wide mechanical voting apparatus, the organized mass dances which are the only kind that survived, the comical search among old books for something on "love," and the steel, concrete, and glass backdrop against which the man of the future lives are hardly offered as a happy prospect. Mayakovsky ridicules the philistine individualism of Prisypkin, but he doesn't seem to believe either in the hardening mass organization that crushes him.

The Bath, produced in 1930, is similar in theme to *The Bedbug*, though it is more simply and pointedly directed against the Stalinist bureaucracy which was taking form at the time. It portrays in one Pobedonosikov the new Communist officials who were moving into positions of power in the government and Party apparatus, to replace the revolutionaries of the Civil War period. They are a narrow-minded and conformist generation, sycophants, opportunists, and timeservers, people of vulgar ambition and vulgar tastes, philistines mouthing Marxist phrases but interested only in power and the exercise of power. It is understandable that neither *The Bedbug* nor *The Bath* was well received by the literary bureaucrats, and one of these, Yury Libedinsky, a leader of RAPP when the play was produced, recently wrote in his memoirs that at that time the "secretariat" of his organization thought Mayakovsky was exaggerating the amount of bureaucratism in the Party apparatus. He later found, he says, that Mayakovsky was right and that he and his comrades were wrong.

Mayakovsky as a Monument

The Vladimir Mayakovsky that we have presented here—and we have tried to be objective—has hardly anything in common with the heroic statue that stands on a pedestal in

Moscow's Mayakovsky Square. Is something missing from our account? Would a Soviet critic object that something vital has been left out? Would he say that we have studied only the bohemian intellectual "who was never really a Futurist," to the neglect of the Bolshevik political agitator? Would he present a long list of poems not mentioned in our brief survey and accuse us of a certain bias in selection?

Indeed he would, and perhaps we should look at that "other side" of Mayakovsky. If Mayakovsky had written only such poems as "Lenin," "Very Good!" and "At the Top of My Voice," would his image for us be quite different, and more like that created by his Soviet biographers and critics, who, on their side, tend to neglect the love lyric? Probably not.

We must remember that Mayakovsky even when performing the function of a "partisan-poet" remained that peculiar and original phenomenon, Mayakovsky, and was always more poet than partisan. The nineteenth-century civic poet Nekrasov wrote: "A poet I may be, but a citizen I must be." Mayakovsky would have reversed that dictum: he was perfectly capable of being a citizen, even a propagandist, but could never escape the necessity of being a poet. The best illustration of this is a famous passage from the poem "Home!" where Mayakovsky attempts to describe his function as a poet. To make the point, the Russian text is here translated and transliterated:

Along with reports on pig iron and *steel*	S chugunom chtob i s vydelkoi *stali*
I want a report on verse production on behalf of the Politburo	o rabote stikhov, ot Politburo chtoby delal
From *Stalin.*	doklady *Stalin*

No doubt these lines written long before Stalin had reached his eminence had much to do with forming the latter's opinion of Mayakovsky as the "greatest poet of our socialist epoch," but the lines do not contain the flattery he saw in them. The name Stalin (man of steel) was chosen, not from political but from poetic considerations: it furnishes both a pun and a rhyme for the word *stali* (steel). At the same time the choice of the person heightens the irony of the line and the humor of the pun, since the prosaic Stalin was the least suitable member of the Politburo to read a report on poetry.

The poem "Lenin," written on the occasion of Lenin's death, is a skillful piece of rhetoric which gives in a rhymed and readable capsule a summary of world history from the Marxist viewpoint and treats the figure of Lenin as a kind of predestined savior who appeared according to history's law at the moment of capitalism's decline and violent fall. Voronsky complained that the Lenin of the poem is a schematic and unreal figure in which no one can believe, and here it would seem that a normally sensitive critic has missed the poetic point. Mayakovsky was not interested in the "real Lenin," in his personal psychology or the nature of his peculiar political genius. Libedinsky reported that Mayakovsky flatly rejected any demand that he portray "individual psychology," and thus Voronsky's strictures on the poem are beside the point, though his remarks convey the spirit of the thing better than anything else that has been written about it: "Mayakovsky's Lenin is a figure of stone, frozen into an emblem. He doesn't walk, he marches; he doesn't act, he performs." Precisely so. The Lenin in Mayakovsky's poem is a myth. He is the messiah foretold in the scriptures of Marxist prophecy, and the story of his great deeds, like the chronicle of the Savior, begins with the creation of the world. To criticize "Vladimir Ilych Lenin" as a serious political poem is wide of the mark.

"At the Top of My Voice" is Mayakovsky's last important poem. It is a colloquy "at the top of his voice" with his comrades of the Communist future, who, he assures himself, will understand him and his verse, which "will break through into their lives like an aqueduct in our day, built by Roman slaves." The stirring imagery and wordplay of this poem remind us of the young Mayakovsky whose fire again flares up in them. But the verses we know under the title "At the Top of My Voice" are not the poem he was actually writing, but only an introduction to it. And they are not even the whole introduction but only the first part of it. "At the Top of My

Voice" is a "civic" poem, boldly declaring Communist beliefs
and presenting the poet as an agitator and a rabble rouser.
There was to be a second introduction, and the few fragments
found in his papers after his death reveal that the Mayakovsky of the second introduction was to have been a lyric Dr.
Jekyll to the civic Mr. Hyde of the first, as soft and tender,
indeed, as a cloud in pants:

> It's after one.
>   You must have gone to bed.
> The Milky Way runs like a silvery river through the night.
> I'm in no hurry
>   and with lightning telegrams
> There's no need to wake and worry you.
> The sea draws back
> The sea goes off to sleep.
> As they say
>   the incident is closed
> The Love boat
>   has smashed against convention
> Now you and I are through
>   No need then
> To count over mutual pains, harms, and hurts.
> Just see how quiet the world is!
> Night has laid a heavy tax of stars upon the sky
> In hours like these you get up and you speak
> To the ages, to history, and to the universe.

Such was to have been the mood and style of the lyrical
introduction. Four lines of this fragment Mayakovsky introduced into his suicide note, with the change of "you" to "life."

About the poem itself for which the "double introduction"
was written nothing is known except that it was to have been
about "The First Five-Year Plan." This final performance
of Mayakovsky contains a symbolic commentary on his life.
There is no easy answer to the question asked by normal
people: who and what was he? Was he a convinced poet of
the Revolution, or was he playing a part? Was he all wounded
tenderness and sensitive to the slightest hurt or was that, too,
a pose? What was the "real" poem to which his thirty-seven
years provided only a "double introduction"? Perhaps there

is no answer to a question such as this. Pasternak, who hated the Mayakovsky monument and was deaf to his Revolutionary poetry, has provided a cryptic answer to our question in his remark that "Mayakovsky, disdaining to act a part in life, played at life itself."

Chapter 3

Prophets of a Brave New World

The Machine and England

MAYAKOVSKY, WHOM STALIN proclaimed "the greatest poet of our socialist epoch," and Eugene Zamyatin, who left the Soviet Union under a cloud in 1931, are both concerned with the problem of how separate items of humanity are to be related to the inescapable "mass." Both devise literary images of the Communist "future," and both deal with the effect on human beings of, in Mayakovsky's phrase, "the machine and England." Both study "love" and investigate "sex," speculating on the modifications that may one day occur in these areas of individual experience as subjective feeling gives way to the rational organization of life. Each is an innovator in his own literary medium, Mayakovsky as a poet, and Zamyatin as a novelist, short-story writer, and critic. Zamyatin is, like Mayakovsky, a declared enemy of fixed philistine values in literature and in life. Zamyatin's hatred for the established and secure was no less than Mayakovsky's, and his contempt for the servants of *byt*, an enemy which he knew under the term "entropy," was equal to Mayakovsky's. And, also like Mayakovsky, Zamyatin has a close affinity with literary bohemia.

Zamyatin is a self-conscious mirror of a world in violent process, and therefore his prose tends to the grotesque in both form and content. His art, to use his own phrase, portrays the world as it might be seen in a storm from the mast of a ship listing at a forty-five-degree angle "when the green jaws of the sea are gaping, and the ship itself is cracking." At such times it is impossible to present land- and sea-scapes of settled Euclidean dimensions.

Zamyatin's writings—his novels and stories as well as his essays—are a systematic defense of heresy as a way of life.

69

Perhaps the best statement of his "philosophy" is the following from an essay entitled "On Literature, Revolution, and Entropy":

If you were to ask the straight question "What is revolution?" you would get many answers.

Some would answer à la Louis XIV: "The revolution, *c'est moi*"; some would answer according to the calendar, giving the month and year; some would answer by spelling out the word. But if we proceed from spelling to speaking, then we must say the following:

Two dead, dark stars collide with an unheard but deafening thunder, and they give fiery birth to a new star: that is what is meant by revolution. A molecule tears free of its orbit and, invading a neighboring atomic universe, gives birth to a new chemical element: that is what is meant by revolution. Lobachevsky with a single book burns out the walls of the thousand-year-old Euclidian world: and that is what is meant by revolution.

Zamyatin, who was educated as an engineer, was sent to England during the First World War by the Russian government, where he took part in the construction of the ship *Alexander Nevsky*, an ice-breaker intended for use in the Arctic Ocean. At the same time he gathered materials for his first novel, *Islanders*, partly written in England during his stay there and published in Petrograd in 1918.

This short novel is a satirical treatment of British middle-class respectability, as Zamyatin, not without the help of Shaw and Wells, was able to perceive that phenomenon. His experience of England was neither wide nor prolonged, and the novel is rather a piece of literary autobiography than an objective commentary on that experience. The work does reveal the main concerns of Zamyatin both as a thinker and as a literary stylist, and it must be regarded as a kind of preliminary sketch for the later novel on which his renown is based: *We*. The British middle class, both the source and the product of industrial civilization, repelled him by the rigid demands of its code of respectability. Under such a regime the individual human personality, held firm in the forms of convention, must either atrophy or rebel. The chief bearer of ideas and attitudes repugnant to Zamyatin is a certain Vicar Dooley, the author of a work called *The Testament of Compulsory Salvation*. In order to achieve both holiness and happiness, Vicar Dooley had worked out a rational schedule for all necessary human activities. According to this schedule, which is displayed in Mr. Dooley's library, certain hours were set aside for taking food, certain days for repentance (three per week), and certain others for charitable activities, and a portion of each day was reserved for walking in the fresh air. There was at the end of the list a final item which concerned Mrs. Dooley and where the modest notation was made: "Saturdays of every third week." Mrs. Dooley, should she invite caresses at times set aside for other things, heard the following gentle remonstrance:

"My dear, this may seem a very slight deviation from the rules, but you must remember what I say in Chapter II of my Testament: our lives should move like graceful and well-made machines, and with mechanical certainty proceed to the desired goal."

For Vicar Dooley the "desired goal" is salvation and the promised bliss. He believes, moreover, that his strict moral regimen should be enforced throughout England, and it is his intention to have Parliament adopt a bill making it obligatory upon all. And why not? Shouldn't everyone be compelled to save his soul? "Far better that we should be slaves of the Lord than free sons of Satan." In Dooley, Zamyatin has created a grotesque caricature of bourgeois respectability braced by religious dogma but having ultimate recourse to the police.

The main character, Campbell, whose life has up to the time we meet him held strictly to the rails of propriety, and who is repeatedly compared to a machine, suddenly and unaccountably loses control when he meets a music hall entertainer by the name of Didi. But he has been so well trained by his mother, Lady Campbell (who thinks the faces of cultivated people should all be alike, in fact, a cultivated person "should not really have a face"), that even this "deplorable and unconventional" liaison he seeks to make regular, respectable, and decent. He would marry the girl. They must have a house in the suburbs with furniture in it, and he will buy her an electric iron. The house, the furniture, and the electric iron must be acquired before the marriage in order to give it a frame of respectability.

The representatives of British respectability are contrasted, following a literary convention that Zamyatin's Russian readers may not have been aware of, with a carefree Irishman named O'Kelley, who is disorganized, funny, and immoral, and who practices nonconformity as a matter of principle. "Have you heard?" he says to Didi. "A bill has been brought into Parliament to force all Britons to have noses of the same length. And why not? This difference in nose length is the only remaining one, and it must be done away with. Then they will all be as alike as buttons, or as Ford cars."

Zamyatin in *Islanders* not only provides a preview of the main themes of *We*, but practices the literary tricks and devices that he would later use in that novel to such good effect. Characters are identified by the device of the repeated metaphor: Campbell is regularly a "lumbering truck," then "a truck out of control." Or they are repeatedly associated with objects that typify them for the reader: for instance Mrs. Dooley's "basic organ" is her pince-nez. Vivid, impressionistic pictures are provided by a few simple line strokes: the "two brows of a face raised to form a triangle." The narration moves in a brisk staccato, with swift ellipses and insistent repetition of key visual images. The "eye" of Zamyatin's camera moves abruptly from one scene to another. Zamyatin is a mannered literary artist whose style belongs to the school of Remizov and Bely, and to that style Zamyatin has given the fillip of his own preoccupation with modern mathematics, which no doubt suggested to him the systematic distortion of visual images based on the old-fashioned geometry.

Islanders is an important event in Russian literary history, for the novel places in clear focus the real nature of Zamyatin's rebellion against the machine and mechanized civilization. The novel *Islanders* was obviously not inspired by an apocalyptic vision of a future society governed by the proletarian mass; rather it describes an industrial society of the present dominated by a smug and conformist middle class. The author of that mass regimentation which Zamyatin in *We* foresaw as the future lot of mankind was not backward Russia but the industrialized West, and the Table of Hours imposed on the people of the twenty-ninth century by the benevolent dictator is nothing else but Vicar Dooley's rules and schedules. Zamyatin's rebellion, then, is not against any particular version of the modern mass society. It is not directed at socialism or Communism as such but rather at forms of the regimentation which has resulted from the growth of a huge and complex industrial civilization. The burden of rebellion against the rational gods of Ford, F. H. Taylor, and Vicar Dooley is carried in *Islanders* by the "disorganized" Irishman, O'Kelley, the demimondaine Didi, and Campbell himself, in whom the irrational forces at last break free of confinement. In *Islanders* Zamyatin rejects "the machine and England," and presents as their antagonists a few unpunctual and happy-go-lucky individualists, themselves conventional bohemians. And the reader is certain that they will be crushed by the Lady Campbells and the Vicar Dooleys. Zamyatin's problem is similar to that of Mayakovsky in his last two plays and in his life as a whole, but the solution suggested by Mayakovsky is, as we shall see, the reverse of Zamyatin's.

The political environment of Eugene Zamyatin, the Russia of 1918–19, was one in which the mass had triumphed—at least according to the official version—and where collective interests transcended the individual. There were self-styled proletarian poets and writers who proclaimed in sonorous verse that there could be no more individual heroes: the great laboring mass of humanity is now the hero, they said, in history, and must be the hero in our literary works. "The collective 'We' has driven out the personal 'I'," shouted the youthful Bezymensky, and among the proletarian poets and novelists there developed a mystic belief in the collective as an entity in which the individual finds happiness by losing himself, like a Buddhist saint in Nirvana. The regimented paradise was a frequent theme of the poet and novelist

Gastev, a member of the Smithy group of proletarian poets, whose eloquence on this subject had a cosmic swing. He wrote:

The mechanization, not only of gestures, not only of production methods, but of everyday thinking, coupled with extreme rationality, normalizes in a striking degree the psychology of the proletariat. . . . It is this that lends proletarian psychology such surprising anonymity, which permits the qualification of separate proletarian units as A, B, C, or as 325,075, or as O, and the like. In this normalization of psychology and its dynamism is the key to the prodigious elementariness of proletarian thinking. . . . In this psychology, from one end of the world to the other, flow potent massive streams, making for one world head in place of millions of heads. This tendency will next imperceptibly render individual thinking impossible, and thought will become the objective psychic process of a whole class, with systems of psychological switches and locks.

Proletarian poets of the Smithy group not only proclaimed the total regimentation of this world as a consummation devoutly to be wished, but celebrated in their verse the spread of such a system to other worlds as yet unknown that are scattered through the cosmos. This quasi-religious tendency came to be known as "planetarity." Its sources were to be found both in literature and in science. The science-fiction fantasies of H. G. Wells and his imitators had a pronounced influence in Russia. A more immediate and more Russian influence were the works of the scientist Tsiolkovsky, who had written popular works on such topics as rocket propulsion, intercontinental missiles, and interplanetary travel, and whose lectures at the literary studios of the Proletcult undoubtedly influenced young proletarian poets. Another probable source of proletarian "planetarity" were the symbolists who taught "verse-making" to these poets. Perhaps the striving for a quite literal "communion with other worlds" through science in proletarian poetry of the early period is only a rationalist version of the metaphysical-religious search of the early symbolists.

At the very moment when the mass man was being celebrated in prose and verse Zamyatin wrote the novel ironically entitled *We*, certainly the most humorous and probably the most perceptive of the twentieth-century negative utopias. Written in Russia in 1919 and 1920 but never published in Russia, *We* belongs to the family of modern novels which forecast for us in the future a dehumanized, machine-made world, a dull world organized for the greatest good of the greatest number, aimed at building paradise on earth. Huxley's *Brave New World*, published in 1932, echoes many of Zamyatin's themes, and George Orwell's *1984* owes a fully acknowledged debt to Zamyatin but differs from *We* in some important particulars. If Zamyatin's novel is compared with either work it turns out to be superior to them in its quality of ironic humor. Zamyatin himself described *We* as his "most jocular" work, and it is best read not as a dire prophecy of modern Fascism or Communism, but as a very funny commentary on the vagaries of reason. It resembles not so much Samuel Butler as Anatole France, who was a favorite of Zamyatin and whose spirit communicated itself to him. Zamyatin might have said of *We* what France said of his own work: "The irony which I acknowledge is not cruel, it does not make fun of love nor of beauty; but it teaches us to laugh at those who are mean and stupid, and without this laughter we might allow ourselves the weakness of hating them."

The story of *We* is based on the diaries of one of the leading mathematicians in a state of the twenty-ninth century. We see the precisely regimented world of that day through his eyes. At first, as a loyal mathematician and as builder of the space ship *Integral*, which is to carry the message of reason to distant worlds, the author of the diaries moves with perfect contentment as an obedient wheel in the social mechanism. But reason breaks down when he finds that not everything in the world is reducible to logarithmic systems. And that is the theme of the novel.

In *We* human beings of the twenty-ninth century are citizens of a city-state known as the Only State. The civilization of that day represents the final triumph of the *city*, the last step in civilization. In the course of a two hundred years' war which the people of the twenty-ninth century have only read about in their history books, the city had finally been victorious over the country. This terribly destructive war isolated one city from another and destroyed existing civilization. Only two-tenths of one per cent of the world's population survived the holocaust. After the invention of an artificial petroleum food had made the city independent of the country, the city dwellers cut themselves off from nature. Almost all surviving human beings were walled up inside cities and sealed off from the country by a wall of glass. Inside the Glass Wall all life is rationally organized and the benevolent state controls everything. There can be no accidents, no surprises: nothing unexpected ever happens, in fact nothing just happens, everything enters into the plan. The human reason, in its Euclidean variant, is all-powerful, and the aspect of the city presents only straight lines, planes, right angles, and neat diagonals. The streets and the houses are of glass, and, like the Crystal Palace which was for Dostoevsky the symbol of scientific rationalism, hard, shiny and square. The inhabitants have never even seen a tangled, mixed-up structure such as a tree, or stepped on any surface that wasn't level and smooth.

Outside the Glass Wall there is only the debris of nature, wild, uncontrolled, free growth, and strange, imperfectly organized beings. It develops that a small remnant of the human race had been forgotten and left behind outside the wall; but these people have fallen in the scale and become like animals. While one part of the human race has developed entirely along rational lines, the other part has preserved primitive, instinctive impulses and feelings. Zamyatin's point in this novel would seem to be that only through the union of the two parts could a fully human being again develop. Zamyatin finds hope in the irrational creatures that had been left "outside the wall"—only they can revivify and rehumanize life within the wall. Revolutionists in the Only State propose to tear down the wall that separates them from nature. George Orwell develops a similar idea when he indicates that a part of the human race in 1984 has been left out of the regimented society. The *proles* in that novel, descendants of the proletarians of our day, have been allowed to sink to a prehuman level and are regarded as no better than slaves. But when a rebel from the civilized community looks for hope for the future of humanity he can find it only in the *proles,* who have maintained the old human feelings of love, desire, and honor, and still have some memory of poetry. O'Kelley and Didi in the *Islanders,* with their fondness for song and story, also represent the human feelings that go on living "outside the wall."

In the regimented paradise of Zamyatin's *We,* the concept of an individual human being has already died out, and it is possible to speak only of "we." The citizens do not have names, but only numbers; they are called "numbers," or "unifs," a corruption of an old word meaning uniform. Politically the organization of the state is so perfect that no thought, no initiative, and no action is ever required of the citizens. The chief officer of the state, the Benefactor, is an iron-willed, mercilessly loving father image and god substitute. He strives always for the welfare of the "numbers," and their whole duty is to obey, honor, and—yes—worship him. His name, and pronouns referring to Him, are capitalized. The name is mentioned only in hushed reverence or in anger: when the citizens swear, it is not by the long-dead gods, but "by the Benefactor." (It will be remembered that in Huxley's *Brave New World* Ford had become a deity to be sworn by.) The earthly paradise has need of security forces. They are called the Guardians, and they hover protectively over the citizen at all times, displaying the most benevolent interest in his reading habits, listening to his conversations, observing the expression of his face for evidence of thought. Every citizen expects a slight delay in the delivery of mail, since all letters must first be read in the Bureau of Guardians. And the Guardians operate a mechanism called "The Machine," a terribly modern contrivance for executing political criminals, wherein those who defy the Benefactor are atomized —an advance over "liquidation." D–503, the narrator, in his moments of rational calm, likens the institution of the Guardians, with its care for the welfare of every citizen, to the system of "guardian angels" in which the ancients believed.

There are elections, regularly held on the Day of Unanimity. The suffrage is universal, and the voting is open and above board. The good citizens of the Only State have no desire for the slinking secrecy in the voting process which the ancients favored, for they want everyone to know that *they* vote for the Benefactor.

All life is social life, and every moment is scheduled. D–503 regards the ancients as having been particularly primitive in this respect, and he finds it hard even to imagine how life would have been without precise regimentation.

I have had opportunity to read and hear many improbable things about those times when human beings still lived in the state of freedom, that is in an unorganized, primitive state. . . . How could a government, even a primitive government, permit people to live without anything like our Tables—without compulsory walks, without precise regulation of the time to eat, for instance? They would get up and go to bed whenever they liked!

He willingly admits that his own society has not yet attained complete perfection, since two hours out of the twenty-four in each day are set aside for the "numbers" to do as they please, but he derives comfort from the reflection that with the progress of science and reason in human affairs at long last all 86,400 minutes of the day will be organized and supervised by the state. "Let them call me an idealist and a dreamer, I believe that sooner or later we shall find a place in the general formula even for the personal hours," he wrote in his diary. He regards the most nearly perfect product of ancient twentieth-century literature to have been the railway timetable.

Love and its sexual expression have been controlled. Hunger and Love no longer rule the world. The *Lex Sexualis* of the twenty-ninth century declares that "any number has the right to use any other number as a sexual article." This law ended the irrational situation (and unjust as well) in which there were some whom everyone preferred and others whom no one preferred. And it is easy to see how much mischief such a law eliminates from human life: the pang of unrequited love, the madness of jealousy, the suicides, the novels of Turgenev, "The Backbone Flute," all of these things have been rendered quite obsolete by the promulgation of this simple, healthful law.

One of the scheduled hours in the Table is the personal hour, the only time of the day when the "numbers," all of whom live in glass houses, have the right to draw their shades.

The rest is only a matter of technique. You are carefully examined in the laboratory of the Sexual Department where they find the content of the sexual hormones in your blood, and they accordingly make out for you a Table of sexual days. Then you file an application to enjoy the services of Number so-and-so (or Numbers so-and-so). You get for this purpose a checkbook (pink). That is all.

. . . The thing which was for the ancients a source of innumerable stupid tragedies has been converted in our time into a harmonious, agreeable, and useful function of the organism, a function like sleep, physical labor, the taking of food, defecation, and so forth.

Literature and the arts have, like love, been freed of the irrational. Poets there are, and tons of poetry are produced, but it is unthinkable that a poet, a member of the Institution of State Poets and Authors, should write about anything that happened to come into his head. Poets have been domesticated and harnessed. They perform a state service, and their poetry is "a commodity."

Music is produced entirely by mechanical means; tunes are turned out in the factory—the same ones for the whole population. George Orwell lived at a time when television and radio had reached a high level of development, and the *1984* "Telescreen" produces programs which are obligatory for all—there is only one channel, and you can't turn it off. Zamyatin could not know of the technological advances which would in the twentieth century convert the media of mass communication into a terrible menace, but he does foreshadow the immediate future with remarkable insight in this repellent image of the Musical Factory producing soothing music to which everyone must listen.

Yet there is revolution brewing even in this perfectly regimented society, and the Number on whose diaristic notes the novel is based, D–503, finds its ferment inside himself. As he writes, his attitude toward life in the Only State subtly changes. He had thought that his relations with other human beings were coldly codified, but suddenly he falls in love—with a particular woman. His love is desperate, irrational and out of control. The turmoil in his mind shows itself in confused and dreamlike images in his writing. He develops a flair for original metaphors. (He could even have written "The Backbone Flute.") He dreams. As his illness grows worse, reality seems to fuse; sometimes the world as he describes it is fragmented. His thoughts occur not in ordered and logical sequence but in swift telegraphic impulses. And he finds that there are many rebels: his pink-cheeked girl friend O–90, who is below the maternal norm but wants a baby anyway; his friend the official poet, R–13; S–4711, a member of the Guardians, who is a secret revolutionary; and the object of his bursting love, I–330, who is actually a leader in the revolutionary plot to break down the wall and let into the city the primitive creatures from the surrounding woods. I–330 it is who initiates him into the secrets of life in the twentieth century. She sheds her uniform for a saffron-yellow dress, smokes cigarettes (very harmful!), and drinks a greenish liquid of queer taste and heady effect. She takes him to a house of that era, preserved in glass outside the wall, the "Ancient House." There is the bust of a poet (Pushkin) in the house and furniture of irregular geometry. She takes him outside the wall where the hairy creatures on whom the future now depends have a meeting. And the builder of the *Integral*, D–503, infatuated with all of this, recovers his sanity only after an operation has removed from his brain the center of fantasy. Only then is he as good as a machine and capable of perfect happiness.

Zamyatin is not entirely pessimistic about the human future, and the novel simply does not contain the frightening prophecy which has been ascribed to it. The leader of the Only State, the Benefactor, only seems to have imperfect control; there are many revolutionaries—in fact almost all the characters we meet are in the movement—and rebellion is still in progress with the issue in doubt as the novel ends. As revolution rages on the streets of the city, D–503 finds refuge from it in the men's room of a subway station:

I do not remember how I got into one of the public rest rooms, in a station of the Subway. Above, everything was perishing; the greatest civilization, the most rational in human history, was crumbling, but here, by some irony, everything remained as before, beautiful. The walls shone; water murmured cozily; and like the water, the unseen, transparent music. . . . Only think of it! All this is doomed; all this will be covered with grass some day; only myths will remain. . . .

I moaned aloud. At the same instant I felt someone gently patting my knee. It was from the left; it was a neighbor who occupied a seat on my left—an enormous forehead, a bald parabola, yellow, unintelligible lines of wrinkles on his forehead, those lines about me.

"I understand you. I understand completely," he said. "Yet you must calm yourself. You must. It will return. It will inevitably return. It is only important that everybody should learn of my discovery. You are the first to whom I talk about it. I have calculated that there is *no infinity*! No!"

I looked at him wildly.

"Yes, yes, I tell you so. There is no infinity. If the universe is infinite, then the average density of matter must equal zero; but since we know it is not zero, therefore the universe is finite; it is spherical in form, and the square of its radius—R^2—is equal to the average density multiplied by . . . The only thing left is to calculate the numerical coefficient and then . . . Do you realize what it means? It means that everything is final, everything is simple. . . . But you, my honored sir, you disturb me, you prevent my finishing my calculations by your yelling!"

I do not know which shattered me more, his discovery, or his positiveness at that apocalyptic hour. Only then did I notice that he had a notebook in his hands, and a logarithmic dial. I understood then that even if everything was perishing it was my duty (before you, my unknown and beloved) to leave these records in a finished form.

I asked him to give me some paper, and here in the rest room, to the accompaniment of the quiet music, transparent like water, I wrote down these last lines.

I was about to put down a period as the ancients would put a cross over the caves into which they used to throw their dead, when all of a sudden my pencil trembled and fell from between my fingers. . . .

"Listen!" I pulled my neighbor. "Yes, listen, I say. There, where your finite universe ends, what is there? What?"

He had no time to answer. From above, down the steps stamping . . .[1]

There is much in common between Mayakovsky's play *The Bedbug* and *We*, written about ten years earlier. No doubt Mayakovsky was consciously engaging Zamyatin in dispute over the importance of the values which, both agree, would probably disappear in a rational world. Mayakovsky ridicules Prisypkin's "heart strings," his individualism, and his dirty indulgence in cigarettes and vodka. For Zamyatin, in both *Islanders* and *We,* in the twentieth as well as the twenty-ninth century, these things are symbols of rebellion against social regimentation. The quality of Zamyatin's rebellion is neither political nor soundly philosophical. It is bohemian. The "Ancient House" where I–330 arranges assignations with her lover, the mathematician D–503, is an apartment in Soho, or a spot in Greenwich Village. And though his vision of future men serried into ranks of human anonymity may seem horrible to us, surely the hairy creatures "outside the wall" are more horrible. And Zamyatin must have known that primitives are never as free as civilized men and that a sense of individual worth has developed as civilizations became more complex.

Defective though it may be as an anti-utopia, Zamyatin's *We* is a truly great book which will probably outlive its relatives in the genre. With satiric scorn, it offers a quintessential image of any and all Establishments, religious or social, bourgeois or Communist, that seek to enforce their particular and temporary values on all human beings as eternal verities. D–503, in his period of naïve adjustment to the Benefactor and the Only State, had believed that the revolution that created that state was the last one. Zamyatin could observe in the Bolshevik revolutionaries of his own day evidences of a developing conservatism and hostility to change. The October

Revolution, they thought, was the last one. The young woman I–330 challenges this doctrine of finality: "There is no such thing as a 'last' revolution. The number of revolutions is infinite."

Zamyatin's influence was felt by many writers of the Serapion Brotherhood, though probably no surviving member would admit this, and he was an esteemed and influential figure in the Writers' Union until attacked as a literary "enemy" in 1929 and relieved of his post as a member of the executive board. His work is hardly known to the present generation of Soviet readers, and his name is mentioned in the recent three-volume *History of Soviet Literature* only in order to characterize him as an anti-Soviet "inner emigré," who joined the "outer emigration." That work quotes his ironic survey of contemporary letters in 1921, *I'm Afraid,* in which he maintained that since proletarian literature was a "step backward," and the real writers, "madmen, hermits, heretics, dreamers, rebels, and skeptics," were silent, it followed that Russian literature had only one possible future: its past. His stories "The Cave" (1922) and "Flood" (1930) are mentioned only as indicating a certain reprehensible tendency. His tales of Petrograd in the grip of hunger—"Mamai," for instance, which catches in lucid metaphor the essence of life reduced to subhuman privation—are passed over without intelligent comment. His *Impious Tales* are not mentioned. Nor is his early work *The Province* (1913) and *Far Away* (1914), set in the Russian backwoods, and featuring a primitive way of life. Zamyatin's brilliant essays on Anatole France, and on the work of H. G. Wells, with whom he had many things in common, as well as his portraits of the literary men he knew, are evidence of fine human and literary sophistication. His own roots reach into the purely Russian style of Leskov, whose ornamental wordplay he admired, and of Gogol, whose manner of narration seems to have influenced him. Zamyatin drew his strength as a writer from the Russian tradition, and at the same time had a lively appreciation of Western literature. The Soviet authorities who have decreed that he is to be ignored are defeating themselves. They have "thrown a pearl away, richer than all their tribe."

Olesha's Critique of the Reason

The creatures who rule the world of *We* rely on the power of human reason to return that world, after its adventure in revolution, to predetermined logical shapes. They would deprive man of his "fantasy," because that faculty is not always obedient to objective reason, containing an element of individual caprice. The man who lives by fantasy creates a private world of his own, and may thus become a subject for medical attention.

Or he may become an artist. Indeed an artist by nature possesses and exercises the power of fantasy; this is the message contained in the work of Yury Olesha, who died in 1960 at the age of 61, having produced only his famous novel *Envy* (1927), a few magnificent short stories, a fairy tale for children, *The Three Fat Men* (1928), one full-length play, *A List of Benefits* (1931), a number of movie scenarios, some critical articles and fugitive literary comments, and brief reminiscences of his contemporaries. His "autobiographical novel," entitled *A Line for Every Day*, was published in full in 1965. It combines reminiscence with intensely personal literary reflections.

The "Complete Works" of Yury Olesha do not bulk large in Soviet literature, nor do they have a prominent place in the consciousness of the contemporary Soviet reader. The present writer in 1956 met with a number of young Russians interested in literature who had never heard of Olesha. After an explosive success with the novel *Envy* in 1927, Olesha fell silent and was largely forgotten during the thirties. The reason for his silence he stated himself with disarming frankness in a speech to the First Congress of Soviet Writers: "The First Five-Year Plan was not my theme. I could have gone to a construction project, lived at a factory among workers . . . but that was not my theme." What, then, was Olesha's theme? The principal object of his artistic interest is the particular and unique quality of every human experience: the individual flavor of a particular person, the shape of daylight at a given place and time, the unexpected look of a clock's face pointing to 3:15, the fantasy effect of long shadows in a northern latitude, sunlight reflected in a bronze vase or broken into its spectrum of color by a mother-of-pearl button. Olesha re-creates the world as a child might see it: a world of direct sense impressions which, unnamed and as yet un-catalogued, still have the freshness of surprise. The formalist critics who influenced Olesha, Victor Shklovsky in particular, emphasized the importance for literary art of such devices as the "estrangement" and the "deformation" of reality. The artist, said Shklovsky, by breaking the fixed pattern of verbal or sensual experience, forces the beholder of art to see again simple things which he had taken for granted, or to hear again the actual sounds of speech. "Estrangement" of reality in Olesha does not, except in the fairy tale written specifically for children, *The Three Fat Men*, consist in the construction of an unreal and nonexistent world. That is not the source of Olesha's "fantasy." Rather it is the rich world of experience which the individual mind can create for itself out of the simplest reality, just by paying attention to it. A stone, for instance. In a wonderful story called "The Cherry Pit" Olesha introduces a fairy tale about a young man who was "in too much of a hurry to throw a stone." He threw it, but in throw-ing it—in treating it according to its definition as a "thing to be thrown"—he had lost forever its special and unique reality:

With the stone in my hand I stood about four paces from the wall. The stone was supposed to fall into the niche and stay there. I swung my arm and let it go. The stone flew away and hit the brick. There was a short spurt of dust. I had missed. The stone fell in the bushes at the base of the wall. It was only then I heard the stone's cry, uttered while it was in my hand and before I let it go.

"Wait!" it cried. "Look at me!" And then I actually re-membered. I should have subjected the stone to an inspection. Why, really, that stone was a remarkable thing. And now it's disappeared there in the bushes! And though I held it in my hand I don't even know what color it was. But maybe it was a lilac-colored stone; maybe it wasn't a monolith but consisted of several separate parts: maybe something petrified was locked into it, the remains of a beetle, or a cherry pit; maybe the stone was porous, and maybe it wasn't a stone at all that I picked up but a weather-beaten bone.

The sudden metaphysical malaise felt by Olesha's young man when he threw the stone anticipates Roquentin's very similar experience with a stone in Sartre's novel *La Nausée*, written many years later. Roquentin has lost the faculty of separating one thing from another and organizing the items of experience into classes by the device of naming. The eyes of his mind are out of focus, and he experiences nausea. The stone, which he picked up at the seashore intending to throw it into the water, was by definition inanimate, but it seemed to touch him, like a live thing, and he could not throw it. The philosophical concern of Sartre is the same as that of Olesha: both men are examining the texture of the human mind as revealed in experience; but for Sartre the detachment from naming and classification results in nausea; for Olesha it is a source of wonder and of new worlds.

In the story "Liompa," the old man Ponomarev is dying and in delirium. The world of things is gradually receding from him until at last he is left only with those things which directly touch his person: the bed, the blanket, the sounds in his immediate vicinity. For everything else he has only "names," arid concepts without weight, color, or texture:

The vanishing things left the dying man nothing but their names.

There was an apple in the world. It was shining amidst the leaves; it was seizing little bits of the day and gently turning them around: the green of the garden, the outline of the window. The law of gravity was waiting for it under the tree, on the black earth, on the hummock. Beady ants were scampering among the hummocks. Newton sat in the garden. There were many causes hidden inside the apple, causes that could determine a multitude of effects. But none of these causes had anything to do with Ponomarev. The apple had become an abstraction to him. And the fact that the flesh of a thing had disappeared while the abstraction remained was painful to him.

In the apartment with him is a little boy who rushes about greeting each new thing as a wonder, though he is already falling into the intellectual trap of classification:

The little boy dropped in on Ponomarev. The child's head bounced around like a ball near the edge of the bed. The sick man's temples were pale, like those of a blind man. The boy came close to Ponomarev's head and examined it. He thought that it had always been this way in the world: a bearded man lying in a bed in a room. The little boy had just learned to recognize things; he did not yet know how to distinguish time in their existence.

For Ponomarev the condition in which he possesses only the *names* for things, only the rational tools for their manipulation and not the real things themselves, is the condition of death.

Envy and Rage

There are novels which catch and concentrate the essence of a particular historical moment. Such was Yury Olesha's novel *Envy*. Published in 1927, it was acknowledged by almost every literary faction as an important artistic statement. The literary critics reacted with interest and sympathy to the picture of an anti-Communist intellectual claiming to belong to the nineteenth century, reduced in the new world to sharing with a colleague a fat widow in a rococo bed. For them that image meant the degradation and death of the old values. The leaders of the Russian Association of Proletarian Writers admired Olesha's reduction of a dissident intellectual to basic ingredients of envy and adolescent rage. These critics, moreover, saw in Andrey Babichev, the Soviet businessman, a satire on power-hungry bureaucrats of the trusts and committees. Intellectuals tended to see themselves in the drunken poet Kavalerov, and they interpreted the novel as a plea for the rights of the individual against the mass pressures of the Communist regime. The mark of genuine greatness attaches to the novel. No one can fail to recognize in it a part of his own human reality.

The fundamental thematic structure of *Envy* is not original, but, rather, typical of its period in Soviet literature. Many novels and stories of the period deal with the conflict between old and new values and the dislocation of sensitive intellectuals in the collective society. Even some proletarian writers, perhaps influenced by Freud and Jung, explored subconscious, nonrational factors in the behavior of their characters. The debate of the intellectual with himself over "accepting" or "not accepting" the Soviet regime, a favorite theme of Olesha in both *Envy* and *A List of Good Deeds,* was already an established one in the work of the fellow travelers. Olesha's originality lies in his statement of the problem. He presents that problem in concrete human terms as a conflict between a successful Soviet sausage manufacturer and two drunken and dissolute poets who envy, hate, and maybe at times love him. The theme when stated in these terms, and enriched with overtones of adolescent sexual attachment, takes on universal significance. One forgets that Olesha is describing the Soviet Union of the twenties and that the big breezy Babbitt of his story (he is actually named Babichev) is a Communist bureaucrat. The Babichev of Olesha's novel is a hardheaded businessman with big ideas and a purely utilitarian set of values. He has little use for intellectuals except as proofreaders and suppliers of interesting but useless bits of information, like the answers to such questions as "Who was Jocasta?" He has two overpowering projects on which he lavishes his wealth of efficient energy. The first is to create a sausage, firm, tasty, nutritious, and just juicy enough, that can be mass-produced for twenty-five cents a pound. His second and more alluring dream is to build enormous communal dining rooms where thousands of people can be served at a nominal price. This creation, which is destined to liberate women from slavery to pots and pans, is actually being realized as the novel opens. The "Ten Cent Piece"—as Babichev has named it for the low cost of the nourishing mass meal which it will serve—is in process of construction, and Babichev, its creator, rushes about in a fever of activity attending to everything.

Andrey Babichev has a protegé, Volodya Makarov, a young

man who represents "the new." He is a famous soccer player, universally admired for his courage and skill on the field. He carries the aroma of sweaty athletic prowess, and when he smiles two rows of perfect teeth appear. He too is deeply involved in building the brave new world, and if he experiences envy, it is envy of the machine. He writes to Babichev:

. . . I am a human machine. You won't recognize me. I have become a machine. And if I am not really one yet, it is what I want to be. The machines in the workshops here are pedigreed! They are terrific, so proud, so dispassionate, nothing like the ones in your sausage factories. Yours are just artisans. All you do is slaughter calves. I want your advice. I want to be working-proud, proud of my work. I want to be indifferent to everything, you understand, everything that is outside my work. And so I have become envious of the machine, you understand? Why am I not just as good as it is? We invented it, designed and constructed it, and it turned out to be much harder than we are. Start it and it gets to work. And it won't make a single unnecessary wriggle. That's the way I would like to be. Understand, Andrey Petrovich, not a single unnecessary wriggle.

Opposed to the new and positive men are Nikolai Kavalerov and the brother of Babichev, Ivan, both aliens in the new world, both poets of a sort, both engaged in a love-hate duel with Andrey Babichev and both devoted to the unnecessary wriggle. Olesha devised the complex structure of the novel so as to present Babichev and his world through the eyes of the alienated pair. In the first part Kavalerov is the narrator, and it is his attitude toward Andrey Babichev that the reader experiences. Olesha consciously adopts for his character Kavalerov the irrational emotional attitudes of Dostoevsky's Underground Man, and he understands better than most of the commentators on Dostoevsky that the Underground Man's hatred of the normal world is the outgrowth of adolescent rage, of the fury experienced by the unfledged young unable to place or define himself. Kavalerov, though not young in years, displays symptoms of a delayed adolescence and of homosexual attachment to his father image and enemy, Andrey. He is surprised, on seeing his own reflection in the mirror, to observe a general resemblance, no more than sexual, to his own father. His thoughts about Babichev, who has befriended and supported him, reveal hatred so special and particular that it is not far from love. His letter to Babichev is a distillation of wounded feeling:

Andrey Petrovich:
You took me in out of the cold. You took me in under your wing. I slept on your delightful sofa. You know how lousily I lived before that. Came the blessed night. You took pity on me, gathered up a drunk.

You put me in linen sheets. The material was so smooth and cool, it was calculated to, and did, soothe my anger and ease my anxiety.

Even mother-of-pearl pillowcase buttons came back into my life with the iridescent ring of the rainbow swimming in them. I recognized them at once. They came back from a long-forgotten corner of childhood memory.

I had a bed.

The word itself had a poetic remoteness for me, like the word "hoop."

You gave me a bed.

From the height of your well-being, you lowered upon me the cloud-bed, a halo that surrounded me with magic warmth, wrapped me in memories, nostalgia without bitterness, and hopes. A hope stirred that I could still have much of what had been intended for me in my youth.

You are my benefactor, Andrey Petrovich!

Just think: a famous man made me his close companion! A remarkable public figure settled me in his home. I want to convey my feelings to you.

Strictly speaking, it's all one feeling: hatred.

I hate you, Comrade Babichev.

I'm writing this letter to bring you down a peg.

From my first day with you, I felt afraid. You stifled me. You crushed me under your weight.

You stand in your underpants giving off the beery smell of sweat. I look at you and your face becomes strangely enlarged, your torso becomes bloated—the lines of a clay idol curve out, swell. I want to shout out:

Who gave you the right to crush me?

How am I worse than he?

Is he more intelligent?

Is he richer spiritually?

Is he on a higher level of organization?

Stronger? More important?

Superior not only in position, but in his essence?

Why must I acknowledge his superiority?

These were the questions I was asking myself. Every day, observation gave me a fraction of the answer. A month went by. I know the answer. And now I'm not afraid of you. You're just an obtuse dignitary. And nothing more. It was not the importance of your personality that crushed me. Oh no! Now I see through you, look you over, having placed you in the palm of my hand. My fear before you has passed, like something childish. I have thrown you off my back. You're not much really.

At one time I was tortured by doubts. Can it be that I am a nonentity compared to him? I wondered. Can it be that for an ambitious man like me he is plainly an example of greatness? ...

The first part of the novel involves a straight presentation of Kavalerov's viewpoint, but in the second part the viewpoint is that of Ivan Babichev. There is an apparent shift to the third person narrator, but his narration is based almost entirely on Ivan's memories, fantasies, notions, and dreams. The shift at midpoint from first to third person recalls the technical tricks of Dostoevsky, as does the orientation of the narrative on Ivan's fevered imagination in both the waking and the dream state. Part Two begins with an account of Ivan's reminiscences of his boyhood, when he thoroughly frightened his father because of an incurable penchant for treating his daydreams as reality. Ivan perversely rejects the real in favor of his own fancies, and he abjures rational counsel if it interferes with feeling. When interrogated by the Soviet Security Police he announces that he is organizing a Conspiracy of Feelings, those feelings, such as pity, tenderness, pride, jealousy, love, which he believes are being liquidated:

"I want to find the representatives of what you call the old world. I mean feelings like jealousy, love for a woman, vanity. I want to find a blockhead so that I can show you: here, Comrades, is an example of that human condition known as stupidity.

"Many characters played out the comedy of the old world.

The curtain is coming down. The characters must gather on the proscenium and sing the final couplets. I want to be the intermediary between them and the audience. I will direct the chorus and the last exit from the stage.

"To me has fallen the honor of conducting the last parade of the ancient, human passions. . . ."

Ivan hates the machine-made world of Edisons, Babbitts, and efficient communal kitchens, but he himself is the inventor of a fantasy machine which will, he says, destroy them all. He has given his machine the sweetest and tenderest human name: Ophelia, the name of a girl who killed herself from love and madness. His creation is the most human of all machines, it is the human source of "the machine" itself, and he places all his reliance on it. But Kavalerov in a dream sees this most human machine turn on him and destroy, not the others, but its own inventor. Perhaps Olesha wishes to suggest in this strange nightmare that human feelings would not really die in the new world but would only reject the Dostoevskian irrationalists who rely on them exclusively. The new generation, represented by the sun-tanned girl Valya, whom both Kavalerov and Ivan yearn to have on their side, rejects the old-fashioned poet and the dreamer. All the beautiful and good things in the world are garnered by the bustling bureaucrat and the young sports enthusiast, and the conspirators are left in the end with only their holy feelings of hatred and envy. Instead of the fresh and tender Valya ("Valya, I have waited for you all my life. Take pity on me!") the two settle on Annie, a petit-bourgeois widow who has a small flat and a high, old-fashioned featherbed. The theme of thwarted manhood appears in the portrait of Annie's husband which hangs over the bed where Kavalerov possesses the woman:

"You do remind me of him," Annie whispered ardently, leaning over him.

The glass-covered photograph hung over the bed. In it there was a man, somebody's youngish grandpa, in formal attire, one of the latest cutaways of the bygone era. One could feel that he had a solid, many-barreled nape to his neck. A man of perhaps fifty-seven.

Kavalerov remembered his father changing shirts. . . .
"You do remind me a lot of my husband," Annie repeated. . . .[2]

Envy, like *We,* contains conscious echoes of Dostoevsky's *Notes from the Underground* as well as of "The Grand Inquisitor." Both novels enter a plea for individual freedom and the autonomy of feelings in opposition to the rationalism of modern mass society. Like Dostoevsky, both novelists rebel against the imagined "Crystal Palace" of the future, where life will respond only to logarithmic tables, and the individual human being, for the sake of happiness, gives up freedom. The principal literary text for Olesha's *Envy* is the passage in *Notes from the Underground* where Dostoevsky lashes out at the "Crystal Palace," the utopian vision of the communist future presented by the socialist critic Chernyshevsky in 1863. Poetry, the human personality, traditional Russian culture are shown in Olesha's farcical fantasy as degraded and discarded. The envious adolescent Kavalerov and the retarded old fool Ivan Babichev, neither of whom has a man's place in the new world, reflect Olesha's pessimistic view as to the fate of the nineteenth-century literary imagination in the twentieth century. Though Kavalerov and Ivan are defeated, Olesha has so contrived the telling of his story that the reader identifies himself with their disreputable human feelings, and never with the Buddha-shaped businessmen in nose spectacles. The bizarre form of the novel conceals a defense of human values which Olesha felt were being trampled upon in the name of building socialism, and a plea for the right to existence of love, a sense of personal honor, and respect for oneself.

Yet Olesha is not without optimism for the future, even should it be socialist. This quality of essential hope, the conviction that organic human growth will break through iron and concrete, is characteristic of him. The "feelings" that now conspire against the state will continue to live though they may change their form. The nineteenth-century imagination may be dying but that does not necessarily mean the death of all imagination. The sausage manufacturer has a real affection for his young protegés, though doubtless different from the feeling of a father for his children. The sausage manufacturer, though presented through the eyes of those who hate him, is a sympathetic character. His sausages are the product of a kind of art, and the creation of the "Ten Cent Piece," his communal dining room, called for idealism and imagination. Olesha's novel seems to have a prescience of new "feelings" coming to birth as the old die out.

Thus in his story "The Cherry Pit," which opposes a fanciful young man living in the "Invisible Country" of artists and poets to a sober Marxist with a set of stable names for his predictable range of experiences, the last scene is an expression of Olesha's deep optimism. The fanciful young man has planted a cherry pit in a city lot in memory of his unrequited love. But he had not taken "The Plan" into account, and on that spot a huge concrete works was to be set up:

Dear Natasha, I forgot about the main thing, the Plan. A Plan exists. But I acted without consulting the Plan. In five years a huge concrete establishment will rise on that spot where there is now only a vacant lot, a ditch, useless old walls. My sister, Imagination, is a rash creature. In the spring they'll start laying the foundation, and then what will become of my stupid cherry pit? But in the invisible country, a tree will blossom, dedicated to you. Tourists will come to see the concrete mass of buildings. But they won't see your tree. Is it really impossible to make the invisible country visible?

The above is an imaginary letter. I never wrote it. I would have written it if Avel [the Marxist friend] had not said what he did:
"The buildings will be laid out in a semicircle. The interior of the semicircle will be taken up by a garden. Do you have any imagination?"
"Yes I do," I answered. "And I see it, Avel. I see it clearly. There will be a garden here. And on the very spot where you are standing a cherry tree will sprout."

Chapter 4

The Intellectuals I

Serapions

THE BOLSHEVIK TERROR of the Civil War years did not fully liquidate the prerevolutionary educated class—the sophisticated and finely cultivated Russian intelligentsia. The bearers of nineteenth-century culture in the Russian world rising from the ruins were young men who had roots in that class. Of those who were born near the turn of the century many took part in the Civil War—sometimes mobilized by the Whites, sometimes by the Reds—and after the advent of peace and the New Economic Policy in 1921 they tried to find a *modus vivendi* with a regime organically hostile to their traditions and their class. A number of hopeful young writers with no claim to proletarian origin or ideology found one another in Petrograd in 1920, and under the inspiration of two older men, Victor Shklovsky and Eugene Zamyatin, consciously sought ways to preserve the heritage of literary culture they had received. Under the patronage and protection of Maxim Gorky,[1] they met regularly in the House of the Arts in Petrograd to discuss literary problems and perhaps even more to develop a strategy for dealing with an unprecedented situation in which a tyrannical regime basing its power on the illiterate proclaimed itself the sponsor and advocate of cultural enterprise. When Lenin's liberalized New Economic Policy had opened the door to experiment in the production of a free and independent literature, these young men moved courageously into the field, at the same time insisting on their sympathy for the Revolution. This was "The Serapion Brotherhood." The date of their first public meeting is an important one in Soviet literature, February 1, 1921; and their first collection of stories and articles came out early in 1922.[2]

Recognizing the anomalous position of these young men,

Trotsky with real perception dubbed them, and others like them, "fellow travelers" of the Revolution. Their manifestoes were ironic parodies of the apocalyptic proclamations which proliferated at the time in the literary milieu. They proclaimed only freedom from proclamations and demanded only that art be allowed to exist and to develop independently of doctrines and parties, camps and classes. They rebelled against the tendency of nineteenth-century Russian literature, too, to serve the aims of ideology, and in this they reveal an affinity with the prerevolutionary symbolist movement, with its insistence on the specific nature of literature:

With whom do we stand, Serapion Brothers?
We are with the Hermit Serapion. We believe that literary chimeras are a special reality, and we will have none of utilitarianism. We do not want to write for propaganda. Art is real, like life itself. And like life itself it has neither goal nor meaning; it exists because it cannot help existing.

It would be a mistake to think of the Serapions as one of the many literary organizations of the day. They were not "organized" in any way. They shared no conviction about literary style. Only in a very limited sense were they "brothers," for they had nothing in common with one another except an organic revulsion against the *use* of literature for nonliterary purposes. Zamyatin, usually considered an elder of the society, maintained that there never was such a society. The Brotherhood "was invented," he said, "partly by myself." There could be no "Brotherhood" since the Brothers all "had different fathers"; they had no common direction, since some moved west and others east; some were realists and some impressionists, while others cultivated Hoffmannesque fantasy. Independence was all they valued, and Slonimsky claimed that they feared only one thing: that some day a "Serapion Brothers Society" would be established in the People's Commissariat for Education.

Whether we think of it as a Brotherhood or not, the membership of the Serapions included the best literary talent of the day. They were violently attacked as enemies of the Revolution. They met in difficult times to find a way of adjusting to a strange and even repellent reality, and the majority succeeded in this, though eventually their success meant critical compromise with the state.

We shall here review briefly the careers and principal contributions to Soviet literature of the Serapion Brothers, then deal in some detail with other important writers of the so-called fellow-traveler movement.

Victor Shklovsky (1893————) is one of the most important figures in the history of Soviet literature. A leading theoretician of the formalist school of critics, he was active during the First World War in the Society for the Study of Poetic Language (*Opoyaz*) in Petrograd, which specialized in a study of the linguistic devices of poetry and engaged in polemics with academic exponents of biographical and historical criticism. After a career during the Civil War which still remains in shadow, though it is certain that he at one time fought on the side of the Socialist-Revolutionaries and against the Reds, Shklovsky appeared in Petrograd in 1920, and his authority was such that he immediately became a leader among the Serapions. He was a close literary friend of Mayakovsky, as we have seen, and when his rather shadowy biography led to attacks on him, Mayakovsky supported him as a critical intelligence whose ideas were important for Soviet literature. At a meeting called to negotiate an agreement between members of the Moscow Proletarian Association (MAPP) and *Lef,* the proletarian leaders demanded before agreeing to anything that *Lef* expel such doubtful characters as Shklovsky and Pasternak. Mayakovsky refused to do this, saying that "even Victor's dubious notions will enter into the history of Russian literature."[3]

And Victor Shklovsky's ideas are certainly stimulating, even when they are demonstrably wrong, whimsical, or fantastic. He is a specialist in paradoxes which, while they may shock or amuse, always point to the essence of a problem. When he says, for instance, that "art has always been free of life, and its colors never reflected the colors of the flag waving over the city," or that "new art forms are simply old and inferior genres elevated to the level of art," and that "Pushkin's lyrics come from album verses, Blok's from gypsy songs, Mayakovsky's from comic doggerel," or when he maintains that a literary work is simply the sum of its devices, Shklovsky raises in acute and original form important problems as to the genesis of art, or the succession of genres, or the nature of creative writing.[4]

Shklovsky's propagation of the notion of *ostranenie,* or "estrangement," of reality as a basic function of all literary art, even the realistic variety, had a pronounced influence on the work of Olesha and of many younger fellow travelers. The artist should, according to Shklovsky, break down the habit of automatic reaction to the outside world and force the reader to see and hear it. His own literary style is subjective and impressionistic and, because of the personal and arbitrary movement of his thought, difficult to follow. Clarity is itself a kind of lazy man's vice, he seems to think, and the reader who would follow Shklovsky's turns must work at it all the time.

Shklovsky has not only survived, but managed a career in Soviet literature. He has long since lost the intransigent fire and recanted the heresies of his youth. Critical reviews and books which he has published in recent years do, however, contain occasional flashes of the early Shklovsky.

Lev Lunts (1901–1924) was a brilliant young playwright and a pupil of Shklovsky. He produced much of the manifesto material which identified and described the Serapion Brotherhood, and four plays of distinction. His essays deplore the indifference of Russian writers to story structure, and his plays, *Outlaws* (1921), *The Apes Are Coming* (1921), *Bertrand de Born* (1922), and *The City of Truth* (1924), have intricate and interesting plots. His slogan "To the West" meant that a new prose revival should arise from the union of Western, particularly French, storytelling art and the raw material of Russian life. Had he lived Lunts might have made an important and original contribution to Russian drama. Gorky regarded him as one of the most promising younger men.

Nikolai Nikolaevich Nikitin (1897———) was a writer of singular power and remarkable range of style whose stories about the Civil War, *Fort Vomit* (1922), *Bunt* (1923), *Flight* (1925), and others, are grotesques of moral and physical horror which the author presents calmly and almost without concern. His naturalistic scenes of sex or violence shock and stupefy the reader, and they might also repel him, but the technique of narration places such things at an artistic distance. His characters tend to be dominated by erotic drives.

Nikitin is different from Lunts in the kind of material he uses and in the manner of narration, but he is like him and like other Serapions in his self-conscious concern with the craft of narration itself, and in his experiments with storytelling method. Nikitin is a practitioner of the verbal somersault: the words normally used to describe a person or an incident are often avoided as too hackneyed, and other words unprecedented in the given context are selected. The influence of Victor Shklovsky is clearly in evidence here, but the effect of that influence is not always happy.

Like the majority of the Serapions, Nikitin made a successful adjustment to the requirements of "Soviet reality." In a novel written in 1950, *Aurora Borealis,* he deals with a conventional theme, capitalist intervention during the Civil War, in a thoroughly conventional manner. In 1958 he published a frankly political essay: *Taiwan—an Inseparable Part of the Chinese People's Republic.*

Vsevolod Ivanov (1895———) was the product of an intellectual milieu, but his biography is more like that of Gorky in the bewildering variety of his experience on the lower level of life. Like Gorky he lived as a kind of tramp from an early age. He had many occupations: compositor, sailor, organ player, poetry reader, clown, sword swallower, and dervish. He is unlike Gorky in that there is some doubt as to his sympathies during the Civil War. He fought with the Whites under Admiral Kolchak, was taken prisoner and sentenced to be shot. Pardoned, he joined the Red Army and fought in its ranks until the end of the Civil War. When he arrived in Petrograd in 1922 he joined a group of proletarian writers, the Cosmists; but he outraged the proletarians by joining the Serapion Brotherhood at the same time. The proletarians apparently attributed this, not to naïveté, but to lack of principle.

And indeed how could a young man coming of age in 1917 find in his world secure moral or ethical moorings? Ivanov's biography and his stories betray the effect on young intellectuals of the catastrophic collapse of values experienced during those days. Something analogous to this happened in the West in the postwar period, but nothing like the Russian experience of being reduced to a bare subsistence level in morality.

His early stories, which brought him fame along with the misfortune of being called "a new Gorky," which he certainly was not, describe guerrilla warfare in Siberia and in the Far East, where Russia borders on Mongolia and China. The setting of the stories is exotic, the cast of characters a mélange of Russian peasants, Kirghiz nomads, Chinese farmers, Mongol horsemen. They are dark and cruel, they have lost normal human feelings of pity. A band of Russian peasant partisans destroys a Kirghiz infant whose mother is favoring it over a motherless white child ("The Child"):

"You want a Russian boy to die for that infidel? You want Vaska to die?"
The peasants began to feel very sad.
Selivanov said to Afanasii Petrovich:
"Take the other one away. To the devil with him, let him die. . . . We've killed a lot of them. Just one more . . ."

A group of peasants driven south by famine and starving on the way await the death of one of their number so they may eat him ("Hollow Arabia"). The stories "Armored Train No. 14–69" (1922), "Colored Winds" (1922), and "Blue Sands" (1923) describe events of the Civil War. The basic human experience in Ivanov is of unbridled passion and violence, and when, as in "Colored Winds," the characters "philosophize," what emerges is a kind of unlettered and ignorant pessimism.

Ivanov, too, in his early period is a conscious literary stylist. Plot and incident are less important in his stories than their lyrical atmosphere. Even when the actions described are harsh and cruel, the language is musical and evocative, and scenes are depicted with an artist's sensitivity to line and color.

Ivanov, never a man to stumble, easily conformed to the new demands on literature which were made in the period of the Five-Year Plan. He was one of the first and most enthusiastic literary celebrants of the industrial achievements under Stalin, taking part in excursions and official visits to collective farms and industrial enterprises as early as 1930. His *Adventures of a Fakir* (1934–35) is a fascinating account of his experiences as a circus performer, full of action, color, and cynical amusement. *Parkhomenko* (1938) is a novelistic biography of a Civil War general, conventional in form and neatly tailored to the Party line. *The Fall of Berlin* (1945) is a long novel about the Second World War. Certainly it is fair to say that it lacks the stylistic interest of his early work as a Serapion.

Mikhail Leonidovich Slonimsky (1897——) in his auto-biography records that his father was editor of the magazine *Vestnik Evropy* (*Herald of Europe*), and that his mother was the sister of a famous professor. "My childhood," he wrote, "passed in an atmosphere permeated by literature and music." His earliest literary teachers were Zamyatin and Shklovsky and his work shows clear traces of their tutelage. *The Sixth Rifles* (1922) is a collection of stories dealing with war and revolution and like the work of Nikitin and Ivanov it presents in a subjective manner pictures of grotesque and senseless cruelty. His novel *The Lavrovs* (1926) depicts the fatal effects of the Revolution on values and on family life in the intellectual milieu. There is a note of compromise and conciliation even in the first version, where it seems clear that the hero will "become a useful Soviet citizen"; and *First Years* (1949) is a retelling of *The Lavrovs* with a more explicit ideological denouement. *Foma Kleshnyov* (1931) presents a model Communist at work.

Venyamin Kaverin (1902———) is another Serapion whose adjustment to "Soviet reality" has been successful. He managed to publish his skillfully constructed novels and stories in every period of Soviet history, and he has recently completed a major work, his trilogy, *Open Book* (1949–56), dealing with the life and education of a Soviet scientist. Lunts he considered his best friend and acknowledged a debt to him for his own literary development. He shared with Lunts an attraction to writers of fantasy and adventure stories: Robert Louis Stevenson, Edgar Allan Poe, and E. T. A. Hoffmann were his favorites, and his early works *Masters and Apprentices* (1923) and *The End of a Band* (1926) reveal his interest in the carefully plotted tale. In the novel *Nine Tenths of Fate* (1926) he tried to present the psychology of the displaced intellectual of his day. His most famous novel of the early period, *Artist Unknown* (1930), develops a conflict between a serious artist and a realistic builder of the new world. The builder, Shpektorov, is contemptuous of ethical values and holds the product of art to be low on the list of requirements for the new state. The artist who insists on the need for a free art is defeated, but he has produced, nonetheless, a single deathless picture. His *The Fulfillment of Desires* (1935) and *Two Captains* (1939) are arresting, well-written, and nicely constructed stories, with just enough of the required ideological element to make them publishable in the Soviet Union.

Other writers who formed part of the Serapion Brotherhood and felt Shklovsky's influence will be dealt with later. Zoshchenko's humorous sketches have a special place in Soviet literature; Fedin and Pilnyak have made important contributions to the modern Russian novel and will be examined at length; Tikhonov, a successful poet and until 1946 president of the Union of Writers, will figure in a later chapter; Vladimir Pozner emigrated to Paris where he was active as a critic and poet; Elizaveta Polonskaya, the only woman among the "brothers," is known for her poetry. Ilya Gruzdev is a well-known critic and literary historian.

Almost all of the young intellectuals who found one another in Petrograd on the day after the Revolution have become eminent in Soviet literature. These men represented, it would seem, that segment of the old intelligentsia which either could not or would not emigrate, and elected rather to try to find an adjustment of some kind to the Soviet dictatorship. For the most part they managed to make such an adjustment. What that adjustment cost in terms of personal morale is difficult for an outsider to judge. In a literary sense, each successful accommodation meant the reduction of an individualistic literary idiom to common terms.

Boris Pilnyak: Biology and History

Boris Pilnyak was not one of those who successfully adjusted to Soviet "reality." The Revolution he never "accepted," though he pretended to welcome its barbarous violence as a cathartic process. With persistent irony he treats the Revolution as the blindly elemental deed of that old Russia of the steppes and deep provinces which never had a part in the westernized culture of the cities, and now would burn out every trace of Europe, translating into "Slavic" terms even the socialist theories of Marx. Perhaps the most sharply discordant note in Soviet literature is the work of Pilnyak, and it is not surprising that he was regularly in trouble over certain of his published works. He was disgraced and dismissed from the Union of Writers in 1929; he disappeared during the Stalinist purges, and while his name is occasionally mentioned in the Soviet press he is one victim of the terror who has not been rehabilitated.

A few passages from his autobiography are interesting for the light they throw on his background and personality:

My real name is Vogau. My father was a rural veterinary whose family came from the German settlements on the Volga. My mother belonged to an ancient Saratov merchant family. She graduated from the Moscow Teachers College. Both my father and mother played an active part in the populist movement of the '80's and '90's.

I carry in myself four blood lines: German with a touch of Jewish on my father's side, Slavic and Mongol (Tartar) on my mother's side. My childhood I spent in provincial towns . . . Mozhaisk, Bogorodsk, Kolomna, and in the home country of my parents, Saratov, and the village of Yekaterinshtat on the Volga.

Pilnyak emphasizes that his parents belonged to the radical intelligentsia and worked among the peasantry in rural areas. It is characteristic of him also that he attaches importance to facts not so much of his biography as of his biology: the mixture of races and "blood lines" in him. This bare autobiographical statement reveals more about his philosophy than about his biography. The Revolution he understands as a peasant revolt, and the setting of his stories is always the small provincial town, backward and barbarous in its ways. He is nationalistic, in fact he has been called a Slavophile, and he sees the Revolution not as a step toward the West but as a rebirth of some ancient "Slavic" quality in the Russian soul. The ancient past of Russia and its survivals far from the city and the centers of culture acquire a kind of religious mystique in the thinking of Pilnyak.

As a writer he was one of the most popular and certainly the most famous of the fellow travelers. His first published work after the Revolution appeared in 1920 under the title *Bygones*, a miscellany containing sketches and stories about events and characters of the Civil War. Most of these were later worked into the novel which made his reputation, *The Naked Year* (1922). Pilnyak later claimed to have been the first "Soviet writer," the pioneer of the literary revival of the twenties, and until he was discredited in 1929 it was a commonplace of Soviet criticism that Pilnyak was the leading figure in that revival. His style had a wide influence on contemporary writing. He is a writer's writer, and his mastery of a particular manner set a literary fashion. Though his style is derivative, owing very much to Andrey Bely, he displays original imaginative power both in the involved, symbolistic, nonrepresentational manner of *The Naked Year,* and in his more normal, stylistically more conventional stories, which are noted for vivid narration.

Pilnyak's characteristic language is a kind of poetic prose, at times personal and lyrical, at times featuring an epic solemnity, with frequent retardation and word for word repetition of key passages. We find also in *The Naked Year* a conscious reminiscence and echo of the Russian folk epic, a national creation, to which Pilnyak refers many times. Sometimes his style becomes ridiculously involved, in fact a kind of carica-ture of literary style, with intricate syntax, parades of exotic vocabulary items, subordinate clauses within subordinate clauses, and obscure, learned allusions. Such passages, read aloud and for fun, are surprisingly effective. At other times his style descends to coarse, vulgar simplicity. And he makes frequent use of the very simplest linguistic devices, the cata-log, for instance, where he simply lists objects or words to create the effect of a particular social or natural environment. Pilnyak, in a word, inherited from his elders a literary style which suited him perfectly, and which he used with versa-tility and verve. To read him is not easy, but it is rewarding.

One of the characteristic devices of Pilnyak is the so-called *skaz* technique. This is a method used extensively in Soviet literature of the twenties, by Zamyatin and Babel and by the numerous imitators of Pilnyak. *Skaz* involves telling the story, or expressing certain feelings or ideas about the events of the story, from the viewpoint and in the speech style of one of the characters. We shall see how this device is used in Babel's *Horse Army* (sometimes translated as *Red Cavalry*), where shocking details of savagery are related by a morally obtuse character whom they do not shock at all. Pilnyak often tells what happened, not in his own idiom, but in that of a vulgar town character, a peasant, a criminal, or a newspaper. The predilection of Pilnyak for the *skaz* manner and the widespread use of the technique in Soviet literature of the twenties is probably explained by the fact that it made pos-sible the inclusion in novels and stories of critical or satirical comments on Soviet life for which the author took no re-sponsibility.

It is not possible to speak of the plot of the novel *The Naked Year,* nor is it possible to speak of a single central idea. It is not a "novel," strictly speaking, but a series of episodes describing scenes of the Revolutionary period. They had been published separately, and are not worked into a coherent novel form. Some of the obscurity is the result of symbolic hinting at hidden meanings, but often enough it is caused by the author's failure to tie the parts neatly together. Sometimes, indeed, the obscurity seems deliberate; for instance, the use of the same names for Donat the Bolshevik and Donat the religious sectarian does something besides establish a symbolic connection—it quite literally confuses the reader and gives him a sense of actual participation in a whirlwind of events when it is impossible to know just what is happening or just who is who—was that Donat the Bolshevik, or Donat the sectarian?

The Naked Year presents a number of scenes from the famine year (1920) in the Russian interior. The decay of old values in the midst of hunger and misery is its central theme, and this theme gives rise to a medley of new ideas, borrowed notions, and old prejudice. Pilnyak's philosophy is frankly visceral. He belongs to that group of Russian intellectuals who called themselves "Scythians" and who insisted that Russians are not European but rather a half-Asiatic people with special characteristics of their own. The special traits of this Slavo-Tartar blood line have only been damaged by the contact with Europe, and Peter the Great, symbolized by the ponderous Bronze Horseman hovering over Russia, had inhibited the growth of native cultural forms. To this idea Pilnyak returns in the novel again and again, and some of the passages that express it have real emotional power:

Once there was a native Russian painting, architecture, music, folk literature. Peter came—and like an impossible clod of earth that Lomonosov [the eighteenth-century classicist] with his Ode on Glass—and the national creative genius disappeared. . . . Since Peter, Europe has hovered over Russia, but under the horse's hooves our people have lived just as they lived for thousands of years.

Certain characters who are the spokesmen for Pilnyak in the novel, the priest Sylvester, for instance, insist that in order to cleanse Russia of contamination the "holy blood bath" is a necessary and healthy thing. The Revolution is like a Russian forest demon whose weird cry Pilnyak hears in the newfangled invented words of the Communists: Glavbum, Kolkhoz, Cheka, Tseka, Gubkom. These are the sounds of the submerged Slavic gods now sweeping over the land to drive out the Western carriers of contamination: priests, czars, landlords, and worst offenders of all, the intelligentsia. "Our days," he says, "are bitter, like wormwood. But with wormwood Russian women purify their huts of unclean demons." The "unclean," it must be remembered, include in their number the principal agents of culture in prerevolutionary Russia.

An important argument of the novel is that the old aristocracy has degenerated, and the Ordynyn family symbolizes this degeneration. Most of its members are diseased and childless: they suffer from syphilis, alcoholism, dope addiction, and in the case of the father, from religious insanity. Gleb, the artist, is a saintly figure, but he is virginal and without issue. Only Natalya is a complete human being, but she has joined the Bolsheviks and will marry the leather-jacketed Arkhipov, a Bolshevik leader wearing the beard of a peasant patriarch, and they will produce a new "line" of healthy children. Here Pilnyak introduces another of his favorite notions, the need for the nobility to regenerate itself through intermarriage with the lower classes, and once again we see his insistence on blood and genes. Pilnyak is at his best in some of the pages dealing with the aristocratic Ordynyns. Seldom has anyone given us the feeling of degenerative despair, of that "nowhere to turn" hopelessness, with such sympathy and skill as Pilnyak when he describes how Andrey Ordynyn is obliged to leave his ancestral home. Bunin and Chekhov had treated the same kind of tragedy, but Pilnyak gives it special and original emotional empathy.

Superimposed upon the Russia of degenerate aristocrats, anarchistic peasant villages, sectarians, and occasional saints Pilnyak presents another kind of human force called "leather jackets" from the conventional dress of Bolshevik organizers during the Civil War period. The "leather jackets" in Pilnyak meet the primitive and elemental forces of revolution and propose to harness and regiment them for rational purposes. His "leather jackets" are not Europeans in outlook or culture, but are Russians of the native soil who have the brains and the courage to ride the whirlwind, to control and direct the passionate hatred and cruelty released by the Revolution.

They are uncompromisingly cerebral men—rational, purposeful, and ruthless. They undertake impossible tasks and succeed in them. Equipped with a "foreign" ideology, they are yet as thoroughly Russian as the religious sectarians, and are symbolically linked with the latter.

Arkhipov the Bolshevik, one of the "leather jackets," spends his nights in study. He carries with him a *Dictionary of Foreign Words in the Russian Language*, and all foreign words he stubbornly Russianizes in pronouncing them. He is reading *Das Kapital*, and will no doubt translate Marx's ideas into a Russian idiom. His peasant followers have no notion of the niceties of theory: they love Arkhipov the Bolshevik (a native Russian word) but hate all Communists (an imported word).

The Naked Year is a virtuoso performance. It is a symphonic structure of themes and ideas—some of them, the Slavophile idea and the degeneration of the nobility, for instance, traditional in Russian literature and some quite new. Passages of description or cerebration on the part of the author or his characters are packed with ideas both expressed and symbolically suggested. The ideas are not necessarily original or profound, and they may be fantastic or repellent, but Pilnyak has contrived to link them with the troubled characters of his novel in such a way that the reader experiences a kind of aesthetic empathy for each fragment in the philosophic medley. In thus personalizing his ideas Pilnyak is a follower of Dostoevsky.

The book displays an amazing stylistic versatility in the various levels of Russian speech which Pilnyak easily commands: that of the cultivated aristocrat, the radical intelligentsia, the simple peasant. It is a textbook of literary devices, and one from which Pilnyak's contemporaries studied their craft. It is one of the most *literary* novels of the period, in the sense that the author never conceals from the reader his function as a craftsman of words and a dispenser of ideas. The author is present in the narrative *qua* author. He comments on his own work and addresses critical remarks to the reader. The linguistic wealth of the novel is enhanced by the great variety of original documents included in it: records of court decisions, newspaper articles, ancient documents, diaries, and notebooks. One of the first Soviet novels, indeed the first, if we are to believe Pilnyak, *The Naked Year* is also one of the most versatile, and of the novels and stories which deal with the Civil War it is the one which, even with all its devices of "estrangement" and "stylization," presents the most immediate, moving, and, if one may be allowed the word, "realistic" account of the period.

Pilnyak, like Olesha and Zamyatin, sees the Communists making a fetish of the machine and industrialization, and in Pilnyak's best work a struggle is taking place between biological, blind forces and the directing hand of rational, organized man—the "leather jacket." In *Machines and Wolves* as well as in *The Naked Year*, Pilnyak seems to be entering an argument for the "leather jacket," but this argument takes place only on the artist's rational surface. Pilnyak's organic subconscious sympathy is not with the Communists, but rather with the sectarians or the anarchists—with those who are seeking freedom from compulsion—even with disillusioned Communists who want to return to 1917, when everything was clear and simple.

His most telling protest against the effort to subject all life to a rational plan was a story bearing the curious title "A Story of the Unextinguished Moon," published in 1926 in the journal *New World*. This story expresses Pilnyak's feeling that the rationale of the "leather jacket" concealed a basic error. A Red Army commander and hero of the Civil War has fallen sick and the party apparatus has ordered him to undergo an operation. The Commander has an instinctive feeling that he should not allow himself to be operated on, that the operation will end in death. He seems to sense the approach of death, and he reflects on the meaning of his own life. He remembers Tolstoy, particularly the desolation of Tolstoy's Ivan Ilych, who when dying found that a life lived according to the pattern of conventional *comme il faut* was no life at all. He converses with a little girl whose fantasy about blowing out the moon seems to him important, though it doesn't fit the fixed rational categories. His own free thoughts and the girl's fantasy are a pleasant contrast to the "apparatus," with its soldiers at stiff attention, giving out orders touching matters of life and death. The "apparatus" is operated by a "troika," the number-one member of which is a ramrod man who sits constantly at a desk over papers and reports and whose speech is an instrument for the transmission of formulas. He is surrounded by soldiers and secretaries who, like himself, are automata. This dehumanized machine demands surgery "in order to repair a good workman," but the Red Army commander, as he himself had foretold, dies on the operating table.

The story when it appeared in print had the effect of holding a mirror up to nature. Stalin thought he recognized himself in Number One, and the incidents of the story suggested to him the fate of the Red Army Commander Frunze, who had died in very similar circumstances a year earlier. All issues of the magazine in which the story appeared were confiscated; Pilnyak and the editors of *New World* were forced to denounce the story as an "error." Many years later Pilnyak tried to clear himself of blame by suggesting that A. K. Voronsky had given him the idea for the story.

But the story is probably not a topical political document. The fact that the characters and events in it are so much like reality is a tribute to Pilnyak's artistic sensitivity. The character "Number One" is most probably not drawn from any living example but is rather a typical image of the party bureaucrat. The soulless *apparatchik*, dead to feeling and sympathy, is a not uncommon character in literature of this period. Stalin's rage at recognizing the image must have been a source of surprise and gratification to Pilnyak.

Ivan Moscow, which appeared in 1927, develops the theme of an individual whose quirks of brain and personality unfit him for a part in the new industrialized society, in spite of his belief in it. Pilnyak's best statement on the inexorable passage of time is contained in this story. Time passing brings death to the old way of life with its superstitions and evil incantations, and brings a new way of life through the unlocking of atomic power. The dead, however, are slow to die, and remain among the living in mummified form. Ivan Moscow, the rational creator of the new world, is himself in the grip of the dead past: he has an incurable hereditary syphilis.

Mahogany (1929) features romantic, individualistic Communists for whom the finest hour was the Revolution itself and who cannot be at home in the tame construction work of the late twenties. The setting is the deep provinces, where modern mechanization confronts an old and semi-Asiatic culture. Ivan, one of the leading characters, lives in a dugout in the yard of a brick factory with a few honest followers who are still faithful to the Revolution as a "cleansing fire" and who practice a kind of basic Communism. This novel, published first in Germany, caused Pilnyak new and serious trouble.

The Volga Falls to the Caspian Sea (1930) is Pilnyak's effort to produce a novel about reconstruction and to make amends for *Mahogany*. Much of the material of that work appears in this new novel. Near the ancient town of Kolomna a great new dam is being constructed which will reverse the flow of the Moscow river, flooding the ancient settlement in order to create a hydroelectric plant and make the river navigable by ocean steamers. The theme is the familiar one of the struggle between "the old and the new," but it is characteristic of Pilnyak that he induces in the reader a lively sympathy for the old culture with its beautiful artifacts and its mysterious links with the deep past. As in *The Naked Year*, on the surface of his thought Pilnyak is drawn to the machine builders, but what fascinated him as an artist was the old and not the new: the old town of Kolomna itself, sluggish and seemingly asleep, with its ancient towers and its ruined Kremlin, is a more interesting place than the planned city that is rising near it. The mahogany collectors who seem peripheral characters in this novel symbolize, in spite of their grubby backwardness, the tender concern for old things: beautiful hand-wrought, carved things of fine-grained wood. Pilnyak has no real sympathy for the builders of the dam who, when they reverse the river's flow, will leave not a trace of the Russian past.

Pilnyak's work after *The Volga Falls to the Caspian Sea* is both sparse and undistinguished. There is the novel *O Kay* (1932), devoted to his travels in the United States, and *The Ripening of the Fruit* (1935), which continues his chronic, inescapable inner conflict over the disappearance of old values, old art, and all old things.

Pilnyak was the most important single influence in Soviet

literature of the twenties, more important, probably, than either Zamyatin or Shklovsky, since he was a more productive writer, and his works, while often published first in Germany, did circulate freely in the Soviet Union. Those works set a fashion for the times. Cultivation of Pilnyak's literary manner was common, not only among the "fellow travelers" in the Serapion Brotherhood, but even among proletarians. "Pilnyakism" was a phenomenon recognized, named, and duly deplored by Communist critics, though some of these acknowledged Pilnyak's greatness. Pilnyak himself was not a retiring man, but was, on the contrary, energetic and active as a writer and as a literary politician. In spite of his generally bad political repute he was chairman of the Moscow executive board of the Union of Writers in 1929, a tribute to the high esteem in which he was held by the writers' community itself.

Precisely at that point he fell afoul of the Stalinist authorities in literature. We have seen that with the adoption of the First Five-Year Plan in 1928 the relative freedom of the twenties in literature began to be eroded. A focus of heterodoxy and free thought was the Union of Writers, which had continued to function as an organization concerned more with the economic welfare of its members than with their political indoctrination. This condition of the Union was symbolized by the fact that in 1929 Zamyatin was head of the Leningrad section, and Pilnyak of the Moscow section. The Russian Association of Proletarian Writers (RAPP), engaged in vicious warfare with "neobourgeois" and "kulak" literature, and enjoying the full support of the Party, turned its fire on the leadership and apolitical program of the Union of Writers.[5] The "struggle against neobourgeois literature" was a 1929 euphemism for a campaign to oust the leadership of the Union of Soviet Writers. That campaign was carried on by RAPP, and took the form of an attack on Pilnyak and Zamyatin, two of the principal leaders of the Union, who had published abroad novels that could not be published in the Soviet Union.

The purpose of RAPP was to exert proletarian and Party leadership over the fellow travelers and to negate among them the influence of that group of writers whom it identified as right wing, or neobourgeois. The list of writers "out of tune with the times" was usually headed by Pilnyak, and it included Zamyatin and Fedin, Zoshchenko, Alexey Tolstoy, and many others. For a number of reasons the leaders of RAPP considered these men to be out of sympathy with the Revolution: Pilnyak had consistently talked and written against the prevalent tendency to write from the viewpoint of an ideology; Zamyatin's works were described as a polemic against the proletarian dictatorship; Fedin had been attacked for his story "Transvaal," which had portrayed a "kulak" of foreign origin as the only source of progress in a Russian village. Such writers as these were influential in the Writers' Union and had a large following among the fellow travelers.

The attack on Pilnyak and his reduction to recanting impotence might have served as a model for later literary campaigns and purges. The technique was the very simple one of associating him with enemies of the Soviet Union. His novel *Mahogany* had been published abroad, and though this was not uncommon in the twenties, this "deed" was represented as evidence of an alliance with the "White Guard." Headlines in the literary press screamed of his "criminal action," and that of his "fellow conspirator," Zamyatin. Under this attack Pilnyak's nerve seems to have broken. He defended himself by pointing out that the history of the publication of his novel abroad itself refuted the charge of "trafficking with enemies," but in his letter to the editors of the *Literary Gazette* assuring them of his loyalty to the Soviet system, he "explained" those parts of the novel which seemed to be critical of the Soviet regime. Pilnyak's prestige as a leader of Soviet literature was permanently damaged.

After 1932, as we have seen, all separate literary groupings were disbanded. The literary groups that have been mentioned, Pereval, Smithy, RAPP, Lef, Constructivists, and others, were dissolved by Party fiat, and all writers were gathered together into a single Union of Soviet Writers with a single program and purpose in order to facilitate centralized control of writing and publishing. "Factionalism," whether based on stylistic affinities or common political interests, was after that considered an unhealthy thing. And yet Pilnyak maintained during the thirties regular contact with a group of writer friends who met at a kind of literary salon in his apartment in Moscow. We know of this from the accounts of people who emigrated during the forties, accounts which are entirely credible.

Throughout the thirties, until the time he disappeared from view during the purges, this literary salon was a meeting place, apparently, where anything was allowed. There was stimulating and quite free debate on literary questions, sharp and at times violent discussion of the Soviet order, all of this mingled with heavy drinking and some debauchery. The meetings went on until the beginning of Stalin's purges. Those events thoroughly terrorized Pilnyak and his friends, and with reason: many of them were swept away in the wake of the trials in 1936, 1937, and 1938.

Our admiration for Pilnyak's great gifts as an artist, and our sympathy for him as a human being crushed by a tyrannical regime, should not obscure the fact that his view of the world would probably be no more congenial to Western democrats than it was to the Stalinists. We may admire his courageous anti-Communism, but we should not forget his attachment to the old and primitive, his mystical belief in the Slavic soul, and his emotional distrust of Western scientific rationalism. Such atavisms in our own generation of Western intellectuals have sometimes led them into the camp of Fascism. In Pilnyak's career there is a double tragedy. He was kept from the full realization of his powers as a writer not only by the Soviet state, but by his own insistence on using the literary form to preach a set of sterile notions. The artistic level he might have reached is evidenced in powerful scenes from *The Naked Year* and in many beautiful short stories. But he always returned to the pretentiously cryptic statement of an arid philosophy.

Chapter 5

The Intellectuals II

Isaac Babel: Horror in a Minor Key

PROSE FICTION of the early twenties, whether written by proletarians or fellow travelers, had one overpowering and ever-present theme: the Civil War. Every one of the writers who created the literary revival of the twenties dealt with that experience from one viewpoint or another. The fellow travelers tend to be more concerned with the literary style than with the political or social content of their work, but they could not be indifferent to the latter. Thus it has happened that the Russian Civil War is thoroughly documented by literary works, some of them stylistically mannered and obscure, most of them featuring verbal and metaphoric ornamentation, all of them agreed on the need to study either in aesthetic or political terms the moral nudity of the times. The generation of writers that witnessed the events of the Civil War felt the need of catharsis and found it, partly, in portraying with aesthetic detachment scenes of horror and blood. Sensitive children of a high culture, they had witnessed the ultimate degradation of human passions, and they had observed the actions of men more cruel than beasts. These writers seem to suffer a compulsion to present scenes of extraordinary violence in literary form.

The Civil War stories of the fellow travelers are interesting also for their geographic and ethnographic content. Their authors had been dispersed in the course of the war to all corners of Russia and even outside of Russia, and this dispersion is reflected in their stories, which deal with Volga settlements, Kirghiz tribesmen, Cossacks on the Polish border, Tambov Province, the steppes of Siberia, the Don country, as well as with the cold caverns of Moscow and Petrograd.

The Marxist critic Kogan, defending the fellow travelers, pointed specifically to this feature of their work:

In a very short time Russia was described more realistically and in more vivid detail than ever before. The majority of the writers had fought on numerous fronts, held responsibilities both in big cities and in the deep provinces, seen with their own eyes pictures of hunger and inhuman cruelty and also inhuman feats of bravery. They had seen sectarians, superstitions, the age-old customs of tribes and peoples scattered over that enormous expanse. . . .

The principal work of Isaac Babel, a series of short stories concerned with incidents in the campaign of Budyonny's First Cavalry Army in Poland, is typical of Civil War literature in the variety of its characters—Cossacks, Polish lords and peasants, Jews, and Russians—and in the cruel reality which it depicts.

Babel was born in Odessa, the son of a Jewish merchant who educated his son in the Hebrew language, and forced him to study the Bible and the Talmud. He records that life at home was difficult because of the father's insistence on serious study, but that he found relief from that in school. There he learned French, well enough to write short stories in that language, and he came to love French literature. Literary ambition and the need to escape at any cost from the narrow orthodox world took him to Petrograd in 1915, where he lived miserably in a cold cellar, constantly on watch for the police, since he did not have the residence permit required of all Jews. Only Gorky would accept any of his stories. The prominent Bolshevik editor printed two of these in his journal *Chronicle* in 1916. Because of these stories Babel was brought into court on the charge of subversion and pornography, but, as he reported ironically, the Revolution of 1917 saved him from prosecution. Of these early efforts, which combined eroticism and a certain wit, Babel wrote: "The complete absence of decency in them was rivaled only by their meager content. Fortunately for well-intentioned people, some of them never saw the light of day." Babel records that Gorky's encouragement was one of the most important events in his life, and he claimed to revere the memory of the famous writer.

After this literary misadventure Babel abandoned the effort to write fiction for a number of years, and though he attributes the ensuing period of varied activity to Gorky's advice it was more likely the result of the troubled times. He fought in the Czarist army on the Rumanian front, then joined the Bolsheviks. According to his "Autobiography," written in 1924, he worked with the Soviet Security Police (the *Cheka*), was a functionary in the People's Commissariat of Education, and in 1918 took part in grain-collecting expeditions. He fought against the Whites on the northern front, did editorial work in Odessa, and was employed in the local Soviet administration there. He was assigned in 1920 to the First Cavalry Army as a political commissar, where he was primarily responsible for political indoctrination of the rough Cossack mass that made up Budyonny's army. Out of this curious assignment came his most powerful writing, the collection of stories known in Russian as *Konarmia* ("Horse Army"), a Soviet neologism for cavalry. The usual translation of the title, *Red Cavalry,* is unfortunate, and may be partly responsible for the Western reader's misinterpretation of Babel's sketches as a criticism of the Revolution itself; Babel's irony reaches well beyond the immediate and the topical.

The book on which his fame rests can best be understood if it is approached in the spirit in which it was written. *Konarmia* was intended as a series of anecdotes, each with an ironic twist. It has often been pointed out that Babel was influenced by Maupassant and Chekhov, and the specific lesson learned in that school was the art of elevating the funny story to the level of irony. In *Konarmia* thoroughly absurd human beings in ridiculous situations are occupied with the slaughter of other human beings. We misread Babel if, searching for open or hidden commentary on the Revolution, or horrified by pictures of barbarism, we fail to see that each story is built around a grim incongruity. Consider these priceless anecdotes: A peasant soldier writes a letter to his mother regaling her with all the adventures of the campaign, including among them an account of how his brothers murdered their father; a Cossack remount officer reassures peasants to whom he has given worn-out nags in return for their healthy horses: "If the animal can stand up it's a horse"; a village artist offers to paint a picture of you as St. Francis and of your enemy as Judas Iscariot for a small fee; the same artist tells of how Jesus lay with Deborah, a Jerusalem maid of obscure birth, and begot a son that was hidden away by the priests; a soldier, sick of the Revolution and the war, asked to be reassigned to Italy where it's warm and sunny or at least to the Cheka office in Odessa; the Jew Gedali wants to found an International of Good People, where every soul would get "first-category rations"; a mild intellectual assigned to a Cossack platoon earns the respect of his soldier comrades by taking and killing a goose that doesn't belong to him; the same intellectual, after spending the Sabbath with a community of Hassidic Jews, returns to his *agit-train* to finish an article for "The Red Cavalryman." After a town is taken a commissar encourages the stunned and plundered populace: "You are in power. Everything here is yours. No more Polish Pans. I now proceed to the election of the revolutionary committee." The hero is upbraided by a Cossack soldier for going into battle with no cartridges in his revolver: "You're a milk-drinking pacifist. You worship God, you traitor." A rabbi's son, who has rejected orthodoxy for the Revolution, still lives in his father's house, "because he doesn't want to leave his mother."

Ilya Ehrenburg, who wrote the Introduction to the one-volume edition of Babel's work published in the Soviet Union in 1957, claims that Babel's diary, which has not been published, contains entries proving that these sketches were based in the main on actual occurrences of the Polish campaign, and are therefore "highly realistic." It is possible to agree with Ehrenburg's statement that the sketches contain much firsthand experience, but the term realistic as applied to them is meaningless. Budyonny, on the other hand, leader of the First Cavalry Army, who appears as a character in two of the sketches, fulminated against Babel for his failure to show the heroism of the Cossack horsemen in their struggle for the Revolution. It would seem that Budyonny in rather naïve terms is criticizing the sketches for their failure as "realism." But perhaps Ehrenburg and Budyonny both miss the point. The sketches do not purport to give a balanced picture of the Cavalry Army or the Polish campaign. They are a series of fugitive anecdotes based on experiences of the author during that campaign, and held together by the deliberate injection into each one of the author's own personality. The picture of the Cossack fighters is impressionistic and subjective. We have to do with a kind of lyric apprehension of absurd violence, seen through the eyes, indeed through the spectacles, of a sensitive intellectual whose work for the Revolution has brought him into the company of innocent savages. And the Cossacks are innocent men: they shed human blood without reason but almost without malice. When the book is examined as a whole it appears that, far from offering a comprehensive treatment of Budyonny's Cavalry or the Polish campaign, only a little more than half of the sketches have to do with that organization or its exploits in war. The rest tell of other things: Hassidic Jews in eastern Poland, the deserted Polish Church at Novograd, an assortment of original local characters, old buildings and cemeteries, pogroms, and other matters.

Conventional Soviet criticism is no doubt right according to its own lights in finding that Babel's work is weighted with the details of brutality, and that he has missed "the rational principle in the Civil War, and the organizing role of the Communist Party." No doubt Babel himself could have constructed a final ironic anecdote featuring the Soviet literary critics who say such things. The great virtue of his stories is precisely their lack of political color, their apparently casual and fragmented structure. Not the least of Babel's ironies is the fact that the ideals of the socialist revolution, wrapped in facile phrases, have come into the possession of Russian peasant warriors incapable of understanding or realizing them. The stories are studded with such phrases as "no more masters," "heroic revolutionary army," "all are now equal," "the teachings of Lenin," "the revolutionary consciousness of the mass," and so forth. Such ideas might have been used by another writer, Furmanov, for instance, to justify and give rational meaning to the bloodshed of the Polish campaign. But in Babel's stories they are always given in mangled, misunderstood form by a moral illiterate who has just performed some needless piece of violence, such as killing an old Jew or shooting a woman in the back. Babel's stories are reminiscent of Blok's poem *The Twelve,* where the world is at the mercy of twelve Red guards who kill and plunder to the tune of revolutionary songs and slogans. The hopes and fears of the reformers, idealists, and revolutionaries of the nineteenth century, in *Konarmia* as well as in *The Twelve,* find distorted utterance in brutish mouths.

The narrator of the sketches in *Konarmia,* whose job is political propaganda, is present in all of the stories, and it is his personal view of things that the reader becomes aware of. The fact that he is a Jew is made explicit in some of the stories, and is suggested in others by the organic hostility toward him expressed by the Cossack soldiers. He is a man of peace, the only one, if we forget Sandy the Christ, a mild syphilitic moron, who travels with the Horse Army, and he finds it almost impossible to adjust to the folkways of violence. He loses his best friend through inability to kill a comrade dying in misery.

Silhouetted against the setting sun, Afonka Bida came galloping toward us.

"We're pounding them a little," he cried out gaily. "What's the fuss here?" I pointed to Dolgushov and rode off.

They spoke briefly, but I didn't hear the words. Dolgushov handed his papers to the commander. Afonka stuffed them into his boot, then shot Dolgushov in the mouth.

"Afonka," I smiled pathetically as I rode up to the Cossack, "I just couldn't do it."

"Get out of here," he said, and his face was white, "or I'll kill you. You fellows in specs have as much pity for guys like us as a cat has for a mouse." And he cocked his revolver.

I went off at a walking gait, without turning around, and I felt the cold chill of death at my back.

"Hey, you," Grishchuk cried out behind us, "are you crazy?" And he grabbed Afonka's arm.

"The filthy snake," Afonka shouted. "He won't get away with it."

Grishchuk caught up with me at a bend in the road. Afonka had gone off in another direction.

"You see, Grishchuk, today I've lost my best friend, Afonka."

He wins their friendship only by brutality, he loses it when he displays a civilized reluctance to kill, maim, or defile another human being. Saddened by his alienation from the Cossacks he "implores fate to grant him the simplest of skills, skill in killing human beings."

Paustovsky's reminiscences of Babel and the latter's own stories about the anguish of the Jewish community during the pogroms in Odessa, "The History of My Dovecote," for instance, reveal with unusual clarity the sharpness of Babel's consciousness that he was a Jew. The scornful remarks of the Cossack about "fellows in specs" are anti-Semitic attacks, and therefore Babel was never allowed to forget the fact of his biography. Paustovsky wrote:

A tear gleamed behind the convex lenses of his glasses. He took them off and wiped his eyes with the sleeve of his drab patched jacket.

"I did not choose my race," he said suddenly in a broken voice. "I'm a Jew, a kike. Sometimes I think there's nothing I can't understand, but one thing I'll never understand: the reason for this black vileness which bears such a humdrum name as anti-Semitism." He fell silent. I too was silent and waited for him to calm down and for his hands to stop trembling.

"I went through a pogrom when I was a child and survived. But they twisted the head off my dove. Why? . . . I hope my wife doesn't come in," he whispered. "Lock the door. She doesn't like this sort of talk. And she might easily cry all night. She thinks I'm a very lonely man and perhaps she's right."

Not only do the stories describe peaceful orthodox Jewish communities, Hassidic rabbis and dreamers like Gedali who talk of an "International of Good Folk," but also young Jews who like Babel himself had rebelled against the ghetto and "joined the Revolution." There were many of them in the Odessa Cheka and in the Red Army during the Civil War, and they often reached positions of leadership. This historical fact is beautifully etched by Babel in a single symbolic image:

Our foot soldiers were entrenched three versts from the town. Before the front line a stoop-shouldered youth in spectacles was walking back and forth. A saber dragged along at his side. He moved with a hopping gait and an air of irritation as though his boots hurt him. This "hetman of the peasants" whom they had chosen and loved was a Jew, a near-sighted Jewish youth, with the thin, concentrated face of a Talmudic scholar. . . .

Babel had many faces: chekist, political commissar, soldier, reporter. The most real and the most important of his many roles was that of writer, and it is the one which he himself took most seriously. The reminiscences of his friend Paustovsky reveal the tortured perfectionism of his attitude toward the craft:

"What I do," Babel said, "is to get hold of some trifle, some little anecdote, a piece of market gossip, and turn it into something I cannot tear myself away from. It's alive, it plays. It's round like a pebble on the seashore. It's held together by the fusion of separate parts, and this fusion is so strong that even lightning can't split it. And people will read the story. They'll remember it, they'll laugh, not because it's funny but because one always feels like laughing in the presence of human good fortune. I take the risk of speaking about good fortune because we're alone. As long as I live you mustn't tell anyone about this conversation. Give me your word. It is, of course, none of my doing that, I don't know how, a demon or an angel, whatever you want to call it, has taken possession of me, the son of a petty merchant. And I obey him like a slave, like a beast of burden. I have sold my soul to him, and I must write in the best possible way. I guess it's an affliction. But if you take it away from me—either my good fortune or my affliction—the blood will gush out of my veins and my heart along with it; I will be worth no more than a chewed cigarette butt. It's this work that makes me into a man, and not an Odessa streetcorner philosopher."

The trick of Babel's art is to find the stuff of life by indirection, almost by accident. The Cavalry Army itself is a kind of side issue in a world which includes a vivid array of individual peasant soldiers, plundered villages, trampled fields, and indifferent nature itself. The task of "political education," of explaining what it means, is abandoned as a grim travesty. The superflux of suffering and violence seems really to serve no rational end, and, therefore, Babel takes the sensations of the moment and transforms them through art into aesthetic experience. One of the means for this transformation is an ornate and elevated style, the texture of which is variegated with elaborate and arresting metaphors. Here are a few examples: "Blue roads flowed past me like streams of milk spurting from many breasts"; "His long legs were like girls sheathed to the neck in shiny riding boots"; "And we were moving toward the sunset, whose foaming rivers flowed along the embroidered napkins of peasant fields"; "Crouching at the feet of huge estates were dead little Jewish towns"; "The orange sun rolled down the sky like a severed head"; "The deathly chill of eye-sockets filled with frozen tears"; "The stars put out by ink-swollen clouds"; "Between two and three o'clock of a spacious July day the rainbow web of heat shimmered in the air." By such lavish use of poetic language Babel screens himself and the reader from direct experience of violence. The device makes it possible to treat as matters for contemplation even Afonka Bida's empty eye socket: "In place of the left eye on his charred face there yawned horribly a monstrous pink bulge."

Ilya Ehrenburg in his reminiscences, *People, Years, Life,* devotes several pages to his memories of Babel and quotes from the diary Babel kept in 1920 during the Polish campaign the following passage, containing raw material which went into the story "Berestechko." The entry in his diary demonstrates the method of Babel, the gathering of impressions which can be given artistic form, but hardly reduced to rational meaning:

The ancient house of a Polish Count, probably built about 100 years ago, horns, old-style paintings on the ceiling, little rooms for the servants, stone blocks, passageways, excrement on the floors, Jewish urchins, a Steinway piano, sofas torn open down to the springs . . . oaken doors, letters in French dating back to 1820.

Like Olesha and many other fellow travelers, Babel produced very little. At the Congress of Writers in 1934 he announced that he was working in a new genre, "silence." In addition to the stories in *Konarmia* he published *Odessa Tales* (1923–24) which describe in his characteristic exotic manner the Jewish half-world of gangsters and racketeers, a number of short stories, many of them autobiographical, and two plays. When he was arrested in 1939—"on a false charge," according to the Soviet edition of his works—he left behind the manuscript of a number of unpublished stories, some of which appeared during the 1960's in various places (see Bibliography). He died in 1941 at the age of forty-seven and was cleared of criminal charges in 1954.[1]

Konstantin Fedin: The Confrontation with Europe

Konstantin Fedin describes himself as an early associate of Zamyatin and the Serapion Brothers, and he asserted in 1926 that the association had meant very much to him. His early novels in their experimentation with time sequence, in their transitions from one narrative tone to another, and in their complex plot structure speak eloquently of lessons learned in the school of Zamyatin and Shklovsky. But Fedin's relationship to the Serapions was solely one of stylistic affinity. He was hardly one with Lunts and Kaverin in their call "To the West!" nor did he belong wholly to the "eastern" or Scythian wing of the movement. His position, rather, is a uniquely personal one somewhere between the westernizers and the Scythians. In the body of his work we find an original, even idiosyncratic statement of the problem which for him overshadowed all others—the relationship of Russia and Europe. This preoccupation of his, also one of the chief problems of the Brotherhood as a whole, has become involved in Fedin's work with a number of other questions: the problem of the individual in history, the fate of the old Russian intelligentsia, and "the superfluous man" in modern Russia.

A fact of prime importance in Fedin's biography was his

civilian internment in Germany during the First World War, from 1914 to 1918. Impressions of the German bourgeois world form an important ingredient of his two most important novels, *Cities and Years* (1924) and *Brothers* (1928), and the profound disturbance engendered by long exposure to Western culture is reflected even in those stories and sketches which describe the deep provinces of Russia. Bourgeois individualism, progressive and rationalistic, is, according to an old model going back at least as far as Dostoevsky, contrasted, sometimes with the backwardness of rural Russia, sometimes with the collective organization of the new society. Fedin's basic sympathies seem to be confused and divided. One of his best stories, "Transvaal," describes a foreign "kulak" who holds Russia in contempt, and, because of his superior cultural background, has managed to gain control of a peasant village. As time went on and history unfolded, Fedin seemed to resolve his dilemma in favor of the Soviet version of socialism and to adapt his art to the precepts of socialist realism without fatally vitiating the former.

Fedin began to write in 1919, and in 1921 was "found" by Gorky and introduced to the Serapions. His first writing of consequence was a play, *Bakunin in Dresden,* conceived as dramatic scenes for reading and intended to present important events in the life of the Russian anarchist. The play was produced under the inspiration of Gorky, who, as head of the publishing house World Literature had developed the grandiose idea of a cycle of dramatic works each presenting a crucial moment in human history. Fedin's dramatic treatment of Bakunin is interesting as an early effort to explore the psychology of a puzzling historical figure.

Fedin first attracted notice in the literary world with the short story "The Orchard," published in 1922. The story is direct and uncomplicated both in plot and style. Interestingly enough, the experimental touch of the young Fedin is absent from it, and it is no surprise to learn that he wrote it in 1919, two years before his introduction to the Serapion society. In its simple laconic realism it resembles the mature Fedin of *Early Joys* and *An Unusual Summer* rather than the self-conscious stylist of *Cities and Years*. A luxuriant orchard once part of a fine estate but abandoned by the owners has been converted into a Soviet Children's Colony. In the character of the old gardener, Silanty, who refuses to accept the ruin of his old master's estate by the new revolutionary regime, Fedin introduces thus early in his career one of his main themes: the resistance of old habits to the new. Silanty's revenge on the new takes the violent form of arson committed against the Children's Colony.

A collection of his stories under the symbolic title *Empty Land* appeared in 1923. These stories are the fruit of his boyhood and early manhood in the provincial towns of southeastern Russia. They deal almost exclusively with old and outworn habits, with characters and a way of life that ought to be, but, one suspects, are probably not entirely dead. The stories are told in an ornamental, mannered style, with frequent use of the *skaz* technique.

The novel *Cities and Years* (1924) is a study of the emotional vicissitudes of an intellectual unable to accept fully the Revolution and the new regime. The novel develops, in the life experiences of a single character Andrey Startsov, the complex of problems which beset the old intelligentsia during the twenties. Cultivated and sensitive, European in his education, Startsov is not so much an enemy of the new as he is a soul at dead center, unable to move in support of either the old or the new. He is an individualist to the marrow and as such cannot find an honorable way into the collective society, which seems to him to violate indispensable humanistic ideals. The novel somewhat resembles Olesha's *Envy* in its theme, though it has greater psychological realism than the latter novel. Like Olesha, Fedin seems to sympathize with his doomed hero, Startsov, whose doubts and misgivings may easily have been shared by the author himself. The determined and well-organized opposite to Startsov, Kurt Wahn, a Bolshevik in thought and action, whose ideas flow in simple prose and whose speech is constructed of proper phrases, lacks the human and individual touch and therefore may repel the sensitive reader. The conflict between the two concerns the importance of individual human beings and the evaluation of one's ties to them of friendship, loyalty, or gratitude.

Startsov, whose revolutionary enthusiasm has quickly cooled, spares the life of a class enemy to whom he owes a private debt of gratitude. Wahn, who had been Startsov's friend, hunts the latter down and coldly kills him as a traitor to the Revolution.

The structural ingenuity of the novel has often been commented on. The chronological order is exactly reversed and the story begins with its final act set in the year 1922, the killing of Startsov by Wahn and the latter's exoneration by a revolutionary court. Time then turns back to 1919, when Andrey, already doubtful and dispirited, is assigned to the Petrograd front to help defend the city against Yudenich. The action then moves farther into the past, to Andrey's young manhood in Germany where, like Fedin himself, he was interned during the war. Thereafter the time sequence is observed with relative regularity and the knot of mystery and suspense created by the opening chapters is gradually untied, though not without frequent digressions by the author on a variety of themes and with great versatility of stylistic cadence. The tone is sometimes elevated and tragic, sometimes emotionally lyrical, not infrequently ironic. There is real poetry in the prose of the early Fedin. He attempted to explain and justify the compositional eccentricities of his novel. The storm through which he had lived forced its will upon the structure of the novel itself. "The seething reality of war and revolutions obliged the writer to seek new and untried artistic methods."

Fedin's treatment of the German world, in spite of his apparent propaganda intent, reveals ambivalence in his attitude toward the two cultures. The neat, bright German towns with an abundance of all good things and a relatively free life are in striking contrast with Fedin's bare and primitive Russian towns. The hero, Andrey Startsov, is at first powerfully drawn to German culture and only as the novel moves toward its object and World War I moves toward revolution does Andrey's—and Fedin's—attitude toward the West change. Under the proper veneer of bourgeois decency another Germany suddenly revealed itself, the narrow, philistine Germany whose banal patriotism brought on the First World

War. And this, it turned out, was the Germany that really counted. And this Germany is fully documented in the novel, which includes diaries, editorials and articles from German provincial newspapers, and also scenes of mass enthusiasm for the war which Fedin had witnessed. Fedin gives himself many opportunities for emotional declamation on the senseless suffering of war, and these passages are often beautifully written, though they come perhaps too frequently and are too long.

After *Cities and Years* Fedin turned his artistic attention again to Russian peasant life in areas far removed from contact with the centers of culture in Europe or in Russia. He spent the years 1923–1926 in what he calls the "deep preserves of the old way of life" in the Smolensk area. The fruit of his sojourn was a collection of three stories which appeared in 1927 under the title *Transvaal*. The story which supplied the title for the collection had actually appeared separately in 1926 in a collection of stories and articles entitled *The Proletarian*. It is the most arresting of the three stories, and it gave rise to a prolonged and violent polemic in the Soviet press, for Fedin, as we have already observed, seems to portray an alien and unsympathetic kulak as the only source of economic progress in a Russian village. The contrast between the resourceful European, Svaaker, and the superstitious, childlike Russian peasants whom he easily controls produces in the story a dominant note of pessimism. Pessimism always disturbs the Communist critics, and Fedin was violently attacked for introducing such a note. But in the course of discussing pro and con its social implications, the real nature of Fedin's Svaaker and of his story tended to be forgotten. Fedin's Svaaker is a powerful creature of dubious past, who claims to be a Boer in origin, and his presence in Russia is mysterious. One-eyed and disfigured, he is a human grotesque, and he speaks atrocious Russian. A charlatan and a resourceful performer, he has won the complete trust of the peasants, who think he is a magician. He exploits not only the peasants but the Revolution itself in order to build a private empire. He disposes easily of the former landowner, marries his daughter, and through unconscious charismatic power and deliberate chicanery reduces the whole area to dependence on him. The story reveals no trace of any native force, Communist or other, capable of opposing this foreign influence.

In his second novel, *Brothers* (1928), Fedin returns to the theme and in part to the manner of *Cities and Years*. The novel deals with the maladjustment of a sensitive intellectual, this time a musician, in revolutionary times. The main character, Karev, is a lonely individualist and remains one to the end, but this seems to be justified by the fact that he is an artist, and as such in need of creative isolation. Free from the pressure of social involvement, he may yet produce a great work, bearing upon it the stamp of his own time. Karev, after unsuccessful efforts to screen his own life from the socialist world, "accepts the Revolution" and tries to adjust to it. But even his artistic success, his symphony, bears on it the stamp of Europe and of the past, and its inspiration has been private and personal.

In Fedin's third novel, *The Rape of Europe* (1935), the confrontation of two worlds, Europe and Russia, is explicit in both theme and structure. The value of Fedin's observations of both worlds is diminished by the patent thesis of the novel, written during the Stalinist thirties, that the capitalist world is in decline and doomed to destruction, while the socialist world burgeons with new people and new strength. It is to be regretted that Fedin was obliged to work under motivations ulterior perhaps to his own purposes. He had traveled and lived for long periods in the West and he might have produced an important novel. As it is, *The Rape of Europe,* which draws on Fedin's long experience abroad, contains many pages of realistic description dealing with the crisis-ridden thirties in Europe, pages that in spite of the author's ever-present thesis do have artistic merit. Most readers and even Soviet critics agree that the pages in which he tries to express in a credible artistic idiom the successes of socialist construction in the USSR have much less merit.

His next novel, *Arktur Sanatorium* (1940), is based on his own sojourn as a tubercular patient at a sanatorium in a Swiss mountain valley. Again the setting and the characters are

Western, and Soviet Russia is here represented by only one important personage. Fedin's purpose in the novel was, he said, to present a picture of Western society "crushed by the contradictions of those years."

This was the last in a long series of novels in which the character of European life, and its contrast with Russian, was Fedin's principal preoccupation. His next publication was his reminiscences of Russian literary life of the twenties, *Gorky among Us* (1941–44), a book which is not only honest and wise, but indispensable for the historian of that period. It was bitterly attacked in the Soviet Union for the objectivity of its tone when describing ideologically "alien" elements, and publication ceased after the appearance of the first two parts. In the autobiographical sketch written for the 1957 edition of his works, Fedin spoke of his intention to complete this work in the near future.

After the Second World War Fedin abandoned Europe as novelistic material and turned to the writing of a trilogy on purely Russian themes. The first two novels in the trilogy were published earlier—*Early Joys* (1945) and *An Unusual Summer* (1948)—and the third novel, entitled *The Fire*, has been serialized in *New World*. The abandonment of what had been a favorite theme, Western Europe, may have been forced upon Fedin by the chauvinistic mood of the Soviet authorities under Stalin; but it is more likely that the experience of Russia—and Fedin personally—with the German army during the Second World War soured him on the values of Western culture and brought about a decisive turn to Russian themes and a search for a Russian hero. Such is Fedin's account, and there is no reason to question the sincerity of his statement that "Western Europe obliged the Russians to think of many things in the course of the war." The obvious answer that it was not all of Europe but only German Fascism that made such havoc in Russia probably seems to him beside the point.

Fedin, while he is probably not a "great" writer, does possess in a high degree the talent for communicating the atmosphere of a particular time and place. His best writing is reminiscent re-creation of his own experiences, and his memory is able to select and retain sensuous elements of long-past scenes which render their telling a rich experience. This quality is found in his memories of his youth among the German students and burghers, set forth in *Cities and Years* and *Brothers*, in the recollections of his boyhood contained in *Early Joys* and a number of beautiful short stories, and especially in the pictures of his early manhood among the doomed literary bohemians which one finds in *Gorky among Us*.

Fedin's talent has been one of the casualties of the Soviet epoch, but it has not been a total loss. His career is unique in that it covers the whole span of Soviet literature. He was on intimate terms with the Serapions, but survived all the purges, and, though drawing criticism from time to time, he has never been in serious trouble. His characteristic theme is the tragic dislocation of individual human beings in a time of catastrophic change, but his efforts to deal with this problem have not, as a rule, led him into ideological dispute. While he has paid his due to the demands of the Party for tendentiousness, he has usually succeeded at the same time in maintaining a modicum of literary merit. In short, he has "managed," and now he is a leading figure in the Union of Writers, and is an editor of the most important literary magazine, *New World*. He is said to be working on a new volume of reminiscences, and these, when they appear, should provide prime material for an understanding of the writer's difficult road in a Communist society.[2]

Leonov and Katayev

Two men whose careers are alike in that both began as intellectual writers of an apolitical hue and eventually achieved acceptance and status as major Soviet writers are Leonid Leonov and Valentin Katayev. Both have originality and power, and both have experimented with the novel form. Leonov began as a practitioner of "ornamental" prose, but in his first, and perhaps his best novel, *The Badgers* (1924), employed a more conventional style, saturated however with the speech turns of peasants. The novel deals with the impact on the village and the peasantry of the Revolution and symbolically pits brother against brother in the struggle. *The Thief* (1927) is a novel containing much powerful writing and full of the real substance of human character, but it is spoiled in execution by the self-conscious literary poses of the author and his transparent derivation of himself from the "irrationalist" Dostoevsky. Leonov nonetheless performs a shrewd psychological dissection upon his main character, a disillusioned commissar who has become a member of a gang of thieves. He produced a thoroughly reworked version of this novel in 1959. In *Soviet River* (1930) Leonov returns to the Russian interior to describe the construction of a paper mill on the banks of a river in the dense, half-civilized northern forest. This novel, Leonov's contribution to literature of the First Five-Year Plan, sets forth the obstacles both natural and human overcome by the Communist builders. *Skutarevsky* (1932), probably one of his best works in style and intellectual power, explores the psychological problems of an eminent scientist working in a socialist state and, in what is undoubtedly an autobiographical statement, traces his development from a skeptical critic of the new order into an enthusiastic supporter. *Road to the Ocean* (1935) presents a kind of philosophy of history in complex novelistic form, with a fantasy treatment of the Communist future and subtle variations on the expected time sequence. The hero, another embodiment of Leonov, meditates on the suffering he has caused and endured and tries to answer the question whether it was worth while in the total economy of history.

In *Russian Forest* (1953), as E. J. Simmons has said: "The majestic forest . . . stands as a symbol of permanence in an impermanent world . . . the eternal forest is Mother Russia embracing all of Russian life, its antiquities, its art, and culture." Leonov has been a versatile and prolific dramatist as well as a successful Soviet novelist. He is like Fedin a case study in the adjustment of an intellectual to Soviet society, and in his novels, though they contain the required admixture of "tendency," it is possible to study such an intellectual's image of himself and the historical problem.

Valentin Katayev (1897——) might very well be treated as a satirist. His first successful novel, *The Embezzlers* (1927), is a Gogolian satire of the new Soviet bureaucracy. The embezzlers of the novel are two Soviet officials, conventional, philistine examples of the breed, who more or less by instinct or by accident conspire to defraud the Soviet state. They are thoroughly respectable and decent officials whose tastes and characters are petit bourgeois and who simply need money to satisfy these tastes. Elegance and style are not to be found in the Soviet Russia of the mid-twenties, and in their journey in search of fine ladies and titled gentlemen the embezzlers turn up only a drunken prostitute and a spurious Czar. They try to retain in their drunken haze the forms of bureaucratic propriety, carefully itemizing all the expenses of their trip.

Time, Forward! (1932), one of the best of the construction novels, describes the building of the huge metallurgical plant at Magnitogorsk in the Urals. The title of the book was taken from a poem by Mayakovsky, and its theme is the speeding up of time in the Soviet Union where the historical development of a century must be completed in ten years. Katayev devised techniques which convey a vivid impression of time in movement. Objects are shown always in motion: inanimate things are blown by the wind, landscapes are seen through the windows of moving trains or from an airplane circling above. Quick cinematic techniques are used to confuse ideas of space and time: old space and time concepts are made to seem inadequate to the new historical period. And the central event of the story is the successful attempt of a brigade of workmen to break the world's time record for pouring concrete. *Peace Is Where the Tempests Blow* (1936), a novel laid in Odessa during the 1905 revolution, is a warm and sensitive study of the psychology of children who witness the events of that revolution. It is the first in a four-volume cycle. Others in the cycle are *A Cottage in the Steppe* (1956), *Winter Wind* (1960), and *For the Power of the Soviets* (1951), a novel about guerrilla activity. His writing of the late sixties, "The Holy Well" (1966) and "The Grass of Oblivion" (1967), is an experiment in recovering the past.

Katayev, like Leonov, has been a successful playwright. His best and probably most famous play is *Squaring the Circle* (1929), a farcical satire of Communist marriage folkways and of the Moscow housing shortage.

Conclusion

"The Russian Intelligentsia," says a character in Pantaleimon Romanov's *Comrade Kislyakov* (1930), "began with Belinsky and is ending with specimens such as us." The pessimism of that remark seems justified by the story of Kislyakov, an intellectual of the finest grain who found a place for himself in the new society only at the cost of degrading his intellect. Romanov's novel is an ironic treatment of a stock theme: the intellectual who "accepts" the Revolution. In that novel the remnants of a fine tradition, individualists to the marrow, are still devoted to the free mind, but this devotion they can express only in furtive conversations and in low tones. Their overwhelming needs are the simple ones: a job, an apartment, clothing. Kislyakov has a job on the staff of a historical museum which is directed by one Polukhin, a "worker" who believes in proletarianizing both the staff and the exhibits. Intellectuals on the staff who won't cooperate are faced with dismissal, but those who will he welcomes as "converts" and comrades. Kislyakov flatters the director, praises his ignorant ideas on reorganizing the exhibits to feature the working class and the "movement," even pretending to hold views slightly to the left of Polukhin's. Having wormed his way into the Party cell, Kislyakov cleverly undermines his boss, and is at last appointed director of the museum to replace him. For Kislyakov "conversion" to the new order meant the disintegration of his intellect and character, and the acceptance, not of the Revolution, but of cynical self-service as a way of life.

No doubt Romanov's novel reflects some part of the truth about the experience of intellectuals under the Soviet regime. Not all of them, however, were able to make a successful adjustment. Zamyatin, Olesha, Pilnyak, Babel, and many others went their own way, and not the way of Comrade Kislyakov. A kind of conversion to the new order was the rule, however, for the great majority, and it would be a presumption to pass judgment on this conversion. The complex of forces that made good Soviet citizens out of rebellious individualists can only be partly understood by one who observes this process from a safe vantage. One may safely assume, however, that the struggle to survive as a writer called into play in many cases a cynical "acceptance" of what could not, at the moment, be changed.

The great tradition of the Russian intelligentsia found its best expression in the work of men who have been called Serapions, or "fellow travelers," and the great majority of them did survive. They are men of broad education, at home in the languages and cultures of Western Europe. Zamyatin was on intimate terms with English literature; Fedin's work is seldom free of German influence and associations; Babel was formed as a writer by his study of French literature; Lunts and Kaverin sought lessons in their craft "in the West"; Valentin Katayev knew English and French literature; Leonov's "plot play" suggests more than an acquaintance with Gide. The fellow traveler "movement," if one can speak of such a thing, maintained contact through almost all its members (even the "Scythian" Pilnyak) with the literature and culture of Europe as a whole.

They were receptive to new method and content in art, and their literary work is, in almost every case, experimental. They avoided established and easy forms in favor of innovation. They wrote, not for a mass audience, but for readers with an intellectual tradition. Their work was published in relatively small editions and read by the culturally literate. Their roots in Russian literature go back through the symbolists to Dostoevsky and Gogol, rather than to the conventional realists, Turgenev and Tolstoy.

What is most important, they have preserved the tradition of regard for the individual human being and respect for the untrammeled mind. The movement began as a reaction against the corporate and the collective in literature, and continued to assert the existence and the rights of particular human beings. In this, too, they were, perhaps, more in the Western than in the Russian tradition.

Chapter 6

The Proletarians I

THE TERM PROLETARIAN is now hardly ever used in the Soviet Union of Writers or in Soviet literary works and is used sparingly and usually without clear definition in other areas. Abandonment of the term in literature occurred suddenly in the early thirties as the result of the bad repute proletarian organizations had acquired through their arrogant efforts to dominate Soviet literature. A contributing reason for the disgrace which overtook proletarian literature under Stalin was the fact that proletarian organizations had close ties to the Old Bolshevik leaders whom Stalin was determined to destroy, and proletarian novels were a frequent source of muffled dissension. When, in 1932, the Russian Association of Proletarian Writers was dissolved by Stalin's edict he accomplished the double purpose of destroying the influence in literature of an "unreliable" element and taking credit for liberalizing literary policy.

Yet the term proletarian literature, properly delimited, is a useful, indeed an indispensable one for the proper analysis of certain literary trends of the twenties. It is not used here to identify writers or works as to "class origin." A proletarian writer is not necessarily one who has sprung from the working-class milieu or writes exclusively about factories and slums. While in the early twenties the class connections of a writer were important and biographical articles never failed to give some details as to social antecedents, yet an examination of those biographies reveals that with few exceptions there simply were no writers of properly proletarian background. Nor is this surprising, since proletarians were, in Trotsky's phrase, "the stepchildren of culture." The writers who belonged to proletarian organizations and prided themselves on the "working class" essence of their writing were, as their biographies reveal, products either of the peasant village or of a lower-middle-class milieu, and many of them came from families belonging to the provincial intelligentsia. Because they were not proletarian in origin they found it necessary to give special importance to Marxist ideology, which was their chief claim to the term proletarian and thus to the material advantage and political mystique that the term commanded in the early days of the Soviet state.

The atmosphere of literary life in the proletarian world was the complete antithesis of that to be found among the Serapions. To the proletarian writer the *raison d'être* of a literary work was its social message. Though many of them showed traces of the influence of the symbolists and of the radical experimenter Pilnyak, the dominant formal demand was for clarity and simplicity, and this meant in practice the cultivation of literary forms already well-established and widely intelligible. The proletarians were deeply conservative, and looked with suspicion on the "tricky" writing of the Serapions and other fellow travelers. They were also committed to organization, and their theoreticians insisted from the start on the comradely pooling of collective strength rather than isolated individual effort. Zamyatin's *We* is a conscious satire of this collectivist tendency among the early proletarians.

The Proletcult

The earliest organization of proletarian writers was the Proletcult, an abbreviation for the Proletarian Cultural and Educational Organization. Founded in 1917 by A. A. Bogdanov (Malinovsky), for many years a theoretician of the Russian Marxist movement, it received warm support after the October Revolution from the Commissar of Education, Lunacharsky, and, in the early period, from Lenin. The "literary studios" set up by the Proletcult served as the center and focus for creation of a literature which was to be an expression of the proletarian "world view," just as bourgeois literature, now about to disappear, had expressed the "world view" of the bourgeoisie.

In order to produce at forced draft and as early as possible this new proletarian literature the new organization spread its network over the country, and during the terrible winters of the Civil War gathered into its heated studios thousands of ambitious proletarians eager to wield the pen. The First All-Russian Conference of the Proletcult passed a resolution which said:

a) In order to acquaint [the members] with the literary heritage of past epochs courses should be given in ancient and modern literature, Russian and foreign . . . and in the history of culture, and at the same time all these courses should be given from the viewpoint of the working class.

b) . . . The writer and working-class reader should become acquainted with the technique, with the practical skills and habits of literary creation, and for this purpose theoretical courses and practical exercises should be given in metrics, rhythm, and the general theory of versification, in the theory of dramaturgy, artistic prose and criticism.

The theories of Bogdanov on the origin and functions of art are an example of a vain attempt to apply Marxism to the production of literature. Today they have the interest of a historical curiosity. He maintained, as do all Marxists, that literature is a social product conditioned by the class environment in which it arises; but he went beyond this in asserting that the principal function of literature has always been to organize the forces of the collective in which it arises. The proletariat, therefore, must have its own "class" art to organize its collective strength. In 1918 he published a lengthy article called "Art and the Working Class" in which he set forth his ideas in detail. Labor, he believed, was not only the source of all economic value, but also the source of all art. Poetry began in the cries of primitive people at work. Nor were their cries ever the pure creation of art for its own sake: "They were not simply an amusement or a diversion. The workers' songs united the effort of the group in a common task, gave to their movements order and rhythm, and in this way served to organize the collective." The same purpose is served by myth-making in primitive societies and science today, the purpose, that is to say, of organizing the practical efforts of the group. Even pure lyric poetry has the purpose of communicating to a large group of readers inner moods and experiences which the individual author has known, by this means organizing the collective psyche, and eventually collective action, in a certain way. What the working class needed was the work of poets who take the viewpoint of the working class, who think and feel in the way that is peculiar to that class. As an example of a genuine proletarian poem, Bogdanov quoted the following, by the proletarian poet Gastev:

> When the factory sirens give forth their sound
>   In the Workers' quarter,
> It is no summons to toil
>   But a song of the future.
> Once we labored in poor little shops
>   And our work began at odd times
> But now at eight in the morning
>   The siren sounds for millions at once
> And at the same instant, the millions
>   Take hammer in hand—
> What are the songs of the factory sirens?
>   They are the matins of unity.

In summarizing his views Bogdanov insisted that the distinguishing characteristic of literary work in the epoch of proletarian power would be "collectivity." In bourgeois times the division of labor and the high level of specialization made for individualism in the process of literary creation, but comradely collective work would be characteristic of the proletarian machine civilization. Thus individual creativity would tend to disappear and "we" be substituted for "I."

For a number of reasons, chief among them Bogdanov's pretension to independence of government authority, the Proletcult soon fell into disfavor. Lenin scotched its claim to independence, and Trotsky wrote with searing contempt of the grandiose but impractical theories and plans originating in its collective discussions. He argued that a specifically proletarian "class" literature simply did not exist and would not have time to develop, since the role of the proletariat in world history would be to do away with classes and create a socialist society throughout the world. Of the proletarian product he had this to say:

There can be no question that even weak, colorless and illiterate verses can show the political growth of the poet and his class and may have considerable importance as cultural symptoms. But weak, and moreover illiterate, verses do not constitute a proletarian poetry, for they are not poetry at all.[1]

The Blacksmith Poets

The Smithy (*Kuznitsa*) was formed in December, 1919, by a group of proletarian poets who seceded from the Proletcult and set up their own organization. Some of them had published before the Revolution. Poets such as Gerasimov, Lyashko, and Kirillov were among the pioneers of working-class literature. Like the Proletcult, the Smithy had a program embodied in a "Declaration of Principles." In a letter published in *Pravda* announcing their withdrawal from the Proletcult, this group of writers gave as their reason for taking this step that the Proletcult "is holding back the development of the creative possibilities of proletarian writers." The real motivation is not known, though it probably had to do with factional Party politics as well as concern lest creative energy be dissipated in mass cultural work.

In their declaration the poets of the Smithy announced that literature was a "weapon for the organization of the coming Communist society." They maintained that writers of the old bourgeois stamp were unable to use the new revolutionary material and that therefore the new literature must be the product of proletarians. In this the Smithy took the same ideological position as the Proletcult. They maintained, moreover, that proletarian art must be a monumental art, an art of large canvases.

The group further declared itself the one and only proletarian literary organization and thus initiated that clannishness which was a characteristic of proletarian literary groups. And yet, in its understanding of art as a means of organizing the new society, the Smithy group reiterates Bogdanov's basic idea, an idea which became an essential part of proletarian dogma. Their manifestoes are prone to statements which cannot be reduced to exact meaning, but do have important emotional effect. The Smithy, like the Proletcult, was another manifestation of early proletarian romanticism, and its literary ideas were cosmic, but ill-defined. Only one thing was clear. Proletarian art must be like the proletariat itself: mighty, monumental, and merciless toward its enemies.

The factory and the working class are the central theme of Smithy poets, both highly idealized. They found in the factory the source of the proletarian's might, "the cradle of a new world." The "factory" of the Smithy poets is not, however, a particular, earthly factory. Nor is their "proletarian" a man of flesh and blood but a romantic idea. The apotheosis of the proletariat led to the peculiar development in proletarian poetry known as "cosmism." The "cosmic" mystique appears not only in the cosmic swing of their poems and declarations, but in an effort on the part of the poetic imagination to go beyond the bounds of earthly life and to include sun, moon, and planets in the ecstasy of earthly triumph. According to the Marxist critic Kogan, the revolutionary cosmism of the Smithy was the result of "the poet's faith in the unlimited power of science and labor." Other observers saw in the tendency a more or less obscurantist effort to escape from this earth for another, purer world. Voronsky interpreted it as "quietism" arising from the need to "drown the living, feeling, seeing human being in a sea of cosmic and pantheistic emotions." A combination of influences made for "cosmism" in proletarian poetry: science fiction as well as symbolist poetry.

The chief criticism leveled at the Smithy poets by the younger proletarians was that they were romantic and abstract, withdrawn from the world of living human beings and quite unconscious in their poetry of the real physiognomy of actual proletarians. Moreover, they developed no new proletarian forms, deriving their poetic rhythms from Briusov, Balmont, Blok and other poets of the symbolist movement. Their poetry was remote from the actual life of proletarians and was for the most part unintelligible to them. Their romanticism was ill-suited to the prosaic NEP period which followed hard upon the victory in the Civil War, and a new proletarian organization was formed by dissidents who wanted to "forget about the cosmos . . . and celebrate the earth and living people." One of the leaders of the new group was Yury Libedinsky.

Yury Libedinsky: Communists as Human Beings

When, in the early twenties, Party representatives queried the ambitious young proletarians as to what literature they were actually producing, they would point with enthusiasm to a short novel, Libedinsky's *A Week,* published in 1922 under the editorship of A. K. Voronsky in a collection of stories and poems called *Our Days.* For a time there was little else to which they could refer with satisfaction, but this work seemed a promise of future production. *A Week* remains, for all its passionate statement of a political point of view, and in spite of inept lyrical excursions in the "modern" manner, one of very few honest literary formulations of life in a Communist "apparatus" of the revolutionary period. The principal characters are members of a local Soviet organization isolated and defenseless in a rural area where the peasantry is murderously hostile to the regime. The Red Army detachment on which they depend has been dispatched to collect fuel to move the trains which will bring in seed for the spring sowing. While they are absent an uprising occurs in which most of the Communists are killed. To deprive the local Soviet of its troops was a hard decision, but it was the only correct one, as Libedinsky assures the reader:

. . . If the troops were to be taken out of the town, there would be no way to prevent an uprising; if they were not taken out the spring sowing could not take place. The correct path was taken—the contradiction was resolved at the price of heavy sacrifices. To sow the fields it was necessary to get seed; to get seed it was necessary to obtain fuel; to get fuel, and bring in the seed, it was necessary to take out the Red Army men; and this might be the occasion for an uprising. But it had to be done.

The violent uprising which followed is reported from the viewpoint of the individual human beings who made up the

Communist organization. Libedinsky explores the personal life and the particular psychological problems faced by each of the more or less willing "sacrifices." The chief merit of the novel is this effort to show the operation of the Party from the inside, not only inside the apparatus, but inside the individuals who formed it. To the extent that it is possible for him, a youthful Party member emotionally committed to the cause, Libedinsky is "objective." He tries to explore the experience of each of his characters in facing death or bringing death to others. He reveals the doubts and inner conflict which they experience. He is ruthlessly frank in communicating their sense of isolation in a "swamp," as one character expresses it, "of hatred."

A Week is an important event in Soviet literary history. It was the first of the "proletarian" novels, though Libedinsky himself was no proletarian, but the son of a provincial doctor. It was the earliest attempt to depict the "workdays" of the Communists from their own viewpoint. Though realistic in approach and basic method it still bears the stamp of Bely. It is laden with political doctrine, but expressed so naïvely and innocently as to be relatively inoffensive even to the non-Marxist taste. The didactic message is more than mere support of Soviet power, but touches, even, upon internal Communist doctrinal disputes. The helplessness of the Russian Communists in the face of the hostile peasant mass suggests Libedinsky's support at that time of Trotskyism: the idea that the Revolution in Russia could gain significance only if supported by revolutions in the advanced countries of the West.

His next novel, *Tomorrow* (1923), is frankly Trotskyist in viewpoint. It describes the inner life of the Communist Party during the period of transition from war Communism to the "normalcy" of NEP. Disillusion and moral deterioration among the Communists are the motif of the novel. Hope for the Russian Communists, sunk in the "swamp" of NEP and a bourgeois revival, is presented in the form of a Communist revolution in Germany, the only possible outlook for "tomorrow" in the mind of the old Bolshevik character in the novel. *The Commissars* (1925) takes up again the problem of "neobourgeois" influences on Communist leaders trained in the hard school of the Civil War. The novel is a valuable historical document, presenting, as it does, scenes from Party debates of the period, and showing the conflict between glamorized "commissars" and the routine discipline of Party machinery. *The Commanding Heights* (1929) is an excursion into playwriting, heavy with propaganda messages. Its value as literature is slight, and it adds little in the way of documentation to the history of the period.

The Birth of a Hero (1930) is Libedinsky's best novel. Vilified and forgotten by official Soviet criticism because of ideological "deviation," it has gone unnoticed also outside of Russia because its author considered himself an orthodox Communist. The novel perhaps deserved a better fate, for it attempted to formulate in literary terms certain basic moral problems, and it was Libedinsky's relative honesty in facing these problems that aroused the suspicion of the orthodox. The themes he touches upon are all of them important, and they transcend the Communist milieu and the Russian locale. He explores the relationship of children to their parents, stating the problems in terms of characters and situations that would be recognized almost anywhere in the Western world. He attempts to eliminate the artificial alienation of one human being from another resulting from ideological or party differences. He deals with the problem of subconscious motivation and its relationship to the rational part of man. His novel reveals the growth of comfortable "bourgeois" complacency in his own Communist milieu. And the most important and pervasive themes seem to echo Zamyatin's *We*, for Libedinsky is concerned with the freedom and integrity of individual human beings and with the continuing and "permanent" revolution. Like Zamyatin, he makes the point that "there is no *last* revolution. The number of revolutions is infinite."

From this description it appears that Libedinsky's novel is a thesis novel, indeed a thesis-ridden novel. Libedinsky used the novel form to say a number of things which he felt very strongly and thought needed to be said. His thoughts, however, do not obtrude themselves in the nonliterary form of

direct preachment. For each of his "problems" he has devised
fully adequate human characters that are interesting in themselves. Influenced in his literary technique by the example of
Tolstoy, he probes the minds and exposes both the ostensible
and the real motives of his characters—and the tools of Tolstoy even in the hands of an imitator are effective literary
instruments.

The Birth of a Hero is a muted protest against the hardening authoritarian structure of the Communist Party and the
deadening effect of this development on Soviet life. It exposes conformism and stagnation in the intellectual life of
the Party milieu, and it is a defense of the revolutionary
attitude against the search for stability and comfort. The
main character, an old revolutionary named Shorokhov, is
in conflict with a new generation of Bolsheviks, whom he
identifies in their standards of behavior as enemies of
the cause he has worked for. These enemies include his young
and beautiful wife, Liuba, whose interests are limited to family, home and reproductive activity, all of it encased in the
petit-bourgeois comfort of pleasant and pretty things. One of
them is his own daughter by an earlier marriage, Olga, herself
married to a grim-faced young Communist named Gorlin
whose thought takes the form of rigid doctrinal assertion. The
most important of Shorokhov's enemies, the one who stands
as a symbol of the inimical element around him, is his assistant, a proper and well-organized young Communist named
Eidnunen, an efficient administrator and conscientious clerk
for whom each problem has its own patterned and symmetrical solution. Lacking a sense of human complexity, Eidnunen
makes frightful mistakes in dealing with human problems,
mistakes of which he is quite unconscious, for he knows he
always has acted according to "correct" doctrine.

The key statement of Libedinsky's ideas as to the inner
complexity of human beings and the infinite possibilities of
variation among them is given in the interior monologue of a
"young pioneer," Valka, who, doing his homework, makes
up arithmetical problems which he works out and demonstrates with matches.

Then Valka tried to make up a problem for some young pioneers. But the problem wouldn't work out. For he couldn't treat the pioneers as he handled the matches. With matches it was simple: you have 52 and you add 36; how many are there? Or you lay the matches out in 12 rows and the total is 240—how many in each row? But the young pioneers were different somehow: they were always doing something. . . . He remembered something which had happened while the pioneers were at camp: some pioneers went to bathe and left some others to guard the camp. But here they are playing leapfrog, and there are so many of them: the problem wouldn't work out. All the pioneers were interested in their own affairs, each one had his own face, his own name, his own voice—and Valka's arithmetical problem just melted away into life.

Under heavy attack from various "Eidnunens" in the Party bureaucracy, Libedinsky acknowledged that his novel was a mistake soon after its publication, though he had earlier said at a meeting of proletarian writers that he considered *The Birth of a Hero* his most successful attempt to embody in a work of art the idea of the dialectic of history. At the same time it was discovered by the dogmatists that other works of his bore the virus of deviation. Some of his short sketches on the Soviet "heroes of labor," part of his contribution to literature of the Five-Year Plan, were criticized for delving too deeply into the psychology of those heroes, revealing with too much emphasis negative qualities, such as doubt and conflict. Libedinsky was in serious disfavor at the time of the dissolution of RAPP in 1932, and he was briefly expelled from the Communist Party during the purge of 1938, which he miraculously survived. *The Birth of a Hero* was his last serious attempt to produce a work of literature. His writing since that time suggests by its subject matter a long sojourn in the provinces, particularly in the Caucasus and Siberia, the locales in which the novels *Mountains and People* (1947), *Dawn* (1952), and *The Morning of Soviet Power* (1958) are set. His reminiscences, published in 1958 under the title *Contemporaries,* are rather sentimental, especially where they touch on memories of his life as a young man devoted to the Revolution and deep in the struggle. The book is not without documentary interest, since it does deal with a variety of important figures in the proletarian literary movement. But the name of Trotsky is not mentioned, nor is that of Leopold Averbakh, one of Libedinsky's closest friends. And the book sheds little light on the mysteries of Libedinsky's own career.

Tarasov-Rodionov: "Our Own Wives, Our Own Children"

Shortly after the appearance of Libedinsky's *A Week* in 1922 another young commissar, who had taken part in the Revolution and the Civil War and returned to Petrograd full of harrowing experiences, published a novel based in part on those experiences. *Chocolate* (1922), which appeared in the magazine *Young Guard*, was an immediate success with Russian readers, earned the admiration of many critics, and was for a number of years the focus of an embittered controversy. Tarasov-Rodionov in this novel faced without blinking the truth about "revolutionary justice" as meted out by the organs of State Security, and with knowledge gained at first hand he revealed the methods used by the Cheka to maintain the Bolsheviks in power.

The novel *Chocolate* has a feature that most Soviet novels lack: an interesting and suspenseful intrigue. The story grows out of a sequence of events all interconnected in a narrative whose outcome is a matter of life or death for the principal characters. These events are presented in an order which gradually heightens the sense of danger to the hero, and his ultimate destruction comes about as an inevitable result of what might be called a tragic mistake: "a moment of pity for a class enemy." The pervasive influence of Bely and symbolist prose writers is obvious again in this tale of life among the Communist secret police. There are three levels on which the main character is presented: his uttered speeches, his conscious but unspoken thoughts, and the unconscious dreamlike images of the life of blood and struggle through which he has passed. The *Chocolate* of the title stands symbolically for luxuries enjoyed by the bourgeois in the midst of proletarian starvation, luxuries which now tempt even the most seasoned of proletarian revolutionaries.

The main character, Zudin, is the chief of the local Security Police (Cheka) in a Russian provincial town not far from the front lines where the White Armies are advancing. His men have arrested a group of conspirators and along with them a beautiful young ballerina who happened to be present, but in the role of prostitute rather than that of conspirator. After questioning her Zudin is convinced that she knew nothing of the conspiracy and orders her released. He pities her, and allows himself moreover to be captivated by the upper-class charm exuded by the delicate creature. The creature pleads with him to let her work for the Revolution, and he hires her as a secretary in the Cheka office, where they have many lingering contacts. The liaison is never consummated, in spite of all her efforts, for Zudin's proletarian conscience at the crucial moment steps between them. He resists, not without a struggle, her passionate advances, then explains himself to her:

You must not feel hurt. Naturally, I'm not a saint. The coarse and tender feelings, all the instincts peculiar to man are not foreign to me. But I have also something within me that you will not understand—how shall I explain it to you? Class feeling! It is an amazing, ever-living, and powerful spring. From it I derive all my strength, from it alone I drink my dearest and most precious happiness. How this feeling was born in me I cannot remember myself. All I recall is how, in the dark cellar where I lived with my mother, who was a laundress, watching through the window the feet of the passers-by, I, a ragged child, understood that in the world there were beautiful people in new boots but with hard, dirty little souls, and that there were many, many others who were always barefoot and dirty but who shone with sincerity and devotion.

Yelena is at the same time having an active affair with another dear friend, one Edward, an Englishman and a suspected spy, wanted by the Cheka, who supplies her with chocolate and silk stockings. She makes a present of some of these things to Zudin's wife, who, in her thoughtlessness and hunger for the finer things, accepts them. Yelena then discovers that one of the bourgeois prisoners being held by the Cheka had actually been cleared of all charges three months before but, through an oversight, had not been released from prison. A simple order from Zudin is all that is necessary, but before calling the matter to his attention she extorts a heavy payment in return for his release from the young man's family, pretending to be acting in the name of her chief. At that very moment Zudin's assistant, Katzmann, is killed by a socialist revolutionary, and in a sudden passion of class hatred Zudin orders the immediate shooting of one hundred bourgeois hostages held in the Cheka jails. This is done suddenly, without a second thought, almost casually.

Yelena's operations are finally revealed to the Central Committee, and Zudin is involved in charges of bribe-taking and collaboration with a class enemy. One of the heaviest ironies of the story is that no blame ever is laid upon him for the casual killing of one hundred innocent people, but the charge that he had accepted chocolate and several pairs of silk stockings, is repeated by the investigators with venomous insistence. The investigating commission reaches its decision by a curious path of revolutionary logic. They doubt very much that Zudin is guilty—and of course the reader knows that he is innocent of the charges brought against him—but they decide that the question of guilt or innocence is unimportant, and the question of "justice" never enters their deliberation. Zudin had, on his own admission, made a mistake in pitying Yelena, he had compromised the Revolution in the eyes of the workers, whose mood because of him was rebellious. In order to win back their good opinion and their support in the struggle against the Whites, it is decided that Zudin must be shot, guilty or not. An old revolutionary comrade of Zudin's explains the decision to him, and he accepts it:

We reasoned it out very simply, just as you did. There is no question of guilt here. But we have to do something, and something cruel, terrible, otherwise our whole cause will perish. You understand, not us, but our cause. What devil ever moved you to take pity on that wench? Haven't we inherited enough of that refuse? But you are an old revolutionary, and you should have looked at the most important things, and gone right past her. But we're all alike, with very few exceptions, and we don't blame you. You know we all have our very own wives, our very own children.

The sacrifice of a single human being without regard to

moral considerations is justified in the supposed interest of "thousands" of human beings, of the "mass" of human beings. Such is the ostensible message of the story, but it provoked fierce opposition precisely because it exposed to public discussion the philosophical assumptions of the terror—both Red and White. It is impossible to suppose that the author did not realize the deadly nature of the questions he raised. The story is prophetic of the purge trials of the thirties, when, no doubt persuaded by arguments not unlike those offered to Zudin, and like him reduced to moral impotence by their own lives of terror and deception, the Old Bolshevik leaders delivered in court confessions of their own guilt—not for their real crimes, however, but for fabricated ones.

Tarasov-Rodionov wrote a second novel, *Linyov* (1924), which develops themes of the Civil War period with his characteristic irony and not without excessive verbal ornamentation, and he projected a chronicle of the Revolution in the form of an autobiographical trilogy. The work, called *Heavy Steps*, was never completed. He was accused of Trotskyism in 1937, when he disappeared from the Soviet literary scene. There is no record that he confessed to any crimes.

Dmitry Furmanov: An Earnest Commissar

Another young man "of pen and sword" who served as a political commissar with red detachments during the Civil War, then settled into the literary calling, was Dmitry Furmanov (1891–1926). His two most important works are *Chapayev* (1923) and *The Uprising* (1925). He also wrote a number of short stories, the story "Red Landing" (1923), and many propagandistic and critical articles. The Soviet edition of his works in four volumes contains his diaries and notebooks and the sketch for a novel about the literary milieu entitled *Writers*.

The novel for which he is most honored in the Soviet Union is *Chapayev,* and it is on this work that his claim to the status of "classic" depends. The novel, based on Furmanov's own experiences as a party representative attached to the headquarters of the peasant guerrilla leader Chapayev, contains the central political idea that the Communist Party bridles and controls the anarchistic force of peasant rebellion. Chapayev is the leader of a senseless and violent "Russian revolt" such as Pushkin deplored in his novel about the Pugachev uprising; Klychkov, the young commissar assigned to Chapayev by Red Army headquarters, represents discipline and order. The practitioners of the latter turn out to be more ruthless and stronger than the elementally brutal Chapayev. Klychkov is an autobiographical character, and his experiences are those of Furmanov himself.

Furmanov's brief autobiography, written in 1926, is a curious document, which throws much light on the character of this young representative of organization and plan:

My earliest childhood, up to the age of eight years, I can remember only in sad fragments. But at that point the passion for reading hit me. I read a great deal, in a kind of hot fever for books. With particular interest and enjoyment I read Jules Verne, Conan Doyle, Maine Reed, Walter Scott, and things of that nature. Education: a public grammar school in Ivanovo-Vosnesensk. A trade school in the same city, and in Kineshma, a town on the Volga. I finished three years of a scientific secondary school. After that, Moscow University. I completed the course in Philology in 1915, but never managed to pass the state examination. I was sent as a medical corpsman (*brat miloserdiya*) to the Turkish front, the Caucasus, to Persia, to Siberia, to the western front. . . .

In the middle of 1916 I arrived in Ivanovo-Vosnesensk and . . . I taught in workers' schools. Then came the Revolution of 1917. My fiery mood, together with a meager knowledge of politics, drove me to be at first a maximalist, then an anarchist. As it seemed to me then, the new and longed-for society could be built with the help of bombs, anarchy, and everyone's unlimited goodwill. But life pushed me into the Soviet of Workers' Deputies—and later into the Party.

It is evident from this that the young man who wrote the classic work on "bridling" the Russian revolt had himself a history of anarchism, and this history, while it may have served him as useful psychological material, caused him to overcompensate in the direction of discipline. The photos published in Soviet editions of his work show a young man of set jaw, whose eyes seem to look at one with grim certitude.

His capacity for work amazed his comrades. He was First Secretary of the Moscow Association of Proletarian Writers, a position in which he demanded punctual production both from himself and from others. He could not endure literary bohemians who were irregular in attendance at meetings or who came to them late. He kept a diary and kept it systematically. Libedinsky, in his reminiscences, reported that "Furmanov's life moved constantly in a brave and happy rhythm of work. It was as though he was marching to the beat of music which came from inside his young and inspired heart." Any irregularity, independence, individuality seemed to him a symptom of bourgeois decadence. He believed passionately in the organization of literature. When some of the proletarian writers complained at a conference in 1925 that organizational pressure was "crushing the initiative" of individual writers, Furmanov stood firmly for collective literary work in which proletarian writers would help one another to develop creatively and protect one another from infection with alien ideology. The one-time anarchist, turned inside-out, had become the most disciplined personality on the literary scene.

Furmanov's own comments on his *Chapayev*, which are to be found in his diary and notebooks, reveal that he approached the task of writing with forethought and a high degree of literary interest. It is significant that he, almost alone among proletarian writers, was interested in the problem of "literary genres" and had asked himself the relatively sophisticated question, "To which of the established genres does *Chapayev* belong: 1) *Short story,* 2) *Reminiscences,* 3) *Historical record,* 4) *Fictionalized historical chronicle,* 5) *Historical ballad,* 6) *Scenes,* 7) *Historical sketch.* What would you call it? I don't know."

Further evidence of literary perception is his high opinion of Isaac Babel's sketches. Babel described people and situations very similar to those we encounter in *Chapayev*, but Babel's approach is the opposite of Furmanov's. Babel views his reality from a near vantage, where each detail can be brilliantly sketched; Furmanov, while not sparing himself the senseless violence of his characters, focuses attention, not on the details of bestiality, but on the rational historical development in which, as he believes, even Chapayev, that "wild horse of the steppes," had an appointed place. The two writers were as far apart in style as in temperament. Babel is "ornamental," his style constantly calling attention to itself; Furmanov is laconic and matter-of-fact. Babel has no explicit ideological task to perform; Furmanov, in his own words, "set himself the practical, revolutionary aim of showing how we carried on the struggle in the days of the Civil War, of showing this without artifice or invention. . . ." Furmanov's appreciation of Babel as a literary stylist, attested to by a close friend, is, therefore, interesting evidence of a certain catholicity of literary taste in the man, and his own writing is not devoid of sensitivity.

The *avant-garde* critics of *Lef* and *New Lef* valued Furmanov as a writer whose works might serve as textbook illustrations of the modern literary mode. Brik and Shklovsky admired his uninvented narrative based on historical fact and constructed out of biography, diaries, notebooks, newspaper accounts, official orders, and other evidential materials. Such work was a perfect example of that "Literature of Fact" in which they believed. Perhaps the most important single factor in the formation of Furmanov's literary style was not his indoctrination with Marxist ideas but his labors in the field of red journalism. The best pages of both *Chapayev* and *The Rebellion* are those which bring to life the partisan movement in the southeastern steppe country. Chapayev himself and the members of his band are portrayed in simple vivid strokes as part of the primitive peasant milieu which produced them. If Furmanov had refrained from injecting his philosophy into the narrative—if he had not editorialized—*Chapayev* would have been a journalistic account of the war in the steppes comparable to the best of Western war reporting. His description of the guerrilla band as it unceremoniously takes over his own quarters is an achievement of some merit:

Soon the boys who had come with Chapayev poured in, in a noisy gang. They tossed their stuff in every corner of the room. On the table, the chairs, the windowsills they threw hats, gloves, belts, laid out their revolvers. Some of them took off their bottle-shaped bombs and carelessly shoved them right among the caps and gloves. Tanned, stern, courageous faces; coarse thick voices; clumsy, unpolished movements and speech. Some of them had such a strange way of talking that it seemed they uttered nothing but abuse; they asked questions curtly and roughly and they answered just as roughly, as though in anger. . . . The whole house hummed with their arguments and their conversation: the new arrivals had soon spread themselves out into all the rooms. . . .

In a few minutes Klychkov observed one of the guests spread himself out on the unmade bed, prop his legs up against the wall, light a cigarette and shake the ashes off to one side, aiming them directly at Klychkov's trunk which stood near the bed. Another slumped onto a fragile "dressing table," which crunched and cracked under his weight. One of them beat out a window pane with his pistol butt; another threw his dirty and stinking sheepskin coat over the bread laid out on the table, and the bread when it was eaten had a sickening smell. . . .

Equally ironic is Furmanov's account of the mysterious power exercised by Chapayev over the peasants. It is to be doubted that the author had ever heard of the modern concept of the "charismatic" leader, but he has presented in Chapayev an excellent case history of such a leader. Chapayev's mastery of the rough peasant mass seems to Furmanov the result of some "magical" power, and the passages that depict him in action as a popular leader are written with mingled irony and respect:

We arrived at a village and stopped at the office of the local Soviet. The peasants, as soon as they heard that Chapayev had come, crowded into the building, all pushing their way forward, hungry for a look at the famous hero. Soon the whole village had learned of his arrival, and the streets were full of a thronging mob rushing to find him, to get a look at him. The entryway was blocked by the numerous throng: boys and old women, even bearded white-haired old men who had crawled out for the occasion. Everyone wanted to greet him, Chapayev, as an old and good friend, many called him by his first name. . . . Swimming on the faces of the crowd were pathetic honey-sweet smiles, and strange, gray faces suddenly sparkled with joy. Some gazed at him seriously and intently as though to be sure of getting the full satisfaction of seeing him and to imprint forever in their memory the image of the heroic commander. . . . The street boys stopped their hubbub and stood quietly, patiently waiting for something. And everybody seemed to be waiting for something— clearly they wanted to hear what Chapayev would say. . . .

"You might say something, comrade commander," the chairman of the local Soviet said to him. "You can see the peasants would like to hear a wise speech."

"What am I going to say?" Chapayev smiled.

"Oh, tell them how people are getting on—all around. You'll think of something."

Chapayev never liked to make a fuss. He could see the peasants wanted to hear him—why not say something? While the horses were being harnessed he made a speech. It would be difficult to state the central theme of Chapayev's speech. He simply repeated commonplaces about the Revolution, the great danger, the great famine. But even these things they liked, and why not? Wasn't Chapayev himself speaking? With strained attention they heard out to the last word his long and confused speech, and when he had finished, they nodded their heads sympathetically and whispered to one another:

"That's the right stuff!"

"That's the way to give it to them!"

"Boy, he's a great one!"

The story interest in *Chapayev*, as well as the central ideological theme, is the development of a working relationship between this ignorant and politically unversed peasant leader and his "commissar" Klychkov. Klychkov's problem is to establish his ascendancy over Chapayev and to direct into predetermined channels his spontaneous revolutionary energy. He has little respect for Chapayev as a man and is dubious as to the Chapayev legend. The rational force in Furmanov's book masters and exploits the emotional energy generated by the peasant leader, and thus Klychkov, not Chapayev, is the real hero. Indeed the end effect of Furmanov's story is to deprive Chapayev and other individualistic swashbuckling Civil War heroes of the glamour that surrounded them. Free-

wheeling filibusters riding the wave of the peasant uprising—
and Chapayev was such a one—are the objects of the commissar's cool and reasoned contempt. And individual deeds
of spectacular courage, he concludes, are to be indulged in
sparingly:

That kind of thing is very good—*but* . . . And at that
point he insisted on a *"but."* At that point he drew a logical,
irrefutable, clear and convincing conclusion: a commander
should never permit himself to be carried away by his own
private action, but always have in view the welfare of the
whole—of the total operation, and all his troops. Particular
action he should assign to someone else. Yelan's personal
bravery might have had a sad outcome for the whole brigade
if he . . . had been shot and his replacement had been unable
to manage the brigades.

On almost every page Furmanov insists on the solid factual
basis of his narrative. Letters, telegrams, official orders, an-
nouncements, and the like are introduced as authentic documents: "Here is a note written by Klychkov on the spot";
"The following letter was then sent to headquarters, and it is
given here word for word"; "This document has been preserved in the archives." Much of the content of *Uprising*,
which describes a rebellion of Red Army troops in the town
of Verny against the local Soviet authorities, is given in the
form of official archive material. Furmanov's method, which,
as we have seen, was related to that "Factography" advocated
by the Left Front of Art, has profoundly influenced Soviet
prose. Gladkov, Serafimovich, Sholokhov, Polevoy, indeed
the majority of successful practitioners of "socialist realism,"
all lay careful claim to *historical truth* for their novels. They
purport to deal with real situations and actual characters.
Not all of them have succeeded in producing books like
Chapayev, which can be read with pleasure even by a non-
Marxist. Furmanov has the advantage over the "socialist
realists" in that his sharp and honest intelligence draws a fine
line between the actual *facts* and his own opinion about them.
By presenting his ideas directly and without disguise he has
produced works which have genuine value both as ideology
and as literature.

A. S. Serafimovich: A Popular Saga

At the time of the Revolution, A. S. Serafimovich (1863–1949) was already an old and established writer, his first stories having appeared in 1889 and 1890, while he was living as a political exile in the far north. Those early stories are documentaries on the life of poor peasants and laborers in many parts of Russia and in various occupations. In 1902 he met Gorky at the home of Leonid Andreyev, and the first volume of his collected stories was published in 1903 by Gorky's famous Znanie publishing house, which was partial to books that described with sympathy and social purpose life on the lower levels. Thereafter Serafimovich, who had already received the accolade of political exile, was associated with the Marxist Social Democratic Party in its Bolshevik variant, though he did not actually join the Party until 1918. He was thereafter active throughout his life in red journalism, editing magazines and contributing regularly to *Pravda* and *Izvestia*. In 1921 he was chief of the literary section of the People's Commissariat of Education under the Commissar, Lunacharsky. In 1924 he published his principal work, *The Iron Flood,* which has become a "classic" of Soviet literature. He planned and labored over a second novel, *The Struggle*, which dealt in documentary fashion with peasant and worker life, but never finished it. His work from 1924 until his death in 1949 consisted of sketches, stories, editorials, and articles on contemporary political and social problems. He worked on an autobiographical novel during the forties but never completed it. He seems to have been a reliable Party man.

Quite apart from its merits or defects as literature, *The Iron Flood* is a significant historical document. It is significant not so much for the events which form the core of its narrative as for the approach and method of the author. *The Iron Flood* has entered into the main arteries of Soviet literary life, and some of its "iron" is still to be found there. Its portrayal of the "mass" as the hero in history; its unconcern with individual personalities; its implacable optimism; its insistence on victory over terrible odds; its tendentiousness—all of these ingredients are to be found in the standard product of socialist realism. That standard product is, however, very inferior to the prototype, for Serafimovich does not shrink from the reality he has chosen to portray. The mixed mob of deserters, mutinous sailors, and Bolsheviks with their women, children, and household goods who marched north from the Taman peninsula, after escaping encirclement by the Whites, is shown as an unruly and bloodthirsty force. Atrocities committed against the enemy are not glossed over. For instance, the following actions are described as part of the capture of an enemy village:

From the priest's house people with ashen faces and golden shoulder-straps were being led—part of the Cossack head-quarters' staff had been taken. Their heads were cut off in the vicinity of the priest's stable, and blood soaked the dung.

The din of the firing, the shouts, curses and groans stifled the noise of the river.

The house of the village ataman was found. It was searched from basement to attic—he was nowhere to be found. He had fled. Then the soldiers called out:

"If you do not show yourself we shall kill your children."

The ataman did not appear.

They began to slaughter the children. The ataman's wife crawled on her knees, with streaming hair, clinging to one of the soldiers' legs.

He slashed at the little girl and then split open the skull of the wildly laughing mother.

The Iron Flood is a relatively honest book; but can anything be said for it as literature? Two writers, Zamyatin and Furmanov, who are nearly at opposite ends of the literary spectrum, have made definite pronouncements as to its merits. Zamyatin said the following:

The Iron Flood is metal torn up out of the earth. Well, you might think, what could be better? But just send a bit of that iron to the laboratory and you'll find that it's been gathering rust for a long long time in the cellars of Gorky's Znanie publishing house. And just as one would expect from the tried and true custom of the Znanie writers, for a solid page or two the workers sing: "Thou hast fallen in the brave and fateful struggle." And again according to the Znanie formula, this time inherited from Leonid Andreyev's *Red Laugh*, we find such locutions as: "the mad sun"; "the mother laughs with an inexplicably gay, ringing laughter"; "she wildly kisses her child"; . . . "madly the light trembles"; "above the sky-blue abyss." . . .

But there is something else there, too—something that wasn't in the Gorkyesque [Znanie writer] Serafimovich. When we read: "Toward the windmills there comes out of the throng with an inexplicably red face, with a black mustache just sprouting, in a sailor's cap. . . ." in such a sentence without a subject we sense an unbridled "modern," almost Pshibi-shevsky. When we find phrases like: "Again among those people who were straining toward salvation there arose an overwhelming astonishment," we must suppose here the be-ginnings of a kind of instrumentation, almost in the manner of Bely.

And another thing: in Znanie there never was the cheap gilt that one observes on Serafimovich's iron, which he mined "from the Depths." The figure of that "rotten compromiser" Mikheladze is fashioned according to all the rules for gilding. And the gilt is especially thick at the end of the story, with the apotheosis of the hero . . . and the "tears streaming down the windworn faces of the crowd . . . and the young girls' eyes shining with tears."

The ore that Serafimovich used for his *Iron Flood* is so rich that even worked up into operatic stuff it is not com-pletely worthless—we do remember a few scenes.

Zamyatin's casually devastating review of *The Iron Flood* was published in 1924, soon after the appearance of the novel. Furmanov's critical reaction was strikingly different and can be given much more briefly:

From his first story "On the Ice" to this last fine novel *The Iron Flood,* Serafimovich has always been a singer of the struggle of labor against capital, the struggle of a free order with the realm of poverty, violence, and exploitation. . . . Serafimovich has no need to be "tendentious." It is enough that he is just himself. . . . Serafimovich combines the mastery of an artist with the rich erudition of an eth-nographer and the wise and sane approach of a sociologist-historian. . . . Serafimovich shows reality in its revolutionary development. . . . Through the darkest ignorance of the masses, through their barbarity and cruelty one can sense the new thing that will come to replace that ignorance, barbarity, and cruelty.

Furmanov speaks of "the symmetrical structure of the novel, its carefully planned composition, the balanced proportion of its parts, the author's economical handling of his material. . . ."

The confrontation of these two "critics" is an important one, for much more is involved here than the difference in literary method or literary taste. The chasm separating Zamyatin from Furmanov is one which probably cannot be bridged. One observes Zamyatin's easy, offhand sophistication, his expert knowledge of literary styles, his sensitivity to literary echoes, however distorted, his acute ear for the peculiar resonance of a political fairy tale, and his contempt for the hard-driving sentimentalist with "weatherworn" face and a "glistening" tear. Zamyatin's most caustic vitriol is directed precisely at borrowed ornaments in Serafimovich's style: the already hackneyed devices of symbolists and populists which he uses to construct his propagandist tale apparently without fully realizing that they are devices and that they are hackneyed. But what of Furmanov's criticism? To dismiss it as the work of a partisan, as one is inclined to do, would probably be a mistake. Furmanov derived enjoyment which he would label "aesthetic" from the reading of *The Iron Flood*, and so did millions of people who have read it in the Soviet Union. These millions were probably not aware of any aesthetic lack in the book, since they, and Furmanov as well, do not have the critical sophistication of a Zamyatin or his sensitivity to the ring of falsehood. Zamyatin's remarks mirror the gently educated taste of an intellectual, Furmanov's the popular hunger for heroic sagas, especially those which claim historic truth. The word *bylina*, which came to be used for the Russian folk epic with its superhuman heroes and marvelous deeds of valor, meant originally "a true event." Those epic stories evoked an emotional credence which had nothing whatever to do with their credibility. In much the same way the modern Russian reader follows with sympathetic, suspenseful interest the epic journey of that filthy and ragged mob (the "proletariat") in its relentless, iron-hearted march out of captivity through terrors both man-made and natural, moving with one will and a massive resolve into the promised land of the Soviet State. Their leader, Kozhuk, is more than human. He has no weaknesses, no doubts, and no hesitations as to the right path. There are no separate distinct personalities in the marching mass. The only individual portrait is that of the "rotten Mikheladze," the Menshevist traitor to the working class, whose egocentric "stream of consciousness" is presented only as a fitting prelude to his death. Furmanov, and the Soviet reader, find in Serafimovich what they put there themselves, a sympathetic identification with the mass hero. Zamyatin simply did not have it.

Chapter 7

The Proletarians II

Fyodor Gladkov: An Autodidact of Literature

THE UNRESOLVED PROBLEM in Soviet literary practice even to the present day is the problem of the individual hero. Questions that were asked during the twenties as to the area of private life and personal motive that might be allowed a proletarian character are still debated. This debate began, as we have seen, with the reaction against the abstract metallic proletarian of the Smiths, but the transition to prose fiction with a realistic thematic base only posed the problem in sharper form. The total abstraction of *The Iron Flood* from the personal lives of its characters was the more striking for the fact that the work, in spite of its emotional charge, is a prose work about ordinary people. Other works of the earlier period exhibited the same indifference to individual character, for instance A. G. Malyshkin's *Fall of Dair* which relates, also in highly charged prose, the military "feat" of the Red Army in recapturing the Perekop peninsula from the Whites. In this heroic tale, as in *The Iron Flood*, there are no individuals but only a massive human force which seems to move according to predetermined historical laws. Similarly, a consciously Marxist view as to the relative unimportance of the individual in history is implicit in Furmanov's account of that "great man" Chapayev.

Critics both proletarian and bourgeois spoke of this neglect of individuals as a fault, and the proletarian literary organization in setting up "demands" upon its writers insisted on their cultivating a literary method which would avoid this particular fault.

The slogan for the presentation of the "living man" . . . on the one hand correctly orients proletarian literature toward the reflection of contemporaneity, and on the other hand ex-

presses the necessity of struggle with stereotypes, with schematic portrayal, with "bare poster art," and of development
in the direction of showing forth the complex human psyche,
with all its contradictions, elements of the past and seeds of
the future, both conscious and subconscious.

The campaign against "poster art" and stereotyped heroes
was headed by Libedinsky, the leading theoretician of the
Association of Proletarian Writers, and Alexander Fadeyev,
a grim commissar of the literary world, who had the following to say about the "faceless" heroes of proletarian literature:

[Works which have recently appeared] represent an advance even over the novels of Furmanov and Serafimovich,
where the "hero" was predominantly the collective, the workers' element or the forces of history which move people. Concrete figures were portrayed in such novels not in their particular and individual traits, but only from the point of view
of those qualities which helped them to fuse themselves with
the collective.

Fadeyev found solid Marxist support for the idea that historical processes, however impersonal, find their concrete expression in individual minds and hearts, and should be portrayed in terms of the actual experience of particular persons.

The psychology of characters acquires great importance in
our eyes because it is the psychology of whole social classes,
or at least of social groups, and because, therefore, the processes taking place in the souls of individual characters are a
reflection of historical movement.

The appearance of two novels marked the emergence of
the new emphasis on the real problems of actual people—
Fyodor Gladkov's *Cement* (1925) and Fadeyev's *The Nineteen* (1927). It is instructive both to compare and to contrast
the two works. Gladkov (1883–1958), an autodidact of literature whose life story is like that of Gorky, was a Party man
before the Revolution, suffered imprisonment and exile and
nurtured a bitter Gorkian hatred of the clean and respectable
world. He read everything, but was particularly drawn to
Lermontov, Nekrasov, and Dostoevsky. The influence of
Lermontov and Dostoevsky, as has been pointed out, is evi-

dent in most of his early work, including *Cement*. Early tales which carry the clearest evidence of Dostoevskian influence in the handling of the characters, and of modernistic tendencies in style—*The Fiery Steed* (1923) for instance—Gladkov finally rejected as alien to him in form and content. Figures of demonic wickedness, revolutionaries with "feverish" personalities, women with an "infernal" hatred of the double standard and their inferior position, families and communities torn by poverty and misery, all of these bear the impress, faint no doubt, of Dostoevsky's style. The presence of such types is likely to escape the reader's attention in the welter of Communist propaganda, topical thematics, and rousing speeches on socialist construction, but Dostoevsky's "infernal woman" is still recognizable in Dasha, the emancipated woman of *Cement*, fighting for the independence of her own will, though Dasha does wear a red scarf.

Cement is, like *The Iron Flood*, a popular saga, but it is a saga not of war but of reconstruction. It is a novel about industry, in which the machine is treated, in poetic prose reminiscent of Smithy poetry, as the proletarians' friend and savior. The hero, Gleb Chumalov, an industrial worker and Red Army commissar, returns to his home after the end of the Civil War, to find that the old forms of life have been destroyed but nothing new has yet taken their place. Zamyatin said of *The Iron Flood* that certain scenes are well-done and memorable. The same thing can be said of *Cement*. Gleb's homecoming is one of these. As he observes the enormous cranes and huge blocks of factory buildings, Gleb experiences a thrill of recognition, but immediately senses something discordant:

Very good! Once more, machines and work. Fresh work. Free work, gained in battle, won through fire and blood. Very good!
The goats scream and laugh with the children. The ammoniacal stench of the pigsty. Weeds everywhere, and the paths besmirched by hens.
What's this? Goats, poultry, and pigs? This used to be strictly forbidden by the management.
Three women were walking towards him in single file, with

bundles under their arms. In front marched an old woman with the face of a witch; behind, two young ones. One of them was fat and full-bosomed. The other with red eyes and red swollen eyelids, her face deeply buried in her shawl. Was she ill or weeping? . . .

As he approached them on the narrow pathway he stood aside in the high grass and gave them a military salute.

"Greetings! Comrades!"

They looked at him askance and stepped past him. Only the last one gave a screeching laugh like a scared hen: "Get on with you! There's enough scamps like you about. You can't greet them all."

"What's the matter with you women? Don't you recognise me?"

Loshak's wife looked gloomily at Gleb—just as an old witch would do—then murmured to herself in her deep voice: "Why, this is Gleb. He has risen from the dead, the rascal!"

And went on her way, silent and sullen.

In this scene of Gleb's rude greeting by an industrial compound overrun with barnyard animals and by emancipated impudent girls, Gladkov has, with a certain sense of structure, introduced the main themes of his novel: the restoration of industry along socialist lines and catastrophic changes in the family. Gleb's mighty socialist feat in making the factory work again, carried out against opposition from relics of the old regime, from bands of White terrorists, from traitors and weaklings within the fold, is only part of his story. He must also, as his wife Dasha pointed out, fight a civil war within himself to conquer the old morality and the old family relations. Dasha believes in free love and complete equality. She wants to work, organize, and fight in the same rank with her men. In a section of the novel called "The Cold Hearth," Gleb experiences the desolateness of this new life:

At nighttime he came home and Dasha was not there. She was not waiting for him on the threshold as she used to in the early days. In those days it was cosy and hospitable in the room. Muslin curtains hung at the windows. The painted floor glittered like a mirror and the white bed and clean tablecloth beckoned to him. And a samovar. . . . The clinking of the china. . . . Here Dasha lived in every corner: she sang, sighed, laughed, spoke of tomorrow and played with her little daughter Nurka.

Nurka, his daughter, is in a children's home, and Dasha insists she is no better than the others and should get the same treatment as any other child: "They're all equal here and they all are lovely." Nurka herself has almost forgotten her father and hardly recognizes the word "home":

"Would you like to come home, Nurka? To play there like you used to . . . with daddy and mama?"

"What home? My bed is over there. We've just had some milk, and now we're going to march to music."

In Gleb's public life he is a hero. In the course of realizing his dream of the reopened cement factory he conquers laziness and disorganization in his own proletarian comrades, and, an even greater triumph, he wins the loyal support of the foreign bourgeois engineer Herman Hermanovich, who was at first his enemy. The following scene, which probably can make no claim to verisimilitude, is a symbolic statement of the Party's policy toward skilled specialists inherited from the old regime:

"Herman Hermanovich . . . now you are one of our best workers—a good head and hands of gold. Without you we couldn't have gotten anything done. Just see what a fine job we have done under your guidance."

"My dear Gleb Ivanovich, I intend to devote all my knowledge and experience—all my life—to our country. I have no other life except that life with all of you; and I have no other task except the struggle to build our future."

And for the first time Gleb saw Kleist's eyes fill with tears. . . .

"Well then, Herman Hermanovich, let's be friends."

"Right, Gleb Ivanovich, let's be friends."

In his private life Gleb is not successful, but that is not the important thing. As the novel ends he has not yet found the way to a "socialist" relationship with Dasha but is still blinded by jealousy and rage at her "new life," and his daughter Nurka has died. Optimism in the face of personal tragedy is, perhaps, the leading motif of the novel, and in Gladkov's world the loss of a separate home, one's own child, and individual happiness counts for little. Gleb himself sensed that no individual could take credit for success in the really important thing, the reconstruction of the factory. Support for that came, he felt, from the mass of laboring men, and he would have been helpless without that support.

The "expendability" of individual human beings in the general economy of history is a variation on the main theme of the book. *Cement* represents an advance over *The Iron Flood* in that it does recognize the existence of private lives. Yet it does so only to show their insignificance as tiny units in a huge sum. Gladkov was influenced by Dostoevsky, but in *Cement* he debates with his master as to the moral weight one should attach to the suffering of history's guiltless, incidental victims. It will be remembered that Ivan Karamazov, in his dialogue with Alyosha, rejected God's world because he could find no way to justify the miseries visited upon the innocent: ". . . If the sufferings of children must swell the sum of sufferings necessary to pay for truth, then I protest that the truth is not worth such a price."

The answer to Ivan Karamazov is given in the meditation of Sergey Ivagin, who has been unjustly expelled from the Party on the ground that he is "an intellectual, and a demoralizing element." Ivagin, still a devoted Marxist, reflects:

Whether he would be readmitted or not made no difference; he, Sergey Ivagin, as a separate personality did not exist. There was only the Party and he was an insignificant item in this great organism. But that day he was going through his old pain once more.

A further stage in his melancholy thought process leads to the conviction that he as an individual owes all of himself to the Party and the historical process embodied in it:

Would he be rehabilitated finally or not? It was of no importance: it would not change his fate. He must work and only work. If he were to be thrown out like refuse, then it meant that this was necessary for the future. He was bound to the whole world, to all mankind, by unbreakable ties.

Wandering and reflecting on his own and man's fate, Sergey

finds himself at a dockside and stops to look down at the pounding waves.

Right at the seawall, placed among the refuse and seaweed there lay the body of an infant. A white scarf was tied about its head, there were stockings on its legs, and the arms could not be seen because of the swaddling clothes around it. It was a fresh corpse, and its waxen face was quiet, almost alive, as though it were sleeping . . . Where did the infant come from? The warm hand of its mother was almost still upon it—in the scarf, the swaddling clothes and the little stockings on its chubby feet. Sergey gazed at it and could not tear his eyes away . . . Where did such a pitiable human sacrifice come from? From a wrecked ship? Thrown overboard by a frenzied mother?

He stood there, unable to tear himself away from the little body. People approached curiously, looked at the corpse and at once continued on their way. They muttered a question to Sergey, but he neither heard nor saw them. He stood there gazing without thought, sorrowful, his eyes full of astonishment and pain, and he felt a deep oppressive grief encircling his heart. Then unconsciously he spoke aloud, without hearing his own voice.

"Yes . . . It must be so. . . . A tragedy of the struggle. . . . To be born anew, one must die."

Cement lacks both verbal artistry and psychological power, yet it had an emotional impact on the Soviet reader, and it became the model and prototype for the vast novels of industrial construction written during the thirties. It was a favorite of Stalin, and as such was circulated in millions of copies. It contained an explicit statement of Marxist philosophy, and in successive editions it quite unsubtly reflected changes in Party policy. Gladkov's fundamental indifference to his novel as a literary product is shown by the ease with which he altered both content and style as times and fashions changed.[1] We shall give two examples of this rewriting. The first of these is amusing evidence not only of the reader's changing taste in the matter of naturalistic detail, but of the Party's changing doctrine on the relative position of the sexes. The parallel passages are from the 1925 edition and the 1950 editions respectively, and the later version reflects in a brutal image the return to a more conventional relationship, in contrast to the woman's struggle for "emancipation" in the early days:

1925 Edition

From the other side of the narrow street muffled drunken voices could be heard coming from the open window of a building. It was the heavy voice of the cooper Savchuk and his hysterical wife Motia, who was cackling like a hen. Gleb left his kit near the fence and crossed over to Savchuk's place. The walls of the room were filthy with soot. Overturned chairs lay helter-skelter on the floor, and clothing was strewn about . . . Because of the sun in his eyes Gleb could not immediately distinguish any person. Then he made out two dirty, convulsed bodies rolling and fighting on the floor. Taking a closer look he saw that it was the Savchuks, man and wife. The man's shirt was torn to bits, his back was bent and his ribs stuck out like barrel hoops . . . The woman's full breast heaved violently as they struggled together.

1950 Edition

On the other side of the street the drunken cooper, Savchuk, was making a row. His wife Motia was screaming hysterically. Gleb listened to it a moment then sprang into action. He got up and went over to Savchuk's quarters. There was dirt and stench in the room. Stools and clothing were strewn about on the floor. A tin tea kettle lay on its side. Flour was scattered all over everything. Motia was lying on a potato sack and hugging it to her bosom, and Savchuk, in a torn and ragged shirt and bellowing like a bull, was punching Motia with his fists and kicking her with his bare feet. Gleb grabbed him from behind under the armpits and dragged him away from her.

The second example of editing was applauded by a Soviet critic, and it illustrates Gladkov's responsiveness to the demand for intelligible and didactic prose even in the remarks of a character under emotional stress. A sudden sharp attack of White "bandits" has just been repulsed. Several workmen have been killed in the action, and Gleb, choked and panting, addresses the proletarian crowd:

1925 Edition

1950 Edition

Again Gleb raised his arms on high.

"Comrades, listen! A sacrifice to labor. . . . With our united strength. . . . No tears or crying! The victory of our hands . . . the factory. We have won. . . . We shall make ourselves heard with fire and machines. The great labor of constructing the Workers' Republic. . . . Ourselves, with our brains and hands. . . . The blood and suffering of the battle—these are our weapons for winning the whole world."

Gleb shouted through his palms as through a megaphone: "Comrades! This has been a sacrifice in labor and struggle. No tears and sobs, but the joy of real victory. . . . Soon the factory will begin to roar with its furnaces and machines. You and I are beginning the mighty construction of socialism. Yes, blood has been spilled, and there has been much suffering. There have been many trials on our path and there will be many more. But this path of struggle leads to happiness, to the final victory over the world of violence. We are building our own world with our own hands. With the name of Lenin on our lips, with faith in unlimited happiness let us double and treble our efforts for the conquest of the future."

The earlier variants provide evidence that Gladkov's style possessed originally a kind of rude emotional power. In an article entitled "My Work on the Novel *Cement*" Gladkov describes the systematic "normalization" of that style undertaken so that the book's message might be intelligible and acceptable to as many Russians as possible. In successive operations on the text of the novel, Gladkov excised substandard vocabulary, vulgar language, and almost all traces of class or local dialect.

Gladkov's work after *Cement* falls into two main categories, "socialist realist" works on topical themes and autobiography. The former are unreadable in the sense that they can be read neither as literary products nor as documentation nor even as honest propaganda; the latter are quite readable reminiscences of Gladkov's boyhood and young manhood with its wanderings and chronic hardship. In the first category, the massive novel *Energy* appeared in installments from 1928 to 1938, was published after extensive revision in book form in 1939, and after much criticism and further self-censorship by the author appeared in a new edition in 1947. It undertakes to describe the construction of the great hydro-electric power plant on the Dnieper river, Dnieprostroy. Gladkov, always responsive to the demands of the Party, spent several years at the construction site accumulating first-hand information on matters both technological and human. He produced during his visit a great many sketches on the great labor taking place at Dnieprostroy, and he seems to have become a kind of expert in the technical details of construction. The result is a formidable novel.

The Birch Grove (1941) deals with the industrial transformation of the provinces, and in it Gladkov attempts to strike a "human" note in the person of the schoolteacher Martin, who lectures the construction manager on the need to create, along with his new project, a more beautiful life for human beings. In *The Vow* (1944) Gladkov portrays the magnificent patriotism shown during the war by Russian workingmen in the rear, who carried out without flinching the collective "vow" made to the great leader, Stalin. Gladkov's autobiographical trilogy, *A Story of My Childhood* (1949), *The Free Way* (1950), and *A Hard Time* (1954), is not without interest, and in some parts, the first volume particularly, displays the power of language that Gladkov originally possessed.

Gladkov's novels, chiefly his proletarian "classic" *Cement*, are read in many parts of the world by the recently literate masses to whom the strictures of cultivated critics or the amused contempt of a formalist writer such as Osip Brik are understandable, probably, only as evidence of their malice. As the "new reader" in Communist countries grows in education and literary sense, will he finally reject these crude collective sagas? It is of course too early to say, but for the moment the novels of Gladkov have an importance in the world far transcending any merit they may have as literature.

Alexander Fadeyev: The Search for a New Leo Tolstoy

Fadeyev (1901–1956), who was a native of Siberia and the son of a village doctor, joined the Communist Party at the age of seventeen, fought in Siberia against Admiral Kolchak, the Japanese, and Semyonov's Cossacks, published his first stories "The Flood" and "Against the Current" in 1923, and at last settled in Moscow to become a close collaborator of Leopold Averbakh, the leader of the Russian Association of Proletarian Writers (RAPP). Fadeyev was from the start a writer with a mission. Though his first novel *The Nineteen* (1927) was a success in the Communist and proletarian milieu, he early showed a preference for the writing of resolutions, speeches, and essays on the theory of proletarian literature. Under his guidance RAPP adopted an attitude toward Gladkov that was distinctly unfriendly, and however justified their criticism of artistic shortcomings in his works, the sharpness of their tone is mildly shocking. Gladkov complained that the critics of RAPP declared his novel *Cement* "beyond the bounds of literature," and he fought them with equal ruthlessness. In the archives of the Institute of World Literature, in Moscow, there are manuscripts in the hand of Gladkov which refer to his constant struggle against the literary theories of Averbakh, Fadeyev, and other semibourgeois "aesthetes," as he called them, and his punishment at their hands by silence, censure, or abuse. Like most devotees of a particular doctrine, Fadeyev believed that contrary doctrines were mistaken and harmful and that their carriers should be corrected. His sternness toward Gladkov was motivated by a conviction that, although *Cement* did reveal personal and family problems, its author had left untouched the inner lives of his characters.

Fadeyev's insistent emphasis on the portrayal of "living men" in their complex psychological reality was solidly based on Marxist doctrine. Marx and Engels had provided texts suitable for use in the ideological struggle against those relentless "human streams" and romanticized heroes of the early proletarian period. Because Marx, Engels, and Lenin had at times expressed a preference for writers of the realistic school, the words "reality" and "realism" came to be clothed with mystical authority. Fadeyev took upon himself the task of liquidating romanticism. He was an enemy, also, of formalism, stylization, "factography," anything, indeed, that smacked of "modernism." He developed the argument that "realism" is the literary expression of a materialist philosophy and devised a slogan to be used against romantics: "Down with Schiller!"

Fadeyev and his friends in their position as lawgivers to proletarian writers urged upon them the value of a realistic approach to individual psychology and prescribed models for them to imitate. The importance of the "classics" and the need to learn from them were a steady refrain. What "classics" did they have in mind? Not even the Proletcult or the Smithy had succeeded in producing a totally new literature, and all proletarian writers had in some degree been learning from past masters. The question clearly was "which classics" should be imitated, and for Fadeyev, the "classics" added up to one author, Leo Tolstoy. Rebelling against the modernism of Bely and Pilnyak, which had infected even proletarian writing, Fadeyev, and with him the leading proletarian writers, reverted to the style of their "grandfathers," the great masters of classical realism.

Tolstoy was made to order for the proletarians. His approach to character seemed "rational" in that his probing tended to reveal the motivation of behavior in terms of environment, memory, hidden needs, and desires. His method had solid sanction from the nineteenth-century socialist critic Chernyshevsky, who called him a "dialectician of the human psyche," and from Lenin, who admired his ability to "remove the masks" from social convention. And his artistic means are so simple and economical in appearance that it would seem anyone might use them with profit. Fadeyev reported that before writing his novel, *The Nineteen*, he reread *War and Peace* in its entirety.

The Nineteen reveals hardly a trace of "Pilnyakian" device. It is free of excited lyrical digressions. Its language is a smooth instrument of communication featuring matter rather than manner. Syntactic distortion, verbal play, self-conscious ornamentation are scrupulously avoided, almost for the first time in Soviet prose. The important thing for Fadeyev is the political *idea* of the book, and he exercises what literary skill he has to express that idea in terms of individual human experience. The result is a novel which, in spite of its reversion to an earlier realistic style, struck the Soviet reader as a new departure, for it described real people rather than a clash of primitive forces or the inexorable historical march of "masses."

The political purpose of the novel is to show, in a small band of guerrillas operating in parts of Siberia controlled by the Whites and the Japanese, the nexus of relations binding together the social forces which made the Revolution. The band contains peasants, workmen, professional revolutionaries, "*lumpen* proletarians," students, intellectuals. The psychology of each "class" is presented in the inner thoughts and feelings of a particular representative. Thus the peasant has a violent hatred of farmer landlords, but so strong a love for his own little plot of ground that he fails to understand larger issues; the youthful intellectual Mechik has a romantic attachment to "the workers" and "the Revolution" but can't be relied upon in a crisis; the unruly proletarian anarchist Morozka develops loyalty and discipline in association with the band. And it is the "real" worker, the miner Dubov, who understands most clearly the great issues of the time, and the leader of the band, the Jew Levinson, lays his greatest reliance on Dubov and his men.

In Levinson Fadeyev created a new kind of hero. Levinson has all the square-jawed ruthlessness of Kozhuk in *The Iron Flood* or Gleb Chumalov in *Cement*, and he presents to his men the image of unbreakable resolve. But he also has a secret inner life and a consciousness of his own weaknesses. The techniques for revealing the private as well as the public thoughts of his characters Fadeyev learned from Tolstoy. He confessed, "When working on *The Nineteen* I often found myself subconsciously imitating Tolstoy even in my choice of words and in the rhythm of my sentences."

Examples of the Tolstoyan technique of the "inner monologue" and other Tolstoyan devices are common in the novel.

The young intellectual Mechik muses about his working-class girl friend, Varya:

His thoughts carried him far away into the bright days of the future, and in consequence they were light and airy, dissolving of their own accord like the soft, rosy clouds over the plains of the taiga. He thought how he would return with Varya to the town in a cushioned, jolting train with open windows, through which they would see just such soft, rosy clouds sailing over the darkening chain of mountains in the distance. They two would sit at the window, very close to each other, Varya murmuring soft words to him, he stroking her head, and her braids would shine like gold, like the noonday sun. . . . The Varya of his daydreams bore little resemblance to the round-shouldered woman of the pump at No. 1 Pit, since all his imaginings were remote from actual things and embodied only what he longed to see.

Mechik sees Morozka and Varya return from a tryst in the woods:

When he saw Morozka again, returning so soon from the forest (the orderly was swinging his arms as he walked, his steps heavy and slow), Mechik, with the subconscious assurance which is based on no concrete fact, but which does not permit of doubt, realized that "nothing had happened" between Morozka and Varya, and that he, Mechik, was the cause. An uneasy joy and an inexplicable feeling of guilt woke in him, and he began to be afraid of encountering Morozka's murderous glance.

The adjutant Baklanov involuntarily reveals his reverence for the leader:

"What? . . ." Baklanov asked again in threatening tones, turning his whole body to the man in the way Levinson would (Baklanov thought that Levinson did this in order to emphasize the importance of his questions, but in point of fact Levinson twisted in this manner because he had been wounded in the neck and could not turn round in any other way).

Fadeyev's novel is simple in its plot and straightforward in its execution. Levinson's band, trapped and hopelessly outnumbered, is beaten and decimated. Only nineteen men escape, and they go on, defeated but not demoralized, ready to fight again for the Revolution. The revelation of that leader's human weaknesses, his fear in battle, his secret failures in self-confidence, and the near collapse of his strength and will in the face of disaster was the new touch that added to Fadeyev's proletarian novel the fillip of human verisimilitude. Fadeyev claimed to have created, in Levinson, not a saint but a "living man." He did succeed, in any case, in jolting the reader with this picture of an abject and miserable commander surveying the poor remnant of his band:

Levinson's eyes remained fixed for several seconds on the men. Then all at once he somehow collapsed and shrank, and everybody at once noticed that he had become weak and much older. He was no longer ashamed of his weakness and he no longer tried to hide it; he sat huddled up in the saddle, slowly blinking his long wet eyelashes, and the tears ran down his beard. . . . The men turned aside in fear that they might lose control of themselves.

Levinson turned his horse and slowly went on ahead. The company followed him.

"Don't cry! . . . What good . . . will that do?" Gontcharenko said humbly, raising Varya by the shoulder.

Whenever Levinson forgot himself he started to look behind him in uncertainty; remembering that Baklanov was not there, he began to cry again.

So they rode out from the forest—the nineteen.

Fadeyev's second novel was planned as an ambitious fictional effort to be published in six substantial parts. Only the first four parts had been completed at his death in 1956, and he was at that time engaged in writing the fifth part, of which one chapter was published. *The Last of the Udegs* has, like *The Nineteen*, an idea which gives it form and content. The Udegs, a remote nomadic tribe of the Russian far east, whose contacts with twentieth-century civilization have been sporadic and brief and whose culture is still on the level of primitive Communism, are suddenly confronted with the "Communism" of a modern world state. Fadeyev planned to demonstrate in telling their story the thesis that an extremely primitive people under the guidance of the Soviet government may experience a leap from tribal Communism to the complex collective organization of the twentieth century, skipping over the intervening "historical stages": family, private property, slavery, feudalism, capitalism and socialism. Lines from Engel's *Origin of the Family, Private Property, and the State* stood as an epigraph in an early edition of the novel. But to describe the novel solely in terms of ideology does less than justice to a work over which Fadeyev labored for thirty years and to which he gave his best as a writer. Uneven though it is, *The Last of the Udegs* contains some of Fadeyev's best pages, and the fact that he spent his energies on literary administration rather than on the completion of this novel is a minor tragedy. In concept it was to be, in a sense, an experiment in the juxtaposition and contrast of various stages in the development of human societies, and each "stage" had its representative in a particular person. There are a dozen or more clearly delineated characters, the merchant-capitalist, the radical intellectual, the peasant revolutionary, the proletarian socialist, the Chinese merchant, and, last, the members of the primitive Udeg community itself whose way of life was to be radically altered through contact with "history" in the form of collectivized farming.

When Fadeyev describes in translucent prose the simple way of life of the Udeg tribes, their adjustment to cruel seasonal changes, their hunting expeditions, the education of their young, their courtship and marriage customs, he covers very skillfully ground which has, no doubt, been gone over before. And yet the story of these simple but hardly innocent people abruptly confronted with the weapons and the violent issues of modern Europe has a power of historical drama not wholly dampened by the author's insistent Marxist message.

The Young Guard, a novel about the guerrilla resistance to the German occupation during the Second World War, has had a sorry fate. Published in 1946, it was awarded a Stalin prize, first class. In the same year a dramatization was presented in Leningrad. Discussion of the novel took place in factories, at meetings of the Young Communist League, and in the Writers' Union. Defects were pointed out, the presence of which Fadeyev acknowledged. In a letter covering his "errors" Fadeyev said:

I was criticized not because the underground fighters were poorly described, but because I should have given a broader picture of the activity of our Party in the underground, and because I should have shown not only Bolsheviks who were weakly organized and who failed, but chiefly such as were capable of organizing a genuine resistance to the German occupationists. The latter were of course more typical, and I shall take this advice.

A "revised and enlarged" edition of the novel was published in 1951. A comparison of the two versions shows that Fadeyev included "new material" giving credit to the centralized Party apparatus for a movement that had in the first edition been presented as a spontaneous manifestation in the young of Soviet patriotism.

The operation performed on *The Young Guard* damaged but did not destroy it. Fadeyev displays in it a stylistic virtuosity that was absent from both *The Nineteen* and *The Last of the Udegs.* An occasional note of romanticism recalls the early Civil War novels, and elements of the heroic national saga have reminded some critics of Gogol's *Taras Bulba.* As in so many of the Civil War novels, including his own *The Nineteen,* the most powerful scenes, those labored over with special devotion and skill, are scenes of disorganization and defeat. Quite possibly the best writing in *The Young Guard* is to be found in those pages which describe the retreat of the Red Army before the Germans and the confused and tragic evacuation of the civilian population.

A study of Fadeyev's career as a writer and as a literary official would throw much light on Soviet society. He was another of the young Red Army commissars who entered proletarian literature in the early twenties with firm convictions and great plans. He was one of the principal leaders of the Russian Association of Proletarian Writers and, along with Averbakh and Libedinsky, devised its literary platform and fought its literary battles. When RAPP was liquidated in 1932 and his comrades fell into disgrace, Fadeyev himself wrote a series of earnest articles (*Old and New*) in support of the new regime in literature. He survived the purges of 1936–1938 while many of those same comrades were shot or sent into exile. His role during this period is impossible to assess on the basis of information we now have. From 1939 to 1954 he was Secretary of the Executive Board of the Union of Soviet Writers. He was thus directly involved in policies that led to the debasement of Soviet literature, and he was the official spokesman of its Stalinist period. He was not re-elected as Secretary of the Union at the Second Congress of Soviet Writers held in 1954, after the death of Stalin. There is evidence that he suffered from alcoholism, and had undergone hospital treatment for that ailment. In May, 1956, early in the de-Stalinization period, he shot himself. Probably the most honest words spoken in public about him were those of the novelist Sholokhov at the Twentieth Congress of the Communist Party:

Why couldn't someone long ago have said to Fadeyev: "The thirst for power is a contemptible thing in the writers' world. The Writers' Union is not a military body, nor is it a punitive battalion, and no writer need stand at attention before you, Comrade Fadeyev. . . ." For a great many years Fadeyev was a "general secretary" and gave his time exclusively to such business. The result is that we lost a good writer, and now we have also lost a "general secretary. . . ."

Mikhail Sholokhov: The Don Cossacks

When the first installments of Sholokhov's *The Silent Don* appeared in 1928 in the magazine *October,* published by the Moscow Association of Proletarian Writers, it was as though some natural phenomenon suddenly burst forth outside the normal chain of cause and effect. Their author, who was just twenty-two, was relatively unknown, and his *Stories of the Don,* published in 1924 and 1925, had given no one reason to suppose that he possessed major literary talent. He was not one of the youthful commissars who had come to Moscow after the Civil War to produce proletarian literature. The son of a merchant whose family had settled in the Don Cossack country, he was unknown in the literary organizations of the capital, and he took no part in literary politics. He was, and always remained, averse to the normal means of publicity available to Soviet writers: his name is not conspicuous in collections of autobiographies or of essays on "How We Write" or "The Nature of the Writer's Work." And as one installment of *The Silent Don* followed another the fascinated Soviet reader sensed that this new star hardly belonged in its proletarian constellation. The story contained no inept digressions on the iron will of the proletariat—in fact the village characters were not proletarians at all in the generally accepted meaning of the term, but Cossacks, the traditional support of the government against the Revolution. One superb scene after another convinced the Soviet reader at last that no clear political thesis would emerge, that no commissar would appear to guide the "elemental forces," that no problems of Communist ethics would be raised and solved. *The Silent Don* became in a very short time the favorite reading of millions of Russians, and such it has remained. In the life-and-death story of a remote Cossack village on the Don the reader could experience the full tragedy of his own war and revolution unhindered by the verbal complexity of a "stylist" or the lucid commentary of a commissar. Events in the lives of ordinary human beings were in the center of Sholokhov's focus, and not from theoretical considerations, but because they entered organically into his design. For instance, a moment just before dawn when Gregor Melekhov is watering his brother's horse is completely captured:

Aslant across the Don lay a waving, never-trodden moon path. Over the Don hung a mist, and above it the grain of stars. The horse set its hind hoofs down cautiously. The drop to the water was bad going. From the farther side of the river came the quacking of ducks. A sheatfish turned and darted over the water above the mud by the bank, hunting in the shallows for smaller fry.

Gregor stood a long time by the river. The bank exuded a dank and sickly rottenness. A tiny drop of water fell from the horse's lips. A light, pleasant void was in Gregor's heart. He felt happy and carefree. The red-tailed dawn was pecking up the starry grain from the dove-colored floor of heaven.

Close to the stable he ran into his mother.

"That you, Grishka?" she asked.

"Who else?"

"Watered the horse?"

"Yes," he answered shortly.

And the haymaking in the Cossack village:

The haymaking began immediately after Trinity. From early morning the meadow blossomed with women's holiday skirts, the bright embroidery of aprons, and colored kerchiefs. The whole village turned out for the mowing. The mowers and rakers attired themselves as though for an annual holiday. So it had been from of old. From the Don to the distant alder clumps the ravaged meadowland stirred and pulsed.

Or Aksinia filling her pails at the river:

Her pails scraping, Aksinia went down to the Don. The foam serpentined along the shore in an intricate yellow lacework on the green hem of the wave. White seagulls were hovering and mewing above the river. Tiny fish sprinkled in a silver rain over the surface of the water. On the other side, beyond the white of the sandy headland, the gray tops of ancient poplars rose haughtily and sternly. As Aksinia was drawing water she dropped her pail. Raising her skirt, she waded in up to her knees. The water swirled and tickled her calves, and for the first time since Stepan's return she laughed quietly and uncertainly.

And the husband when he is deserted by an unfaithful wife:

He stared around the room, and at last he understood. He dropped the lamp, tore his sabre down from the wall, gripped the hilt until the veins swelled in his fingers, raised Aksinia's blue and yellow jacket on its point, threw the jacket up in the air and with a short swing of the sabre cut it in two as it fell.

Gray, savage, in his wolfish yearning he threw the pieces of old jacket up to the ceiling again and again; the sharp steel whistled as it cut them in their flight.

Then, tearing off the sword knot, he threw the sabre into a corner, went into the kitchen, and sat down at the table. His head bowed, with trembling fingers he stroked the unwashed table top time after time.

When war and revolution come, they seem to enter these

individual lives like drought, flood, and other natural calamities. The author's Marxist viewpoint can be discovered if one looks for it in his selection of detail and system of emphasis, but through most of the book this viewpoint is neither explicit nor obvious. The long and multiplaned story of his heroes' lives is told with objectivity and in a mood of reflective detachment. Political viewpoint becomes obtrusive in the later portions of the novel when the background of war and revolution must be given, and in the edition of 1953 passages of an offensively tendentious nature were inserted under pressure from Stalin.

But those who in 1928 read the first volume of the novel as it appeared in *October* were struck first of all by its freedom from the familiar idiom of proletarian art. Surprise was expressed in many quarters at its originality and power. Serafimovich published a review in *Pravda* in which he likened Sholokhov to a baby eaglet who suddenly spreads enormous wings. Others were incredulous, and rumors soon began circulating that *The Silent Don* was actually the work of a White officer killed during the Civil War whose manuscript Sholokhov had appropriated and presented as his own. This accusation was so widespread and so persistent that it was felt necessary to answer it publicly. A statement appeared in *Pravda* in March, 1929, signed by Serafimovich, Fadeyev, and Stavsky, who claimed to have seen Sholokhov's own notes for the novel and the rough draft of his manuscript. But the story of plagiarism is still heard in Russian émigré circles, and many still refuse to believe that the proletarian writer Sholokhov is the author of *The Silent Don*.

The vast design of the novel as it began to emerge in the published installments was equally surprising. Prose fiction as it revived in the twenties had been largely confined to short, concentrated pieces centering on particular events and relatively few characters. None had yet attempted an epic of "war and peace" rivaling Leo Tolstoy's in the dimensions of its canvas and the number and variety of its characters. Sholokhov's "epic" in its final form consists of four volumes in eight parts totaling 1500 pages, and is thus somewhat longer than *War and Peace*. The first two parts deal with life in a Cossack village before the First World War, the action of the novel beginning in 1912. In its portrayal of the manners and mores, and in its reproduction of the dialect of these Cossacks, the novel has some claim to merit as an ethnographic document, and as such it was read by many critics. Conversations are reported in the actual dialect of the speakers and even descriptive passages are laced with vocabulary and phrase-turns peculiar to the Don region. Because the novel was difficult reading for its Russian audience, it was provided, when published in book form, with a glossary giving the Russian equivalents of about three hundred local words.

The third part, which concludes the first volume, describes the intrusion upon the Cossack community of the First World War, and the disturbance in its normal life brought about by the loss of its men to the front lines. The moment of excitement and tragedy at the beginning of the war is given in the following image, where the late summer haymowing is interrupted by the news of war:

As they crossed the field track Piotra glanced to his left, and noticed a tiny cloud of dust moving swiftly along the distant high road from the village.

"Someone riding there!" he remarked to Natalia, screwing up his eyes.

"Fast! Look at the dust!" Natalia replied in surprise.

"What's up? Daria!" Piotra called to his wife. "Rein in for a minute, and let's watch that rider!"

The cloud of dust dropped down into a hollow and disappeared, then came up again on the other side. Now the figure of the rider could be seen through the dust. Piotra sat gazing, his dirty palm set against the edge of his straw summer hat. He frowned and took his hand away; "He'll kill that horse—riding at a gallop like that."

Now the horseman could be seen quite plainly. He was riding his horse at a furious gallop, his left hand holding his cap, a dusty red flag fluttering in his right. He rode along the track so close to them that Piotra heard his horse panting as it breathed the overheated air into its lungs. As he passed, the man shouted:

"Alarm!"

A flake of yellow soapy foam flew from his horse and fell into a hoof print. Piotra followed the rider with his eyes. The heavy snort of the horse, and, as he stared after the retreating figure, the horse's croup, wet, and glittering like a steel blade, remained impressed in his memory.

The second volume (parts four and five) describes the growth of discontent and the outbreak of revolution both in the army and in the village. The third volume (part six) deals with the struggle in the Don country between the revolutionary Cossacks under Podtyolkov and the Whites under Kaledin. The fourth (parts seven and eight) has as its central theme the uprising against the Reds in the Tatarsk area and its bloody suppression. In the last three parts much attention is given to the fate of individuals and of Cossack families torn apart by the changing fortunes of civil war. The central figure in the novel, its "hero" Gregor Melekhov, is a young man whose rebellious love affair with his married neighbor Aksinia Astakhova runs as a single thread through the narrative as its focus shifts from the village to the war fronts or to the capital in the days of the Revolution and again back to its structural center, the village.

Sholokhov's panoramic novel has been compared both to Tolstoy's *War and Peace* and to *Anna Karenina;* though there are similarities the comparison is not helpful, since the two writers are far apart in their style and in the kind of world they portray. Sholokhov's concept was undoubtedly influenced by *War and Peace,* and the movement of the story is reminiscent of Tolstoy's work: the fortunes of a few Cossack families are traced through upheavals of world-wide significance, the scene shifting back and forth from "public" to "private" events and lives. Like Tolstoy, Sholokhov introduces historical personages, the Cossack general Kaledin and the revolutionary Podtyolkov, for instance, as characters in the story, and actual historical documents, for example, Lenin's statements on imperialist war, are worked into the text of the novel. The battle scenes, especially those seen through the eyes of Gregor Melekhov, owe much to Tolstoy. Sholokhov has learned the trick of using the viewpoint of the "naïve" observer to convey an impression of violent confusion. And Melekhov's groping search for the right path to take in the confusing clash of armies and parties, his adherence first to the Reds then to the Whites, and at last to no party, does have a tenuous likeness to Pierre's search for truth. But the ways in which Sholokhov is simply himself and quite different from Tolstoy are more interesting and more significant.

Sholokhov was born in 1905 and grew to manhood in a period of constant bloody strife in which he himself was a participant. His sensitive artist's vision preserved and re-created innumerable scenes of violence. The novel opens with the savage stamping to death by the villagers of Prokoffey Melekhov's pregnant Turkish wife, suspected of being a witch, and Prokoffey's revenge on one of the instigators:

"Drag the bitch into the yard!" came a roar from the steps. A regimental comrade of Prokoffey's wound the Turkish woman's hair around one hand, pressed his other hand over her screaming mouth, dragged her at a run through the porch and flung her beneath the feet of the crowd. A thin shriek rose above the howl of voices. Prokoffey sent half a dozen cossacks flying, burst into the hut, and snatched a sabre from the wall. Jostling against one another, the cossacks rushed out of the porch. Swinging the gleaming, whistling sabre around his head, Prokoffey ran down the steps. The crowd shuddered and scattered over the yard.

Lushnya was heavy of gait, and by the threshing floor Prokoffey caught up with him; with a diagonal sweep down across the left shoulder from behind he clave the cossack's body to the belt. Tearing out the stakes of the wattle fence, the crowd poured across the threshing floor into the steppe.

Some half hour later the crowd ventured to approach Prokoffey's farm again. Two of them crept cautiously into the porch. On the kitchen threshold, in a pool of blood, her head flung back awkwardly, lay Prokoffey's wife; her lips writhed tormentedly back from her teeth, her gnawed tongue protruded. Prokoffey, with shaking head and glassy stare, was wrapping a squealing, crimson, slippery little ball—the prematurely born infant—in a sheepskin.

Violent emotion that issues in cruel attack upon the persons of other human beings is the stuff of which *The Silent*

Don is made, and it is made with great skill. The action is punctuated at regular intervals with scenes of irreparable injury committed by one human being on the body of another. As Stepan Astakhov beat and kicked his faithless wife: "You would have thought, watching him from a distance, that it was someone doing the Cossack dance." Aksinia's father, after raping her, was beaten by her mother and brother, and they "went on beating him steadily for half an hour." The despised Ukrainians are beaten by Cossacks in a fight over a turn in line at the flour mill: "At the door of the weighing shed a young Ukrainian boy lay with a broken head in a pool of blood; bloody strands of hair fell over his face." A troop of Cossacks drag a young girl into a shed and rape her one after another, and afterwards: "She lay on her back, her legs crossing and uncrossing like scissor blades, her fingers scrabbling in the snow by the wall." Podtyolkov's men slaughter their captured White officers; Podtyolkov's men are themselves slaughtered and their bodies piled into a hastily dug hole. The Red Misha Koshevoi kills the father and grandfather of his enemy, Mitry Korshunov; Mitry Korshunov returns after the Whites recapture the town and kills all the remaining Koshevois, old and young: "And Mitry throws a rope around the old woman's neck and drags her along the ground, just as though she was a dog—and she, poor thing, doesn't make a sound."

Scenes such as these are recurrent in the novel and are dwelt on by the author with detached horror. Tolstoy no doubt witnessed such events, but the conventions of Tolstoy's "realism" did not admit the literary treatment of such matter. Gorky, rather than Tolstoy, is here the model, but Sholokhov has left all his models far behind in mastering the techniques of raw naturalism.

Sholokhov probably has no masters in one other area: the expression in physical terms of overpowering human emotion. Sometimes the effect is humorous, as when Pantaleimon Melekhov, in a frenzy of rage at his sons, "slobbers his beard, and dances up and down in the field." And grief at the death of a loved person in Sholokhov's world literally strikes men to the ground: "Like a blind man he ran into the gate, gave a hollow cry, fell down . . . and crawled along the ground on all fours, moving faster and faster, his face almost touching the ground." And the onset of sexual love literally "moves" his characters: "A wave of rapture and heavy joy carried Bunchuk away. He bowed his head as though before a blow, and said, half seriously, half in jest: 'Anya, you're as good as someone's happiness.' "

His chronicle of human disaster Sholokhov projects against the background of nature—of *The Silent Don* flowing endless and unperturbed to the sea. Nature he perceives in moments of lyric clarity and reduces it to fresh and unusual, if at times somewhat strained, metaphors. The poetry in Sholokhov's roughly realistic prose is its most original feature.

The Silent Don is a much better book in its earlier than in its later chapters, and most commentators agree that there is a decline in imaginative power in the last two volumes, where it becomes necessary to tie together the threads of the chronicle. The novel then becomes an account of the victory of the Reds over the Whites, and the author, a conscious Marxist, includes documentary material and commentary intended to illuminate the historical significance of that victory. Unlike Tolstoy, who believes that there must be an iron necessity in history but does not claim to know the laws of its movement, Sholokhov has at his disposal in Marxism a scientific explanation of those laws, and a forecast of the future. His Marxism does not vitiate, however, Sholokhov's feeling for certain basic realities. His hero, searching for the right path, does not find it in Communism. He finds no answer to his questions, and after his tortured journey returns precisely to that spot which he had left as the novel opened and which remained for him the only reality, his own home and family.

And now had come to pass that little thing of which Gregor had dreamed during so many sleepless nights. . . . He was standing at the threshold of his own home, holding his son in his arms.

This was all that was left to him in life and that still made him kin with the spacious earth that lay glittering under the chilly sun.

The final emphasis on a separate, individual existence independent of nations and "history," so reminiscent of the ending of *War and Peace* on a note of family happiness, argues that Sholokhov is philosophically close to Tolstoy and that in him Marxist historical doctrine is less than skin deep. Though the Reds do beat the Whites (and indeed who in Sholokhov's world is not "beaten"), *The Silent Don* is not a happy or a hopeful book. Life's movement we sense in it, but (even though his characters tell us about it in confident terms) we do not have a sure sense of its direction. The interpretation of the novel according to which Gregor's individualism is "wrong" and the outlook and behavior of the Communist hero Koshevoi "right" belongs to the Soviet critics rather than Sholokhov. The novel is so contrived that the reader identifies himself and sympathizes with Gregor and with no other character.

Yet Sholokhov has been responsive to Party demand upon his talent. Recent studies have shown that the text of *The Silent Don* suffered during the Stalin period from emendations aimed at eliminating vulgarity in its language or deviations in its politics. The most damaging alterations of the text occurred in the edition of 1953, but in the edition of 1956 older readings have in almost all cases been restored.

He was responsive to the Party's literary needs in 1930, when, on a visit to Moscow, he was persuaded to interrupt the writing of *The Silent Don* in order to produce a novel on the collectivization of agriculture in the Don region. The first part of this novel, the title of which, *Podnyataya Tselina,* has been translated as *Seeds of Tomorrow,* or *Virgin Soil Upturned,* was completed in 1931. After publishing the first part Sholokhov returned to the writing of *The Silent Don,* which he completed in 1940, and the second and final part of the novel on collectivization did not appear until 1960. The latter has been translated under the title *Harvest on the Don* (1961). During the nearly twenty years while he worked on it rumors were rife as to the reasons for the failure to finish it. There was speculation abroad that Sholokhov was not in sympathy with the direction of Stalinist policy and that changes in the novel had been dictated which he refused to accept. Inside the Soviet Union scarcely veiled charges were made from time to time that Sholokhov had not been able to finish the novel because he did not "really understand" socialism on the land.

In the years from 1940 to 1960 Sholokhov wrote little. During the war he traveled on various fronts as a correspondent, but found that he had no skill in the writing of newspaper sketches. A short story, "The Science of Hatred" (1942), has some historical significance in that it shows the transformation of a good-natured Russian officer, disposed to tolerate and even to like his fellow man, into a furious hater of all Germans. Sholokhov in this story draws heavily on his resources for the portrayal of extremes of emotion. A few chapters from a novel about the Second World War, *They Fought For Their Country,* planned as a major production, appeared in 1943 and 1944. The short story "Fate of a Man," published in *Pravda* in 1957, has been translated into many languages and made into a distinguished film. The story is a powerful and tender treatment of the resilience of human love under adversity. Utterly unpretentious in its manner, Sholokhov's story is one of the best things in recent Soviet writing.[2]

A Scatter of Minor Deities

Out of the Proletcult, the Smithy, and the RAPP organization there emerged a number of proletarian poets and prose writers whose very names have in many cases been forgotten. The principal poets have already been mentioned. The prose writers are not without a certain literary and historical interest and should perhaps be restored to memory. P. K. Bessalko (1887–1920) belonged to the older generation of proletarian writers and spent many years in exile in western Europe. A pupil of Bogdanov, he became a fanatical theorist of proletarian exclusiveness in the arts, and is the author of a work on proletarian poetry. In a series of autobiographical novels he traces the growth of a working-class child into a conscious revolutionary. N. Lyashko (pseudonym of N. N. Lyashchenko, (1884——) began to publish in provincial magazines before the revolution of 1905, and, like Bessalko, he sentimentalizes the worker in a manner peculiar to proletarians of the older generation. His most important work, *The Blast Furnace* (1924), is a predecessor of *Cement* in the depiction of proletarian reconstruction in industry, and it outdoes *Cement* in romanticizing the proletarian collective at the expense both of individuals and of other social groups. In this novel the toiling mass, heroic in its devotion and faith, brings to life again a decaying industrial plant.

V. M. Bakhmetyev (1885———) qualifies as a proletarian writer through early membership in the Bolshevik faction of the Russian Social Democratic Party. He is one of the best representatives of the proletarian school of "psychological realism." His most important work, *The Crime of Martin,* is a genuinely interesting psychological study in the motivations of a Communist functionary revealing the clash of his instinctive drives with carefully learned rules of behavior. It is a study in the dominance of instinctive behavior.

Alexander Neverov (1886–1923), whose promise for Soviet literature was ended by his early death, was closer to the peasantry than to the proletariat. *Tashkent, City of Bread* (1923) is an account of the search for survival of a young boy who during the famine year leaves his village on the Volga and, always displaying courage and cleverness, makes his way to the "city of abundance," Tashkent. Neverov was the author of numerous sketches and stories of peasant life, and his plays were awarded a prize in the State Publishing House competition of 1920.

A number of new writers appeared in the pages of the RAPP publication *October* at the end of the twenties. Some of these displayed the promise of new talent, but, in most cases, have been lost to Soviet literature. L. S. Ovalov (1905———) wrote a number of stories in which the central characters are rank and file Soviet workers whose lives and thoughts are honestly explored. The story "Chatter" (1929) is in the form of casual notes describing the everyday activities of a printer, a man of the older generation whose comments on the contemporary scene are pointed and sharp. A second story, "Hunters of Doubts" (1930), dealt with the underground Trotskyist opposition movement, and Ovalov took his readers inside that movement to reveal the kind of people who were drawn to it. He represents them as "mistaken" but as honest revolutionaries, and his story documents the underground political life of the times.

A. Mitrofanov is the author of stories and sketches on the life of the young Communists, and his best product was the story "June-July," the first part of which appeared in 1930, though the work has never been published as a whole. Mitrofanov in this story presents sympathetically a number of young people who are disillusioned with the direction the Revolution has taken. A cruel campaign against Mitrofanov as an apologist for such attitudes was launched soon after the appearance of the first part of his story.

An able and interesting proletarian writer, now largely forgotten, was Sergey Semyonov, whose best and most popular work was *Natalya Tarpova* (1928), a long novel dealing with the private and personal as well as the official lives of Communist party functionaries during the NEP period. Semyonov was one of the best practitioners of "psychological realism," and his lancet frequently lays bare the inner lives and thoughts of his characters; in fact his chief skill is in reporting the stream of unspoken thoughts and desires that lie behind their actions. The central theme of the novel is the conflict inside a Communist woman between the natural affection she feels for a "bourgeois" engineer and her strict set of Bolshevik values. The novel is a valuable historical document in that it gives an entirely credible account of the problems of marriage and morality as they were examined at that time and in that

Finally, the proletarian novelist Fyodor Panfyorov (1896–1960), a very prolific writer, gave his principal attention to the collectivization of peasant life. The long novel *And Then The Harvest* (1928–37), on which his fame largely rests, develops its thesis from the processes which militated against individualism and in favor of collective enterprise. Panfyorov is like Furmanov in the frankness tive enterprise. Panfyorov is like Furmanov in the frankness with which his thesis is stated and developed, yet he gives vivid portraits of a great variety of village and Party types, showing the tensions that existed between the peasant who simply loved his land and the organizers possessed by a theory

192 / **Russian Literature Since the Revolution**

and a program. The novel, especially in its early chapters, is interesting and rewarding reading. The non-Soviet reader finds less rewarding those sections that describe the efforts of peasant leaders to overcome "petit-bourgeois individualism" in the village. Panfyorov has keen powers of observation and his peasants are real and interesting people.

The Struggle For Peace (1945–48) is a long novel about operations behind the German lines during the war. *Mother Volga* (1953) returns to the theme of peasant life and the struggle for production. Panfyorov's frank realism in the treatment of peasant character and setting is one of the most interesting features of this novel, as it is of the story "In the Name of the Young" (1960). Like so many Soviet novelists his work is painfully uneven. Pages of excellent writing regularly yield to journalistic statement.

Conclusion

Few of the writers in the proletarian literary movement had ties either to the urban working class or to the intelligentsia. Many were of peasant stock, but the majority came from middle-class provincial families. This is true of the most prominent among them: Fadeyev, Sholokhov, Furmanov, Libedinsky, Averbakh, and Serafimovich. Their education was purely Russian. They had few contacts with Europe, and only rarely betray awareness of Western literature. Fadeyev speaks with great respect of Balzac, but that is no doubt an echo of Engels' favorable opinion, and there is no evidence that Fadeyev himself had any interest in French literature. Averbakh knew German and wrote about Goethe, but from a narrowly proletarian point of view. They were on the whole exclusively Russian in culture and outlook.

They settled easily into group work and placed their literary talents at the service of the movement. They welcomed the organization of literature. Libedinsky's satire of the "soulless" bureaucrat was directed more at his soullessness than at his bureaucratism. Even Sholokhov, who lived apart from the writers' hive, was, as a Party man in good standing, always available for "Party tasks." And so were most of the others.

Narrowly conservative, they recognized only the established

traditions of Russian realism. Some of them showed traces of symbolist contamination, but that was superficial and accidental. They were uneasy with strangeness or originality of form, and preferred writing that was intelligible to the great mass of readers. They were influenced by Tolstoy rather than by Gogol or Dostoevsky, and they carried on the Russian tradition of literature as a social value.

Few of them were satisfied with the "mass" hero, and their tendency was to seek for individual human experience and to find in their characters thoughts and feelings that were particular and personal. Sholokhov reported that in his initial version of *The Silent Don* the novel was to center on "event" and on generalized portraits, on a historical panorama of Cossack participation in the Revolution. But he rejected that form, he said, and chose to reveal historical events through the lives of the leading characters, who then became the principal elements in the plot. Proletarian literature as a whole underwent an evolution similar to that described by Sholokhov. The idealized metallic sculptures of the first proletarian poets early gave way to Libedinsky's living and suffering human beings, and Serafimovich's faceless monolith broke up into the vivid likenesses of *The Silent Don.*

Chapter 8

The Critic Voronsky and the Pereval Group

Soviet Literary Criticism

LITERARY CRITICISM during the Soviet period has, paradoxically enough, produced a rich harvest of ideas and literary theories. It is true that original and independent criticism was more common during the twenties than in any other period, and that during the years of Stalin's ascendancy the Russian critical spirit was in a state of suspension from which it is reviving only very slowly. The most powerful stimulus to critical thought came from the formalist school and writers close to it in spirit, whose activity pre-dates the October revolution. Shklovsky's contributions to literary criticism on the pages of *Lef* and *New Lef* have already been mentioned. His works on literary theory were equally important: *On the Theory of Prose* (1925), *The Technique of the Writers' Craft* (1927), and the collection of essays *The Knights' Move* (Berlin, 1923) contain some pregnant observations, ideas, theories, and critical *bons mots*. Formalists who are primarily literary scholars have contributed new ideas in a number of areas: Boris Eichenbaum, with his investigation of the works of Leo Tolstoy and his studies of romanticism; and Boris Tomashevsky, with his essays on Pushkin and on the theory and practice of verse-making. The works of critics whose view of literature was similar to that of the formalists make an original contribution to an unusually productive period: Yury Tynyanov's study of the *Theory of Parody* and L. P. Grossman's works on Dostoevsky, for example. These are just a few of the critics and literary scholars whose serious and original studies have added a bright new page to literary history.

Marxist criticism, too, has been more varied and stimulating than might be expected. There has never been, even among official spokesmen, full agreement as to the meaning for literature of Marxism; yet certain basic tenets are shared by Marxist critics who will disagree on almost everything else. They hold that the social structure of a given society depends on the manner in which that society satisfies economic needs. Upon the basis of production and the relationship of social groups to one another in the process of production there is erected, according to their theory, the "superstructure" of religion, art, and literature which constitutes the culture of a given society. If the society is divided into classes this cultural superstructure will reflect the view of life of the dominant class. Only after a classless society has been established will literature, for instance, express the thought and feeling of humanity as a whole. The critic who maintains that the Soviet Union is a classless society must also maintain that Soviet literature has general human significance.

Within this general ideological framework a number of schools of thought developed during the twenties and thirties. Strict application of sociological criteria in literary criticism was the method of A. Bogdanov (1873–1928), V. F. Friche (1870–1929), and V. G. Pereverzev (1882–?). Bogdanov was the founder and leading theoretician of the Proletcult, whose purpose as we have seen was to develop through the training of working-class writers a specifically proletarian "class" literature. The dominance of the proletariat in all cultural fields, was, Bogdanov believed, a prerequisite to the establishment of the power of the proletariat over society as a whole, and art is simply a "means of organizing its forces." This position found no sympathy among higher Soviet officials, who were concerned that the Russian proletariat acquire the barest elements of human culture before attempting to create "its own" literature.

V. F. Friche was a sociological critic who tended to reduce sociology to simple economics. Typical of his approach is an essay on the *Sociology of Literary Styles*, in which he accepts the idea (advanced by Spengler and others) of the unity of styles in all fields of culture during a given period, but rejects as "idealistic" any but the economic interpretation of this unity: "The first task of sociology in this field

[literary criticism] is to work out the relationship of a particular poetic style with a particular economic style." Friche
believed that in the coming socialist world man would become
a purely rational being and that literary style would reflect
the "rationalization" of his life.

V. G. Pereverzev was an exponent of strict economic de-
terminism in literary criticism, though he rejected Friche's
belief in the imminent "rationalization" of literature. He
maintained that in order to understand a given writer the
critic should direct his attention not to his biography or his
conscious view of the world, nor even to his social and political environment, but exclusively to the position occupied
by the given writer in the process of production. Thus Dostoevsky's frequent split personalities he explained as so many
projections of Dostoevsky himself, a declassed nobleman
torn between the values and standards of bourgeois productive
relations and his own aristocratic traditions and antecedents.
Pereverzev maintained, further, that the process of literary
creation is subconscious and that the writer cannot by taking
thought himself or by responding to directives from the Party
alter the class nature of his "system of images." Indeed the
writer works within a "charmed circle" of images, subconsciously determined by his economic environment. If the
writer is a proletarian his images are certain to be of proletarian characters. The writer of one economic "class" cannot
even imagine a character of another "class." Since the creation of literature is directly determined by productive processes and the author's place in them, such creation cannot
be mediated by educational, political, or governmental bodies.
Pereverzev thought that the proletarian state can affect literature only by silencing the literary voice of "hostile classes."

Even strict Marxists like Friche and Pereverzev when they
analyzed specific works were sometimes able to see them in
an original light and reveal important factors, both cultural
and psychological, in their production. Pereverzev's work on
Dostoevsky and Gogol is a contribution to our understanding
of those writers, couched though it is in a strange and seemingly ritual Marxist idiom. Other Marxist critics have made
contributions of a more modest nature. P. S. Kogan (1872–
1932) and V. Polonsky (1886–1932) are the most compe-

tent Marxist literary historians of the Soviet period. N. Pik-
sanov is a scholar who concentrates on the study of literary
texts and the process of their production. And two critics associated with the Pereval group, D. A. Gorbov and A. Lezhnev,
emphasize psychological factors in literary style.

Voronsky

A strikingly humane tendency in Marxist criticism was
represented by Alexander Voronsky (1884–1943), the main
object of whose study was the individual writer and creative
processes not reducible to terms of economics or sociology.
One of the most important literary groups of the twenties was
that associated with his name, *Pereval* (The Divide), and
the group is important because its members risked everything
and lost in their effort to remain free of a vulgar and dogmatic
Marxism. The history of Soviet literature offers some examples of heroism in the face of terror. One such example is
the behavior of the Pereval group, and that story should be
better known.

Alexander Voronsky, the most sensitive and genuine Marxist critic of the twenties, belonged to the group of Communist
intellectuals who supported Trotsky and opposed Stalin.
According to a recent survey of literary trends in the twenties
Voronsky belonged to the Trotskyite opposition from 1925
to 1927.[1] He was a courageous man whose opposition, at first
clear and sharp, may have been ill-concealed even after
Stalin's control of the Party was established. When the opposition was defeated in 1927 Voronsky was arrested and sent
into exile with other members of that group. After a formal
recantation he was permitted to return to Moscow in 1930,
where he continued to write and worked as an editor in the
State Publishing House but was never again prominent as a
critic. He was arrested again in 1935 and, according to the
1958 edition of the *Small Soviet Encyclopedia,* he died in
1943. No details of his death have been published, but it
probably occurred in prison or in a labor camp. His name
has been posthumously cleared of criminal charges, though
the influence he exerted on Soviet literature is still described
as heterodox and harmful.[2]

The debt which Soviet literature owes to Voronsky is very

great. He deserves more credit than any other literary man for the revival which took place during the twenties. As a Party assignment he edited the magazine *Red Virgin Soil* from 1921 to 1927. This magazine carried important essays on history, economics, and politics along with a generous assortment of contemporary poetry and fiction. The publication was a Soviet version of the so-called "fat" journals which served the Russian intelligentsia during the nineteenth century. As an editor Voronsky soon earned the suspicion of "proletarian" literary groups, and the reason would seem to be that the criteria he followed in the selection of stories and poems for publication tended to be literary rather than social or political. The result of his policy was that non-Communist and nonproletarian intellectuals were able to make their contribution to Soviet literature. Rigid dogmatists attacked him as a fool or a traitor because he had opened the pages of the Soviet press to an "alien" element. In the course of a long and bitter controversy Voronsky examined his position and that of his opponents, presented an analysis of the nature and function of imaginative literature, and defended his own activities—always with courage and sometimes with patient scorn.

Voronsky was, during most of his adult life, an active Marxist revolutionary, and his ideas about the nature and function of literature developed at first within the framework of Marxist thought. The defense of his own liberal publishing policy he based on the writings of Belinsky and Plekhanov, both acceptable in the Soviet Union of the twenties as authorities on literary questions, and in his polemic with the organizers of art he restated certain ideas that had long been current in the Russian Marxist milieu. These ideas are still recognizable as Hegelian, even after having been filtered through the thought of Belinsky, Plekhanov, and finally Voronsky.

Voronsky maintained, first of all, that art provides knowledge of the world in the form of sensible images. The artist, the scientist, and the philosopher are alike in that they all deal with "reality"; but while the scientist investigates and analyzes its nature, and the philosopher generalizes about it, the artist presents his knowledge of reality in the vesture of sensible form. Philosophy and science offer their truths primarily to the mind, art to the sensuous nature of man, but what both offer is truth. It followed from this that any genuine work of literature, though conditioned by the social origin of the writer and the historical period in which he lived, has an objective value as "cognition of life." And Voronsky pointed out—as in that time it was necessary to point out—that the great literature of the past, though it may have been the product of slaveowners or feudal lords, was a revelation of human experience and, as such, a permanent possession of all mankind, including the Russian proletariat. The works of supposedly bourgeois social origin which he published in *Red Virgin Soil* should be judged, therefore, by their value as artistic products first of all, rather than as social commentary or propaganda. And the aesthetic value of a work of art depends, he maintained, upon the validity of the images presented in it, their faithfulness to the nature of that which is portrayed.[3]

Voronsky's basic views do no offense to Marxist ideology and need not have troubled the state. Indeed he carefully eschewed any claim to a possibly dangerous originality in propagating such views, maintaining that he was a more orthodox Marxist than were his opponents, the champions of "proletarian hegemony" in art. Many of the most important political figures of the day supported him in this contention, among them Trotsky and the Commissar for Education, Lunacharsky.

But to those government figures who saw in literature and art only weapons to be used in the service of the state, the activity of Voronsky both as editor and as critic seemed close to treason. Averbakh, one of the leaders of the proletarian literary movement, was one of the first to observe that though Voronsky protested his innocence of unorthodox views, he "seemed to find the Marxist uniform too tight and close-fitting." Indeed an ideological uniform, whatever its color, would not have fitted Voronsky, and Averbakh was no doubt correct in his observation that the critic sometimes introduced into literary discussion ideas which lacked adequate Marxist sanction, often enough leaving them unrefuted. There was a disturbing tendency in Voronsky to range freely over literary topics and to entertain ideas from a variety of sources. He maintained to the end that he was a Marxist; yet he valued the Indian philosopher Rabindranath Tagore, who was not; he had studied Freud, and acknowledged the Freudian contribution to the understanding of the unconscious; he had certainly read Bergson; he drew upon Tolstoy for insights into the nature of artistic creation; his own reminiscences of his childhood suggest the possible influence of Proust; and at the same time he could confute his opponents, if need be, by citing texts from Belinsky, Marx, and Plekhanov. The dogmatists were right to distrust him.

Views that seemed heterodox crept into Voronsky's literary essays whenever he attempted to explain the process of artistic creation, though he always maintained that there was Marxist precedent for those views. The behavior of the artist was to him rather mysterious, and not fully explicable in terms of conscious rational purposes. While his polemical articles stressed the role of literature as knowledge and made confident use of Belinsky's definition of the artist as one who "thinks in images," his theoretical essays explored the possibility of unconscious psychological processes in the creation of art. He concluded that something he could only call "intuition" was an essential part of this process. In propagating such a view Voronsky was, in the jargon of Bolshevism, out of tune with his epoch. Such words as "creativity," "inspiration," "intuition," were suspect in the Soviet literary lexicon of the twenties, as indeed they are now, for it was feared that such concepts smacked of bourgeois mentality. The idea was widely accepted that the new literature would be, not "created," but produced, by verbal craftsmen cognizant of the facts of life and instructed in Marxist ideology. Their products would be so fashioned as to satisfy the "social demand" of the socialist epoch. As we have seen, the Left Front of Art contended that the highest form of literary creation was good factual reporting and that in the dynamic present the daily newspaper had already taken the place of the great epics of former ages. The Left Front was no doubt extreme, but there were other groups which spoke of the central importance of "device," literary technique and method, and still others presented a theory of literature as the "making of artifacts." The "constructivists" spoke of planned literature, wherein the verbal material would be "loaded" with the latest scientific and technical connotations. Eager bureaucrats in the literary field suggested that the Party, when drawing up a resolution on collectivization, for instance, should add a final point directing that a certain quantity of poetry and prose on the given topic be "ordered." With the adoption of the first Five-Year Plan in 1928 it became official doctrine that literary men must devote their talents to propagandizing the plan "in great works of art." The idea that artistic production, both collective and individual, could be directed by a rational plan received wide acceptance in the Soviet Union of the twenties.

Against this current Voronsky argued that "intuition," an activity independent of rational intention, was basic to the artistic process. He defined intuition as the sum of knowledge which we have arrived at without conscious analytic investigation. Such knowledge is not "contrary to reason," but may consist of truths discovered by the human reason in former generations, and stored in the subconscious. These intuitive truths reveal themselves in the consciousness of the artist suddenly, unaccountably, and often contrary to plan. To illustrate his thought Voronsky quoted a passage from Tolstoy's *Anna Karenina*, where the painter Mikhailov finds that an accidental smear on one of the figures in a drawing gave him a sudden insight into his picture not revealed to experiment and analysis. From Tolstoy, Voronsky borrowed the phrase "removal of veils" to characterize the process of artistic creation. In moments of freedom from the control of his rational ego, the artist is receptive to "direct, childlike impressions" and, "removing the veils" from the real world, is able to see it as it is. Shortly before the end of his career as an editor, Voronsky developed the idea that reality is deformed by our conscious cerebral processes, the purpose of which is not to *know* but to *use,* and that the artist, by shedding his social integument, recovers fresh and unspoiled images of a world which is beautiful in itself.

It is obvious that Voronsky could lay no claim to originality as a theorist of aesthetic experience. Of course he never
identified the main sources of his ideas on the intuitive
activity of the artist, for they were suspect. It was eagerly
pointed out, however, that he had an affinity with Kantian
aesthetics and that he was indebted to both Freud and Jung;
and a major article in the magazine *Literature and Art* in
1930 "unmasked" Voronsky as a follower of Bergson, which
he may indeed have been.[4] Yet Voronsky claimed to be a
Marxist, a title generally denied him not only by Soviet historians, but by some Western intellectuals who have admired
his work. He maintained that his ideas on the importance of
subconscious factors in art were quite consonant with Marxist
philosophy, and had indeed been discussed by Plekhanov. If
we conclude that his position is inconsistent with "Marxism,"
it can only be that we accept a rigid definition of what a
Marxist is. Voronsky did not regard Marxist philosophy as
a closed and complete system of beliefs, and he reached out
into the stream of Western culture for ideas in areas not
adequately explored by the founders of Marxism, such as psychology and aesthetics. Voronsky was a Marxist; but he was
also a man of great intellectual scope and wide human interest, and as such he has never been acceptable to those Soviet
authorities on Marxism who tend to convert it into a set of
dogmas.

Pereval

Along with Voronsky the group of young writers who had
looked to him for support and encouragement were castigated in the official press of the early thirties and passed over
in silence for two decades. Some of them were imprisoned or
exiled for criminally subversive activities. (One of these, Ivan
Katayev, was, like Voronsky, posthumously cleared of such
charges in 1956, and a new edition of his collected works
was published in 1957.)[5] Pereval, as the group was called,
means literally "a narrow pass over a mountain range" and is
usually translated as "defile" or "pass." By their choice of
the name the writers of Pereval dramatized their own view
as to the transitory nature of the reality they were describing.

The Soviet state of the twenties was not, for them, a static and established fact, but a moment in human development, and they viewed their time as a difficult journey toward new horizons. Perhaps "the divide" expresses the overtones of meaning suggested by the word *pereval*. The members of Pereval proclaimed their devotion to the Revolution and their intention to work for its aims. More than half of them were, in 1925, members of the Communist Party;[6] but they insisted that the individual writer must find his own social content and work out his own style, and so the group issued no directives and announced no program, confining itself in public to general statements favoring such unexceptionable qualities as "sincerity" and "artistic realism" and deploring the prevalence of literary stereotypes. Their statements of belief and policy, though cast in the apocalyptic revolutionary jargon of the twenties, declare that the writer as such must be free of programs and parties. Certain recurrent ideas and phrases in their public declarations betray a close relationship to Voronsky: they reiterate the special importance of the writer's "inner world," of his "subconscious," and of intuition in the literary process; and they emphasize the primary importance for the writer, not of "the Party spirit," but of "the human spirit."

This quality of "humanism" was admired by their friends and severely questioned by their political foes. There was a danger that the direct portrayal of real human situations might suggest to the unwary reader the inadequacy of certain desirable political stereotypes. Various "class enemies" sometimes emerged in their stories as complex human beings on familiar terms with suffering and death, while workers and peasants might be portrayed as culturally or morally underprivileged. The Perevaltsy were not—as their enemies sometimes claimed—engaged in conscious sabotage of the official ideology; but it is a fact that the images of reality which appeared in their stories and poems were presented as the product not of conscious cerebration but of "immediate impressions," and it might have been difficult for the thoughtful reader to make those images fit the vulgar folklore of the state.

Voronsky's influence in this respect is written large in the work of the Perevaltsy. His sympathetic interest in human beings, regardless of party, is evident in his autobiographical works, in his literary essays, and especially in a casual article he wrote in 1920 about a chance meeting with a former member of the Social Revolutionary Party who had once violently opposed the Bolsheviks. This article, which makes certain political assumptions and contains definite political judgments, reveals at the same time Voronsky's zest for understanding human situations. He manages to convey the bitterness of the old man's opposition to Bolshevism, his defeat and destitution, and the fear of complete disillusionment with "the cause of socialism" which had brought him to embrace the Soviet state. Voronsky displays such power of empathic writing that in his account pathos touches not only the converted socialist revolutionary but even the Bolsheviks, themselves caught in the general tragedy.[7]

No doubt the most original of the Pereval writers, and a skillful practitioner of "Voronskyite humanism," was Ivan Katayev, and the best of his stories is one called "Milk" published in 1930 and immediately singled out for special disfavor by the editors of *Pravda,* who regarded with suspicion Katayev's portrayal of a "class enemy" as a sympathetic character. The story is told in the words of a Soviet organizer whose job it is to set up dairying collectives and who has just eliminated a clique of kulaks from control of a dairying community near Moscow. But the organizer, nicknamed "The Calf" either because of a certain softness in him or because he had raised the norms for calving in his district, he's not sure which, is disturbed by what had happened. He had grown quite fond of the leading kulak, a Baptist named Nilov, a handsome, intelligent, and highly civilized peasant, the most efficient dairyman he had ever met and also a kind of Tolstoyan religious philosopher who spoke persuasively about that "great unifying force, the universal milk of love and brotherhood." Such was the power and prestige of Nilov in the district that the efforts of the "poor and middle" peasants to dislodge him from control at first got nowhere. But during a crucial meeting there occurred a sudden act of violence— quite unconnected with politics—against Nilov's son, who was brutally attacked by a personal enemy. After Nilov's misfortune the peasants suddenly turned against him and overwhelmingly passed a resolution deposing him from the executive board and installing a "committee of the poor and middle peasants." The peasant mass appears in the story as primitive and inarticulate: "Our peasants don't have any respect for bad luck," says the thoughtful organizer, "and a man who's unlucky will never get their trust. You see, as long as you are strong and healthy, they'll honor you and believe in you and trust you. But just as soon as you slip a little they're disgusted with you. . . ."

Such was Ivan Katayev's contribution, in the critical year for collectivization of 1930, to the literature which described that development. The narrator had not only expressed interest and sympathy for the kulak Nilov, but ended his story on a questioning note: "Lord! How dark and confused everything still is! You can't find clear boundaries or sharp lines anywhere. . . . You can't understand the beginning or the end . . . and men and their lives are devoured in the torrent. . . . It can't be helped. But still it's chilling and frightening."

Katayev's "Heart," published in 1928, is a story in a similar vein, the hero of which is a Communist functionary who has abandoned the various hammer-and-sickle stereotypes, whether of language or manner, in favor of a simple human speech and natural behavior. Like the narrator of the story "Milk," he has a spot of softness in him and is not impervious to feelings of compassion. There is more than a suspicion that Katayev is attempting in this and other stories to portray an alternative to the image of the Bolshevik as a "man of steel."

Eight collections of stories were published by the Pereval group between 1922 and 1932, when all autonomous literary groups were liquidated.[8] Among the contributors were a number of young writers whose talents have, in many cases, been lost to Soviet literature. In these stories the locale is frequently the small provincial town or the distant village, and the inhabitants of these places are portrayed with the prescribed "artistic realism," but sometimes with a distinct undertone of moral horror. Yekaterina Strogovaya's "Country

Women" deals with the working class in a provincial manufacturing town. The characters and events are presented as though from life, with no attempt to organize the material according to any preconceived social thesis. The style is harshly and laconically realistic. Ostensibly the story concerns "survivals of the old way of life" and the activity of "antisocial elements," the work of the Party cell and the factory committees; all the material for the tendentious social treatment is present, but somehow the thesis never appears. We see the peasant women now become workers as illiterate, ignorant, savagely bigoted and ready to persecute a "fellow worker" who has lost favor with the group. They are gossip-mongers who poison life with suspicion and hatred. One of the younger girls is ostracized because of a rumor about "a rich kulak uncle," though she and her family are destitute. A girl of masculine build and manners is driven out as a "half-and-half." And through the fog of meanness and stupidity one can see moving and occasionally having an effect such strange organisms as "womansec" (*zhenatdely*), "partycell" (*partya-cheiki*) and the people from something called the "faccom-mit" (*fabzavkom*).

Boris Guber's "Corpses" is the definitive treatment of the melancholy aimlessness of life in the deep provinces. The heroes of his story, two country schoolmasters, are Gogolian grotesques of vacant boredom. Sleep, adventure stories, and vodka fill their free time. They have forgotten how to want anything or do anything. One of them cannot manage to finish a letter and in several false starts makes deliberate semi-literate spelling mistakes.

Zuev's "Tien" describes a Russian peasant community of the remote north, where the chairman of a village soviet struggles in vain with old and rooted tradition. In the works of many of the Perevaltsy we become vividly conscious of the elemental, savage, and desperately poor villages of the deep interior, an aspect of Russian life which seems to have escaped the attention of the nineteenth-century writers, who, with some few exceptions, idealized the Russian folk—and which, of course, is not emphasized either in Soviet literature. As one unfriendly critic of the thirties put it, their stories of village life demonstrate the triumph of "biology" over "sociology," of primitive instinct over the forces of reason.

Thus in their stories, as in their critical thinking, the Perevaltsy tended to lay stress on areas of human experience not easily susceptible to rational explanation or control. If leanings in that direction had been confined to a small splinter group, the authorities might not have been disturbed; however, the Pereval writers and critics commanded respect in the literary world, and their ideas and their manner of writing spread like an infection even into the proletarian literary organization. Ideas identified as "Voronskyite" began to appear, after Voronsky had left the scene, in the critical articles published by the leaders of Averbakh's organization, the Russian Association of Proletarian Writers (RAPP). These ideas often appeared in vulgar, sloganized form, but there could be no doubt of their origin. Thus Voronsky's "removal of veils" became "the tearing off of masks," and his phrase "immediate impressions" was used by Libedinsky in a statement of the proletarian platform in literature. The "humanism" of Pereval was expressed in the RAPP slogan "For the Living Man in Literature," a call to treat human beings as complex psychological structures. This curious development, in which the sworn enemies of Voronsky and the Pereval had begun to mouth their favorite notions, was described in ironic terms by Lezhnev, a critic associated with the Pereval group:

Time has shown that we were right after all. The principles of Pereval have been embraced by those who fought against them most bitterly. . . . These principles are being put out now by a new firm, under a new label. Many people seriously think that the idea of the necessity for psychological analysis, about "the living man" . . . or the thesis that we must do battle with stereotypes or mere sketches for the sake of a more realistic art—that all of these things were advanced by the Association of Proletarian Writers. But Pereval, of course, has never taken out a patent on its own ideas. . . .[9]

The dangers, imagined or real, presented by Pereval were such that leading organs of the Party and press turned their attention to the group in 1930. When attacks were published, the Perevaltsy demanded a hearing, and a public "debate" was held in Moscow in May, 1930. The printed record of this event, though written from a partisan point of view and unfriendly to the Perevaltsy, shows that the latter defended themselves with spirit against a succession of slanderous attacks on their Marxism, their loyalty and their honesty.[10] A second discussion was held at the Communist Academy, the upshot of which was a resolution published in May, 1930, condemning among other things their "humanistic phraseology." The language of the resolution marks a stage in the evolution of the Stalinist intellectual patterns:

The use of humanistic phrases is one manifestation of the vacillation and panic experienced by certain intermediate petit-bourgeois and intellectual groups, who, unable to keep up with the rush of events, cannot find their place in the ranks of the fighters for socialism.[11]

After the dissolution of all literary groups in 1932 Pereval disappeared as a separate entity, though a number of writers who had belonged to the group continued to write, even satisfying, occasionally, the socialist realist demand of the "epoch." Since the middle thirties and until 1954 there had been, as far as the present writer can determine, only occasional references either to Pereval or Voronsky, and these couched in vituperative terms. It is especially interesting to note, therefore, that the spokesman of the Soviet Union of Writers, Surkov, sensed in some of the post-Stalin critical writing—especially where it spoke of sincerity, directness, the immediacy of impressions—a recrudescence of long-silent thoughts. The Party is still vigilant against any autonomous, unorganized activity on the part of its writers. Yet it will soon become evident that the current of "humanism" associated with the name of Voronsky and Pereval has not dried up but is again a major force in Soviet literature.[12]

Chapter 9

The Levers of Control

Resistance

THE HISTORY OF VORONSKY AND PEREVAL is clear proof that Russian literature did not easily accept regimentation by the state for collective purposes. If writers and critics who were members of the Party openly resisted encroachment on the autonomous preserve of literature, it is clear that resistance was widespread in the literary world. Shklovsky's warning, "You cannot control the unknown," was fully understood and accepted not only by the Serapion Brotherhood and other individualists but by active Marxists, the recipients of official funds.

Even more surprising than the resistance of Voronsky was the behavior of the Russian Association of Proletarian Writers under the leadership of Averbakh, Fadeyev, and Libedinsky during the years of the first Five-Year Plan. Their "dialectical materialist method" in literature had given rise to a number of slogans reiterated constantly during those years for the benefit of proletarian readers and writers. Libedinsky, Fadeyev, Semyonov, Mitrofanov, and other writers who belonged to the school of "psychological realism," provided in their works concrete examples of how these slogans should work out in practice.

RAPP, the mass organization of proletarian literature, was the lever upon which the Central Committee of the Party placed its chief reliance. But the Party did not find that organization amenable to a grossly utilitarian program. The leadership was narrow, doctrinaire, and dogmatic, but it did not accept the idea that literature could be produced by directive. Their first and basic slogan was that literature must provide honest pictures of the material world, and since that world is in a process of "dialectic" movement, since things develop by way of internal contradiction and conflict, these conflicts will be reflected in the individual human personality. Such conflicts, they said, take place inside every "psyche." Even a proletarian Communist is not *all* good but has many traits that are historically backward, and the conflict inside him between "good" and "bad" should be shown in literature. The bourgeois, on the other hand, though a class enemy, should never be portrayed as *all bad*. That wouldn't be true to life, since everyone has *some* good qualities working in his particular set of dialectical conflicts. Motives moreover are not always clear and simple. A man contains subconscious irrational drives which may be just as important as his rational surface. The writer should never glorify or romanticize his heroes; positive heroes, models of desirable behavior, might be the material of propaganda, but never the material of literature. All of this they summed up in the slogan: "For the Living Man."

Other slogans of the late twenties were "Against the Varnishing of Reality" and "For the Removal of Any and All Masks." The proletarian leaders insisted that it was the right and the duty of literary men to expose vice and corruption wherever they found it. Incompetence in the bureaucracy, corruption and hypocrisy in the Party, brutality and ignorance among the workers—all of these things should be revealed by the writer wherever he found them. The actual world should be shown as it "really is." The proletarian theorists, it will now be obvious, owed much to Voronsky. Many of the slogans they mechanically repeated were neat capsule versions of his leading ideas.

Under the guidance of these slogans the proletarian writer sometimes behaved in strange ways. A fairly common object of his artistic attention was the disillusioned Communist, who regrets the passing of the period of strife, when life held promise and the world revolution seemed near, and who is disappointed at seeing life settle down into conservative and respectable ruts. Another negative type they portrayed was the ignorant and complacent Communist bureaucrat, capable only of thinking in terms of the latest slogans and of expressing himself in the language of the latest official statements.

They occasionally wrote novels and stories in which the sordid side of Russian life was not glossed over. But literature of this kind was not at all what the Party wanted during the period of the first Five-Year Plan. It wanted books about construction and collectivization; it wanted positive heroes, and bright, hopeful perspectives; it wanted literature not to reveal what people are like and how they experience life at a given moment, but to inculcate lessons, to propagandize very simple ideas, to inspire and mobilize the workers, to "put across" to them in quasi-literary form the current propaganda line of the Party. The proletarian organization, narrow though it was in its devotion to a few simple slogans, was not narrow enough for the Party. So the Party's own organization had to be liquidated in 1932, and all writers, proletarian and others, were gathered into a single Union, the first Secretary of which was Shcherbakov, a political man close to Stalin. "The Dialectical Materialist Method in Literature" was rejected as a very dangerous approach. The slogan "For the Living Man" was buried; the slogan "Tear Off the Masks" was condemned as potentially counterrevolutionary because, as one Party representative said: "One must not raise such a slogan without indicating from whom the masks are to be removed." A new slogan and a new method became compulsory for all Russian literary men. That slogan was "Socialist Realism." From 1932 until the present "socialist realism" has been the required style for Soviet literature. Though the term did not appear until 1932, the method of "socialist realism" was actually applied during the first Five-Year Plan. Once the Politburo severely censured a publishing house because the books it had published did not show the "*heroism* of socialist construction.*" An editorial in *Pravda* in 1930 asserted that "literature, the cinema, the arts are levers in the hands of the proletariat which must be used to show the masses positive models of initiative and heroic labor." The writer was expected to draw inspiring pictures of the great enthusiasm and heroism displayed by the Russians working on the Five-Year Plan. He was expected to show how magnificent the future would be, even if he couldn't get excited about the present. Writers went out in "brigades" to visit and report on construction or agricultural work in a given district. A typical brigade promised that it would present "not less than four plays dealing with the completion of the spring sowing." Agitation vans were sent out to the collective farms to recite poems, sing songs, and present plays intended to inspire greater efforts on the part of the farmers. Most of the literature produced in this campaign was of low quality. It was admitted several years later by the head of the State Publishing House that seventy-five per cent of the output of this first Five-Year Plan period was worthless as literature. But the Party didn't care about that. What was needed above all was a literature which would publicize and propagandize the program. It was a practical program engineered by practical men who neither knew nor cared much about literature. If there were Russians around who could write, they could write about the Five-Year Plan. And they'd better write in a simple, down-to-earth style, so the workers would understand them. It was a cynical and brutal program. What these practical men tried to do was take Russian literature in their hands and force it into a mold of their own making.[1]

The Purge

The great reform of 1932 involved the liquidation of all independent organizations in favor of a single Union closely tied at every level to the Party itself. From the viewpoint of the "fellow travelers" the reform was not unwelcome, for it meant the end of the arrogant pretension to authority of the Russian Association of Proletarian Writers and of proletarian orthodoxy as interpreted by the leaders of that organization. The reform could have meant a liberalization in the literary world, but in practice it did not. For the Union took over not only the defense of the material welfare of writers, but their ideological guidance as well. At the First Congress of Soviet Writers in 1934, which inaugurated the new Union, the leading literary figures, both proletarian and fellow traveler, took the platform to speak of literary problems, and though there were moments of the old controversial fire the keynote of the meeting was harmonious agreement on all essential points. The assembled writers heard the bright sallies of Bukharin at the expense of proletarian poetry, the sophisticated commentary of Radek on Western literature, the honest self-questioning of Olesha, and the cryptic phrases of Pasternak, but the tone of the meeting was set not by them but by a representative of Stalin, Andrey Zhdanov, who made the principal speech. In terms that could not be mistaken he voiced the concern of the Politburo with the content and form of Russian literature. He said:

> Our Soviet literature is not afraid of being called tendentious, because it *is* tendentious. In the age of the class struggle a nonclass, nontendentious, apolitical literature does not and cannot exist. . . .
>
> In our country the outstanding heroes of literary works are the active builders of a new life. . . . Our literature is permeated with enthusiasm and heroism. It is optimistic, but not from any biological instinct. It is optimistic because it is the literature of the class which is rising, the proletariat, the most advanced and the most prospering class.

No one could doubt after the First Congress in 1934 that the Stalinists were in control of Russian literature, and the direction in which they sought to move that literature was clearly marked out. No one could doubt either that they would deal firmly with opposition, but until the purge trials of the middle thirties it was impossible to guess how far they would go.

In the course of the three public trials held in Moscow in 1936, 1937, and 1938 the most important leaders of a former political opposition to Stalin were denigrated as spies, traitors, and Fascists. With some notable exceptions, and in one case only after an initial frantic denial of any guilt, all these former leaders of the Bolshevik movement confessed their crimes and threw themselves on the mercy of the Court and the "Soviet People." Most of them were sentenced to be shot.

They were men who had held positions of great power. Zinoviev and Kamenev had been rivals of Stalin; Radek was a brilliant political writer; Bukharin had been a member of the Politburo since the early days of the Soviet state, and was the author of widely circulated works on the theory of Communism; Tomsky as leader of the trade union movement had been a potent figure; Yagoda had, as head of the Security Police, organized many such trials himself.

The episode in the history of the Russian Communist Party is now well known, and the real nature of the trials has been documented in the Soviet Union since the death of Stalin. What is perhaps not so well known is how deeply the purge extended into the ranks of the Communist Party itself. Each of the major victims at the trial had a numerous following of small-calibre bureaucrats, and thus a large group of minor Bolsheviks was discredited as the result of the moral and physical destruction during the thirties of their friends, comrades, and sponsors. With the head of the opposition severed at the trials no doubt this body of dissident intellectuals, fallen minor officials, Marxist but not Stalinist theoreticians, proletarian writers and the like would have faded from view naturally and quietly. This, however, was not allowed to happen. Watchdogs at the lower levels were soon at work. One of the areas that attracted their attention was literature. Here was a rewarding field for the work of investigators and accusers. The opposition to Stalin, now firmly branded as disloyal and traitorous, had included at one time the most prominent of the Party intellectuals, many of whom had been active in literature or literary criticism. Among them was Trotsky, a brilliant literary critic, whose influence in the early days had helped to hold in check the intolerant proletarian-izers of literature. Another suspect was Alexander Voronsky, who had once been a member of the Trotskyite opposition. Voronsky's literary enemy, Leopold Averbakh, had himself bridled at Stalin's raw intention to make literary men into obedient propagandists of Party policy. There were many young writers whose loyalty to Stalin's ideas was at best doubtful, and many of them had been discovered or fostered by Trotsky, Voronsky, or Averbakh. A few of these were very good writers. One of Voronsky's protégés was Ivan Katayev, whose picture of collectivization in the Russian village had aroused the official ire of the highest literary authority, the newspaper *Pravda*. Occasionally a talented writer emerged from the ranks of Averbakh's proletarian organization, and one of these, Libedinsky, had depicted the progressive ossification of the Party mind and the intellectual cowardice spreading among orthodox Party men.

Reverberations began in the literary world soon after the close of the first trial in 1936. The chief investigator, accuser, and judge at the meetings of the writers' organizations was a proletarian writer of peasant origin named Stavsky, the author of Party-oriented stories and sketches about collectivization. Grimly loyal to the Party program, Stavsky had gained a reputation as early as 1932 for savage denunciation of straying colleagues, and by 1936 he had advanced to the post of Secretary of the Board of the Union of Writers. Fearing neither truth nor falsehood, he publicly branded a score of writers as Trotskyites and traitors, and his accusations were fully reported in each issue of the *Literary Gazette*, which, as leader of the Union, he controlled. The men he named disappeared from the Soviet scene, and many of them were hardly remembered when, in the period of de-Stalinization, they were rehabilitated. One was Voronsky; another was his younger colleague and friend, Ivan Katayev. Most of the crimes charged to them had been committed much earlier. For instance Katayev had, in 1928, visited Voronsky while the latter was in exile "in order to get directives from him." What "directives" was never stated nor indeed was the question ever asked; for when two such prime suspects come together could they have any but an evil purpose? Boris Guber and N. Zarudin, also of the Pereval group, were caught in the net of accusation along with their colleagues. And the net swept wide enough to drag in even Semyon Rodov, a proletarian intransigent and one of the bitterest enemies of Voronsky and Pereval. Still another victim was Tarasov-Rodionov, whose novel *Chocolate* (1922) had raised serious questions of Communist morality.

The end result of Stavsky's campaign against unclean writers was an editorial in the *Literary Gazette* which pointed out that a number of "Trotskyite bandits" and "agents of Fascism" had in the course of many years entrenched themselves in literature. The "agents" and "bandits" had wormed their way into important positions as magazine editors, publishing executives, and leaders of literary organizations. From these positions they had plotted to turn Soviet literature onto a false and fruitless path.

Early in 1937 a second trial was held and another batch of former oppositionists held up to public obloquy before being sentenced to death. Again the literary repercussions were immediate and violent. Alexander Fadeyev gave an ominous hint of things to come in a public speech to a gathering of writers. Fadeyev declared that there were still "enemies" active in the literary field. He warned that these elements carefully mask themselves and are not easy to detect. He demanded that great vigilance be exercised in dealing with all writers, for it is not easy to tell the bad ones from the good. He offered as a good method for making this distinction the investigation of those who express uncertainty or doubt as to the Party program. The carriers of such moods should be sought for and rooted out, he said.

Soon the editors of several literary periodicals were called to task because they had not exercised sufficient vigilance in the selection of articles for publication. The unhappy editors were obliged to explain why they had so often in the past printed works by writers now unmasked as "enemies of the people." Their defense was necessarily weak. One of them nervously pleaded that it was impossible to detect in all cases the subconscious intent of an article or story. This was characterized as "political blindness."

It soon developed that one of the chief literary villains was Leopold Averbakh, who from 1927 to 1932 had been the leader of the Association of Proletarian Writers and had exercised considerable power as interpreter of the current literary line of the Party. Averbakh had fallen into disfavor himself as early as 1932, chiefly because he had not shown enough enthusiasm for the regimented production of a literature glorifying the achievements of the Five-Year Plan. Many of his literary protégés had revealed disillusionment and degeneration in the ranks of the Party itself, and Averbakh had stoutly defended them on the ground that "Bolsheviks are not afraid of the truth." His association had been liquidated in 1932, and all the Party's literary sins had at that time been heaped on his not always guilty head. Now, in

1937, he was "unmasked" as an agent of Trotsky, whose literary ideas he had always opposed, and as a brother-in-law of the notorious chief of the Security Police Yagoda, which indeed he was. One of his accusers, the popular and patriotic playwright Vishnevsky, offered as evidence against him that Averbakh's first book, published in 1923 when the author was eighteen, had appeared with a preface by Trotsky, proof that Averbakh, out of gratitude, had always followed Trotsky's line. No other evidence was offered to convict Averbakh of Trotskyism. Averbakh's part in the plot had been to persecute the "best Soviet writers," the nonproletarian fellow travelers, always, of course, at the behest of Trotsky. Stavsky contributed his mite to these accusations, too. He maintained that the errors for which Averbakh's organization had been liquidated in 1932 were actually a pattern of Fascist subversion in Soviet literature, a dark, underground plot against the Soviet Union itself. It was unnecessary to argue this point or to produce evidence to substantiate it. Pavel Yudin, head of the Institute of Philosophy of the Academy of Science and since 1931 a literary activist, published a violent personal attack on Averbakh mingling accusations of treason with snarling caricatures of Averbakh's speech, gestures and manner of movement. The accent of anti-Semitism could hardly be missed. There could be no defense against such charges as: "It is now known to everyone that Averbakh and his paltry literary school were an agency of Trotskyism in our literature," for by this time the word "Trotskyism" had lost all denotative value and had become an ugly weapon with which to beat the alien, the dissident, or the unpopular.

Once Averbakh had been blackened as a devil of disloyalty, those who had been closely associated with him during the six years when he was a leading literary authority were under terrible pressure to divert suspicion from themselves. His best friends and closest collaborators rose in public to condemn him and excoriate his name and to assure the Soviet people that they had long since severed all ties with him. Libedinsky, a novelist who owed his public success in no small part to Averbakh, and who had been very close to him in the leadership of the Proletarian Association, was implicated in the "plot" by innuendo. One man suggested that there were "many dark places in Libedinsky's personal and political biography"; another suggested that certain proposals he had once made for the formation of a literary bloc "looked very suspicious"; another called upon Libedinsky to be frank and open with his comrades, to "tell all he knows." It was revealed as a suspicious circumstance that he had lost interest in the Party and had been remiss in paying his dues. Under pressure of this kind, Libedinsky at last took the floor at a meeting in Moscow where he dissociated himself from Averbakh, condemning him in language very much like that used in the *Literary Gazette* editorial. This was part of the price Libedinsky paid for survival.

Others were not so fortunate. The playwright Kirshon had grown up with Averbakh in RAPP. He was the author of highly successful plays on Soviet life such as *Bread, The Rails Are Humming*, and *Red Rust*, the last of which was produced on Broadway. He was fanatically devoted to the idea of developing new writers "from the work bench and the plow," and had never wholeheartedly accepted the decision of the Party in 1932 to liquidate the Proletarian Association. He had never attacked Averbakh and had often defended both himself and his friend when they were jointly accused of errors and heresies. When in 1932 the "dialectical materialist method" in literature came under an official interdict, he defended the method as sound and helpful. Once Averbakh had been identified as the devil himself, Kirshon was attacked as a minor demon. The instrument of his undoing was Vishnevsky, author of the revolutionary drama *'Tis the Final Conflict* and *First Cavalry Army*, written as a corrective to Babel's *Horse Army*, in which the heroes of Budyonny's cavalry are shown as men of high morale who knew what they were fighting for. Vishnevsky and Kirshon had been rivals as playwrights and members of opposing literary factions.

Vishnevsky demanded at a public meeting that Kirshon explain how it had happened that for fourteen years he had been associated with an "enemy of the people"—Averbakh—without ever having had a serious disagreement with him and had aided him in the management of literary affairs with complete and unbroken harmony. Why had he, five years before, criticized the decision of the Politburo to liquidate the Proletarian Association? How did it happen that sixteen years ago, when the Party was debating the role of the trade unions, Kirshon had voted against Lenin's motion? Why had he supported Averbakh in 1934 as a delegate to the Writers' Congress? How would he explain the circumstance that he once recommended for employment in the Soviet film industry a man who later left the Soviet Union and refused to return? Why had he, in addition to all these things, used his influence to promote his own plays and thus hindered the development of rival dramatists?

Kirshon attempted to defend himself. In his desperation he appealed to facts and reason, but such an appeal could hardly stand up against the gathering momentum of charges, epithets, innuendoes, suspicion and hatred. Kirshon was expelled from the Party and soon disappeared for good from Moscow. And a few weeks later at a meeting of the wives of members of the Writers' Union it was heard that his relations with his wife had always been very bad and that his behavior toward her had been abominable.

Another playwright whose work had been favored by the leaders of RAPP was A. Afinogenov. His plays *Fear* (1931) and *A Far Place* (1936) were immensely successful with Soviet audiences, and he is distinguished among Soviet playwrights for his interest in personal psychological problems. He, too, fell into the nets cast by Vishnevsky and Stavsky. He was expelled from the Party in 1937 but restored to membership a year later. His recently published notebooks give us some idea of his experience:

I kept walking around, then came home tired out and fell asleep, then I got up and went out to walk some more, and I kept this sort of thing up just so I wouldn't have to think about my fate, about what had happened to me, so unjust and unfair. I grew up an honest Soviet artist, a Party man and an activist, and now . . . they've thrown an orange skin under my feet, they've tripped me up and I've fallen and broken my head and other people stand aside and watch and laugh and they think: There's another one knocked off his feet—and he won't get up again, or if he does get up he'll be a wounded enemy. . . .[2]

Each of the accused reacted in his own way. Some attempted to divert suspicion from themselves by confessing former errors and implicating others in them. Such a policy was adopted by the novelist Chumandrin, and he, too, saved himself for literature. Some managed to live through the storm without saying much of anything. Others tried to defend themselves, and of all the suspected and accused these last seem to have suffered worst. One such was the literary historian and critic Prince Dmitry Mirsky, who had fought in the White armies until 1921 but had later become converted to Communism and returned to Russia under the patronage of Maxim Gorky. Yudin dredged out of his past the fact of his service in the White armies, characterizing him as "nothing but a filthy White-Guard officer." Several speakers publicly accused him of being a traitor and a spy on the ground that he had had many contacts with foreigners from the West. It is a fact that he was frequently seen in the company of Americans and Englishmen. A rather naïve visiting American Communist who was present at this meeting sought permission to defend Mirsky against these vicious charges, but the chairman of the meeting, Stavsky, would not give him the floor. Mirsky took the floor to defend himself but was so shaken that he could produce only weak and incoherent phrases.

Even in the Soviet Union hysteria is finally mastered. By the end of 1938 the purge of the little men had run its course, and Zhdanov admitted at the Congress of the Communist Party in 1939 that there had been excesses and errors of judgment as a result of which many innocent people suffered. The excesses were explained as the work of Trotskyites who had wormed their way into Soviet organizations and were using the purge as a weapon to discredit the Soviet Union. But Stavsky and Yudin were never punished for their terrorization of the literary world. In fact they stood higher than ever in the estimate of official histories. The novelist

Sholokhov, at the same Congress which heard Zhdanov deplore the "excesses," made a fervent political speech in which he maintained that the ranks of Soviet literature, now cleansed of "enemies," were stronger and healthier.

The Literary State

A nearly universal literacy had been achieved by the Soviet dictatorship at about the time of the great literary purge in the thirties. Practically everyone can now read, and most Russians do at one time or another. The question of what is to be written, published, and read—and why—is a rather complicated one. It is answered in an "open" society by the operation of a relatively free market. A writer in our world when he sets to work has to aim at producing something that somebody will want to read, and the publisher as a general rule will publish only what a fair number of people will buy and pay for. Admittedly this arrangement falls far short of any ideal. As a practical matter it limits the creative artist to writing for a particular audience, an audience whose tastes and demands he must—however perfunctorily or subconsciously—take into account. The audience with which he must successfully communicate is the writers' cabin, crib, confine. He can escape from it if he likes by abandoning the writers' trade—by going up into the garret or by writing for himself alone.

We are fortunate however in having not one but many audiences, and so there is a place for writers of many and various colors, and off colors. Even though the variegated and motley nature of our audience may have changed in the direction of greater sobriety and uniformity of hue, the fact remains that there are different kinds of readers interested in different kinds of writers. Moreover, the writer can still create his own audience—with luck and persistence.

As a result we in the Western world still have some variety. We have a literature that does many things for many kinds of people. There are various levels of skill and artistry. One can buy and read books and stories which inculcate important civic and moral lessons, which, for instance, inspire patriotic and emulative respect for the heroes who fight our battles and lead our armies; or, one can occasionally buy and read a book expressing cynical contempt for the military life and its practitioners. There is a vast and widely read periodical literature which has as its chief purpose to inculcate moral lessons; and this is balanced by an equally vast and growing product which seems to inculcate immoral lessons and foster feelings of violence and sadism. In short, the free democracies have everything. We even have—though only occasionally and for a limited audience—a literature that explores the world of human beings, their loves and hatred, death and forgiveness. We are rich indeed if the vast gray flood of our published books and stories occasionally deposits a work of art on our shores.

When we turn to look at the literary situation in the Soviet Union, however, we find that it is not like this at all. One lesson has been burned into the Soviet intellectuals through successive purges of their ranks: it is dangerous to be alone. And indeed it is almost impossible to be in any way lonely— in idea, in style, in subject matter—if one is a professional writer in the Soviet Union. Probably no other state in history has exercised such active and pervasive control of the literary product. At no point in his career does a Soviet writer lack the support, encouragement, and active inspiration of the collective. He must of course belong to the Union of Writers, which cares not only for his material needs, but for his ideological improvement as well. The Union supplies him with an apartment in town, a villa out of town, trips to the seashore, journeys around the country to gather material, and generous allowances while at work. Through the Union of Writers the collective watches over the growth of a Soviet novel from its conception in the writer's mind to the moment of its birth and after. How does this work? Themes for novelistic treatment are regularly suggested in speeches and reports by leaders of the Union. It was not just a happy accident that in 1955 and 1956 a number of novels, plays and stories appeared in which an inventor with a new and vital idea is shown in conflict with authoritative officials whose interests are narrow and selfish. At the same time there were editorials in the newspapers and cartoons in the humor magazines with a very similar tendency.

A member of the Soviet Writers' Union, once he has begun to write, has the benefit of consultation with fellow writers and committees of the organization, and his manuscript before it is submitted may be carefully scrutinized for artistic and political shortcomings. This the writer willingly submits to, for it is known in the Soviet Union as "comradely criticism," and the result usually, but not always, is that the writer is placed firmly on the rails of established ideological and artistic practice. Occasional individual deviations from the norm are—ideally—ironed out in prepublication conferences. After the first publication, usually in a magazine, the novel is criticized and changes are often made before it is brought out in book form.

One would think that once the novel is in manuscript form and finds a publisher—say a monthly literary magazine—the author's worries would be over. Quite the contrary. He must then face the editorial office of the publisher, and the editor, blue pencil in hand, normalizes the style (strange, colloquial, substandard, nongrammatical or overly original language is usually questioned), and since editors are thoughtful Marxists, well-grounded in the Party program, they look for evidence of hostile influences, alien philosophies, decadence, pessimism, or other occasional peccadilloes which show themselves in the work of writers. Very often they find these. A young boy in a novel submitted for publication explains that he has a "hobby"—the raising of pigeons—and explains to a comrade that "hobby" is something that has nothing to do with your chief interest in life. "Just think about that word 'hobby,' " said the editor. "Isn't a 'hobby' characteristic of the philistine who lives in his own little world separate from the collective?"[3]

One must admit that in the Soviet Union, though literary experimentation has been officially deplored, something really new under the sun has been discovered: the novel of collective authorship. Literature as we understand it is traditionally the product of an individual human being—conditioned, it is true, by his own social existence as part of a group. The necessary characteristic of a piece of literature—a novel, a play, or a poem—is that not a group of men, not several men, not an organization, but *one* man has something to say

224 / Russian Literature Since the Revolution

about life—he has an idea, a feeling or a vision which he expresses in concrete literary images. During the Stalin period in the Soviet Union, and to some extent even today, that kind of literature tended to become outmoded, and to an astounding extent the collective, confident and strong, replaced the lonely and often tragic writer of our own Western world. A. Kron in his "A Writer's Notes" made the following observation: "The administrative method of guiding the artist has not aided in the development of an individual style."

The history of Russian literature during the Soviet regime is the record of a ruthless campaign, wasteful of people and of talent, to impose upon literary men this collective viewpoint. But Russian literature, let us repeat, did not easily submit. The resistance of Voronsky and Averbakh, the underground opposition of many other figures and of literary groups opposed to literary policy of any kind, the fierce purge of intellectuals in the thirties, all of this gives evidence of will and courage in the opposition. Most writers and artists think of themselves as men of a particular and precious vision, be it tragic, ironic, or humorous; the Soviet state insists on regarding them as employees who purvey approved doctrine to the literate citizenry. To reinforce this lesson it was found necessary after the end of World War II once again to cleanse the ranks of "cultural workers." The man who, not unwillingly, undertook this task was Andrey Zhdanov, and between 1946 and his death in 1948 he castigated deviationists in all the arts: not only writers, but clowns, composers, and movie directors felt his ideological scourge.

Andrey Alexandrovich Zhdanov (1896–1948) belonged to the generation of party men who rose to power as creatures of Stalin and who encouraged his maniacal tendencies. After the mysterious assassination of Kirov in 1934, Zhdanov became Stalin's deputy as the Party Chief of Leningrad. The destruction and subsequent rebuilding along purely Stalinist lines of the Leningrad Party organization had been Zhdanov's chief task, and when it was completed he was elected to full membership in the Politburo (1939). When the German armies besieged and blockaded Leningrad from 1941 to 1943 he defended the city with brute courage, maintaining a labor force in the factories and troops at the front while half a million citizens died of starvation. Stalin regarded Zhdanov as his successor, and the fact that he was made a kind of commissar for cultural affairs is evidence of the importance assigned to that area. Zhdanov was a Soviet bureaucrat and was typical of the breed. If we look closely enough at him he can help us to understand the people with whom a Soviet writer must deal.

As the war ended, the people of Russia looked forward with intense hope to an end of their prolonged ordeal and release from regimentation. There were signs that pointed to such a development. The Western democracies and Russia had been allies against Fascism, and if they should remain allies in the postwar world a softening of the Soviet dictatorship might result. During the war years there had been an apparent dilution of the Party's ideology as a result of the need to cooperate with democracies and to enlist all the forces of "Mother Russia" against the invader. This dilution might result, it seemed, in some tolerance for opposing ideologies. The mood of the people in 1945 has been eloquently stated by Boris Pasternak. Zhivago's friends Dudorov and Gordon are holding a book of his writings and looking out over Moscow:

And Moscow, right below them and stretching into the distance, the author's native city, in which he had spent half his life—Moscow now struck them not as the stage of the events connected with him, but as the main protagonist of a long story, the end of which they had reached that evening, book in hand.

Although victory had not brought the relief and freedom that were expected at the end of the war, nevertheless the portents of freedom filled the air throughout the postwar period, and they alone defined its historical significance.

Magazines and writers' organizations reflected the demand for a rest from the grim rigors of socialist realism even before the war's end. Fedin's freely ranging reminiscences of the twenties, *Gorky among Us,* appeared in 1943; *Before Sunrise,* Zoshchenko's novelistic search through childhood experiences for the sources of a chronic and peculiar melancholy, appeared in 1943; and after a long silence Anna Akhmatova was able during the war to publish again her reflective lyric poetry. At meetings of the writers' organizations a new spirit of liberalism was freely expressed, and bureaucratic interference in the creative process was openly deplored by writers of unquestioned loyalty.

But the fragile hopes of the people and of the writers were very soon destroyed. Stalin and his men were so acutely aware of Russia's mortally weakened condition after the war that they became convinced a new attack would be launched against them, and that, therefore, relaxation could not be allowed. Stalin's speech on February 9, 1946 warned the Russians that the days of their harsh trials had not ended: "As long as capitalism exists there will be wars," he said, "and the Soviet Union must be prepared." Relaxation of effort was unthinkable, and he announced a series of three new Five-Year Plans to raise production in basic industries. Not long after this speech attention was given to events in literature, and Andrey Zhdanov came forward to read the Party's indictment of those writers and editors responsible for the laxity of recent years.

An edict of the Central Committee was published on August 14, 1946, condemning two literary magazines, *Zvezda* (*Star*) and *Leningrad*, for having published the "shallow and insipid" works of Zoshchenko and the "decadent, apolitical" verse of Anna Akhmatova. Both writers were expelled from the Union, the editors of the magazines were replaced, and Tikhonov was removed as Secretary of the Executive Board of the Union of Writers. In articles and public speeches Zhdanov explained the necessity for these actions. Zoshchenko's story "The Adventures of a Monkey," which had been published in *Star*, received his special attention:

If you will read that story carefully and think it over, you will see that Zoshchenko casts the monkey in the role of supreme judge of our social order, and has him read a kind of moral lesson to the Soviet people. The monkey is presented as a kind of rational principle having the right to evaluate the conduct of human beings. The picture of Soviet life is deliberately and vilely distorted and caricatured so that Zoshchenko can put into the mouth of his monkey the vile, poisonous anti-Soviet sentiment to the effect that life is better

in the zoo than at liberty, and that one breathes more easily
in a cage than among Soviet people.

Is it possible to sink to a lower political or moral level?
And how could the Leningraders endure to publish in their
magazines such filth and nonsense?

Zoshchenko had of course done nothing to deserve this
lethal abuse, nor could he rightly be called "a vile hooligan,"
a practitioner of "filth and obscenity," or the "dregs of literature." Zhdanov had simply not understood his whimsical story
about a monkey who escapes from a zoo and, after many
misadventures in a Russian town, is finally adopted by a wonderful little boy who undertakes to educate him, teach him
to blow his nose with a handkerchief, to refrain from stealing
grandma's candy, to eat meat with a fork, in short to behave
like any cultured person—and better than some. Devoid of
humor and burdened with official crime, Zhdanov could see
in the farcical events of this children's fable only a projection
of his own guilt and suspicion. Zoshchenko had not intended
to imply that life in a cage is better, but what if the shoe
should fit?

Turning to Anna Akhmatova, Zhdanov quoted one of her
love lyrics:

> I swear to you by all the heavenly angels
> By the wonder-working ikons I swear
> And by the sweet delirium of our flaming nights—

and commented on it:

Akhmatova's subject matter is individualistic through and
through. The range of her poetry is pathetically limited. It
is the poetry of a half-crazy gentlelady who tosses between
the bedroom and the chapel. . . . Half-nun and half-harlot,
or rather both nun and harlot, her harlotry is mingled with
prayer.

Zhdanov's criticism of Akhmatova reveals both the man
and the society. It reveals his hatred of the sensitive, cultivated gentry who should all have been destroyed but still
find readers among the Soviet people. It reveals his coarse
puritanic revulsion at the frank expression of a woman's ex-

perience in love; it reveals his disastrous lack of literary sense or taste. It reveals the pathetic state of a society whose cultural life could stand at the mercy of an ignorant and violent clown. His positive demands on literary men can be briefly stated. They must produce an educational literature, intelligible and acceptable to the people, saturated with the ideas of the Party and loyal to the program of the Party.

The results of his intervention were immediate. Yarmolinsky's study of the period, *Literature under Communism* (1960), reveals that editors who had contracted with writers for fiction on historical themes scrapped their contracts and their publishing plans to concentrate on novels dealing with the one theme of reconstruction. Similar events occurred in the theaters: plays already part of the repertory were dropped in favor of hastily written pieces of more obvious propaganda intent. Semyon Babayevsky's novels *Cavalier of the Golden Star* and *Light Over the Earth* (1947–50) were awarded three Stalin prizes but were rejected as dishonest propaganda after Stalin's death. The hero of these novels is a young Party member who returns to his collective farm village after the war with ambitious plans for electrification according to the goals laid down by the Central Committee. The chief obstacles to fulfillment of the plan are the individualistic leanings of the farmers, who prefer to work for private goals, and personal ambition in Party leaders. All such obstacles are overcome, however, when the collective will is at last awakened, and Semyon's own dream of success is realized when he is elected Secretary of the District Committee of the Party. Chakovsky's *Here It Is Dawn Already* (1948) deals with the life of fishermen on the island of Sakhalin. Any rebellion of the individual against the collective is resolved in favor of the collective, and the villains of individualism are converted to healthy ways in the end. In Pavlenko's *Happiness*, the hero, demobilized after the war, comes to the Crimea to find a life of peace and contentment in a home of his own but is drawn into the agricultural work of the district where he finds that "happiness" is indivisible and that he can enjoy it only as a member of the larger group. Plays of the period hammered the same lesson. Sofronov's play *Moscow Character* (1950) recounts the conversion of a plant manager who has fallen into the vice of regarding the plant as *his* enterprise and ignoring the interest of his workers, other plants, and society as a whole.

After socialist economic development, the second major theme of the Zhdanov period was anti-Americanism, or, more broadly, antiforeignism. Dangerous thoughts from the West may have entered the heads of Soviet citizens during the period of collaboration, and the regime was concerned over the admiration for Western achievements and Western culture which it had itself encouraged during the war. K. Simonov's play *Under the Chestnuts of Prague* (1946) carried the grim lesson that behind the spectacles and under the capitalist hat of every Czech burgher there might lurk a Fascist enemy. Simonov's *Russian Question* (1946) shows the American newspaper world as the source of anti-Soviet bias in the United States. *The Mad Haberdasher* (1949), by A. Surov, attacks President Truman as a Hitler-like warmonger. Many of the books, stories, and plays that appeared during the period warned the good Soviet citizen of the treachery he would find in Western politicians, journalists, and scientists, and "exposed" the cultural poverty of Western life.

Zhdanov's campaign on the front of Russian music devastated an area that was rich in new talent and original creation. The story has been told in detail in a number of books and articles. The Politburo itself condemned modernistic tendencies in Russian music, especially the works of Shostakovich and Prokofieff; and the language of its "resolution" suggests that it was probably written by Zhdanov himself. The Politburo said of Shostakovich and the modernists:

The characteristic traits of such music are the denial of the basic principles of classical music, the propagation of atonality, dissonance and disharmony, as though disharmony were an expression of "progress" and "innovation" in the development of musical form; the rejection of the all important bases of music, such as melody. The modernists are carried away by confused, neurotic combinations, which transform music into cacophony—into a chaotic conglomeration of sounds. This is the spirit of modern American and European music—which reflects the decay of bourgeois culture. . . .

Many Soviet composers . . . have become alienated in their

music from the demands and the musical tastes of the Soviet people, have shut themselves up in a closed circle of specialists . . . limiting [the function of music] to the satisfaction of the depraved tastes of individualistic esthetes.

At meetings of the Composers' Union Zhdanov himself appeared to explain the Party's needs in music as he had already explained its needs in literature. At these meetings an effort was made to represent him as an authority on music, too. His enthusiastic supporter, Zakharov, a writer of popular songs, pointed out that while Zhdanov was not a professional musician he was a great authority on the folk song, and he reported the following conversation with Zhdanov:

"Is it true, Comrade Zhdanov, that you know six hundred folk songs?"
"No, it is not true. But I suppose I do know about three hundred."[4]

The effects of Zhdanov's campaign were not long in appearing. The novels and stories written to the recipe of a rigorous socialist realism failed to engage the attention of the Russian reader. Literary works in which conflicts are attenuated, suspense eliminated, language normalized, and endings standardized left him bored and indifferent. The Party program had inhibited the production of good literature and (what was far worse!) did not even produce good propaganda. In 1951 and 1952 a reaction set in, and the Party press for those years revealed that floundering efforts were being made to correct a disastrous situation. Editorials and critical articles called for the injection of "new life" into literature, spoke of the need to portray "living men," demanded that writers show life "as it is," featuring the "bad" as well as the "good," and deplored the "varnishing of reality." The reader of such articles is appalled by the break in cultural continuity of which they give evidence: for their authors show no awareness of laboring over ground already covered in the controversies of the twenties about Voronsky and the RAPP program.

Chapter 10

Zoshchenko and the Art of Satire

THE PROLIFERATION in the Soviet state of Stavskys, Yudins, and Zhdanovs suggests that a fertile field has existed there for the satirist. Yet these very characters, the natural objects of satiric attack, have been in a position to discourage the labors of the satirist. Satire has shown the same pattern of growth as other literary forms: it developed richly in the twenties, then settled into a domestic routine as a handmaiden of the state, directing its barbs at preselected "bourgeois" or "imperialist" targets. And even in the twenties the satirist could expose the stupidity of evil fools only at some risk, and usually he chose to avoid prime targets in favor of generalized vices, fantastic rogues, or the ever-present "philistine."

An exception to this rule was Zamyatin's *We*, which contained, as we have seen, a satire, not on the "Communist future," but on the prophets of the collective who held forth in his own time. Mikhail Bulgakov resorted, like Zamyatin, to science fantasy in *The Fatal Eggs* (1924) and *Devilry* (1925). In *The Fatal Eggs* a Soviet scientist has invented, but not yet thoroughly tested, a "red ray" which will greatly increase the growth rate of living organisms. No sooner has he announced his discovery than a leather-jacketed commissar appears in his laboratory with an official order to make immediate practical use of the ray in poultry-breeding on the state farms. Over the scientist's objections the order is carried out, but the wrong eggs are used, and huge snakes and crocodiles are grown on the farms instead of hens. The life of the republic is threatened by these ignorant and premature attempts to apply scientific knowledge. *Devilry* (1925) mingles reality and fantasy in telling the absurd troubles of a Soviet clerk who has fallen afoul of the paper apparatus. Bulgakov's play *Zoya's Apartment* (1926), the setting of which is a fashionable bawdy house catering to the needs of the "new class" of Red officials, was considered too pointed in its satire and was closed. Bulgakov's satire was, like that of Zamyatin, unpalatable to the Soviet authorities.

Other satirists of the twenties were more careful in their selection of targets. Ilya Ilf and Evgeny Petrov, whose *Twelve Chairs* (1928, also known as *Diamonds to Sit On*), *The Little Golden Calf* (1931), and *Little Golden America* (1936) have been popular with the Soviet readers and only briefly during the Zhdanov period were suspect to the Soviet authorities, shrewdly directed their ridicule at rascality of a bourgeois stamp. Their satire is akin in spirit to that of Valentin Katayev in *The Embezzlers,* and their finest creation, Ostap Bender, is an engaging and ingenious adventurer with the lofty ambition of becoming a millionaire. The two earlier novels describe his travels and farcical misadventures in a society where it is impossible to satisfy such a simple aim. *Little Golden America,* based on a transcontinental tour of the country, is basically satirical, but favorable to many aspects of American life, and it provides fresh and illuminating views of our society.

Mikhail Zoshchenko is sometimes included among the satirists, and it has already been mentioned that Zhdanov understood his *Adventure of a Monkey* as ridicule directed at "Soviet reality." And perhaps his work does fit in a general way the concept of satire, but it is in no sense a humorous attack on a specific social organization, or on particular contemporary characters, or on a way of life. There is no evidence in his work that Zoshchenko believed in Soviet "values." There is no reason to think that he held firmly to beliefs that ran counter to those values. He feels neither anger nor scorn as he observes his contemporaries, but only perverse pity and baffled amusement both at them and at himself.

For the Russian humorist Zoshchenko sadness was a way of life. He is an intentional caricature of the melancholy clown. The fact that both his sadness and his humor were organic to him is demonstrated by the autobiographical novel *Before Sunrise,* which is a search for the explanation of his chronic melancholy. All his life Zoshchenko had suffered, he said, from fits of depression, which at times became so acute that he could not function. He was unhappy, and he could not understand why. He concluded that in this respect he was different from other people, and therefore sought in his own life some cause or explanation of a condition peculiar to him. The novel begins with this explanation of how it happened to be written, then moves to an investigation of significant memories beginning at the age of sixteen, each one a self-contained unit of experience. In the selection of memories lies the ironic meaning of the story. Zoshchenko recalls his attempted suicide over a low mark in composition, his experience of wounds and gas poisoning during the war, the succession of ridiculously unsuitable occupations from cobbler to detective from 1917 to 1920, and incidents of his life as a literary man in Petrograd. His brief, bare account of the literary great whom he met among the Serapions is in its way appalling. The face of the poet Blok expressed only sadness and apathy; Yesenin recited his poetry dressed in a velvet blouse with lips and eyebrows made up; Gorky wearily expounded truisms on literature and culture while someone behind him carefully wrote it all down; the editor and poet Kuzmin turned down Zoshchenko's funny stories because they were "exaggerated"; his girl friend, also a writer, asked him to wait for her on the embankment while she visited another lover "for just twenty minutes" and came back feeling wonderful; Mayakovsky turned out to be a hypochondriac, excessively afraid of infection from drinking glasses, forks, and spoons. These and other memories are told in short clipped sentences which lack the rational organization imposed by syntax. They are presented as raw, untreated items of memory and while there is no explicit reflection on their meaning, the sum of all the memories covering the years from 1912 to 1926 is a lifetime of quiet desperation. But with a detached air of scientific curiosity and with his tongue in his cheek Zoshchenko asserts that he cannot find in any of this the reason for his melancholy, so he decides to carry the search farther back into his childhood. The section dealing with memories from the age of five to sixteen is entitled "A Terrifying World," and it relates memories of family and childhood, each one in some way sad. Still not satisfied that he has found the answer, he carries the search back "before sunrise," to the dawn of consciousness, the earliest years of life. But still he cannot explain his sadness. He proceeds then to study the psychologists and gives the reader a brief elementary statement of the Pavlovian theory of the conditioned reflex and of the Freudian sexual theory. He looked for the specific event which caused his unhappiness in "associations" arising from dreams and found that in them water frequently had an association with strong emotion. Certain, he said, that he was on the track of the early conditioning process that had made him an unhappy man, he promised in the sequel to tell of this, but the publication of *Before Sunrise* was stopped before he reached that point.

Even in its unfinished state the novel is his most elaborate exercise of humor. In his ironic search through the well of recollection, aided by modern tools of psychological analysis, for the one single thing that had caused his melancholy, Zoshchenko has laid before us a texture of consciousness that is all woven of normal human melancholy. Perhaps that is what he discovered—that the melancholy he experienced was a general human condition and not peculiar to himself. Perhaps that is what he meant when he said in the Introduction to *Before Sunrise* that "he had become a happy man." His stories are evidence that he was so sensitive to the incongruities of the human predicament that he had no recourse but good-natured and sympathetic laughter.

While Zoshchenko's humor arises from his observation of the general human situation it is obvious that the Soviet predicament provided the data upon which he worked. Situational and linguistic absurdities from Soviet life are the subjects of his hundreds of short tales. Zoshchenko is himself authority for the statement that he introduced the language of the street into his stories, but as Soviet linguistic scholars have pointed out, that statement is itself an absurdity. The stories are stylized both as to language and form, and only in fairy tales or narrative folk songs do characters speak with the intonation, the pauses, the retardation and repetition, and the mock-pithy asides that characterize Zoshchenko's people. No one has ever spoken the language of Zoshchenko's heroes. It is an invented speech made up of newspaper rhetoric, the pronouncements of Stalin and other heroes, misunderstood fragments of Marx or Engels, all mixed up in a weird linguistic brew and laced with the catchwords of popular prejudice. Zoshchenko's technique has been labeled as *skaz*, and his work has been compared to that of Damon Runyan and Ring Lardner, whose stories are told in the speech style of a character who represents a particular milieu. But Zoshchenko is radically different from other practitioners of *skaz*. His narrator is not the Soviet "man in the street," nor is he a representative of the Soviet "lower middle class" or any other social group. He is not a character at all. He is the mask through which Zoshchenko himself speaks to the reader.

Each of the stories is told—one might almost say confided to the reader—by the absurd narrator, who, like the wise fools of folk stories, says much more than he seems to know. The device of the wise fool enabled Zoshchenko to comment on Soviet life without attracting fatal attention from the state. His fool is pompously loyal to the latest and most pompous Soviet notions and full of obvious wisdom on such subjects as the decay of the intelligentsia, proper management of public baths, civilized behavior on streetcars, health, true love in Soviet conditions, the housing shortage, and correct grammar. But the items of reality that he selects as illustrations offer a ridiculous contradiction of his wise pronouncements.

The stories are frequently constructed according to a pattern which can be studied in a few examples. Following a somewhat pompous formalistic scheme, the stories may be divided into three parts: 1) exordium, 2) epic narration, 3) moral conclusion. Let us examine one that is typical: "Not All Is Lost." In that story the "exordium" consists of general comments on "melancholics" who have no interest in this "teeming" life: "All around us are various entertaining facts, a struggle is in progress, various events are, you know, unfolding . . . accidents, thefts. All around us nature with a lavish hand distributes her free gifts. The sun is shining, the grass is growing, the ants are crawling." The narrator reflects that such "melancholics" are "rootless intellectuals" suffering from overeducation, who would have been miserable under any regime. So you can't blame current events. The "epic narration" begins with the self-critical comment that perhaps one should forget all this "empty philosophy" and get down to the case in hand, one Innokenty, an intellectual who found new interest in living and stopped being a "melancholic." The change in Innokenty's life occurred when the chairman of his apartment house committee announced that additional tenants would be assigned to live in his apartment, and Innokenty went off to the housing office to complain. While he was away his apartment was burglarized and some things stolen. As a result he had to visit the police station twice a day to get help and look around in the second-hand markets to see if his stuff had come up for sale. One day as he hurried about this business he fell downstairs and dislocated his arm and then had to go regularly to the doctor's office for examination and massages. So he had many things to occupy him: mornings the business of tracking down lost articles, afternoons the clinic, and evenings discussion of the day's activities with friends. And this rootless intellectual began to take an interest in things and changed radically for the better. Then comes the "moral conclusion," with the fool's comment on the meaning of the story:

Of course it's impossible to say whether he will continue to possess such spiritual boldness all his life. But maybe he will possess it all his life. It all depends on how his affairs develop. Maybe the house chairman will take him to court for nonpayment of rent. And then again maybe the Criminal Investigation Department will summon him about those goods that were stolen. And then again, maybe, as he rushes about on his affairs, Innokenty will break another arm, or dislocate his leg. And then, maybe he will die happy, in full contentment. And, dying, he will reflect on the affairs that filled his life, and on the struggle that he bore on his shoulders with honor.

Not without reason did Comrade Budyonny once exclaim: "Our whole life is nothing but struggle."

Zoshchenko wore the fool's mask in almost everything he wrote—in his essays and novels as well as in his short stories. In an article published in 1922 as part of a symposium by the Serapion Brothers, he wrote:

In general, it's kind of hard to be a writer. Just take ideology. Nowadays a writer has got to have an ideology.
Here's Voronsky (a good man) who writes . . . "It is necessary that writers have a more 'exact ideology.'"
But that's downright unpleasant. How can I have an "exact ideology," when not a single party among them all attracts me?
I don't hate anybody—that's my "exact ideology."

The mask served him well. He was attacked from time to time, but those attacks, even Zhdanov's vicious assault, did him no permanent harm. Serious charges could hardly affect a writer who offered no serious target. After his eclipse during the early fifties he reappeared again in 1956 as the author of skits performed by the popular Moscow satirist Raikin at the Hermitage Theater, and he published a few rather weak stories in the literary magazines. He died in 1958.

Zoshchenko's style is a reduction to the absurd of solemn hypocrisy in whatever form. It exposes the false and trivializes the pompous. It brings to the ground all lofty sentiment loftily expressed. It reveals the vulgarity under official heroism. Through the mask of his clown-hero, Zoshchenko uttered judgments on the Soviet variant of modern life that, coming from a serious man, would have been an offense to the majesty of the state.

Chapter 11

After Stalin: The First Two Thaws

Pomerantsev, Panova, and *The Guests*

EVIDENCE OF DEEP unhappiness among the Soviet intellectuals, and of the Party's dissatisfaction with them in their unhappy state, antedates by three years the death of Stalin. The first effort to mitigate distrust and regimentation of the intellectual world—a condition especially acute in the Zhdanov years—was made by Stalin himself in 1950 when he intervened in the specialized field of linguistics to smash with his ineffable "hammer blows" a sterile dictatorship which the Party had itself established in that field. That the orthodox Marxists in control of language faculties in universities and in scholarly societies were both dictatorial and unproductive may no doubt be taken as a fact, since we have the evidence of Stalin's own words for it. And Stalin was anything but mild in dealing with them: in fact one feels that his condemnation was perhaps a little too severe. "An Arakcheev-like regime" was what he said existed in the area of linguistic studies, with this ugly name evoking the shade of a nineteenth-century political general and martinet remembered chiefly for his brutal barrack-room attitudes and personal cowardice in battle. Even the mildest attempts at criticism of the dominant regime in linguistics had been persecuted, and Stalin deplored that. He enunciated on this occasion an important truth, that "no science can develop and flourish without a struggle of opinions, without free criticism." Brave words and true, even though Stalin's own. And yet Stalin's intervention did not result in the development of free and vigorous debate in Soviet linguistics.

It was obvious that the Party-state had failed to produce a controlled literature, though they did produce the appearance of loyal uniformity. Crippled and terrorized though it was, the writers' community maintained a separate existence and still cared for variety and individuality. Indeed, Soviet literature, when freed from the worst rigors of Stalin's winters, revived the major theme of Russian literature since the revolution: the fate of the individual human being in a mass state.

One of the first statements was an article by a young student of cinematography, Olga Shmarova, published in May, 1953, in which she deplored the absence of "love" from Soviet films. She complained that the theme of love had been replaced almost entirely by the theme of labor and construction and that the conversation of a pair of lovers in a film instead of being full of lyrical nothings was about bulldozers, tractors, generators, and dynamos. She complained of the depersonalized characters: that problems of production take precedence over individual life and individual experiences of all kinds, even the common human experience of falling in love. She quotes dialogue typical of recent Soviet films: "If you exceed the production goals for the spring quarter I'll be your wife." Such dialogue, she says, is not "true to life."

In November, 1953, in the official Soviet publication *Soviet Music* an article appeared by the famous Soviet composer Aram Khachaturyan, an article which was amazing and encouraging by its frankness. It, too, contained much Soviet jargon, expressions of obeisance before the Party and devotion to the idea of the "socialist content" of music; but the main import of the article was that a stifling bureaucratic regime was making the production of good music nearly impossible. The article is a plea for the rights of the individual composer. Khachaturyan calls upon the authorities to take the small risk of trusting him: "Let the individual artist be trusted more fully and not be constantly supervised and suspected." He revealed that Soviet composers work "with a worried glance over their shoulder, always afraid that something bad may happen to them if they make a mistake." He describes how the heads of bureaus and directors of theaters interfere with the work of the actual composers, so that the latter refuse to take the responsibility for anything. "For instance, if the composer delivers a song to some institution everyone considers it his duty to 'advise' him about it. . . . And strange as it may seem the composer usually agrees to all the changes suggested. Only if individuals are allowed to work out their own musical styles, free of bureaucratic intervention, can Soviet music thrive," said Khachaturyan.

At about the same time others began to speak of the dismal prospect offered by Russian prose and poetry. A Soviet poetess, Olga Berggoltz, in a "Discussion of Lyric Poetry," complained that in searching through recent issues of the literary journals she had not been able to find a single poem on the theme of love. And she found that the "lyric" note, the expression of particular and personal emotion, was nowhere to be found. Even a bulldozer operator, she reflected, has a personal life, and the people engaged in construction projects are, after all, *people*. Her article was a plea for consideration of the individual human being—for "the living man"—apart from the life of the collective. One reflects that in the Soviet Union the rediscovery of alphabets is a regular occurrence.

This was soon followed by the remarks of another Soviet poet, Tvardovsky, an editor of one of the leading literary journals and an official poet of some note and considerable skill. One of his best known works is a poem celebrating collectivization, "Muraviya Land." The main import of one section of his long poem *Horizons beyond Horizons* was that the great mass of Russian readers hold the writers in contempt for their insincerity. The main criticism of the readers who had spoken to him frankly was that Soviet literature does not reflect life, that it is "contrived and unreal." Tvardovsky went on to declare most eloquently that Soviet literature had everything that was required of it. It was full of social motivation, construction, the new socialist man, positive heroes of labor and defense, the new life—but unfortunately, it was a dead product.

Finally, lending greater prestige to these complaints, one of the deans of Soviet literature, a spokesman of Stalin and the Party line for many years, an apologist for all the crimes of the Soviet regime, Ilya Ehrenburg spoke out loud and bold to the effect that Soviet literature is pale and uninteresting, and that a Soviet textile worker prefers to read, not modern novels, but *Anna Karenina,* which she reads not because

Tolstoy tells her about the latest victories in socialist construction but because he understood and could convey the reality of childbirth, death, and love, and because he gives her living human emotions. There is only one area in which a writer must be an expert, says Ehrenburg, not in describing construction, but in creating the inner life of particular human beings. "Such books cannot be ordered or planned. They can only be created. Can anyone imagine *ordering* Tolstoy to write *Anna Karenina*?" Ehrenburg when he wrote that sentence was probably unaware that in 1924 a very similar thought had been uttered by Bukharin in the form of an ironic question directed at a proletarian organizer: "Did a Politburo of the nobility order Pushkin to write *Eugene Onegin*?"

How far would writers and critics be allowed to go in stating boldly such obvious truths? Indeed they went very far. In December, 1953, a major article, "On Sincerity in Literature," was published in the magazine *New World*. Its author, a young critic named Pomerantsev, registered casually his impressions of Soviet literature, interposing pregnant and humorous comments on life and people. The article was remarkable for its style. He abandoned the rigidly paragraphed and patterned system of the didactic critic to present his ideas impressionistically, moving gently from one idea to another without apparent ulterior purpose, and giving the effect of immediate contact with thought in process. The article was like an electric shock to the Soviet reader. Instead of a series of good points well taken, leading to inevitable conclusions, Pomerantsev provided something new: ideas of his own about literature. Pomerantsev became the center of a controversy, and though it was never admitted publicly, the approach of the author and his style, rather than the actual idea content of the article, were most likely what really disturbed the pontiffs. Sincerity, said Pomerantsev, is lacking in many novels and plays. Boldyrev's novel *Decisive Years* is a poor novel because the author's heart is not in it: there's nothing either new or exciting in that story of the struggle to make blast furnaces more efficient. What's wanted is a statement of what the writer has really felt and thought instead of constant preachment and propaganda. Readers are bored by lessons and arguments. Elementary psychology cries out against these contrived novels and plays, because they have no effect on anyone. People don't believe our writers because they varnish life, they try to slick it up, make things look better than they really are. Sanctimonious critics are not alone to blame for this. The writers do it willingly. The habit of improving on reality has become deeply ingrained in Soviet writers. They have become their own best censors. They gild reality by presenting pictures of prosperity and well-being. We should not try to transport people into a dream world. Any scene in a newsreel tells a great deal more about our prosperity than a scene in the feature film because we are incapable of expressing in it the truth to be found in the newsreel. We suppress the real problems. Don't carefully spell out conclusions, and don't let yourself write a single line that you do not feel. Be independent.

In an imaginary colloquy with an author: "Your heroes are carried by the ideas, not the other way round. They even dream only logical dreams. Normal confused dreams are not for them. And how they talk to one another! In their conversations your characters sound like radio announcers. Is human conversation like that? Do speeches and harangues pour forth like that, especially when there are no more than two people present? Do you remember how one of your heroes gave his daughter a watch because, as he said, 'his living standard had risen?' This is a phrase straight from the columns of a newspaper: the man who wrote it forgot that in the family circle a man would never say that 'his living standard had risen'; he would say that he was better off or that he had more money now."

"In my opinion," wrote Pomerantsev, "the primary task of criticism today is that of leading writers toward a broadening of themes and a change in the treatment of problems. This is the chief thing, because the reader must be able to get something from literature that he can't get elsewhere."

Pomerantsev's article was a cause for consternation. At first the official bodies seemed not to know just how to take it, or even whether to condemn it. An article appeared criticizing it, then shortly after, another appeared defending the point of view it expressed. There was an interval, not of freedom, but of vacillation in the high councils of the Party, and during that interval a number of things were published which departed radically from the established patterns of Soviet literature and threw light on the realities of Soviet life.

During this first period of "thaw" the publication of Vera Panova's novel *The Four Seasons,* Leonid Zorin's play *The Guests,* and Ilya Ehrenburg's novelette *The Thaw* marked a change in the weather. The first of these, *The Four Seasons,* is the work of a woman whose powers as a writer are very great, but who has, so to speak, emasculated herself for the sake of the Party. She has written both fact and fiction for Communist newspapers since she was seventeen. She has tried her hand at verse, and had some success with drama. Her first successful novel, *The Train,* was written as a direct assignment from the Union of Soviet Writers. It describes in simple, utterly convincing language life on a hospital train behind the front lines during World War II. The human suffering and courage she portrays in that novel have the taste of truth, a truth which is not wholly negated by her Party-oriented selection of character and incident.

In her novels about the construction of new industries and building the new life Panova has somehow managed to maintain the immediacy of experience. Her characters are concerned not only with industry, but with their private homes and real problems; the textbook scenes she includes are often a harsh interruption of human drama. Panova sees life from a woman's angle of vision: to her the home is important, and children are important. Her best writing is about children, their problems and their way of looking at the world. Her "good" characters do say the right things, and her "bad" ones are likely to be converted to better ways, or, if *too* bad, defeated by the good ones. And yet the accident of sex lends to the work of Panova a warmth and sympathy which is not denied even to the "negative" characters and improves her insight into the "positive" ones.

Because of Panova's pervasive femininity some important Soviet literary leaders have never understood or fully accepted her. When her novel *The Four Seasons* appeared in 1953 it was an immediate success with the reading public, and was selected for translation into foreign languages; but there was some distress at the highest level. An attack on the novel appeared in *Pravda* over the signature of V. Kochetov, who compared it to novels published in the twenties during the NEP period and attempted to kill it with a label:

> If the author of *The Four Seasons* undertakes simply to show "how things are in life sometimes," without passing any judgment, then she has taken the direction of naturalism. And naturalism explains nothing. Naturalism can entertain, astound, arouse emotion, but it cannot ever make profound and true social and artistic generalizations.

This is a fair criticism because what Panova is trying to do in her novel is to give, without preachment or propaganda, an immediate sense of the Russian experience. Each of the characters has an accent and an inner life of his own, each is different from the others, each one experiences life in his own way. They fall in love, or out of love, they marry, have children, work, find friends and think uncomplicated thoughts— on life in the Soviet and outside of it. Panova does succeed in capturing some part of the reality, in giving us, as Kochetov puts it, some sense of "how things were."

The unifying idea of the novel is that power corrupts those who wield it. One of the leading characters is the top-level Communist bureaucrat, Bortashevich, a scoundrel and a grafter who lives in fear of exposure. But this scoundrel is treated sympathetically, and the reader doesn't, as he reads the novel, blame him very much. He's a good fellow who has fallen into crime because of the effect of environment: specifically the environment of upper-class Communist society. His criminal activity had begun very gradually, almost imperceptibly, with nothing more than a wink, just because he needed money in order to live in a style better than that of his colleagues, and after a few years he was so deep in crime that he couldn't get out no matter how much he wanted to. He was the victim of social evil, and Panova identifies this evil as the atmosphere of irresponsible power. At one point this is carefully spelled out.

Another character with a problem is Dorofeya, a peasant girl who has risen in the course of an adventurous life to be a high Communist official. Her son, Gennadi, is a lazy wastrel who expects to take from life but never give anything back. Through selfishness and weakness he falls in with some gangsters, Soviet version, and Panova's novel reveals the activities of the Soviet criminal underworld, a form of life hardly ever touched upon in approved novels. But Panova is sympathetic even to this spoiled and selfish young criminal, whom she portrays as basically good, but the victim of bad environment and bad education.

The Four Seasons ends on a note of indomitable feminine optimism. In contrast to her novel *Kruzhilikha,* in which the builder Listopad meditates on the marvels to come in science and industry, Panova in *The Four Seasons,* sensitive to the demand for attention to individual human beings, ends her novel with a lyric apostrophe to her characters:

"We'll soon be feasting. Even nondrinkers will have a drink tonight. When the Kremlin bells ring out at midnight, who would not drink a toast? Let's drink to the happiness of Sasha and Yulka and their friends, to the success of their plans, to the well-being of the town of Ensk. Let us wish Dorothy courage in facing her new trials. Let us wish a great success to comrade Kosykh and the whole machine-building factory, and to all those who honorably work for life, for eternal, ever-young, ever-renewed life.

"Happy New Year, Comrades!"

The novelist Panova is a sensitive woman, whose interests are those of a woman, and whose comments on life have feminine gentleness and tact. She is a "Party writer," but one with sentiment. She wears the "leather jacket," but hers has yellow ribbons on it. Her work is important because she must be credited with having introduced and insisted upon some of the most important themes of the immediate post-Stalin "thaw." Her chief themes are those that have special interest for women: love, the need for human tenderness and consideration, the reality of private emotion, the family, the education of children.

Leonid Zorin's play *The Guests,* published in the magazine *Theater* (No. 2, 1954) and presented in Leningrad and Moscow, is the most direct attack on the Soviet bureaucratic state that has appeared since the death of Stalin. In this play the contemporary rulers of the Soviet Union were held up to public obloquy for having turned their revolutionary inheritance into a source of bourgeois comfort and power. The message of the play is radical: it is a frankly aimed attack at the Party and the government in the name of the lost ideals of the Revolution. The Ministry of Culture lost no time in condemning such a thing and in terms reserved for genuinely subversive material.

The play is built around a single character, a high official of the Ministry of Justice, who has the speech, the manner, and the way of thinking of a man habituated to arbitrary power. The action takes place in a summer house owned by the father of the minister, an old revolutionary toward whose ideals the son feels a kind of tolerant contempt. "Old granddaddy" with his ideas that go all the way back to 1917, seems foolishly old-fashioned to the new generation. For Pyotr political power is the only reality, and he uses his to build advantage for himself. He and his family are full of possessions: a car (with chauffeur), a fine summer house, a luxurious apartment, and to all of this they are jealously attached. The minister himself in his vulgar pursuit of privilege has learned to hold ordinary citizens in contempt. The action of the play revolves around a miscarriage of justice which Pyotr and his cronies intend to conceal because exposure would be a threat to them. The innocents who had been condemned and ruined must stay ruined, the wrong would not be righted.

Three generations are represented in the cast of characters: the old revolutionary, his son the minister, and the minister's son. The minister belongs to the generation of "careerist" bureaucrats, and his father directly accuses him of having betrayed the Revolution. "There is something alien and insulting in their life," comments one character, "a life in which the important thing is not labor, but pride of place." And when the minister's family are discussing a newly acquired piece of property one of the good characters says: "How I hate these filthy little bourgeois." The minister's family and his social set are exposed in the play as an uncultivated and arrogant ruling class. An optimistic note is struck when, near the end of the play, the minister's own son turns on him:

"I hereby declare war on you. Wherever I meet you—in whatever guise you may appear, wherever you show yourself, whatever name you bear—I will recognize you and I will fight you to the death."

No doubt this is rhetoric, and not very skillful rhetoric, but the sentiment expressed was perhaps the most powerful indictment of the Stalinist bureaucracy published in the Soviet Union. Directed ostensibly at "criminal elements" in the Ministry of Justice whose crimes were investigated and exposed after the execution of Beria, the playwright subtly contrives that the portrait of these "elements" resembles a whole new class of criminal careerists.

Ilya Ehrenburg and Alexey Tolstoy

The novelette which gave a name to the post-Stalin period was Ilya Ehrenburg's *The Thaw*, published in the first months of 1954. Ehrenburg in this work provided a concise guide to the themes and theses of post-Stalin literature; as a matter of fact his work sums up so neatly in credible artistic form the main points of "de-Stalinization" that one is obliged to assume a degree of political guidance, direct or indirect, in its writing. The argument of *The Thaw*, taken up again by many authors in subsequent works, runs as follows: 1) Soviet life has become cold and rigid; let us warm up toward one another. 2) Soviet political and industrial heroes are often tyrants indifferent to the popular weal; let us expose them. 3) People are important, and they exist as individuals; let us cherish each one. 4) Emotions are real and cannot always be neatly catalogued and contained in rational categories; let us feel them: love, pity, fear, envy. It is a fine argument, indeed, but it is so well organized that one can sense in it a remnant of ice under the "thaw."

Ehrenburg has been since 1954 the most important advocate of liberalization in Soviet literature, and he has made a not inconsiderable contribution, even though the points he laboriously hammers on the nature of artistic "creation" and the needs of literature are generally so obvious as to induce either laughter or tears. But in Soviet literature someone is always obliged to stress truisms.

Ehrenburg's biography is itself a kind of commentary on the Soviet regime. His personal history is interesting, not only as the development of a complex and cryptic personality under the pressures of the twentieth century, but as a commentary on the relationship to the Soviet regime of intellectuals whose education and outlook is individualistic and West European. A brief biographical digression on Ehrenburg is indispensable for an understanding of Khrushchev's "thaw," and may throw some light as well on the history of the Soviet state.

Ehrenburg was born in 1891 of a bourgeois Jewish family. His father was the first of his line to break away from the folk and the faith, "to leave the ghetto," as Ehrenburg phrased it, and had received his own father's curse for the crime of attending a Russian school. His Jewish family origin has been, all his life, one of the most important factors in Ehrenburg's view of the world. In an autobiographical sketch written in 1926, he said:

I was born in 1891. A Hebrew. Spent my childhood in Moscow, Khamovniki, near a brewery. Warm, sour beer. The workers curse and fight in the barracks. . . . In the spring we went to visit grandfather in Kiev. Imitating him, I prayed, my whole body swaying, and I sniffed clove from a silver vessel. Then the First Moscow Gymnasium. The boys around me said: "The little kike sits on a bench, we'll sit the little kike on a fence." At home I raised mischief—more than was necessary. Set fire to a summer house.

The effect on a growing boy of such experiences may easily be imagined. The fact that he was a Jew, and as such the object of a special, inevitable, and undeserved injury, goes far to explain Ehrenburg's career. The traumatic effect on him of the boyhood shocks he met with is borne out by the fact that he refers to such matters again in his more recent autobiography, written in 1960; but the years had mellowed his memories, and though he mentions the *numerus clausus*, the pale of settlement, the residence permit, and the pogroms, he would have his readers believe that "things were not really bad," and he provides a new version of that first day in a Russian school:

I had somewhere read that the Jews had crucified Christ; uncle Leo told me that Christ was himself a Jew; aunt Vera told me that Christ taught us to turn the other cheek. But I didn't care for that teaching. When I first entered the gymnasium one of the preparatory students began teasing: "The little kike sat on a bench, let's sit the little kike on a fence." Without a moment's hesitation I hit him in the face. But soon we became friends. And no one insulted me again.

Note that an important mnemonic revision has occurred in the account of that boyhood incident written in 1960. In the first version, a number of boys sang the unbearable ditty; in the later account it is only one—a preparatory student at that —and Ehrenburg immediately silenced him. He goes on in that passage to insist that there was no great anti-Semitism among the Russian intellectuals of that day. But the experience of life symbolized by the obscene ditty was really unbearable, and Ehrenburg never became reconciled to it. The culture that contained such injustice has been, most of his life, the victim of his cynical mockery. His consistent support of the new regime in Russia was motivated, perhaps, by his contempt for the values of European bourgeois culture, and a certain fellow-feeling for the new barbarians. His occasional doubts as to the latter appear in a number of works, and after the death of Stalin he undertook to correct some of the damage that had been wrought in literature and art. His voice since 1954 has consistently championed individualism and artistic integrity, and in his reminiscences, *People, Years, Life,* published in 1960 and 1961 in the magazine *New World,* he has tried to revivify the ties with modern European art which were a normal part of the Russian cultural tradition. Like the "theses" advanced in his novelette *The Thaw,* the points he gently emphasizes in *People, Years, and Life* have a programmatic ring.

The refusal to treat with due seriousness the alternatives offered by the bourgeois world is amply illustrated in Ehrenburg's biography. He was a student agitator during the 1905 revolution, and was imprisoned in 1907, at the age of 16. From 1909 to 1917 he lived abroad, spending much of his time on the Left Bank in Paris, talking and "working" at all hours in the Rotonde, the Closerie des Lilas, and other Montparnasse cafés. From 1910 to 1914 he moved in French symbolist circles, was overcome with admiration for Francis Jammes, discovered Paul Claudel and Leon Bloy, became a convert to a kind of mystical Catholicism, and seriously considered entering a Benedictine monastery. The latter thought was perhaps his most respectable attempt at rejecting the values of the bourgeois world. When the war came in 1914 his reaction was original—he tried to enlist in the Foreign Legion, but was rejected as physically unfit. His first response to the October Revolution, "A Prayer For Russia," was a stylized poetic exercise in the neo-Catholic vein on the mystic agony being suffered by "la pieuse Russie" at the hands of infidels. He spent the years 1918 and 1919 in Kiev, Tiflis, and other southern localities where he barely escaped on the one hand the Cheka and on the other the pogroms. He returned to Paris in 1921 on an official Soviet "artistic mission," but was expelled by the French police and went to Brussels. There he wrote *The Extraordinary Adventures of Julio Jurenito and His Disciples*, a book of which he said: "This is the only book I wrote 'in earnest.' Neither the critics, nor the readers, nor even myself can tell in that book where the mockery ends." Without doubt Ehrenburg's best work, *Julio Jurenito* relates the adventures of a nihilistic philosopher who undertakes the mission of destroying finally the culture of Europe. His instruments of destruction are, ironically enough, typical products of that culture: an American Bible-thumping business man, Mr. Cool; a methodical and ruthless German, Schmidt; the French rentier, M. Delhaie; a melancholy Russian intellectual in search of his own soul. Auxiliary instruments and positive characters are an anarchist Bambucci whose only purpose in life is to violate all rules, and an African savage who believes absolutely in his own gods. Bourgeois culture is scathingly attacked in the novel, but the new order in Russia does not escape Ehrenburg's barbs.

During the twenties and thirties he lived for the most part abroad, producing stories and journalistic articles for the Soviet Press. *Trust D. E.: The Story of the Ruin of Europe* (1923) deals with the conquest of Europe by American capitalism. The novel *The Adventures of Lasik Roitschwantz* (1927) is a mockery of the bourgeois—and Communist—world given in the idiom of a poor Jewish tailor who is arrested by the Communist police and imprisoned, then escapes from Russia and travels in Western Europe where he is mistaken for a Bolshevik, and at last dies of starvation in Palestine. Lasik's amused contempt for both West and East is expressed in homely Jewish wisdom, and the novel is peppered with proverbs, sayings, Talmudisms, and the like. *The Summer, 1925* (1926) and *A Street in Moscow* (1927) give a depressing picture of society in the days of NEP, when the Revolution seemed to have reached a dead end. *The Conspiracy of Equals* (1929) is a historical novel about the life of Gracchus Babeuf. *The Factory of Dreams* (1931) is a satire on Hollywood. *Out of Chaos* (1933), Ehrenburg's contribution to Five-Year Plan literature, is second only to *Julio Jurenito* in importance and interest. It is important because it represents for Ehrenburg a decisive step beyond the nihilistic mockery of his earlier work. It is more "in earnest" than *Jurenito* and represents an effort to establish a rational basis for Ehrenburg's pro-Soviet position. The scene of the novel is the great Kuznetsk metallurgical combine in the days of its construction. It preaches the usual moral of Five-Year Plan literature, that a new Communist world will grow out of the industrialization program. The novel is important because of the main character Safonov, a young intellectual and a confirmed individualist, whose ideas at times echo *Jurenito* and who is certainly Ehrenburg himself. Safonov's sophisticated intellectual conscience is outraged by the crass materialism of the new collective. He cannot accept the world being created by the Soviet Five-Year Plan. In Safonov's private diary Ehrenburg pronounced an indictment upon the "anthill" culture being built in the Soviet Union, and in the personal history of Safonov he has illustrated the helplessness of the lone intellectual before the onslaught of that culture. That feeling of helplessness was reinforced by Ehren-burg's conviction that no confidence could be placed in in-tellectuals either of the West or of the East.

Safonov's imagined speech to the "collective" confided to his diary expresses the thought and summarizes the tragedy of Ehrenburg himself:

You are accustomed to silence. Some are silent because you have frightened them; others because you have bought them. . . . As in the days of Galileo simple truth can be spoken only at the stake. You want to discuss the question of culture. It is unlikely, however, that anyone among you understands what culture is. For some, culture is blowing one's nose in a handkerchief; for others it is buying the Academy publications, which they do not understand, cannot, indeed, understand. You have established universal literacy and equally universal ignorance. After this you gather to-gether and prattle about culture. Of course your not blowing your nose through your fingers deserves praise. But it has little to do with culture. You build a thousand blast furnaces and you are still ignorant. The anthill is a model of reason and logic. But it already existed a thousand years ago. Nothing in it has changed. There are ant workers, and ant specialists, and ant leaders. But there never was an ant genius. . . . The Acropolis was not built by ants. The law of gravitation was not discovered by an ant. Ants have no Senecas, no Raphaels, no Pushkins. They have a hill, and they work. They build, they carry twigs, they lay eggs, they devour one another, and they are happy. They are far more honest than you are— they don't talk nonsense about culture.

Safonov did not deliver this speech before the collective, but another and thoroughly acceptable one. And Safonov's sym-bolic suicide had its real counterpart in the demise of Ehren-burg as a satirist. His work during the thirties need not con-cern us since it is for the most part patterned strictly and skillfully to the Party line.

In his journalistic articles during the Second World War he attacked all Germans so violently that the Soviet authori-ties found it necessary to check him, pointing out that there were both Fascist and anti-Fascist Germans. Immediately after the death of Stalin the most fruitful period in Ehrenburg's life began, the period of *The Thaw* and of his articles in defense of a literary and artistic culture that seemed threatened with extinction in the Soviet Union. The cynical nihilism of his young manhood had no part in the campaign he now waged, with a sure sense of the Soviet environment, to educate the recently literate but still uncultivated "Soviet man."

The shock produced throughout the world by Ehrenburg's novelette when it broke the long winter of Stalinism should not be forgotten. To observers in the year 1954 the story seemed a miraculous occurrence, a fantastic piece of writing which gave a glimpse behind the Iron Curtain and revealed Soviet life in its real colors and contours. In this work Ehrenburg wrote according to a recipe which he had himself drawn up in the article "On the Writers' Work," which we have already cited:

> Let us suppose that the novel deals with Ivanov, the reader's next-door neighbor. Neither Ivanov's appearance nor his everyday life is a secret to the reader. The reader has often seen Ivanov, heard him speak at meetings of the *aktiv*, perhaps even dropped in on him from time to time. Yet Ivanov remains unfamiliar and undiscovered territory to him. If the writer is able to show what this distant neighbor is thinking about, how he bears grief, how he works, loves and makes mistakes, the reader will feel enriched by reading this novel; he has come to know Ivanov and therefore has become better acquainted with himself.

The "inner world" of each character is the subject matter of *The Thaw*, and in this it is a conscious polemic against official Soviet literature and a return to the methods advocated in the twenties by Voronsky and the theorists of RAPP. The story is told in a succession of episodes, each presented from the viewpoint of a particular character, whose personal idiosyncrasies and unspoken thoughts are basic to the narrative pattern. Zhuravlyov, an industrial manager and an autocrat who destroys those who disagree with him, is a complex character. The chief villain of the piece, he is still not entirely a villain. He even has feelings. He is in love with his wife, Lena, and cannot reason himself out of such foolishness. Lena is in love, too, but not with her husband, whose faults she sees too well in spite of his production miracles. Sokolovsky, a lone eccentric who thinks his own thoughts, has had a bitter disappointment in love that accounts for his bristling nature. Vera Scherer is a doctor who, like Sokolovsky, lives alone with her sardonic reflections on life. Volodya Pukhov, a cynical artist, paints large canvases ("Feast on a Collective Farm") to order for the government, but secretly envies his colleague Saburov, who has given up success for the lonely path of true art. And other characters are presented in terms of *private* rather than *public* life.

The technique adopted by Ehrenburg effectively conveys the main idea of *The Thaw*. Each character seems to warm up a little toward the others, each becomes less hard and "rational," more sympathetic and understanding. Each feels the need of giving and receiving love.

Ehrenburg was attacked for his revolutionary departure in *The Thaw* by no less a figure than Konstantin Simonov, who found objectionable his portrayal of the artist Vladimir Pukhov as a hack and a careerist. Simonov, with remarkable perspicacity, felt that Pukhov represented all of Soviet art and discerned Ehrenburg's intention to show him as a good character corrupted by environment: "As seen by the author," said Simonov, "Pukhov . . . is a victim who loves real art but is forced to do hack work because he has not the moral strength for heroic opposition to some enormous machine which mercilessly drags him down." Ehrenburg answered Simonov and others who attacked him, and he was at no time forced to recant or repent, but he did, in 1956, publish Part II of *The Thaw*, in which the incongruities of Soviet life as reflected in Part I tend to disappear: the true artist Saburov at last gains public recognition; the plant director Zhuravlyov has a new assignment and, while he may not be an entirely new man, he has learned a few lessons. Having once said the important things, Ehrenburg seems to have been willing to appease his critics by the relatively optimistic tone of Part II. He was awarded the Order of Lenin in 1961, on the occasion of his seventieth birthday. He died in 1967.

In order to see clearly the quality of Ehrenburg, an intellectual who, though he compromised, at last threw his weight onto the side of cultural freedom, we should compare him to Alexey N. Tolstoy (1883–1945), who was also highly successful as a literary supporter of the Stalin regime. A scion of the aristocratic Tolstoy family and a distant relative of Leo, he bore the title of Count, and though he had served with Denikin and emigrated to Paris in 1919, he was welcomed back to the Soviet Union in 1923, where his career moved forward with only occasional hindrance from those proletarian critics who attacked him as a "gentleman" and a "White Guardist." His return to the Soviet Union has been explained in various ways. Some say that, lacking principle, he abandoned the ascetic rigors of the emigration for the fleshpots of Soviet fame; but it was not as simple as that. Others explain that he belonged to the "Change of Landmarks" group of scholars and writers who accepted the current Russian regime while rejecting its Marxist ideology; but Tolstoy was much less cerebral than the "Change of Landmarks" intellectuals. He probably returned because of a special feeling for Russia which one can detect in his novels and which might be called "patriotism." Russia was still Russia, even under the Bolsheviks, and if Tolstoy could upon his return live as a kind of "workers' and peasants' Count," what was even more important for him was that he could remain a Russian "Count."

Tolstoy as a writer had a brilliant narrative flair combined with thematic versatility and a command of pellucid prose, but it is probably fair to say that he had no serious intellectual concerns. He proliferated interesting stories from Russian provincial life, and Wellsian fantasies like *Aelita* (1922), which tells of a visit to Mars by a sensitive intellectual and a crude Russian proletarian who wants to annex the planet to the Soviet; *Engineer Garin's Hyperboloid* (1925–26) in which a scientist who has invented a death ray seeks to impose his own brand of Fascism on the world; and *Blue Towns* (1925), another kind of fantasy in which a romantic idealist, the architect Buzheninov, is defeated in his conflict with philistines. *Nikita's Childhood* (1920), written while he was still in Germany, is widely regarded as his best and most genuine work. A fictionalized account of his childhood on a Russian estate, it is permeated with the charm of distant, remembered places and people, and conveys a kind of naïve joy in the recall of the most ordinary events. His most ambitious work, *The Road to Calvary*, begun in the emigration and not completed until 1941, relates the vicissitudes of a group of intellectuals who at first reject the Revolution, then learn to "accept" it. The earliest sections of the novel contain fascinating accounts of the years of hunger and war as they affected intellectual bohemians and artists, and many vivid pictures of people and events: an unforgettable portrait of the peasant anarchist leader Makhno, for instance, with his entourage of cutthroats and intellectual "idea men." The last volume shows a distinct drop in originality and power, and the novel ends on a depressing note of Soviet affirmation. His unfinished historical novel, *Peter The First* (1929–45), is the fruit of an intensive labor of love over a vast body of Russian historical evidence. Tolstoy in this novel re-created Peter and his period in concrete, realistic images which, as a result of his long study of historical sources, he easily commands. Its power as a work of historical fiction is not vitiated by the parallels Tolstoy sees between Stalin's and Peter's Russia, nor by his conscious rehabilitation of the cruel Czar. Tolstoy's deep and real feeling for Russian history converts this book into genuine art, just as his feeling for the distant "motherland" made *Nikita's Childhood* a thing of real beauty.

Tolstoy secured a place for himself with Stalin through conforming to the dictator's literary tastes and prejudices, and he made no effort to defend himself or other writers against the insane persecutions of the thirties. Ehrenburg tells of Tolstoy's behavior when in 1936 the sudden onset of a campaign against "formalist distortions" and "cynicism" created tortured consternation in the whole writers' community. Tolstoy's reaction was one of decisive and complete acquiescence in the charges and ready repentance for having himself written a "formalistic" play. Ehrenburg explains that Tolstoy wanted only "peace and quiet," and implies that Tolstoy would go to great lengths to achieve them (*New*

World, No. 4, 1962, p. 61). How far he would go became clear in 1937 when, as insurance against the purge, he produced the novel *Bread*, which falsified history in order to present Stalin as the heroic defender of Tsaritsin (Stalingrad) during the Civil War. Stalin's successors have stigmatized this work as shameless flattery, and they have even changed the name of the city.

Tolstoy lived well, enjoying, we have been told, the good food and fine wines that belonged to his station in life and his title. Ivan Bunin described him as "the Bolshevik poet laureate." He is supposed to have been so rich that Soviet banks granted him an open account upon which he could draw without limitation. In return for all this he placed his talent at the total disposition of the regime and of Stalin personally. He was a shallow man even in comparison with Ehrenburg, and compared with Pasternak his work and his thought are only ankle deep.

The Second Thaw[1]

The works we have discussed were published in the period from March, 1953, to about March, 1954. By that time the reaction of the conservatives was already under way. Their counterattack began deviously, taking the form of a series of attacks on writers for ethical and moral lapses, for scandalous behavior, public brawling, drunkenness, and other such peccadilloes. The writers attacked may indeed have been grafters, brawlers, and drunkards and a disgrace to the writers' profession, but the interesting fact is that the campaign for an improvement in their morals took the more general direction of warning writers against individualism, bohemianism and the like. Several writers, whose conduct may have been open to censure, were disgraced and expelled from the Writers' Union.

By August of 1954 the leaders of the Party had apparently decided that matters on the literary front had gotten out of hand, and vigorous action was taken to bring the writers to heel, especially since the Second Congress of writers was scheduled to take place soon and all doubts about the correct literary line should be resolved before that public event. The

editorial board of the magazine *New World* which had published much dubious material was censured and the editor
Tvardovsky removed from his post. A meeting of the col-
legium of the USSR Ministry of Culture was called to consider Zorin's play, *The Guests*. The Ministry of Culture condemned the play because "it presented an important Soviet
official as a rascal and as a typical representative of the
whole Soviet apparatus."

At the Second Congress of Soviet Writers held in December, 1954, the chief spokesman of the Party, Secretary
of the Union A. A. Surkov, reasserted the rigid Zhdanovite
line on ideological purity and insisted on the use of literature
for socialist purposes. Surkov, poet, patriot, and Stalinist to
the core, from his tribune of authority, announced that the
Party would continue to guide the work of writers, and
deplored certain recent "manifestations." But Surkov's rigidities did not fully characterize the Congress. Many writers
in their own prepared speeches spoke out freely and with
surprising frankness. And the reliable Simonov, who had replaced Tvardovsky as editor of *New World*, seemed for the
moment to have joined the dissidents. He called for a "broad-
ened" socialist realism within which greater variety might
appear; he deplored the constant revision of old novels in
the light of present needs; he called for republication of
Soviet satirists of the twenties, such as Ilf and Petrov. There
was no wholesale punishment of the dissidents, nor were there
any public apologies; and the poet Anna Akhmatova, who
had been outraged by Zhdanov, reappeared at the Congress.
Simonov's conversion was evidence that strong forces within
the Writers' Union were moving in the direction of liberalization, although the organization itself was still controlled by
old-line Stalinists. The issues between the two factions had
not at that time been settled, and the highest authority in the
Party, for the moment, held aloof from the contest.

At the Twentieth Congress of the Communist Party in
February, 1956, the Congress at which Khrushchev's speech
on the crimes of Stalin was delivered before a closed meeting, there were two speeches on literature. The first, by
Surkov, contained the time-tried formulas on the educative

function of literature, but the second, by Sholokhov, was a humorous and at times obscene attack on the pretensions of Soviet writers and on all literary generals and general secretaries. "There isn't anything," he said, "that a writer can learn from Surkov. Why do we need such leaders?"

During the year 1956 the liberals seemed confident of their own strength and that year witnessed the publication of a number of poems, plays, and stories subjecting the Soviet way of life to critical examination. Nineteen fifty-six has been called the "Year of Protest," and that it certainly was, though it was also a year of high optimism among Soviet writers as to the prospect for literary freedom. The revelation of the crimes committed by the Party and government under Stalin was the catalyst. To many Russian writers it seemed incredible that men who had accused themselves of such crimes that no moral credit was left to them would presume to guide the creative labors of poets and novelists. The Soviet writers did make an effort to free themselves from Party tutelage. During 1956 the magazine *New World*, which had earlier offended with Pomerantsev's article, published Dudintsev's *Not By Bread Alone*. Pasternak submitted his novel *Doctor Zhivago* to the editorial board of *New World*, apparently in the expectation that it might be accepted and published. This was perhaps the highest point of optimism reached during the year, and Pasternak received, not a reprimand, but a politely worded though stern letter of refusal from the editors. The second volume of the collection called *Literary Moscow* was published. *Day of Poetry, 1956* appeared. And a young writer named D. Granin published his story "One's Own Opinion." The literary product of that brief interval, which ended with the Hungarian revolt in October 1956, deserves careful scrutiny. Since the twenties Soviet writers had never been as free of official direction as they were during that year.

Neither the first nor the second thaw released any serious rebellion against the Soviet state, and it would be fruitless to look for evidence of a radical rejection of Communism or even of the basic forms of Soviet society. Though there may have been exceptions to the rule, the writers who produced the dissident literature of 1956 were loyal to the "ideals" of Communism and in rebellion only against practitioners of power who had debased those ideals. Like Zorin in *The Guests*, these writers suggest that the apparatus of the movement has fallen into the hands of opportunists who despise the people and degrade the state. An individual human being —even an individual Communist—can preserve his integrity only if he holds himself apart from a collective dominated by careerists and criminals. Such is the theme of Dudintsev, Granin, and a dozen or so poets and prose writers whose material was published in the collections already mentioned. The nature of their message explains the fact that in all of these works emphasis is placed on the freedom and responsibility of individual human beings. "You yourself must find the answer," said the poet Semyon Kirsanov. And when you have found the answer, the dissidents insist, you must take the responsibility of acting—even if you are alone. There is in all of this a tragic irony, for the ground these young men traveled with so much courage was country already discovered and explored. Thirty years earlier a controversy had arisen over the so-called "Sten Letter," published in *Young Communist Truth* in 1929, which urged the young to "check and verify on the basis of their own knowledge and experience, every decision and every policy of the Party." Sten, a publicist and educator, was accused then of inviting the young to cultivate Trotskyism and other vices. There was no reason to expect a different kind of answer in 1956.

Dudintsev's *Not By Bread Alone* is not really a very good novel. The style is simple, direct, and competent, but it is also undistinguished, and over long stretches it is flat. We expect mediocrity in Soviet writings of the postwar period, yet Dudintsev has less verbal power than a number of his contemporaries: Panova's style has lucidity and charm; both Ehrenburg and Granin have an ear for the rhythms of contemporary Russian speech. With the exception of the careerist villain, Drozdov, Dudintsev's characters do not emerge as visible images, nor can we recognize them by the sound of their voices or the inner movement of their thought and feeling. Lopatkin, the lone inventor who carries on an eight-year fight against "the system," is a fine idea but not a living being, and it is difficult to sympathize with his fanatic devotion to the centrifugal casting and mass production of large-diameter iron drainpipes. The plot has a kind of textbook simplicity; suspense is not maintained; accident or coincidence plays a vital part in the development of the story. Things happen in the novel as the result of the inner needs and purposes not of the characters but of the novelist himself, who has very much to say and manages to say it all honestly and forthrightly.

It is at first sight not easy to understand why this novel was singled out for special censure and condemned by Khrushchev for overemphasizing the negative features of Soviet life. Dudintsev's central theme was already standard fare in Soviet literature: the scientist-innovator who must fight for a new idea against vested interest had appeared in the work of Kaverin, Ehrenburg, Granin and others. In their treatment of the lone inventor at grips with monopoly these Soviet novelists have many points of contact with Mitchell Wilson, author of *My Brother My Enemy*, who is widely read, admired and imitated in the Soviet Union. And the literary attack on petty dictators had already been accepted in such things as Korneichuk's *Wings*, a popular play of the period, as part of the de-Stalinization program.

Dudintsev's call for love and mutual understanding among human beings, his insistence that the powerful must consider the rights of men lower in the scale, his dictum that a man must speak his mind regardless of consequences when the right is at stake—all of these ideas had formed the principal substance of Soviet literature since Ehrenburg's *The Thaw* appeared in 1954. Where, then, did Dudintsev go off the ideological rails?

Dudintsev's novel presents a conflict between an individual who has a vital idea and a Soviet collective dominated by men whose chief interest is in protecting their own preserves and furthering their own careers. And the novelist, discarding approved literary clichés, honestly faced his hero's problem. Drozdov and his cronies who dominate the collective are able to frustrate him at every turn and even imprison him on fabricated evidence. He is ultimately freed through the efforts of individuals who act independently, and in one case violate Soviet law, in order to see justice finally done. The official euphemisms which cover the abuse of power are resolutely abandoned in this novel. The phrase "cult of the individual" does not appear even once, and when a character, in order to account for a bureaucrat's behavior, uses the formula "survivals of capitalism," the effect is clearly ironical. Careerists and opportunists appear in this novel as an indigenous Soviet growth and as creatures of the Soviet power system. To present the problem in these terms was Dudintsev's first "mistake" and the Soviet writers' "collective," the Union of Writers, dominated by A. A. Surkov, insisted that Dudintsev "see" his mistake.

Not only is the novel a defense of the rights of the individual against entrenched and irresponsible power, but it also exposes to ridicule and shame the vulgar materialistic standards and low cultural level of the barbarians who wield this power. In the best tradition of Russian revolutionary literature Dudintsev derides them for their bourgeois attachment to creature comforts, for their fine clothing, lavishly furnished apartments, television sets, sleek black limousines, and all the rest. The hero Lopatkin could have had all of these things if he had been sensible, given up his original idea, and joined the "collective," but he chose instead his own way, the "endless, austere road" where he remained poor but independent, and free to work out his own thought. There are some interesting remarks on independence and freedom in the novel. Speaking of his trip to the Siberian labor camp, Lopatkin says, "No need to fear journeys. Anyone who is afraid of travel of course will not go. But in that case he will not get far either." And again, "The words *deprivation of liberty* are inaccurate. Whoever has learned to think cannot be completely deprived of liberty." Dudintsev's second "mistake" was that he portrayed the managerial group as a kind of "new class" with values that set them apart from the people and interests that have nothing to do with basic human values, such as freedom, equality, individual integrity. The exceptions to the rule are occasional idealistic individuals who refuse to conform to the values of "vulgar Communism." And the ending is not a hopeful one. The Drozdovs are still in power and the issue is in doubt.

Perhaps the most damaging accusation brought against the Drozdovs is that they are "worker ants" who jealously guard their anthill against the intrusion of strong and original individuals. In a speech which might be an echo of Sutyrin's remarks to Mayakovsky upon his entrance into RAPP, Drozdov expressed his distrust of "cranks and geniuses":

> "You know, Comrade Lopatkin, if I were a writer, I would write a novel about you. Because you are a truly tragic figure. You are the impersonation of a whole epoch, and one which has irretrievably disappeared into the past. You are a hero, but a solitary one. . . . We can see through you, but you don't understand us. You don't understand, for example, that we can get along without your invention, even if it is a genuine and great invention. We can do without it, and, just imagine! without suffering any loss at all. . . . Our designers' and technicians' collectives will find a solution. And this solution will be better than yours, because collective efforts always lead to the quickest and best solution of any problem. The collective is more of a genius than any individual genius. . . . We worker ants are necessary, while you solitary geniuses with your great ideas standing on feeble legs are not necessary."

Dudintsev's novel caused a sensation in Moscow, and when it was translated into Western languages it was widely read throughout the world.

There were many heated discussions of the novel in the days immediately following its publication, evidence that the issues it raised went to the heart of Soviet life. Many of the arguments turned on the question whether "the Drozdovs" were presented in the novel as typical or as exceptional, and the final authoritative judgment, pronounced by Khrushchev himself, was that Dudintsev had exaggerated and "generalized." But before the official mind was made up, the public discussion of the work occasioned some frank speaking. The writer Konstantin Paustovsky's speech on "the Drozdovs" was the high point of that discussion:

> This is a new group of acquisitive carnivores, a group which has nothing in common either with the Revolution, or with our regime, or with socialism. . . .
> There are thousands of these Drozdovs and we should not close our eyes to their existence. Dudintsev's great merit lies in the fact that he has struck a blow at the most vital link in the chain. He speaks of the most terrible phenomenon in our society, a phenomenon to which we cannot at any price close our eyes, unless we are willing to allow these Drozdovs to overrun our entire country.

The collection of fiction, poetry, and criticism published in *Literary Moscow*, II (1956) was a deliberate reproach to the forces that have dominated Soviet literature since the thirties. In it were published a story of Ivan Katayev, who perished in a labor camp; the notebooks of Yury Olesha, who had been silent for almost twenty years; Ehrenburg's sympathetic introduction to a projected volume of verse by Marina Tsvetayeva, who committed suicide in 1941; some sharp commentary on Soviet drama and literary criticism by Mark Shcheglov and Alexander Kron; the short stories "Levers" by Alexander Yashin and "A Journey Home" by Nikolai Zhdanov, which expose the effects on human beings of life in the "apparatus"; and many other disturbing items.

Daniel Granin's story "One's Own Opinion," published in *New World*, dealt in a single sharply focused episode with the demoralizing psychological effects of conformity to the pressure of power.

A number of poems published in *Literary Moscow*, II, in *Day of Poetry* (1956) and in other literary magazines embodied like themes: Semyon Kirsanov's "Seven Days of the Week," an allegory on the need for honest human hearts, Yevgeny Yevtushenko's examination of his own conscience, *Stantsia Zima,* and his poem of hope for the future, "I Know Not." The most passionate statement published of the revulsion felt by the literary community at the debasement of literature was V. Goncharov's poem, "I Hate":

I hate the retouchers,
There's nothing more horrible
Than their work—
For money they'll put
Truth itself to death.
A child is weeping—
But always ready at hand
Is a sly scalpel,
And the boy
Suddenly
To everyone's joy
Is smiling.
There's a dwarf
Who never grew up.
But that's no matter.
It's all quite easy.
Here he is!
Bigger than life
And higher than
The poet's honor.
And there's the dull face

Of a murderer and scoundrel;
Again the instrument
And whose portrait is it?
Our friend and comrade!
I hate the retouchers
Of the day's own light.
They're ready
To mask
The planet itself.
But what about us?
We laugh and cry—
We are the children of light.
The planet
Is dear to us
Without ornament.
No matter how you retouch it
The earth
Is still the earth.
You know the truth,
And like your own heart
It's always with you.

The last line of Goncharov's poem might serve as an emblem of the literary thaw. "The truth is like your own heart—it's always with you" states in a single image the thought that pervades the works of that period. The men who produced them felt anger, not only at the deception that had been practiced on them, but at themselves for allowing it, and they appeal to individual human minds and hearts to judge truth hereafter for themselves and act on their judgment. This new thought in Soviet literature seems a belated echo of French existentialist thought. It was perhaps inevitable that the idea of an individual human being as both free and responsible should have occurred to many thoughtful people when the crimes committed in their name by the "collective" had become known, just as in France during the period of national degradation an escape from collective guilt seemed to offer itself through individual will and action. The fact that, during the Stalin period, men of talent and reputation had supported oppressive policies that damaged literature as a whole and destroyed human beings could be explained only by the absence from Soviet life of a sense of individual responsibility. The latent purpose of the works examined here was to revive in individuals a feeling of involvement in collective deeds. The message is insistent. The managers of collective farms should not be "levers" in the hands of a higher echelon, but human beings with minds of their own; a man who insists on his own idea may be valuable, even though he seems a "crank" and "troublemaker"; it is important not only to have "one's own opinion," but to express and defend it; and the real heroes are those who even though alone carry the good fight against "the Drozdovs"— whose number is legion.

The "Drozdovs" soon reacted. Khrushchev's program to denigrate Stalin and those who had been close to him in the recent past had required a certain latitude for criticism, but there was always a danger that criticism would get out of hand, that negative characters might be treated not as deviations from the norm but as something inherent in "our Soviet reality," and that demands for radical reform of that reality would then be heard. The delicate power balance in which the leadership found itself explains the pattern of vacillation which we have observed: the relaxation of 1954 was followed by reassertion of control and the branding of certain kinds of criticism as out of bounds; the new relaxation following the Twentieth Congress, which reached its high point in 1956, was ended soon after the Hungarian revolt in November of that year. The fact that Hungarian Communist intellectuals had a prominent part in that revolt was not lost on the Party leadership, and Khrushchev, in talks with Soviet writers during the early months of 1957, assured them that if anything of the sort happened in the Soviet Union "he would know what to do with them, and his hand would not tremble."

At meetings of the Writers' Union the limits of permissible criticism were more or less clearly marked out, and writers who had overstepped those limits were named and invited to recant their errors. Among these were Dudintsev, Granin, N. Zhdanov, Yashin, and the editors of *Literary Moscow*, II (1956), Margarita Aliger and Venyamin Kaverin. They were not easily brought to heel. They sat silent at meetings called for the express purpose of "clarifying their position." As late as May, 1957, Khrushchev complained that Dudintsev and Aliger had not reacted "properly" to criticism. The fact that they remained free and unharmed was evidence that there had been real changes since the days of Stalin.

Events, however, did not favor the dissidents. After the first sputnik was launched in October, 1957, the authority of the Party in literature was to some extent rehabilitated. Some of the rebels of 1956, the poetess Aliger, for instance, who had incurred the displeasure of Khrushchev for her failure to acknowledge errors, submitted declarations of complete loyalty only a few days after the launching. Evidence of astounding scientific progress, provided by the first artificial satellite, seemed to weaken the case of those writers who had attacked the bureaucracy as hostile to new ideas and an impediment to progress. The answer to Dudintsev's novel was given by Victor Shklovsky, the formalist critic of the twenties, when he said: "The earth's gravity has been overcome, and signals are coming to us from the first cosmic laboratory in history. ... What we find in Dudintsev's novel is directly contradicted by the great scientific events which followed its publication."

Yet the struggle for the right to write one's own thoughts continued. The year 1957 saw the publication of the novel *Cruelty*, by Pavel Nilin, which has been translated into English under the title *Comrade Venka*. That novel, which relates the adventures in Siberia of two young Soviet detectives, is a well-made, exciting adventure story. We find in it something only rarely provided by Soviet literature: a thoroughly absorbing plot structure. And it is interesting, also, on the moral plane. Nilin's hero, Comrade Venka, is an idealistic young Communist whose simple idea of justice and human decency comes into conflict with the cynical cruelty of the power he serves. Rather than go on serving it Comrade Venka, a warm and appealing character, ends his life.

The Khrushchev regime has felt it necessary to discredit the liberals of 1956 with the Russian masses. It has done this in a number of ways. In 1958 a novel appeared in an important literary magazine, authored by the editor of the

Literary Gazette, V. Kochetov. *The Yershov Brothers* was not only an answer to Dudintsev's *Not By Bread Alone* but a primitive and savage attack on the liberal intellectuals who perpetrated the rebellion against Party controls in literature. Its devices are so transparent, and its dishonesty so palpable and repellent, that even *Pravda*, while approving its ideological position, complained that it lacked "artistry." The author underlines his thesis on every page. He sees two tendencies struggling in the Soviet Union, the socialist tendency which promises a bright future for all mankind, and the dark forces represented by the "intellectuals" and "aesthetes" who are at war with the future and who preach individualism, egoism, and hatred of humanity.

Khrushchev indicated that affairs in the literary world had reached a satisfactory posture in his speech at the Third Congress of Soviet Writers in 1959. He casually rehabilitated several writers who had been under a cloud and announced that "angels of reconciliation" were on the wing. His new liberalism was based on the assumption that those writers who had taken false ideological positions had abandoned them. In calling for an end to attacks against writers like Dudintsev who had "generalized the negative aspects" of Soviet life Khrushchev emphasized that those writers had seen the error of their ways and "you shouldn't kick a man when he's down." Khrushchev's speech to the writers was offhand, rambling, studded with proverbial wisdom, and cheerfully ignorant of all literature. It was liberal in Soviet terms, but it contained a crudely dogmatic statement of the Party's demand for ideological support from the writers and betrayed no sympathy for their recent examination of conscience.

The Way of Pasternak

Boris Pasternak, whose world renown was one of the accidents of the thaw, stands as a refutation of Lenin's famous dictum, "It is impossible to live in a society and be free of it." To a degree he did preserve his inner freedom while managing to live as a Soviet citizen. Yet, at the same time, and paradoxically, he is vitally bound to Soviet history and to contemporary Russian literature. Pasternak cannot be imagined apart from the formalists and the Futurists, and his fate as a writer is bound up with the tragic misadventures of the Stalin period. He has influenced many "accepted" Russian poets, and the better ones have been ready to acknowledge that influence.

The literary historian Prince D. S. Mirsky, writing in 1926, maintained that Pasternak was at that time acknowledged among Russian poets as the greatest living member of their fraternity, and Bukharin, at the First Congress of Soviet Writers in 1934, called him "the greatest poetic master of our times." Displaying great insight, Bukharin went on to say that Pasternak's subjective apprehension of the world enabled him to produce original, but overly personal, images and metaphors. Chastely secluded within the poetic laboratory of his own mind, the poet, according to Bukharin, labored meticulously over the verbal form of his thoughts, memories, and associations, and produced poetry rich with intellectual experience, but necessarily narrow and individual.

Bukharin's analysis of Pasternak was both perceptive and fair, though the Marxist theoretician mistakenly sets up an implicit requirement that any poet, even a "laboratory worker," be consciously involved in social life. Pasternak's "noninvolvement" was a necessary condition of his own, possibly more important, work. Early in life he embraced poetry, not as a trade but as a vocation, not to produce useful linguistic artifacts but to discover new truth and new beauty. He not only worked at this calling, but lived it, and this meant a certain estrangement from the world of immediate relevance, the world, that is, of established truth and old beauty. He was odd; he did and said strange things. Ehrenburg records that when he attended a Writers' Conference in Paris, Pasternak maintained his own eccentric daily schedule, with breakfast at two and very late dinners. He once took the floor at a meeting of the Russian Association of Proletarian Writers in the early thirties to make a speech in defense of genius and to chide the organization for tending to reduce all writers to common terms. In his autobiography *Safe Conduct*, his experience of the cataclysmic years from 1914 to 1920 is covered in three words: "Six years passed." His Zhivago-like noninvolvement in the external events of his time had in it, perhaps, an element of purely Russian *khitrost'*, that cynical wisdom which makes for survival in difficult times. For Pasternak not only survived the cruel warfare of his time, but, unobtrusively and as though by accident, he prospered. Many stories have been told to explain this, but the basic reason was no doubt his unfeigned indifference to all significant issues of the immediate present. Charming and childlike in manner, Pasternak did not fit anyone's notion of an "enemy," and his friends are as one in testifying that his warmth of human love was broad enough to include even the cruel maniac Stalin, grieving over his dead wife. Had he been in touch with the real world in the period of the literary "thaw" he would probably not have submitted his novel, *Doctor Zhivago*, for publication in the Soviet Union. That novel, while it was a triumph of poetic creation, fell short at precisely that point where Pasternak abandoned his subjective stance and commented directly on events and issues. In those pages of direct commentary he betrays the effect on him of the long exile inside himself.

Pasternak records in his autobiography that his first love was music, which he gave up for philosophy, and that his interest in poetry grew out of his experiences in Marburg as a pupil of the neo-Kantian philosopher Cohen. Like the young Blok, whose flirtation with *Sophia*, the Divine Wisdom, was an adventure in epistemology, Pasternak's concern as a poet is with the nature of knowledge. The *method* of Pasternak's quest for truth and beauty was not consonant with philosophy as a discipline. He belonged as a younger member to the generation of Russian artists—Scriabin, Bely, Blok—who seek ultimate truth not through the strict mediation of the reason, but through intuition, association, suggestion, image, and metaphor. Through the medium of poetic language Pasternak investigates, invents, and foreshadows new paths in the human apprehension of truth. He unlocks possibilities in the mind that may not yet be reducible to the categories so far discovered. "Locked in his laboratory," to paraphrase Bukharin, Pasternak carried on research, so to speak, in the nature and extent of the human resources that are available in the quest for truth. Pasternak's description of the room in Marburg where he wrote papers on philosophical themes suggests (as he would say) his method:

But from my very ardor an experienced observer would have said that I would never make a learned man. I lived through the learning of a subject much more intensely than the theme warranted. A kind of plantlike cerebration took root in me. Its characteristic lay in the fact that any secondary concepion unfolding excessively in my interpretation would begin to demand nourishment and care, and when, under its influence, I turned to books, I was drawn to them not from any disinterested attraction for knowledge, but for literary quotations to its advantage. In spite of the fact that my work was accomplished with the aid of logic, imagination, paper and ink, I liked it best of all because the more I wrote the more it became overgrown with a constantly thickening ornamentation of bookish citations and comparisons. But since a time limit compelled me at a given moment to renounce written extracts and as a substitute simply to leave my authors open at the places I needed, a time arrived when the theme of my work materialised and could be reviewed at a glance from the threshold of the room. It lay outstretched across the room rather like a tree fern which spreads its leafy coils over the table, the divan and the windowsill. To disorder them meant to break the thread of my argument, but a complete tidying up would be equivalent to burning an uncopied manuscript. The landlady had been strictly forbidden to lay a hand on them. Towards the end my room was not even cleaned. And when I imagined the appearance of my room . . . I really saw my philosophy incarnate and also its probable fate.

In his autobiographical remarks and prose works Pasternak frequently reverts to the definition of art. The following concerns the genesis of art:

We cease to recognize reality. It appears to us in some new category. And this category seems a condition belonging to it rather than to us. Apart from this condition everything else in the world has been named. New and unnamed is it alone. We try to name it. The result is art. . . .

The clearest, most memorable and important thing about

art is its inception, and the finest of the world's production, dealing with the most diverse things, are really telling of their own birth.

One of the basic features of a work of art is, therefore, the question that called it forth, the new form or quality or condition, whether in reality or in ourselves, presented to the mind as a problem of naming. Pasternak's literary life is a record of concern with such problems, and that is why he is important. Pasternak does not describe what is already known and named—that he leaves to the writers of socialist novels. Instead he concerns himself with naming what is as yet unnamed. His work as a "Soviet writer" is like Olesha's tree that grew out of concrete, or, as McLean suggests, like a mastodon perfectly preserved in a cold Siberian waste, or like a rich jewel in an Ethiop's ear.

The novel that crowned his artistic labor, *Doctor Zhivago*, had an original fate. He completed it at the end of 1955, after working on it for about twenty years. A chapter had been published in 1938 in the *Literary Gazette* under the title "Fragment of a Novel." No more was seen in print until 1954 when there appeared in the magazine *Znamya* (*The Banner*) the set of poems which make up the last chapter of the novel. Early in 1956 Pasternak submitted it to the Soviet magazine *New World*, the editors of which, as we have seen, politely but firmly rejected it. Considering the nature of the novel, their criticism was a model of restraint. Since he could not publish it in the Soviet Union Pasternak offered it to a Milanese publisher, Feltrinelli, who brought it out in an Italian translation in 1957. Urgent messages reached him from Alexey Surkov of the Union of Soviet Writers, and from Pasternak himself, asking that it not be published but returned for, as they put it, "revisions." These messages the publisher ignored.

The novel was then translated from Pasternak's Russian manuscript into French and English, and it was published in the United States in September, 1958. Finally, by arrangement with the Italian publisher, who holds the rights to the manuscript, the novel was published in Russian by the University of Michigan press at Ann Arbor. The history of publication of *Doctor Zhivago* parallels in many respects that of Zamyatin's *We*, which was never published in the Soviet Union, published first in an English translation, then translated into Czech, partially translated from Czech back into Russian, and finally published in Russian in the United States. Pasternak was awarded the Nobel Prize in 1958, *Doctor Zhivago* became a *cause célèbre* in the West, and, like Dudintsev's *Not By Bread Alone*, was employed as a psychological weapon in the cold war. Pasternak, like Dudintsev, publicly deplored this outcome, and there is no reason to doubt the sincerity of his statements. Indeed, the last irony of his life was this use of his finest literary art for political advantage.

Zhivago is a poetic novel. The body of the work, written in poetic prose, relates the misadventures of the hero on the stage of history and his tragic fate; the last chapter is a collection of poems, which constitute Zhivago's real work. The hero was Hamlet-like in his refusal to undertake official actions or to involve himself in public affairs that needed to be set right, and so the plot of his life is spun by the actions of those others who thirst for mundane power. In every important crisis Zhivago temporizes, yields, retreats from action. His life in historical terms is a failure. Even his doctor's skill has not been put to use. He has had two families, but took care of neither, and the woman he loved he surrendered to a scoundrel who could save her life. Yet Zhivago's testament, his thin volume of poetry, is assembled and preserved as a special revelation by his friends and followers. The life that he lived had little importance; the life that he created in art was a priceless treasure bequeathed to all men.

Zhivago is, then, a final statement by Pasternak on his own life and creation, and it is no wonder that he risked much in order to have it published. The poet insists that creatures like himself who produce nothing of immediate use value, do have a use. The originality and strangeness of the poet's view of things may contain the germ of new thought. Yury Zhivago's power of *intuition* is underlined in the novel;

he is a "thinker, and a seeker, a man of a creative and artistic frame of mind," but one whose thoughts do not move along direct, logical lines. And in order to think thoughts that are his own Zhivago holds himself at a distance from state, community, and family; he finds a refuge from movements and parties, with their purposeful and ephemeral jargon. And perhaps everyone needs a "Siberian retreat," such as Zhivago's *Varykino*, where the poet gives birth to thoughts and images which are themselves pregnant with new birth. But then a problem arises. If you cut yourself off from the social body how will you survive? How can the individual human being, however precious his unrepeatable experiments in the laboratory of thought, survive outside of society? Pasternak's answer is a poet's answer and is rather whimsical. He suggests that there are more things in heaven and earth (Horatio!) than are dreamed of in your philosophy. Magic and miracle are not to be ruled out, and marvelous coincidences may alter history or save a life. In his autobiography *Safe Conduct* Pasternak relates that his own life was saved in Moscow in 1920 when an old Marburg friend miraculously turned up, and, an even greater miracle, as a member of the Party and an official in a commissariat. ". . . Time is permeated with the unity of life's events," he wrote of another such occasion, "that is, with the crisscross movement of the hypnosis of being." Magic and miracle are "the Lord's way" of providing. Zhivago has, not *one* guardian angel, but two, who can provide for him because in some mysterious way they have power with the regime. San Donato (of which Samdeviatov is a corruption) turns up when needed to take care of Zhivago's material needs, and Zhivago's half-brother Yevgraf, who gives him spiritual advice and preserves his testament, was sent to him from above, as the account of his first appearance makes very clear:

Footsteps sounded above him. Someone was coming down the stairs, stopping frequently, as though hesitating. At one point, he actually changed his mind and ran up again. A door opened somewhere and two voices welled out, so distorted by echoes that it was impossible to tell whether men or women were speaking. Then the door banged and the same steps ran down, this time resolutely.

Yurii Andreievich was absorbed in his paper and had not meant to look up, but the stranger stopped so suddenly at the foot of the stairs that he raised his head.

Before him stood a boy of about eighteen in a reindeer cap and a stiff reindeer coat worn, as in Siberia, fur side out. He was dark and had narrow Kirghiz eyes. His face had an aristocratic quality, the fugitive spark and reticent delicacy that give an impression of remoteness and are sometimes found in people of a complex, mixed parentage.

Thereafter, Yevgraf also is at hand when needed, and at the end, at no loss to his saintly character, he has become a major general in the Red Army and a figure of real power. A symbolic meaning in Yevgraf has been seen by most of the commentators on *Zhivago*. Edmund Wilson, for instance, constructs a system of religious symbolism out of the details of his characterization. Whether one accepts or not the religious symbolism suggested by the American critics of *Zhivago*, both Yevgraf and Samdeviatov stand as symbols of a force that maintains and cares for us and toward which every human being should feel gratitude.

In Pasternak's world miracles do take place, and that is the simple explanation of the fact that there are in the novel *Zhivago* many coincidences of low mathematical verisimilitude. Pasternak is not concerned with mathematical but with symbolic truth. The miraculous chances on which the plot of *Zhivago* turns symbolize the intertwining of all lives in the common human web; they represent also the role of the unpredictable in human life. Not every chance can be foreseen and worked into a rational plan for "remaking" the world, as the Bolsheviks would have it. Every new individual is an unforeseeable accident. Life, like art, is autonomous and rich in chances.

Zhivago's poems, which make up the final chapter of the novel, are the Doctor's real and substantial contribution to life. Some commentators have attempted to show a connection between the poems and specific events and characters of the novel, and ingenious efforts have been made to tie certain poems to particular themes of the novel. Labor such as this remains unrewarded. Pasternak himself provided the key to the poems when he introduced them in 1954: "Zhivago's thoughts are expressed in a set of poems which constitute the final chapter of the novel." Those poems are Zhivago's created vision. The central and persistent thought in them is the renewal of life, symbolized by the passion and burial of Christ and the triumph of resurrection.

The prose of Pasternak is a poet's prose, as Jakobson insists. Rich with metaphor and symbol, it grows out of the normal rhythms of spoken Russian. Pasternak suggests through subtle variations of diction and idiom distinctions of personality, changes of mood, personal idiosyncrasy, geographical differences, class gradations. There is a language typical of Bolsheviks, formal, logical and tending to the "dead letter"; and that language is contrasted with the live rhythms of poetry and of untrammeled thought.

In *Zhivago* Pasternak has given us God's plenty in the form of an infinite variety of "names." Like the first man in the Garden of Eden, he names everything he sees. And the novel *Zhivago* creates an apprehension of love and beauty, and joyful optimism at the prospect of living.

Chapter 12

Another Thaw?

The Literary Parties

THE ONE IMPORTANT CHANGE in the literary world since the death of Stalin is the tolerance of disagreement and debate. This is apparent in spite of Surkov's authoritarian pronouncements on "socialist realism," or Kochetov's primitive novelistic patriotism, or Khrushchev's crude demands. When Ehrenburg's *The Thaw* was published in 1954 there were differing opinions as to its merits, lively public debate took place, and the principle was enunciated by Simonov that "the author has a right to argue with his critics." The publication of Dudintsev's *Not By Bread Alone* in 1956 was the occasion for violent disagreement. A discussion of the novel was held in a jam-packed auditorium, and according to reports, those who could not get into the auditorium climbed ladders placed against the walls and listened through the windows.

The existence of more than one "party" and more than one idea in Soviet literature was recognized at the Twentieth Congress of the Communist Party in 1956, when reports from the literary field were delivered to the delegates by Alexey Surkov and Mikhail Sholokhov. Sholokhov not only took issue with Surkov, but covered him with ridicule, to the loud amusement of the delegates, whose "laughter and prolonged applause" is immortalized in the stenographic report.[1] This was the first time since 1930 that two opposing viewpoints in literature had been represented at a Party Congress. At the Sixteenth Congress in that year a report on the state of literature had been presented by a leader of RAPP, Kirshon; then a poem attacking the slogans of the leadership was read to the delegates by a member of an opposing literary faction, Bezymensky. Revived in 1956, the practice of recognizing and presenting to the delegates two opposing viewpoints in literature was again in evidence at the Twenty-second Congress of the Party in 1961, when reports were given by Vsevolod Kochetov and Alexander Tvardovsky, a leader of the liberals, who had been removed as editor of *New World* in 1954 for publishing Pomerantsev's article "On Sincerity in Literature." It is significant of the political trend that he was restored to the editorship in 1958 and awarded a Lenin Prize in 1961. Tvardovsky's speech at the Congress called for a literature sincerely engaged with the life of real people and free of political tutelage; Kochetov's rejoinder reminded the delegates of the past achievements of "socialist realism" and demanded a literature permeated with Communist ideas and presenting heroic perspectives.

The debate continued and the "parties" formed. By the early sixties the two main factions were clearly identified as to personnel and principles. Literary publications tended to belong to one or the other "party." At opposite extremes are the very conservative and neo-Stalinist *Neva* and Tvardovsky's liberal *New World*. The magazine *Youth* is liberal and publishes excellent stories by new writers, while *Moscow* and *October* are generally conservative and in their criticism deplore the "bare realism" and "naturalism" of much contemporary writing. Novels and stories dealing with contemporary life sometimes offer evidence that the lines of dispute are well established and factional symbols widely recognized. In a novel called *The Ends of the Earth* (1961), by Ivan Shevtsov, the "positive" heroes visit the Russian Museum, which is devoted to Russian art, read the magazine *Neva*, and bear simple Russian names. The negative character prefers the Hermitage (the postimpressionists), reads *New World* and *Foreign Literature*, and has a name that is not quite Russian, along with thick brows and a slightly hooked nose. The liberal wing is thus crudely identified with intellectual sophistication and "cosmopolitan" tastes.

The existence of factions explains the apparently vacillating literary policies of the Party since 1954. Probably for the first time since the twenties opposing literary groups were able to make their influence felt, and Khrushchev leaned first toward one, then toward the other.

The present writer had an opportunity, not long after the Twentieth Congress of the Party, to meet leading representatives of both the liberal and conservative parties in literary administration. On successive days interviews were arranged in the Writers' Union with Boris Polevoy and A. A. Surkov. It was evident that Polevoy, the author of *The Story of a Real Man*, who is usually regarded as a routine "socialist realist" if not a hack, was actually of the liberal school. Surkov was of course clearly identifiable with a firm policy of control.

Polevoy was at that time an important member of the Executive Board of the Union of Writers, while Surkov was First Secretary; the allotment of these posts seemed also to reflect a split in outlook and policy within the Party itself.

Polevoy's personality provided a shock of surprise. His books prepare one to meet a competent but dull purveyor of heroic personalities and perspectives, but he is quick, clever, and breezy in manner. He is a combination of Jack London (his favorite writer) and a proletarian Jim Tully. His hair is recalcitrant to the comb; his suit, though of excellent material, was casually worn, and somewhat crumpled; he wore no tie, and his shirt—also of fine material—was open at the neck. Very friendly to foreign guests, he produced a bottle of Armenian cognac for their entertainment. Refreshments appeared. He invited "tough questions" and "abuse." He defended his novel *The Story of a Real Man* against the charge that it lacked human verisimilitude. Everything in it, he said, was based on accounts of actual events given him by living people. Images of selfless devotion to work in Soviet novels—the example he used was Krymov's *Tanker Derbent*—he insisted were "realistic," and would not seem exaggerated to anyone who knew the desperate poverty of those days and the need to give oneself completely to labor. The transformation on the tanker *Derbent* of a shiftless gang of individualists into a disciplined crew was not an exaggeration: such things happen to people, he said, when they are under great emotional pressure. Among Soviet satirists Polevoy thought highly of Ilf and Petrov but disparaged Zoshchenko. Challenged on his statement that Zoshchenko "satirized Soviet life from the viewpoint of the philistine" by the argument that it is precisely the Soviet philistine that Zoshchenko satirizes, Polevoy did not pursue the argument, saying that many people, even in the Writers' Union, did not agree with him on Zoshchenko, and "everyone has the right to his own opinion." His remarks and gestures betrayed honest indifference to Zoshchenko, who did not take "an advanced socialist position." "But," said Polevoy, "he's being republished, and people read him." Yury Olesha's allotment of "criticism" was an indifferent shrug. He had never accepted the role of educator; his theme was the lost intellectual in conflict with the new order and his work has little interest for the new generation. But "he's being published, too." Toward those writers whose sophisticated literary style has attracted attention in the West, Boris Polevoy expressed not distrust or contempt but only indifference. He thinks of himself as an educator of the masses. "Realism" he understands as an effort not only to portray reality but to influence its development. Of literature as a craft or a vocation he apparently has no notion whatever. Yet the views he expressed were, by the standards of the Soviet literary administrator, liberal in the extreme, especially his insistently tolerant statement, "You have your opinion and I have mine."

Alexey Surkov was a very different man. He fitted well his two roles of Party poet and implacable critic. He tends to be strict and correct in speech and manner. Rather short and neatly dressed in a blue-gray business suit properly buttoned, he wore a tie and gold-rimmed spectacles. His greeting was stiffly formal, complete with quick bow and brief, cold handshake. Almost, but not quite, a heel-click. The military attitude intruded itself in his bearing and conversation. There was no cognac for us and no refreshments. He waited for the first question, an easy one about the discussion then going on regarding the "varnishing of reality," then gave his answer in the form of a speech suitable for platform delivery and not to be interrupted. While Polevoy had invited objections, Surkov allowed no time for them. The tendency to "pretty up" reality he explained as a symptom of the youth both of Soviet literature and of the Soviet state. For a young and

struggling society *affirmation* is more important than criticism. He thought American literature "in its period of youth"
exhibited the same tendencies. Rapidly changing "reality"
explained the difficulty Soviet writers found in orienting themselves. The fact that for so many years the Soviet Union
had been at "war" explained its need for a positive, affirma-
tive literature. The war against "imperialist intervention"
lasted until 1921, the war against the neobourgeois lasted
through the twenties, the war against the kulaks began
in the early thirties, and these violent campaigns were only
a prologue to the great war against Fascism and, though he
did not say this, the "cold war" against "American imperi-
alism." The note of military urgency was strong in the content and manner of his talk. His metaphors and illustrative
examples were taken in many cases from the military life.
"Soviet literature is loud and assertive because in time of war
one doesn't urge on the soliders with Brahms melodies." The
difficulty some Soviet writers had in accepting the liquidation
of the kulaks arose from the fact that they didn't understand
"we were at war with them."

Surkov, like Polevoy, was hospitable in his way, but his
long and vigorous speech, delivered without interruptions to
two Americans in a small room, was somewhat chilling. Even
during the great Moscow thaw, with the theme of every slogan
"peace and coexistence," one felt the presence of narrowly
intransigent ideological forces, for whom that thaw was a temporary and probably unwelcome diversion of their strength.
This very same emphasis on literature as a weapon in the
struggle is to be found in the novels of V. Kochetov, published in 1958 and 1961.

Both Polevoy and Surkov impressed one as equally loyal
to the Party program, but Polevoy seemed to move in circles
that have knowledge of the outside world. Surkov, and those
like him, can preserve the purity of their faith only by isolat-
ing themselves in their own world.

New Voices

The difference in attitude and approach observed in two
high administrators of the Writers' Union was significant of

basic and far-reaching changes in the apparatus of power it-self, and subsequent events confirmed that tolerance of dis-agreement within broadly defined limits was the order of the day in Soviet literature. Proof that this liberal tendency would continue, and that parties would continue to exist, was the election of Konstantin Fedin, a writer whose career began in the Serapion Brotherhood, as First Secretary of the Union at the Third Congress in 1959, while the main report at that Congress was given by Surkov, who was elected a member of the powerful Secretariat.

The practical result of the policy of tolerance was the ap-pearance of a new accent in Soviet literature. This new accent is to be heard in the stories and poems of some older figures but is characteristic of many young writers who are starting their careers. They do not represent the dominant trend, which is still conventional socialist realism, but there are enough swallows, so to speak, to make a summer. After examining some characteristic novels and stories of the period, it should be possible to make a tentative generalization as to the nature and probable outcome of the new trends.[2]

The oldest of the writers clearly identified with new trends is Venyamin Kaverin, who was one of the editors of *Literary Moscow* (1956), where the third volume of his trilogy *Open Book—Searches and Hopes* was published. The trilogy de-tails the life history of a Soviet woman medical researcher, and the third volume tells of her struggle against careerists in medicine who employ every means including political slander to hinder her work on the development of penicillin. Kaverin was attacked in 1957 for having presented the Soviet scientific scene in dark colors. His story "A Piece of Glass," published in *New World* (1960, No. 8), describes an episode in the life of a young research scientist on a visit to Lenin-grad to obtain a rare kind of glass necessary for his experi-ments. Immersed completely in his scientific work, Uglov is unprepared for the emotional problems he encounters and unable to deal with the personal rivalries that beset his simple quest. His two-dimensional method for dealing with problems is not wholly adequate, and a third dimension, the dimension of personality, is indicated as lacking. He does not understand how his own emotions work—he doesn't "know himself," and therefore finds it difficult to understand others. The story manages to convey the idea that art, music, and literature can be a help in developing such understanding.

Victor Nekrasov, who achieved both popularity and controversial status in 1946 with his war novel *In the Trenches of Stalingrad,* has recently published two interesting and original stories. His war novel is noteworthy for the relative lack of either explicitly patriotic or ideological motifs. Told in the first person from the viewpoint of a participant in the battle, it describes, not heroic events or characters, but the "gray workdays," so to speak, of a Soviet battle unit. The events of each day are experienced directly by his characters, who tend to lose sight of the larger meaning of the war. His story "The Second Night" (*New World,* 1960, No. 5) is focused on a single emotional experience in battle. A sensitive young man has killed a German soldier on a night raid. The belongings of the German include a wallet containing photographs of the young man and his girl friend. The picture of the man he has just killed, a man so much like himself, upsets the young soldier. He is repelled by the callous indifference of his comrades. To his captain, who urges him to drink to the success of the mission, he says simply, "May I leave now, Comrade Captain?" The story strikes a note of compassion for the fallen enemy as a man like oneself, and feelings of brotherhood extend even to the Germans. Such things have been rare in Soviet war stories.

Nekrasov's "Kira Georgievna" (*New World,* 1961, No. 6) is an exploration of emotional indifference in a woman whose deepest feelings have been wounded too many times. Her husband had been exiled on a false charge, and this experience among others has so crippled her that she has at last reached that state in which emotions are not felt but only toyed with. She has learned the knack of avoiding real emotional involvement. Like so much of contemporary writing, this story is concerned with an individual's inner life, but in this case that inner life is damaged, perhaps beyond repair, and Kira is not likely to improve.

A story by B. Bedny, "The Girls" (*The Banner,* 1961,

Nos. 7–9), also deals with the problem of emotionally deprived young people whose feelings do not measure up even to barely civilized standards. But the heroine in this case refuses to accept the moral barrenness of her life. A war orphan, uneducated, barely literate, indifferent to "study," she yet has a sense of her own worth and is willing to fight against the indifference and cynicism that surround her.

Vladimir Dudintsev, of *Not By Bread Alone* fame, published in *New World* (1960, No. 1) his "A New Year's Tale," a story which continues his satire of the materialistic values of the Soviet upper class, in the form of a fable about a scientist who finds his short span of life enormously lengthened and enriched by unselfish labor for humanity. Ideas which in his earlier novel were given explicit and literal statement are developed in "A New Year's Tale" through symbolic images. Thus the inventor in both stories is the hero, but in the "Tale" he is a bringer of light to the dark side of a planet. In both stories the inventor experiences real joy in carrying out his ideas and for the sake of those ideas rejects the conventional "bourgeois" style of life with its competition for material things and for prestige and position. The scientist in "A New Year's Tale" finds a cure for his own death in the light he brings to others. Dudintsev's story is evidence of a quiet determination among Soviet writers to experiment and to search for new directions. His story, like his novel, is a didactic tale, but it is a radical departure from the usual procedure of socialist realism.

Among the younger writers who speak with the new accent, V. F. Tendryakov has attracted the attention of critics in the Soviet Union and outside, and one of his works has been the subject of an unfavorable editorial in *Pravda*. His work consists for the most part of short sketches about life in the remote countryside and in the *kolkhozes*, and he deals with problems of personal morality, giving much attention to individual differences of character and personality. Stagnant habits of the old way of life—attachment to selfish interests and to creature comforts, hatred and violence—he exposes in Soviet men with reticent scorn. Two of his recent stories are especially interesting. "Three, Seven, Ace" (*New World*, 1960,

No. 3) is a story set on the banks of a wide river in a log-
ging settlement in the interior. A man who has been saved
from drowning in the river and become a member of the
colony turns out to be an ex-convict and professional gambler.
Having infected the laborers with gambling fever, he cleans
them out thoroughly, hides the money in the bunk of Leshka,
one of the laborers, then is killed when he attacks their chief,
Dubinin. The chief is suspected of having killed him in a
quarrel over the money, and suspicion is strengthened by the
circumstance that the money cannot be found. Leshka, though
he idolizes the chief, is in such panic at the thought of being
suspected himself that he throws the money into the river.
Dubinin is taken away, and as the story ends Leshka sobs
disconsolately.

The laborers in the story are not bad men, but they are
low on the human scale. They lack not only education and
intelligence, but also the barest minimum of moral responsibility. They live on the fringe of civilization. News of the
launching of a sputnik weighing a ton stirs them less than
gossip about a bear in the neighborhood. The story is a simple
one of primitive passion and violence, and, as the author
reflects, could have been told in much the same way a thousand years ago. The men who figure in it are in no way
"positive" characters, and no "idea" is developed in their
story. Like many of the younger writers, Tendryakov is consciously avoiding the socialist clichés. Some of them manage
this by writing about children and the very young, Tendryakov
by writing about primitives.

"The Trial" (*New World,* 1961, No. 3) is a brief excursion
into the remote Russian forest where life is as yet not fully
under the control of civilized legal formalities. A hunter who
belongs to the primeval woods makes the acquaintance on a
bear hunt of a Soviet construction director whose "enterprise"
is slowly destroying the habitat of both the bear and the
hunter. They are joined on the hunt by Mityagin, a village
simpleton who has never before handled a gun. The description of the hunt is one of the most exciting passages in Soviet
writing. It is a mosaic of human experience: the hunter's
courage in the face of danger as he tracks the great beast,

suspense and fear as the dogs corner the animal, and the moment of finality when two men fire at the enraged and advancing monster. Then suddenly tragedy strikes, for one of the two misses the bear and kills a man who happened to be walking in the woods. The police and the prosecutor are called in, and the dry formalism of legal procedure invades the forest. Apparently trivial matters, not even noticed at the moment of danger, now become very important—the determination, for instance, of the exact position of each man when the shots were fired. The question to be answered is, who killed the man, the construction director or the village simpleton. The hunter, who has cut out of the bear's skull the bullet that killed him, knows that it came from the simpleton's gun. But no one wants to believe that the director and not the simpleton had missed the bear and killed a man. The hunter, certain that the evidential bullet would only cause trouble for him, throws it away in a swamp and denies in court that he ever found it. He fears that the truth can only cause him trouble. The author reflects on the long and painful road still to be traveled:

People change more slowly than life itself. . . . A metallurgical combine can be built in two or three years, but human character changes only after decades. It's not enough to build factories, lay down roads into the wilderness, move people into well-built houses. That's necessary, but it's not everything. People must also be taught how to live.

Yury Nagibin, whose stories "The Khazar Ornament" and "Light in the Window," both attacks on the Stalinist bureaucracy, were published in *Literary Moscow* (1956), has written in recent years about simple, unpretentious people who feel emotions of pity, love or sympathy in basic human terms. His story "Love" is typical. It portrays the constancy of a nice boy's love for a girl in spite of her cheap and vulgar cynicism. The story explores the working of a mysterious emotional process, but Nagibin eschews any effort to explain or pass judgment on it. The author, like his youthful characters, is reverent but tongue-tied.

His story "Echoes" (1960) is a reminiscence of a child-

hood encounter with a little girl named Vitka, who collects
echoes as other people collect stamps or coins. Somewhat
strange in appearance and original in manner, the girl, as she
scrambles over rocks looking for the best places to produce
echoes, seems a bit crazy, but she has imagination and good-
ness, and she is a real friend. Yet the narrator recalls that
when his properly stodgy contemporaries made fun of her he
did not have the courage to take her part. His story is a
melancholy rumination of regret at his failure to recognize the
beauty of this little offbeat sprite. There is a deep human
sadness in it, and no obvious moral.

Yury Kazakov, born in 1927, is one of the youngest Soviet
writers, and his style displays in their purest form the new
tendencies in Soviet literature. His most characteristic story,
"Blue and Green," written in 1956, is told in the words and
thoughts of the central character. That character relates in
direct, naïve terms his love for a girl whom he met acciden-
tally, the irreplaceable happiness it gave him, and his grief
at losing her. The young man's story, somewhat reminiscent
of Yury Olesha, relates entirely to his own consciousness, and
the author, scrupulously inarticulate, offers no wise comment
on his character's experience.

"The Deer's Antlers" (1958) is another exploration of a
single mind, in this case the mind of a young girl recovering
from disease and separated in thought from her comrades.
She experiences a fantastic fairy-tale hallucination, sees trolls
and other wonders, and has a purely subjective vision of
someone she might love. Again, the story is constructed out
of the thoughts and impressions of a particular consciousness,
and the atmosphere of wonder is related to the young girl's
clinical condition. The story has no discoverable moral but
only imaginative interest.

Vladimir Voinovich is a young writer whose work is evidence of new and fresh forces waiting to be released. His
story "We Live Here" (*New World*, 1961, No. 1) is a minor
masterpiece. The author's modest purpose is, as he puts it,
"to write about Goshka and the other people" who live in the
remote collective farm village of Popovka. He brings each
of them to life in a few casual, humorous strokes. Goshka, a

good fellow, is taking extension courses to finish his high-school education. He hates slackers and phonies, and punches them when he can, but has no general observations to offer on any subject. Liza and Sanka, both construction workers, are in love with him. In simple physical terms, he loves Sanka, but she goes off to Moscow to become a singer and broaden her horizons. He does think of life and death:

"Here today and gone tomorrow."
"Are you afraid of death?
"Yes."
"Why? If you die there's nothing to worry about. No German to study."
"I don't know. Maybe I'm curious. I want to know what'll happen tomorrow."

Goshka is a good fellow by instinct, as are most of the characters in the story. Two characters are inspired by "perspectives and history," Ilya, who is in charge of the Cultural Club, and Vadim, a city poet who has come to Popovka in search of "practical experience." Ilya, who secretly writes poetry on "agricultural themes," has managed to get an expensive grand piano for the Cultural Club. On this precious, shiny instrument he has placed a sign: "Do not touch!" Vadim, the lyrical "I" whose verse sings of toil and sweat "in the mines," loses the workers' attention when they learn that he was never actually employed there. The efforts of the village to acquire culture are pathetic or ridiculous and are never sentimentalized. Slogans, inspirational thoughts, socialist exploits are lightly satirized by Vadim's inept verses, and it is no doubt symbolic of the remoteness of literature from the masses that Vadim himself, disconsolate and unappreciated, leaves the village for his native habitat, Moscow.

Voinovich is a master of humorously creative dialogue. His characters tell their own story, not in their thoughts, for they have none to speak of, but in their innocent conversation. The main burden of narrative and characterization is borne, without the author's intervention, by the dialogue, which is reduced to the simplest elements of basic communication. Take, for example, the following conversation between the

Farm Chairman and the spokesman for a work gang who has just asked one hundred rubles a day per man:

"Well, you won't pay it?"

"I won't," said the Chairman positively.

"You won't?"

"I won't."

"Give me a light. . . . All right. For the last time, will you or not?"

"I will not," said the Chairman.

Voinovich is evidently abreast of the literary culture of his day. The influence of Zoshchenko can be felt in his satire of perennially ridiculous humanity. His teen-age characters have a nihilistic naïveté that reminds one of Salinger, and his laconic dialogue suggests that he has learned from Hemingway. But he has an individual style and a spring of optimistic fun that sets him off from all these.

V. Aksyonov is another new voice whose notes are much like those of Voinovich. His novel *Ticket to the Stars* (*Youth*, 1961, Nos. 6–7) deals with teen-age characters who think, and talk, in a teen-age idiom that instinctively rejects established formulas. Some critics have suspected in Aksyonov himself an ironic attitude toward high ideals and serious purpose; but his young Dimkas and Mityas, who clip and cut the accepted grammatical forms and mangle the socialist idiom of their elders, sound much like adolescents anywhere. They are in love with jazz, sports, and falling in love. The purposeful aimlessness of their existence is itself a kind of system—a deliberate method of searching for independence and self-expression. The seventeen-year-old Dimka answers his older brother's reproach: "Your career was decided for you before you were born, but I'd rather be a tramp and suffer privation than spend my whole life as a little boy doing what other people want me to do."

Among younger Russian poets the one who has attracted attention and stirred controversy is Yevgeny Yevtushenko. His *Stantsia Zima*, published in 1955, has already been mentioned. His poem "Babi Yar" was published in the *Literary Gazette* in 1961. As a poem it is technically undistinguished, but it is a powerfully earnest meditation on the tragic fate of the Jews of Eastern Europe, thirty-three thousand of whom were slaughtered by the Germans in 1941 at Babi Yar, a ravine near the city of Kiev. The poet reflects that the ugly prejudice that led to Babi Yar is not confined to Fascists or Germans but is nurtured in many Russians, too, and still "rises in the fumes of alcohol and in drunken conversations. . . . There is no Jewish blood in mine, but I am hated by every anti-Semite as if a Jew, and for this reason I am—a true Russian." Yevtushenko has been violently attacked by literary conservatives for this poem, which they regard as a slander on the Russian people, who gave their blood to destroy Hitlerite Fascism. But he has had many defenders and "Babi Yar" is an immensely popular poem. The controversy it aroused has significance for literature, where two parties exist and engage in warfare. The conservative party when it attacks the opposition uses labels such as "aesthete" and "alien"—which suggest the explicitly anti-Semitic term "cosmopolitan" applied to Jewish intellectuals in the late forties. There has been a tendency in some novels to identify the partisan of a liberal taste in literature with alien elements bearing non-Russian names and having vaguely Jewish physical characteristics. The honest poem "Babi Yar" is evidence that the appeal to anti-Semitic prejudice is being broadcast in various ways and used against liberal tendencies and their bearers. Yevtushenko has had the "boldness," as he puts it, "to speak the simple truth."

A clear strong note was heard when Alexander Solzhenitsyn published his novel *One Day in the Life of Ivan Denisovich* (*Novy Mir*, November, 1962) and the two stories, "Matriona's House," and "An Occurrence at Krechetova Station," (*Novy Mir*, January, 1963). As a revelation of the daily misery experienced by the inmates of Stalin's concentration camps, the novel had an immediate and sensational success. Yet it does not attempt to deal directly with the problem of tyranny and oppression, and, like much of recent Soviet writing, avoids explicit polemical statement of any kind. Solzhenitsyn transmits an intense, particular, and awful human experience. This account of "one day" in the life of a prison camp—and not one of the worst days—brings to life in the vivid four-letter language of the inmates themselves (the editor of *Novy Mir* in his note introducing the story felt it necessary to "explain" the presence of so many vulgar expressions) an array of characters: on the one hand the supervisors, guards, and their toadies, brutalized by the terror they themselves employ; and on the other hand the prisoners, some of whom may have been guilty of something, though most are innocent of the crimes charged to them. All of them, however, have been stripped of liberty, dignity, and elementary human rights. The story gives a credible account of life reduced to an animal level, where "it was every man for himself," and everybody has his own little racket and expects his "own little cut." The very existence of the camp, and the level of life of the inmates, is a tragic irony in a land supposedly motivated by "socialist ideals." The warmest and most sympathetic character is a Baptist named Alyosha, the only one who is selfless and meek. "Matriona's House" is much like *One Day* in its language and style. The central character, Matriona, is a simple woman, who isn't interested in "owning things," who helps people and expects no pay, who is meek and soft-spoken. She is an eccentric member of a collective farm community where the rule of life is selfish and savage conflict over power and the ownership of things. In this story, as in *One Day*, the implicit tragedy lies in the distance between such a village community and any ideal human organization. Solzhenitsyn's writing has great power, both descriptive and evocative. His realistic pictures of milieu and character are the most vivid things in contemporary Soviet literature. (See Chapter 13.)

The new trend in Soviet literature features above all *individuality*. This is to be seen both in the content and in the apprehension of experience. The important thing is the individual experience of love, pain or fear, and that experience the new writers enrich and intensify by narrowing their focus to the frame of a single mind—or to a succession of these. A second characteristic of the latest writing is *simplicity*. This is not the same thing as intelligibility, which was insisted on by the socialist realists. It is rather a kind of ideological naïveté, genuinely experienced by some of these writers and adopted as a literary style by others. This simplicity shows itself in the ideological bareness of stories about young love or forest villainy and in the unpretentious language of the narration. Simple human beings in a primitive locale are often chosen for literary treatment. Children, peasants deep in the primeval woods, loquacious but inarticulate adolescents, tongue-tied village poets, are likely to figure as the central characters. In one of Kazakov's stories the rejection of the verbal and rational is complete: the central character is a dog —a blind one!

In all of this one can discern the features of a literary movement. The new writers are probably not symptomatic of political opposition, but they do rebel, quietly and firmly, against the "style" of their elders. They have reacted strongly against declarative rhetoric and the ringing phrase. If one of their characters declaims on "socialist creativeness" or "the heroism of labor," the effect is certain to be humorous. Nor do they, like Dudintsev in *Not By Bread Alone,* inveigh against injustice and abuses. That song, too, seems to have lost its appeal: one could not go very far with it in the Soviet state. Literature, judging by these new voices, is tending to reject positive heroes or villains and programmatic statement in favor of exploring the lives of simple human beings.

There is exciting evidence that the new trend continues to draw adherents and to gain in strength. It is true that conventional writing concerned with public propaganda and the collective life is the dominant product of belles-lettres, but the writers we have examined, like crocuses pushing up in a weed patch, draw attention and interest, and even invite cultivation.

Chapter 13

Russian Literature in the Sixties

The Literary Establishment

THE LITERARY SITUATION during the sixties was shifting and precarious. The contest between "liberals" and "conservatives" continued, with sharp and unpredictable variations in the policy of the Party toward the two groups, and many serious casualties on the liberal side. And many had the courage to take action against censorship and control.

In December, 1962, Nikita Khrushchev, then Chairman of the Council of Ministers of the USSR, visited an exhibition in Moscow featuring contemporary artists, a few of whom offered non-representational canvases. The visit was a planned move against "modernist" tendencies in Soviet art, and Khrushchev was accompanied by several members of the government, including Comrade L. Ilychev, the head of the Party commission on ideology. Khrushchev's remarks at the exhibition (published in the magazine *Encounter*, April, 1963) revealed his aggressive crudity and his lack of information or taste, but they also signaled a broad campaign against liberal tendencies in all the arts. Here are some samples of his commentary:

On jazz: "When I hear it, it's like gas on the stomach."

On Nikonov's painting "The Geologists": "Are we going to take these blotches into communism with us?"

A question to the painter Zheltovsky: "Are you a pederast or a normal man?"

On the "modernists" in general: "Judging by these experiments, I am entitled to think that you are all pederasts, and for that you can get ten years."

Soon after Khrushchev's excursion into art criticism there were a number of meetings between Party leaders and literary men, the central purpose of which was to mount a propaganda campaign against modern art in all its manifestations.

Ilya Ehrenburg was a special target of criticism, since his reminiscences, *People, Years, Life,* published serially in *New World* during the sixties, was a conscious attempt to revive the ties with modern European art that had once been a normal part of the Russian cultural tradition. Rambling, garrulous, and chronologically irregular, his reminiscences are at times fascinating, often dull, and usually a bit obvious in their commentary on people and events. But they were, nevertheless, a revelation to young Soviet intellectuals, for whom the recent past had become a *terra incognita.* Ehrenburg's work is a casually organized directory of modern art during the early part of the century; it rehabilitated Russian artists who were part of that movement; it provided a plethora of names, both Russian and foreign, some of them almost forgotten: Burlyuk, Baltrushaitis, Tsvetaeva, Léger, Malevich, Meyerhold, Mandelshtam, Tatlin, Rodchenko, Apollinaire, Roman Jakobson, Braque, and scores of others. As such, it offered a prime target for the conservatives in the campaign of 1963.

A dependable wielder of the official hatchet, the critic V. Yermilov, was chosen to demolish Ehrenburg with the charge that his favorable presentation of cubism and surrealism tended to subvert the basic principles of Soviet art. Yermilov's article (*Izvestia,* January 30, 1963) was vicious and destructive, but his intended victim wrote a courageous reply, which was published in the same newspaper. The fact that Ehrenburg never recanted is evidence that the movement he represented had wide support, and perhaps even a measure of political power.

A series of meetings organized by Party leaders and the Executive Board of the Union of Writers during 1963 did, however, lead to recantations, or at least to expressions of loyalty to the Party's leadership, by a number of writers and artists. The sculptor Ernest Neizvestny, the composer Dmitri Shostakovich, the poets Robert Rozhdestvensky, Yevgeny Yevtushenko, and Andrey Voznesensky, among others, published statements to the general effect that they had learned useful lessons during the discussion inaugurated by Khrushchev, and that they recognized the educative role of the artist in a developing Communist society. It is noteworthy, however, that recantation had no palpable result in the actual writing of many who had been criticized, as we shall soon see.

The one event of the sixties that reveals most about the condition of Soviet literature was the Fourth Congress of Writers, which took place in Moscow during the last week of May, 1967, and was treated as one of many functions celebrating the fiftieth anniversary of the Soviet state. That Congress was drastically different from earlier ones in the quality and interest of the reports presented at it. Although it is true that all four Congresses were marked by outward unanimity encouraged by the strong hand of Party control, the record of the First Congress, in 1934, offers stimulating and sometimes controversial statements by Bukharin, Babel, Olesha, and Pasternak; at the Second, in 1954, literary problems were to some degree discussed, and there was debate over the merits of certain works; the Third, in 1959, featured the ramblingly ignorant and overbearing speech by Nikita Khrushchev in which he discussed recent troubles in the literary world and restored to grace certain writers who had "repented" of errors. But the Fourth Congress differs from the earlier ones in that there was, as far as one can judge from the printed record, a dead calm at all of the sessions. There was no debate; there was no discussion of problems and difficulties; there was no serious discussion of literature, though long speeches were devoted to the ritual recitation of approved titles and names, accompanied by impassioned exhortations to produce a "socialist" literature for the people. Georgy Markov, Secretary of the Union, made a report on Soviet prose in which he mentioned about forty names. He brushed lightly on vexed questions. He mentioned Vasily Bykov's much discussed novel, *The Dead Feel No Pain*, but his remarks were only gently disapproving and were calculated to assuage the polemical bite of that powerful story. He seemed determined not to raise any embarrassing issues. In a similar spirit the critic Leonid Novichenko, who reported on the development of criticism, softly chided the liberal journal *New World* for "mistrust of the heroic and lofty, and attempts to justify theoretically a dismal and prejudiced carping." But in the very next breath he partially removed the sting from this by the comment that the arch-conservative journal, *October*, was also guilty of something—"oversimplification."

The keynote speech was made by the novelist Konstantin Fedin. He touched ever so lightly on the disputes that rage beneath the surface of Soviet literary life. His speech, if read with careful attention to its interlinear content, reveals that there are two distinct currents even in Soviet Russian literature: official socialist realist literature, and a literature not yet clearly defined, partly underground, and struggling for a free development of literary styles and genres. It also reveals that the traditional concept of the realistic novel is being subjected to critical analysis. But though he distantly alluded to such problems, Fedin did not discuss them; his speech struck an untroubled major chord of pride in the "positive achievements," the "successes," of fifty years. It was a speech given in a jubilee mood.

All of the other statements but one followed more or less the pattern set by Fedin. The one exception was the speech of Mikhail Sholokhov, who had recently been awarded the Nobel Prize for literature. Sholokhov's speeches at such gatherings are as a rule offbeat and somewhat indiscreet, even though they have usually supported the most backward tendencies and ideas. At the Party Congress in 1966 he branded as traitors Andrey Sinyavsky and Yuly Daniel, who had just been sentenced to long terms at hard labor for publishing their works abroad under the pseudonyms Tertz and Arzhak, respectively. On the present occasion Sholokhov broke through the bland facade arranged by the organizers of the Congress and talked about certain portents of sedition. A careful reading of his crudely but cryptically worded speech reveals that three unpleasant recent developments were troubling Sholokhov. He was disturbed in the first place by the fact that a number of writers were not taking part in the Congress. One of these was Ilya Ehrenburg, and with heavy sarcasm Sholokhov deplored the absence of that former stalwart comrade: "I don't know how the other Congress delegates feel, but I for one am greatly distressed by the absence of my dear old friend, Ilya Grigorievich Ehrenburg. I look around and look around and I feel something is missing; I feel a certain malaise, a gnawing at my insides, and sadness settles down like a black cloud on my otherwise cloudless mood. Where is Ehrenburg? It turns out that on the eve of the Congress he departed for Italian shores. Somehow this was not a nice thing for my friend to do."

The record shows that there was laughter in the hall. Sholokhov singled out Ehrenburg, but his remarks no doubt reflected concern at a much more serious defection from the Congress. According to a report printed in *Pravda* on May 26, 1967, 525 delegates had been elected to the Fourth Congress, and 473 were present. This can only mean that for one reason or another 52 elected delegates found it inconvenient to attend. Ten per cent seems a rather high rate of absence from such an important affair, and we may be sure that Sholokhov was exercised at the absence of many others, whom he chose not to name. It does seem that the self-congratulatory ritual of the Congress was boycotted by a substantial number of writers.

The second matter troubling Sholokhov was the disaffection of an undetermined number of young writers, and this he laid at Ehrenburg's door. "Bad example," he said, "is infectious." He spoke very sternly to the young writers: "They have on their consciences a certain defiance, a rejection of generally accepted norms of behavior, and *some other things*." (Italics mine.) One notes the menace in the final phrase, "some other things." One can only speculate as to exactly what kinds of behavior Sholokhov had in mind: perhaps the public protest at the conviction and sentence of Sinyavsky and Daniel. Perhaps he was also concerned at a kind of boycott of official Soviet literature by the young writers. At any rate he cited some interesting statistics in his speech which, he said, "make one pause and think." At the First Writers' Congress in 1934 71 per cent of the delegates were under forty; at the Second, only 20.6 per cent; at the Third, 13.9 per cent; and now at the 1967 Congress only 12.2 per cent of the total were under forty. Commented Sholokhov: "The average age of the delegates to this Congress is almost sixty, and that makes a rather sad impression." Sholokhov's remarks amount to a tacit admission that official Soviet literature in its organized form—the Writers' Union, publishing houses, journals, etc.—has been losing the support of the younger writers. It is clear, therefore, that the voice of this Congress was not at all a boyish falsetto or a young man's confident tenor but a complacent middle-aged bass-baritone—complacent, but not really confident.

Still a third matter troubled Sholokhov: the demand of some Soviet writers—he doesn't name them—for "freedom of the press." Here too it is necessary to decipher his remarks a bit. What he said was the following: "Recently quite a few voices have been raised in the West in favor of 'freedom' of creation for us Soviet writers. These are uninvited cheerleaders, who include the CIA . . . some United States senators, rabid White Guards, the defector Alliluyeva, and the notorious Kerensky, who has long been a political corpse. It is in this bizarre company that our zealots of freedom of the press find themselves."

This is the most reprehensible passage in Sholokhov's speech, and it is not too difficult to guess at the object of his attack. These remarks are his answer to a letter circulated at the Congress by Alexander Solzhenitsyn, author of *One Day in the Life of Ivan Denisovich*. In this letter, addressed to the Presidium of the Congress and all Soviet writers—a letter that had not been officially acknowledged—Solzhenitsyn demanded a measure of "freedom of the press" and an end of that "oppression, no longer tolerable, that our literature has been enduring from censorship for decades" and that the Union of Writers "should not accept any longer."

The third cloud on Sholokhov's mood, then, was Solzhenitsyn's eloquent letter, with its defense of freedom for all writers and its evidence that repression, injustice, and official slander of dissident writers are still the rule rather than the exception in the Soviet Union. The obtuse state of Sholokhov's ethical sense and the spurious character of his remarks at the Congress become evident when we realize that he implicates Solzhenitsyn, and all others who complain of the Soviet censorship, with CIA plots, White Guardist bandits, and even the old man Kerensky. They are all traitors to their country. Nevertheless, Sholokhov's speech did the service of giving the delegates a look behind the scenes and helped them and us to see some of the things that the bland surface of the Congress was intended to conceal.

There is clear evidence that the bureaucratic structure of Soviet literature as it was developed by Stalinist administrators during the 1930's is in real danger of collapse, and can be shored up only by police action. The trial and sentence of Sinyavsky and Daniel aroused angry indignation and even led to public protest on the part of eminent Soviet writers—not all of them young. The most interesting of several such protests was a letter addressed to the Presidium of the XXIII Congress of the Communist Party and signed by sixty-two writers. This letter, like Solzhenitsyn's later one, complained of the narrow limits within which literary men are allowed to work, and asserted that the trial of Sinyavsky and Daniel had already caused more damage than all of their mistakes. Among the writers who signed this letter were Korney Chukovsky, Ilya Ehrenburg, Victor Shklovsky, and Venyamin Kaverin, all of them old and established, and all of them over seventy. Sholokhov's imputation of rebellious defiance to youth and inexperience was a deliberate misrepresentation: the disaffected group includes both old and young writers. The older writers were joined in signing this statement by some of the most talented younger ones now producing: the poets Bella Akhmadulina and Bulat Okudzhava; the promising prose writer Vladimir Voinovich; a scholar whose reputation is substantial, A. A. Anikst; the gifted playwright L. A. Zorin; and many others. It should be difficult, even in the Soviet Union, to turn aside such a document by the slander that it is the work of CIA agents and traitors.

A number of actions undertaken during and immediately after the Writers' Congress of 1967 provide evidence that some writers are ready to take resolute steps in order to end their automatic subservience to the Party and the State. The immediate and harsh reaction of the Writers' Union and the Security Agency (KGB) in almost every case revealed the Party's concern over any erosion of its authority and its determination to punish those who question its policies. Among those who defended Solzhenitsyn was the poet Andrey Voznesensky, who offered a proposal that all of Solzhenitsyn's work be published in a new edition. As a result of his action Voznesensky's long-planned visit to New York for a poetry reading in June, 1967, was abruptly canceled by the Union on the ground that the poet was "ill." He answered with a letter of protest to the Executive Board of the Writers' Union in which he said, among other things, "I am ashamed to be a member of the same Union as these people." This letter was never published in the USSR, but it reached the West, like so many other documents of this period, by uncharted underground channels.

One of the organizers of the public protest against the trial of Sinyavsky and Daniel was the young writer Alexander Ginzburg, who compiled a "White Book" consisting of the trial proceedings and a collection of statements, signed by many outstanding people, protesting the verdict. The "White Book," too, found its way to the West, and was published and widely read. Ginzburg, along with his friend Yury Galanskov and two others, was himself brought to trial in January, 1968, and sentenced to five years in prison. Equally brutal and uncompromising was the treatment of Vladimir Bukovsky, who had been arrested for the specific offense of organizing a street demonstration in September, 1965, to demand a fair trial for Sinyavsky and Daniel. His heroic speech to the court in defense of freedom of speech and of the press as rights guaranteed to Soviet citizens, recorded and sent abroad by Pavel Litvinov, the grandson of Maxim Litvinov, the former Soviet foreign minister and ambassador to Washington, was published in *The New York Times* on December 27, 1967. "What the prosecutor would like to hear from me he won't hear," said Bukovsky to the court. "There is no criminal act in our case. I absolutely do not repent for having organized this demonstration. I find that it accomplished what it had to accomplish, and when I am free again I shall again organize demonstrations, of course with complete observance of the law, as before."

Other statements complaining about the travesty of justice

in the trials of the writers were directed to Soviet organizations, to the Supreme Court of the USSR, and to Communist publications in the West. The most startling of these was a letter sent to the Presidium of the Conference of Communist Parties held in Budapest in 1968 and signed by twelve Soviet citizens, among them Pavel Litvinov, Larisa Daniel, the wife of Yuly Daniel, and Piotr Yakir, son of the Red Army general executed in the 1937 purge of the Army. This letter called attention to "the danger which results from the complete disregard of human rights in our country," and it revealed the harsh administrative measures that had been taken against many of those who had signed letters of protest: "Those who were most active in their protests received replies in the form of notices terminating their employment, summonses to the KGB with the threat of arrest, and, finally, the most shocking form of punishment, compulsory confinement in a mental asylum."

The events of the middle sixties, fully described and heavily documented as a result of the boldness and civic sense of many Soviet citizens, clearly reveal that a cruel struggle takes place beneath the official surface of Soviet literature, a struggle whose outcome it is difficult to predict. Once this is realized, it becomes perfectly clear why the leaders of the Union of Writers, in the jubilee year, organized their Congress in such a way that there could be no public discussion of the issues that agitate Soviet intellectuals in private. Yet the facade they arranged concealed nothing. Solzhenitsyn's letter and Sholokhov's indiscreet remarks ruined some well-laid plans.

Solzhenitsyn's Letter and His Forbidden Works

Solzhenitsyn's now famous letter is pregnant with the tragedy of modern Russian literature in its Soviet variant. The facts adduced in it concerning the destruction in labor camps of "the pride of Russian poetry," along with uncounted numbers of young writers who were never allowed to blossom, are not even contested by the Soviet literary establishment. And the letter contains the revelation, based on Solzhenitsyn's own personal experience, that the State Security Agency still interferes with writers who have incurred its suspicion. His most serious ground for indictment of the Union of Writers is the fact that its leadership has acquiesced over the years in the crippling of Russian literature:

Our literature has lost the leading role it played at the end of the last century and the beginning of the present, and the brilliance of experimentation that distinguished it in the 1920's. To the entire world the literary life of our country now appears as something infinitely poorer, flatter, and lower than it actually is, than it would appear if it were not restricted, hemmed in.

The losers are both our country, in world public opinion, and world literature itself. If the world had access to all the uninhibited fruits of our literature, if it were enriched by our own spiritual experience, the whole artistic evolution of the world would move along in a different way, acquiring a new stability and attaining even a new artistic level.

The letter set forth in detail the harassment to which Solzhenitsyn himself had been subjected by agents of the Security Police. They had confiscated his literary archives, including a play, *The Feast of Victors*, which presented Red Army men in an unfavorable light; they had taken his novel *The First Circle* and circulated it in a special "closed" edition for perusal by unidentified officials; they had prevented publication of his novel *The Cancer Ward*, although its publication had been approved by the prose department of the Writers' Union. A number of his plays and scenarios had been unable to find producers or publishers. Slanders had been circulated against him and doubts cast on his patriotism and his sanity.

Solzhenitsyn served during World War II on the western front as a captain of artillery and had been awarded two decorations for bravery in action. He was then arrested in February, 1945, on a political charge. He spent eight years in a concentration camp and three more in exile, after which the charge against him was retracted as groundless, and he was fully rehabilitated. His novel *One Day in the Life of Ivan Denisovich* (1962) has been discussed in Chapter 12. Three of his short stories were published in *New World*, but a substantial body of his work is unknown to the Soviet reader. Some of it—*The Cancer Ward, The First Circle,* and fifteen pieces called *Studies and Brief Stories*—has been published outside the Soviet Union.

The *Studies* is a series of lyrics in prose which convey with great felicity of language Solzhenitsyn's feeling for nature, for human history, and for some undefined existence, a "being" of some kind, immanent in the universe. It may have been this barely palpable "religious" interest that helped bring the writer to the attention of the Security Police. These prose poems deal with the beauty and mystery of nature ("Lake Segden," "The Duckling"); they suggest the wonder of creation itself ("A Storm in the Mountains"); they express a personal loss in the death and disappearance of great poets— Sergey Yesenin, for instance, "who looked around amazed and found so much raw beauty" ("Yesenin's Birthplace"); they speak awesomely of the beauty created by human beings ("The City on the Neva"); and one of them ("A Journey down the Oka") conveys a sense of the historical and architectural ambience of central Russia:

When you travel the by-roads of Central Russia you begin to understand the secret of the pacifying Russian countryside. It is in the churches. They trip up the slopes, ascend the high hills, come down to the broad rivers like princesses in white and red, they lift their belltowers—graceful, shapely, all different—high over mundane timber and thatch, they nod to each other from afar, from villages that are cut off and invisible to each other they soar to the same heaven. And wherever you wander in the fields or meadows, however far from the habitation, you are never alone: from over the hayricks, the wall of trees, and even the curve of the earth's surface the head of some belltower will beckon to you from Gorki Lovetskie, or from Lyubichi, or from Gavrilovskoe. . . .

Solzhenitsyn's novel *The Cancer Ward* we know only from an unfinished and obviously unedited copy, but even so, it places him without question in the front rank of Soviet writers. The work deals with the Security Police, with repression and rehabilitation, but it presents these matters from the viewpoint of a Soviet official who has been deeply involved with "security" during the Stalin period. The highly placed official, Rusanov, is beset by a tumor in his neck which increases in size so rapidly that it leaves him no time to utilize his good "connections" in order to get to a Moscow clinic or arrange for private treatment. He is obliged to enter a crowded cancer ward that he must share with lesser men, whose presence irritates and upsets him. Accustomed to giving orders, indeed to disposing of the lives of other men, Rusanov is suddenly bereft of authority and subjected to procedures that he doesn't understand but must accept because they offer the only hope of life.

There are explicit reminiscences of Leo Tolstoy, especially *The Death of Ivan Ilych* and the moral tales. Tolstoy's Ivan Ilych, when he faces death from cancer (his ineluctable pain), discovers that his former life with its systematized proprieties has lost all value; like him, Rusanov finds that his model Soviet family, his well-organized and useful official activities, his nicely furnished apartment, all seem remote and unreachable, somewhere beyond the great "swelling" that has become his intimate companion, perhaps his death. But unlike Ivan Ilych, who in the end experiences salvation through relaxing his grip on life, Rusanov holds on with obdurate desperation. A note of factitious optimism is sounded by his daughter, a budding Soviet writer, who visits him in the cancer ward and even in the face of the suffering and certain death that surround her still preaches the official Soviet literary creed of positive thinking: "All right, father, struggle for health! Carry on the struggle, get rid of that swelling . . . and *don't worry about a thing*! Everything, just everything, is going to be great!"

The most striking feature of *The Cancer Ward* is its penetrating investigation of a Soviet bureaucrat's fashion of life and especially of his mind, his interests, his tastes, his view of himself. Through the device of inner monologue Solzhenitsyn provides an imaginative re-creation of the thought process, memories, and reflections of a man who, in the interest of state security, has brought ruin to many people and is now threatened (the action takes place in 1955) by the rehabilitation and return of many of his victims. We are given the opportunity of imagining his fear, his guilt, his arrogant self-justification. We experience the dismal amalgam of platitude and prejudice that fortifies him. A man named Kostoglotov, another cancer victim and an unwilling neighbor of Rusanov, is in every sense his antipode and enemy. Caught up in the police terror of the thirties because of some frank comments on the "Father of Peoples," Stalin, Kostoglotov has spent his whole life in physical exile and moral alienation from the society managed by Rusanov and his colleagues. He values neither life nor death, and having nothing more to lose, he has nothing to dread. Kostoglotov may be taken to represent those intellectuals and others who have always stood apart from the official world, many of whom are now in open conflict with it.

But *The Cancer Ward* has a deeper symbolic meaning in the sense that death and its pain are the central concern of all the characters. Death as the reality that transforms all values is the abiding presence in the story, and attitudes toward it range from the advice of Aunty Stepha, an ignorant peasant woman, who simply counsels resignation before the will of God, to the thoughtful query suddenly introduced by a character who has been reading Tolstoy: "What do men live by?" Only the apparatus-man has an assured answer to this question, and his answer takes the form of an official plati-tude: "Man lives by his ideology and his social concerns."

Critics both in Russia and abroad have as a rule been impressed by the originality and artistic power of Solzhenit-syn's verbal art. It has been pointed out that in *One Day in the Life of Ivan Denisovich* Solzhenitsyn set for himself, and solved, an intricate problem of narration: he presents the whole story from the viewpoint and in the characteristic language of a rather limited person, into whose speech pat-terns he carefully works general features of peasant dialect, as well as the special piquancy of criminal and concentration-camp jargon. Virtuosity of a similar kind is evident in *The Cancer Ward*, though the narrative viewpoint, and with it the language and thought patterns, constantly shifts from one character to another. Rusanov's viewpoint and his bureau-

306 / Russian Literature Since the Revolution

cratic style of thought and expression regularly yield to the contrasting attitude and idiom of many other characters, including the doctors and nurses, each of whom experiences the clinical inferno in his own way. And the author himself presides over this world of disease and death, never losing control of its many facets, and contemplating it from a lofty moral level.

The Cancer Ward was published in the West in spite of Solzhenitsyn's repeated objections, and he has stated that he has had no control over the publication process and therefore takes no responsibility for what has appeared. In view of this, one should perhaps not pass final judgment on the book. Publication of the novel offered the pretext for a particularly vicious and slanderous attack on him in the official newspaper *The Literary Gazette* (June 26, 1968), and must have added to his difficulties with the Security Police.

The First Circle (1968), also published in the West, returns to Solzhenitsyn's obsessive theme, the Security Police and the concentration-camp system. We have seen that the various "circles" of the Stalinist inferno are the locale of almost all his work: the war front, the brutal and backward village, the labor camp, the cancer ward. *The First Circle* deals with the Soviet analogue of Dante's "first" circle, a prison into which scholars and scientists, all sentenced as state criminals, have been gathered to work on special projects. Like *One Day in the Life of Ivan Denisovich*, the novel reveals an existence so dreadful that its realistic details hold the mind of the reader in a kind of fascination. The suffering depicted at this level of hell is not physical—the prisoners are housed and fed decently, and they have opportunities to read, to write, and even to discuss philosophical questions. Their miseries are mental, and by that very fact, unbearably acute. Among the characters are Stalin, the chief demon and jailer, whose mind is revealed as cruel, base, and banal; Abakumov, the secret policeman directly in charge of this particular camp; and a weird gallery of minor demons who have carved a place for themselves in the system through flattery and service to the major ones. This novel, direct and conventional in its literary method, is an important document on the Stalin era in Russian history. Since its locale is the "first" circle, where the best representatives of human reason have been imprisoned, its characters are unusually articulate on the genesis, development, and philosophy of the police state.

Sinyavsky-Tertz, Daniel-Arzhak, and Others of the "Underground"

One of the most fascinating features of the sixties was the regular emigration by underground routes not of writers (though a few of these did emigrate) but of poems, essays, stories, and documentary materials. The hope has always existed that Russian writers whose thought or style transcends the tight line imposed by the Soviet censorship might still be writing—not for publication, but, as the Russians say, for the "drawer." However, the expectation that literature of vital importance would emerge from that drawer for publication outside the Soviet Union has not always been encouraged by the samples that have appeared. Yesenin-Volpin's book of verse, published in 1961, is the poor product of a peculiar personality and hardly deserves to be included in any literature. Stories entitled "The Blue Bottle" (1962) and "Ward No. 7" (1963), first published anonymously and later acknowledged as the work of Valery Tarsis, do not match in literary quality the fine indignation they express at political and intellectual repression. The underground collections, mainly of poetry—entitled *Syntax 1, 2,* and *3, Phoenix 1961, Sphinx,* and *Phoenix 1966*—have been published in a West German *émigré* periodical (*Grani*). Such work is uneven and often not very good, but the collections are an important expression of contemporary intellectual life inside the Soviet Union. Stories and memoir literature have reached New York by various routes and been published in *The New Review*—for example, V. Shalamov's *Stories of Kolyma*, based on prison-camp experiences, and Lidiya Chukovskaya's *The Deserted House*, a beautifully poignant account of one woman's experiences during the year of the purges.

The everflowing stream of *émigré* manuscripts often contains prose items of high literary quality and some of the best poetry now being produced in the USSR. The first stories of a writer who called himself Abram Tertz came to light in 1959, and it was not revealed until September, 1965, when he was arrested, that "Tertz" was Andrey Sinyavsky, a literary scholar and critic of distinction. His short novel *The Trial Begins* was published in a French translation in the magazine *Esprit*, then in an English translation by Max Hayward in *Encounter* (January, 1961). This story had been preceded by an ironic essay, "On Socialist Realism," and was followed by six *Fantastic Stories*, the short novel *Lyubimov*, translated as *The Makepeace Experiment* (1965), and a volume of aphorisms entitled *Thoughts Unaware* (1966). The work he has published under his own name in the Soviet Union includes a number of excellent critical articles, the best of which is his sensitive and sophisticated introduction to the poetry of Boris Pasternak.

Sinyavsky-Tertz has a sophisticated knowledge of literature, both Western and Russian, and he has a program for Soviet literature which, in his isolated underground, he had worked out both in theory and in practice. The theory is more or less clearly stated in the essay "On Socialist Realism," and the stories serve as its practical demonstration. Sinyavsky-Tertz maintains that Soviet literature has been dominated since the thirties by the great "Purpose" of building the socialist future, and that its "positive heroes" are ideal types intended to point the way to that future. But he points out that under socialist realism a certain hypocrisy also entered literature, in the pretense that these ideal types were true and typical representatives of the "Soviet Man." There was no escape from the lie; socialist realism was never realistic nor did it frankly or honestly romanticize the socialist hero. He sees a possible way out only in the abandonment both of the "Purpose" and of realism, and in the development of a "phantasmagoric art, with hypotheses instead of a Purpose, an art in which the grotesque will replace realistic descriptions of ordinary life. Such an art would correspond best to the spirit of our time." He would seek truth in a new dimension "with the aid of the absurd and the fantastic." Literary art, he seems to say, must seek truth through distorting the given reality and inventing its own.

Many of the stories seem intended to illustrate his program. They contain grotesque caricatures of Soviet police "operatives," naturalistic scenes of Soviet upper-class debauchery flavored with the weird or the fantastic, dream sequences of brilliant power, frequent and frank treatment of sexual activity, usually with overtones of impotence or perversity, and, in the story "You and I," an exploration of both paranoid delusion and confused sexual identity. The stories contain many pages of superb writing, and they do succeed in evoking the political and cultural reality of the Soviet Union without resort to realistic treatment of character or situation. Yet they are very uneven in quality. Too often Sinyavsky-Tertz, in his reaction against the official tendency of Soviet literature, falls into direct statement of an opposite tendency. This is true of *The Makepeace Experiment*, in which a young bicycle mechanic, having succeeded by magic in taking over complete control of a Soviet town, casts a hypnotic spell upon its citizens, causing them to believe they have everything they want. The party-line writers Sofronov and Kochetov appear in that novel—under their own names—as agents and informers, and though this device offers a satisfying satiric bite, it is too obvious for comfort.

Perhaps the best of the *Fantastic Stories* is a strangely moving and mysterious piece entitled "Pkhentz." Its central character is a being who lives in Moscow, speaks its language, and functions as a bookkeeper there while totally alienated in spirit from Russian, and indeed from all terrestrial, life. The outward form his body takes is that of a hunchback, which further separates him from common humanity. He is fastidiously clean, and so chaste that he drives Veronika, a woman who pursues him, to the desperate measure of undressing herself in front of him: "It was awful. It turned out that all over she was the same unnatural white as her face, neck, and hands. In the front a pair of white breasts hung down. At first I thought they were a second pair of arms, cut off at the elbows. . . ."

His revulsion at the sight of the female body might suggest latent homosexuality, but this character's isolation runs far deeper than mere sexual inversion. The male human body is no less repellent to him: "If I were like them, I would never take my suit or even my overcoat off, day or night." His own body, when released from the straps and halters that hold it in a near-human shape, spreads out freely like a graceful palm tree, with many eyes and a multiplicity of hands and feet. He is, as it turns out, a native of some planet in a far-off galaxy who had been shipwrecked on earth many years before and lost all hope of returning to his homeland. The story is an original modern treatment, with an admixture of science-fantasy, of an old romantic theme: the human consciousness of an origin beyond the spatial confines of a particular planet. It is also a poignant symbolic treatment of spiritual isolation, and it expresses, as Sinyavsky-Tertz has said, some part of the loneliness that he himself feels.

Sinyavsky-Tertz is an uneven and undisciplined writer who obviously suffers from the lack of regular contact with an immediately present and critical audience. This is the tragedy of the "drawer" and the "underground." Sinyavsky-Tertz has never been able to function as a fully participating member of a literary community. His work has not been the object of clear, dispassionate examination either at home or abroad; and now, convicted of anti-Soviet activities, he is undergoing a long term of years at hard labor.

Judging by what is written for the "drawer" or for publication abroad, and judging also by some things that are published in the Soviet Union, it is clear that should Soviet literature achieve a measure of autonomy, there would be a resurgence of satire, and the promise of a great satirical literature offered in the twenties by Zamyatin, Bulgakov, Zoshchenko, and many others would now be redeemed. The work of Sinyavsky-Tertz and his co-defendant, Yuly Daniel, a translator who published abroad under the pseudonym Nikolay Arzhak, gave offense to the state, as the record of the trial shows, chiefly because of their satiric barbs aimed at the Soviet way of life. The judge, the prosecutor, and what appears to have been a selected audience were outraged at satiric scenes of everyday life in the Soviet Union, and in particular at one of Daniel's stories, "The Man from MINAP." That story features a young Communist student who claims he can determine the sex of his offspring at the moment of coitus. His services are in great demand among Soviet wives, some of whom wish to conceive sons, and some, daughters. When the Party discovers his talent and queries him as to his technique, he explains that for a male he thinks of Karl Marx at the crucial moment, and for a female, of the revolutionary Klara Zetkin. The young man is promptly employed by the state for the sake of accomplishing a new leap in Marxist-Leninist genetics and encouraged to exercise his talent under the most favorable conditions. The objects of Daniel-Arzhak's satire include Soviet housewives, puritanical Comsomol leaders determined to defend "the Soviet family," and Party scientists eager to establish control over a still unpredictable area of human activity.

Daniel-Arzhak sent three other stories abroad during the 1960's. In the story "Hands" the hero undertakes to explain why his hands are "constantly shaking" by recounting his experiences as a member of the *Cheka*, when those hands were involved in the execution of condemned prisoners. "Atonement" deals with the guilt and isolation experienced by a man who is suspected of having denounced people under Stalin. Perhaps the best of his stories is "This Is Moscow Speaking," a macabre invention which opens with a sober official announcement on Moscow Radio that August 10, 1960, has been declared "Public Murder Day," and that between the hours of 6 A.M. and midnight on that day any citizen will have the right to kill any other citizen. The story explores the reactions of various institutions and individuals to this sudden, inexplicable decree of the Supreme Soviet. The official newspaper *Izvestia* greets the announcement with a shower of Soviet clichés: "the rising level of life . . . genuine democracy . . . for the first time in history . . . the bourgeois press. . . ." A careerist Party man characterizes the decree as an important step in the direction of developing the "creative initiative of the masses." Another Soviet citizen understands the measure as evidence of democratization, in that the state is now granting certain of its functions to the people themselves. The hero's mistress suggests that they do away with her husband on "Public Murder Day." Even the hero and first-person narrator, whose moral level is relatively high, has a violent daydream in which he imagines a mass killing of those responsible for the purges of 1937 and for Russia's other agonies. An artist friend of his has already produced a picture celebrating and illustrating the Day. So inured are they to official murder that it occurs to hardly any of the characters that the whole idea should be rejected on moral grounds.

The trial of Sinyavsky and Daniel has thrown new light on the Soviet literary underground and has helped us to understand what motivates its members in sending their manuscripts abroad. Sinyavsky insisted at his trial that he was not moved by anti-Soviet sentiment or by any desire to damage the Soviet image abroad, but simply by the imperative need of a Russian writer to find readers somewhere for his most characteristic work when that work cannot be published in the Soviet Union. Sinyavsky's defense of himself at his trial was brilliant. He offered his judges many elementary lessons on the nature of the creative process, and his final words to them reveal the tragic isolation of the Soviet "underground": "In my . . . story 'Pkhentz' there is a sentence that I feel I can apply to myself: 'Just think, if I am simply different from others, they have to start cursing me.' Well, I am different. But I do not regard myself as an enemy; I am a Soviet man and my works are not hostile works."

Buried Treasure: Bulgakov and Others

Solzhenitsyn's letter to the membership of the Union provided in a lengthy register the names of writers whom official Soviet literature had persecuted or neglected over the years, and whose works had either been forgotten or never published. Among those he mentioned were Mikhail Bulgakov, Isaac Babel, Boris Pilnyak, Andrey Platonov, Osip Mandelshtam, and Anna Akhmatova. Another "underground" activity, if we may bend the metaphor somewhat, is the officially sanctioned excavation through the archives of departed writers in the search for unpublished manuscripts of value. Encouragement for such enterprises was provided during the 1960's, when selections from the correspondence of Maxim Gorky with Soviet writers was published (in *Literary Heritage* and

the *Archive of Maxim Gorky*). The letters revealed that
Gorky had great admiration for unorthodox writers such as
Platonov, Bulgakov, Pasternak, and Babel, while expressing
cool reserve toward some who followed more closely the precepts of the Party. Since Gorky's authority is not questioned,
there is no doubt that his favorable opinion of certain writers
had much to do with the decision to republish their works.

Andrey Platonov, a highly original prose stylist and once
a prominent member of the Pereval group, has been republished in many journals, and two collections of his prose have
appeared, one in 1965 and one in 1966. The latter collection
contains the short novel *Gradov City* (now published complete from the author's manuscript), a sly satire on bureaucratic tendencies in the revolutionary state, as well as a
number of stories that had not been republished for many
decades. Boris Pilnyak's unpublished novel *The Salt Ware-
house* appeared in the journal *Moscow* (1964, No. 5), and
Pilnyak was sympathetically introduced to "young readers
who have never heard of him" and "older ones who have forgotten him" as a writer who had been unjustly ignored. The
novel deals with a theme that had concerned Pilnyak throughout his career: the revolutionary movement in the deep
provinces. A number of previously unpublished stories by
Isaac Babel have appeared in the literary magazines, and in
Volume 74 (1965) of *Literary Heritage* important items from
the diary Babel kept when he served with the First Cavalry
Army, some preliminary sketches and notes for the stories that
appeared later under the title *Red Cavalry*, and two new
stories were published.

A major rediscovery in poetry was the work of Osip Mandelshtam, a poet of the Acmeist school who was regularly
published during the twenties, but who fell afoul of mediocrities in power, for a time lived in exile, and died in 1938. A
thick typewritten volume of his poetry, much of it unpublished, was widely available in the Soviet Union during the
sixties, and some of his work began reappearing in the journals. An edition of his poetry has been planned and projected
for some time in the Soviet Union, and his *Collected Works*
(in three volumes) in Russian have been appearing in the

West under the editorship of Gleb Struve and Boris Filippov.

Anna Akhmatova published a collection of poems in 1965 under the title *The Rush of Time* (*Beg Vremeni*). Her magnificently tragic poem "Requiem," published in Munich in 1963, was also available in the Soviet Union in many handwritten and typewritten copies, and is to be included in the volume of Akhmatova's poetry currently in preparation. That poem rose out of the deep well of Akhmatova's bereavement at the hands of a pitiless police apparatus. It is a moving poetic account of her grief, and the grief of Russia, during the years when she frequented the long queues that formed outside the jails of the NKVD.

The most startling rediscovery of the period was the prose fiction of Mikhail Bulgakov, who has already been mentioned as the author of satiric fantasies and as a playwright. Two of his novels, which had lain unpublished for almost thirty years, appeared in 1965 and 1966 and were immediately acknowledged as the work of a superb literary craftsman. A third novel was published for the first time in an English translation in 1968. The first of these, entitled *A Theatrical Novel*, was published in *New World* (1965, No. 8), and has been translated under the title *Black Snow* (1968). Written during the thirties, it was based on Bulgakov's experiences as a playwright and a member of the famous Moscow Art Theater, then presided over by Stanislavsky, the renowned originator of "the method." The novel succeeds in bringing the sacred institution and its director firmly to the ground. Its central character is Maksudov, a promising Moscow writer who has fallen in love with the theater and who pursues his mistress with constancy in spite of suffering and disenchantment. Maksudov is an autobiographical figure, and many of the incidents reflect Bulgakov's own experiences with the Soviet theater. The novel is important and interesting, not only as a deft deflation of a revered theater and its sainted leader, but also as an intimate account of a play-maker's creative processes. Bulgakov conveys his enthusiasm for the theater and for the complex art of writing and producing plays.

The appearance of the second novel was an event of prime

importance in Russian literature. *The Master and Margarita* has had curious misadventures in the history of its publication both in Russia and abroad. Published first in the literary journal *Moscow* (1966, No. 11, and 1967, No. 1), it immediately caught the attention of literary critics as a magnificent accomplishment, especially since Bulgakov wrote it during the Stalinist thirties, when he was suffering from chronic rejection as a writer alien to the Soviet mode as well as from uremia and partial blindness. Arrangements to translate the novel into English were made by Grove Press and by Harper and Row soon after its appearance, and when both translations appeared at approximately the same time, it was discovered that the *Moscow* version, which the Grove Press edition had followed, had excised some 23,000 words. The Harper and Row translator, however, had managed to obtain access to the full text. The Grove Press edition, strangely enough, can only be described as an expurgated one. The omissions are arbitrary and not always explainable in terms of political or editorial considerations. Many reflect the special reflexes of the Soviet censor, his prudery both political and sexual. Certain scenes involving nakedness (there is an inordinate amount of this in the novel), lechery, or spectacular drinking have been tampered with; the line addressed to Pilate by Yeshua (Jesus), "the greatest crime is cowardice," was dropped in one context and retained in another; the wonderful comment of a swinish character named Nikolai Ivanovich when he is being transported to Satan's ball, "I refuse to attend an illegal meeting," and the line "destroy the document and you destroy the man" have both been deleted in the *Moscow* version. A rather long passage in which the devil discusses the question whether Moscow residents, in spite of their technological advances, have really changed inwardly, and some references to police activities, were censored. Some though not all of these deleted passages are important for the meaning of the novel.

The story is a fantastic tale featuring the devil and his retinue, Christ and Pontius Pilate, numerous characters from the literary and theatrical world of Moscow, the "Master," and the woman who loves him, Margarita. Its satire of contemporary life is aimed chiefly at the pharisaic mediocrities who dominate the Soviet literary world and whose official function it is to discourage literary talent. Like *A Theatrical Novel, The Master and Margarita* is concerned with the creative process itself. The Master has conceived and written a novel about Christ and Pilate, the creation of which gave him great joy, but he is driven to distraction when bigoted officials attack him for "dragging in the Christ theme." In a fit of desperation he destroys the manuscript, then has himself committed to a mental asylum.

This story about the strange destiny of a book contains a series of complex and bewildering involvements with the devil himself under the medieval name "Woland" and a number of his traditional minor demons—Behemoth, Azazello, and others. The devil plays infernal tricks on bureaucrats, time-servers, and literary hacks, and he throws Moscow into a state of hysteria, but he figures paradoxically as a source of good. His magical tricks at the Variety Theater expose the petty avarice of the citizenry, especially their attachment to such bourgeois matters as fine clothes of foreign manufacture and money. He interferes with base projects, he frees the Master from confinement, he reconciles Pilate with Christ, and, most important, he is the messenger who first tells us of Christ and who reconstitutes the manuscript of the Master's novel. *The Master and Margarita* is a kind of philosophical meditation on the nature of good and evil, and Bulgakov gives as its epigraph a quotation from Goethe's *Faust*: "Say at last—who art thou?" "That Power I serve which wills forever evil yet does forever good."

The story of Pontius Pilate and Jesus Christ we learn from the devil, from a madman's dream, and from a mad artist's manuscript. The rampant fantasy of the scenes in Moscow is skillfully counterpointed by the story of Jesus (Yeshua Ha-Notsri) and Pilate, which is given directly in human and natural terms. The details of Yeshua's character are both strange and appealing. He has a fanatical idea that "all people are good"; he sympathizes with those who torture him; he offers Pilate good advice; and his physical suffering in the process of crucifixion is frighteningly realistic. Bulgakov has given us an adaptation of the gospel story which renders the figure of Christ tragically human and utterly lonely. The cross on which he hangs is cordoned off by a detachment of Roman soldiers, and no one can approach it. Except for one half-mad "disciple" who loves him but garbles and misunderstands his message, he has no followers. The great sin is that of Pilate, who allows an innocent man, a good and generous if somewhat strange character, to be executed because Pilate can allow nothing to threaten the advancement of his own career. His sin is cowardice.

The Master and Margarita has often been acclaimed as one of the great novels of the twentieth century. Judged in the context of Soviet literature, it is certainly a magnificent *tour de force* and a demonstration of what that literature may still accomplish if the current movement against censorship and restriction is successful.

Bulgakov's third "rediscovered" novel, *The Heart of a Dog,* written in 1925, develops a satiric theme in a science-fantasy setting. A Soviet specialist in the transplantation of organs selects for his experiments a mongrel dog from the Moscow gutter. He successfully transplants in the dog the testicles and pituitary gland of a human being, with the result that the animal rapidly takes on the semblance of human form and acquires something like human speech. But he remains a dirty, slothful, mean, and lascivious animal. His speech is an amalgam of curses, abuse, and slander; he reads approved Marxist works and mouths slogans; he learns of his "rights" and demands a share of his master's goods; he acquires some skill at writing denunciations to the Secret Police; he becomes an employee of the state. Like George Orwell's *Animal Farm,* the novel provides a satiric picture of vileness and stupidity grasping for power. The setting and the idiom of this particular story happen to be Soviet, but its satiric reach is broader than that. Indeed, the bitter point of the novel is that a dog's heart is "human, all too human."

The Production Line: Poetry and Prose

We have so far been concerned with underground and rediscovered literature, and some of the most interesting recent publication in modern Russian literature has taken place in those areas. An examination of the output of Soviet literary magazines and publishing houses reveals that in the homeland, itself and under official aegis there have been many interesting and original departures. A complete survey of what has been published in the sixties might degenerate into a dull bibliographic catalogue, and therefore it has seemed preferable to select for discussion certain authors and works that represent important contemporary trends. Both in prose and in poetry there are writers who speak with a new accent, who experiment with new themes and ideas, and who raise questions in their writing that have significance for the present day.

Curiously enough, it is the contemporary poets who create the greatest stir and receive the widest acclaim both at home and abroad. Public poetry readings attract enormous and enthusiastic crowds—large enough, even, to fill the giant Luzhniki Sports stadium in Moscow. Certain poets, Yevtushenko and Voznesensky, for instance, have a devoted following among the young and obviously regard themselves as "tribunes" of the people. They "speak out" on issues with a certain frankness, and the political regime finds it expedient to tolerate them—within limits—and even to use them.

The name of Yevgeny Yevtushenko is perhaps associated most vividly in the minds of foreigners with the struggle for liberalization in the Soviet Union, and his own exuberance in taking intellectually honest positions has caused him some trouble, as we have seen. The main tendency of his life and his writing is an effort to escape from chauvinistic isolation. He has frequently traveled abroad. He was severely called to task in 1963 for the publication in Paris without authorization of his *A Precocious Autobiography*, and a projected visit to the United States was canceled at that time. His work began appearing again in 1964, and in 1966 he visited the United States and toured the country, giving a number of poetry readings.

We have already mentioned his two famous poems, "Babi Yar" (1961) and "Stantsia Zima" (1955). His poetry is characteristically "topical," as is the prose of his *Precocious Autobiography*. That work is naïve, but like so much of

Yevtushenko, beautifully so. Consider this quotation, the innocence of which is not lost in translation: "Gradually I came
to understand that some people who called themselves Communists and were fond of quoting Lenin and Stalin were not
genuine Communists at all." The story of his own literary
education is significant. His mentor, Barlas, he says, "revealed
to me that Hemingway existed." He also revealed to him
writers who were at that time "bibliographical rarities":
Hamsun, Joyce, Freud, Proust, Steinbeck, Faulkner, Re-
marque, Saint-Exupéry. He goes on: "I drank in the might
of Whitman, the violence of Rimbaud . . . the tragic in
Baudelaire, the magic in Verlaine, the subtlety of Rilke, the
sensitive visions of T. S. Eliot, and the healthy, peasant
wisdom of Robert Frost." Frost specialists will of course question the terms "healthy" and "peasant" as applied to him, but
what Yevtushenko means is that he managed to make the
acquaintance of European and American literature and found
it a revelation. At another point he writes:

I don't want borders.
It's awkward
    not to know Buenos Aires
    and New York.
I want to wander
As much as I like
Around London
And talk to everybody, even if only in broken English,
And hanging on the back of a bus like a little boy,
I want to ride around Paris in the morning.

Yevtushenko dedicated one of his best poems, "An Encounter," to Hemingway, and this is symptomatic both for
him and for many of his contemporaries, who prize Hemingway and try to learn the craft of writing from him. Hemingway has offered them, perhaps, an example of how to use
words sparingly and with direct reference to experience. He
is a reproachful contrast to Soviet writing of the Stalin period,
specifically to its hagiographic and homiletic varieties, and
that is why he is so inordinately popular in the Soviet Union.
    Yevtushenko's image of himself as a poet is, nevertheless,

deeply in the Russian tradition and, in fact, rather old-fashioned. He is a "civic" poet, one with a mission and messages. His poetry is declamatory and can be eloquent. Its surface meaning is usually the essence of the matter. He tends to shy away from verbal experiment or formal play, and it is difficult to see that he has learned much from the modern poets he claims to revere. Occasionally a sudden cadence or a striking rhyme recalls Mayakovsky, but by comparison with Mayakovsky he is a timid poet. He has published in the magazine *Youth* (1965) a lengthy poem entitled "The Bratsk Hydroelectric Station," in which he contemplates the enormous dam and installations on the Angara river, one of the most powerful sources of electricity in the world. The poem itself is set in monumental proportions and delivers an important didactic message: the pyramids, the deep past of Russia and her history, man's fate in general, his struggle and labor—all this and much more enter into the poet's lines about a major industrial project. The unifying theme of the poem is the opposition of cynical "disbelief," expressed in the monologue of the Egyptian pyramids, to that "faith" in mankind and in the future which the Bratsk station sets forth. It is an ambitious, even a pretentious poem, and it is not devoid of interesting thoughts and new turns of phrase. In the Prologue Yevtushenko appeals to Mayakovsky as his "muse," but the poem lacks completely the latter's boldness, creativity, and verve. Set beside Mayakovsky and other poets of the early part of the century, Yevtushenko seems nothing if not "square."

Andrey Voznesensky is more original and more enterprising as a poet than Yevtushenko. He came to poetry from architecture, having graduated from the Moscow Architectural Institute, and his work was first published only in 1958. He has published a number of collections of poems, *Mosaic* (1960), *Parabola* (1961), *The Triangular Pear* (1962), *Antiworlds* (1964), and *The Achilles Heart* (1966). The poem he himself considers his most characteristic is one entitled "Parabolic Ballad," which offers the idea that in poetry the shortest distance between two points is never the straight line of direct statement, but a curve. The poem takes as a case in point the painter Gauguin, who,

> To reach the royal Louvre,
> Set his course
> On a detour via Java and Sumatra.

In Voznesensky's poetry the "meaning" of a poem is often incidental to its texture of imagery and language, and can be arrived at only after a more or less lengthy detour, which takes in the scenery of the poet's lyrical personality, and only after many a subtle linguistic twist and turn. Situations, statements, sights, and sounds often enough seem to exist in his poetry for their own sake—sometimes only for the sake of rhyme, assonance, or alliteration. In translation his work is usually distorted and can be destroyed, since translation must be concerned with *what* is said. Each Voznesensky poem is a tightly woven unity of verbal image, metaphor, and symbol, and in each one an item of reality is refracted in such a way that its shape and body become matters of speculation. A case in point is the nearly untranslatable "New York Airport at Night," which begins

> My own self-portrait, a neon retort,
> Apostle of the heavenly gates—
> An airport.

The long poem "Oza" (1964) is the poet's intellectually most ambitious piece of work. It explores philosophy and history, touches on the poet's intimate life, and deals with the confrontation of human values by the soulless world of machines and practicality. Its texture is constantly variegated by reminiscences from the work of many poets: Poe, Mayakovsky, Goethe, and others. Voznesensky is indeed a poet of the parabola. He seldom matches the straight, demonstrative rhetoric of Yevtushenko, but perhaps for that very reason his work is stronger. In the words of Robert Lowell, "he is full of invention, fireworks, and humor . . . a first-rate craftsman who has had the heroic patience and imagination to be himself."

Bella Akhmadulina, who was once married to Yevtushenko, has enjoyed much less notoriety than he but is held in higher esteem as a poet among Soviet intellectuals. Her work has been published only sporadically, and one of her best things, "A Fairy Tale about the Rain," has been published at the present writing only in part and only in a Georgian literary magazine, *Literary Georgia.* A volume of her poetry was published under the title *Struna* in 1962. Akhmadulina's work is interesting and original for the use she makes of concrete things: a thermometer, aspirin, icicles, a gramophone, the rain, a shiny parquet floor, a motorcycle—each of which plays in her poetry a special, personal, and paradoxical role. Nature is a favorite theme, but so are sickness—even the "coming on of a cold"—and neurotic states of mind. Her "Fairy Tale about the Rain" is an allegory of the poet, whose inspiration ("the rain") follows her wherever she goes, and embarrasses her by splashing the floors in fine philistine houses. The poem has been interpreted as an attack on the literary philistines, and specifically on Khrushchev's entertainment and instruction of writers. It does lend itself to such an interpretation, but its wonderfully original imagery and deepfelt disdain for the safe, the comfortable, and the obvious cannot be narrowed to the purely local and topical. The following translation of one section may give some notion of the poem's power:

The hostess said:
"I must scold you.
For heaven's sake,
What talent!
And you walked through the rain!
So far."
And all the guests shouted, "Over to the fire with her!
  The fire!"
But on another day and in another time,
On a public square,
To the sound of curses and of music,
We might have met together, you and I, as the drums rolled,
And you would all have shouted: "Into the fire with her!
  Into the fire!"

Akhmadulina has a strong sense of both language and form, and it is her purpose, in part achieved, that every line be an unobtrusive *bon mot*. She delights in intricately unusual end rhymes, some of which have the effect of neat puns.

Boris Slutsky, who was born in 1919, can hardly be described as a young poet. He began to write and to publish before the war, but his most important work is that which appeared after 1953. His published collections—*Memory* (1957), *Time* (1959), and *Today and Yesterday* (1961)—contain his most characteristic work. A selection of his poems was published in the collection *Pages from Tarusa* (1961). His thematic range is wide. He has written many lyrics that present scenes of war simply and vividly. He writes of construction work in Moscow, of schools, of how he came to write poetry, and of how poetry ought to be written. His vision is childlike at times in his clear enjoyment of the world. Both in his language and in his images he seems to aim at the obvious, almost at the banal, then deliberately to miss banality and arrive instead at something simple but slightly offbeat and surprisingly interesting.

There are many other poets who might be mentioned and whose work does represent an effort to create out of verse, as Slutsky would say, "the truth and happiness." Among them are Evgeny Vinokurov and a young lyric poetess whose first work appeared only in the sixties, Novella Matveeva. She is a highly gifted and disciplined poet whose themes cover a wide range of interest and experience: art, architecture, world history, literature, and other things. Her latest collection is entitled *The Spirit of Things* (1966). Matveeva deals in her work with what might be called a "lyrical problem": the relationship of the poet to the welter of experience, to "Mars, Athens, and an old shoe, a squall, a basket, and building lime, the day of judgment and mud on the road." In each of her poems there are rich layers of symbolic meaning.

The revival of poetry in the sixties featured a number of older poets as well as young ones. Alexander Tvardovsky, the editor of *New World*, published in that journal his "Tvyorkin in the Other World," which follows the hero of his earlier poem "Vasily Tvyorkin" into the nether regions, where he

324 / Russian Literature Since the Revolution

finds an inferno organized along the lines of a Stalinist bureaucracy. Bulat Okudzhava is enormously popular as a singer of his own songs, which he writes simply and without didacticism about intimate and personal things. Leonid Martynov and some others have published interesting and unhackneyed lyrics. Iosif Brodsky is an especially interesting case. Because he had no regular employment and worked only at the poet's trade, he was brought to trial in Leningrad in 1964 on the charge that he was a "parasite" and sentenced to five years at hard labor, a sentence that was later commuted. A collection of his poems was published in the West, and since his release from confinement he has written a cycle of poems dedicated to the memory of T. S. Eliot, an acknowledged affinity. Only a scattering of his work has appeared in the Soviet press. Contemporary Soviet poets regard his talent highly, and Anna Akhmatova considered him the outstanding poet of the younger generation. He stands apart both from his contemporaries and from his predecessors; it is difficult to find in him traces of any influence from earlier Russian poets, though some critics have observed a debt to Nikolay Zabolotsky. There is a deep and serious religious strain in his work, and he has clearly been affected by a study of the Bible. Gravely conceived and solemnly executed long poems such as "Isaac and Abraham," and the poem "Procession," resemble nothing else that is being done in the Soviet Union today. The partial loss to the public of Brodsky's poetic talent is surely one of the tragedies of Soviet literature.

In spite of distrust and frequent harassment, Soviet writers are producing a literature. The most interesting feature of prose writing in the sixties has been a slow, hesitant, at times timid, often tortured search for release from banality—release, that is, from the hackneyed, the obvious, and the false. Just as in the earlier period when successive "thaws" opened up new possibilities, the new tendencies are probably not symptomatic of political opposition. Writers of course must have freedom to think about many things, but the important thing at the moment is the objective of being free to write as one pleases and to develop one's own individual style.

Prose fiction continued to develop new themes, to focus on individual experience, and to experiment with new forms. We have mentioned Yury Kazakov, who began writing during the fifties, but whose best work was published during the following decade. In *Pages from Tarusa* (1961) Kazakov published three new stories, one of which, "The Smell of Bread," is characteristic of his sensitive recording of fleeting mental states so intimately personal that they elude verbalization. It is the story of a Moscow woman who hears that her mother, whom she had not seen for fifteen years, has died in her far-off native village. At first she seems to feel nothing, but when she returns to the village in the spring to sell her mother's property, sensory memories of childhood—the smell of bread and of her mother's old clothing—gradually invade her consciousness, and when, as a kind of afterthought, she visits her mother's grave, a deep source of grief suddenly wells up in her, and she keens over the grave like any peasant woman. The spell of grief passes quickly, however, and she returns to Moscow the next day in a contented frame of mind. In this story as in many others Kazakov subtly traces apparently erratic emotional shifts, showing their connection with accidental sensory impressions of sight or smell.

The poet Bulat Okudzhava is also the author of a short novel entitled *Good Luck, Boy!*, which is an authentic *tour de force* in the unheroic treatment of war. It sets forth, from the viewpoint of a young volunteer who entered the army before he had finished school, the ugly, monotonous, and dangerous workdays of a front-line soldier. The focus is narrowed to the frame of a single mind, and a rather simple one. The boy's needs are modest and very basic. He doesn't want to be killed and he is afraid he will be killed. He needs sleep and wants to be warm, to eat something, to be liked by a girl. The problem of his spoon figures as an ironic symbol of a soldier's real life and real concerns. The hero has no spoon and must use a piece of wood to feed himself. In the end, when a comrade dies in action, the boy inherits a spoon and has his heart's desire. The story is a continuous inner monologue interrupted by thoughts of the past and repellent events of the present. The movement of the boy's thought and the recorded conversations reflect the state of near mental collapse that is the everyday experience of a soldier in combat. He lives in a kind of trance induced by frequent death, noise, and insuperable fatigue. He never knows what he is doing, where he is going, or what the war is all about.

Vladimir Voinovich has already been mentioned in connection with the story "We Live Here," published in *New World* (1961, No. 1). His story "I Want to Be Honest" (*New World*, 1963, No. 2) was very unfavorably reviewed in the Soviet press because it supposedly revealed serious flaws of attitude and ideology. Its central character, Samoikhin, offers a continuous first-person reflection concerning his work and his problems, most of them slight and seemingly unimportant. He simply chatters on, describing a life that has many things in it—everything but interest and enthusiasm. The story gradually develops in a very low key a distinct undertone of tragedy, a sense that something essential is missing from Samoikhin's life, that his very activity only serves to fill a kind of vacuum. The pseudophilosophical reflections of one of the characters—an *autodidacte*—on the "nonexistence" of external objects and other people provide humorous interludes, but they also contain the *leitmotif* of the story, the persistent sense of unreality.

Voinovich's "Two Comrades" (1967) offers a frightening portrait of a future careerist, hypocrite, scoundrel, and "poet" in his first adolescent efforts at "making it." The young man who narrates the story is intelligent, interested in poetry, and not too selfish. His "comrade" is a vulgar hunter after flashy clothes, money, and girls. When they are both caught by a peculiarly vicious set of hooligans, this "comrade" beats his friend without mercy at the order of the gang in order to escape a beating himself. In the end he turns to literature, because poetry "pays well." The "comrade" is an embodiment of those grubby and mean qualities that spoil life.

A number of writers not as well known as those so far discussed have published short stories and novellas that contain original traits of both style and theme. One of them is Lev Slavin, whose story "A Presage of Truth" (*New World*, 1966, No. 5) is, like so much of contemporary fiction, told from the narrative viewpoint of a very young mind. In this case it is a Jewish boy; through his eyes we see the life of his Jewish family and come to know the character of his grandfather Simon—a pillar, very nearly a saint, in the local Hassidic community. The story is told with gentle humor and is remarkable for the naïve and at the same time sympathetic view of this Jewish community before the revolution. The young boy who narrates the story expresses wide-eyed wonder at everything that happens. A number of original characters are brought to life: for instance, the grandfather, a Talmudic scholar who can cite a learned instance in every crisis of faith or judgment, and the great-grandmother, with her memories of the family's deep past, as well as many uncle and aunts, who play a variety of roles in the community. The incongruous juxtaposition of the child's real concerns with those of the adult world is the thread of humor which holds the story together. The young boy experiences a growing sense of the presence of God, and we are made to feel the boy's awe at the interest God takes in every action of his. The story seems at first to promise a kind of autobiography of religious feeling, but a contrived ending—one might almost say a *deus ex machina*—converts the boy at an early age to atheism. In spite of the contrivance, the story is an excellent piece of work—restrained, humorous, full of sympathy.

Another interesting practitioner of the short story and "short novel" form is Nikolai Dubov, whose story "The Escapee" appeared in *New World* (1966, No. 4). This is an entertaining, instructive, and very well made story. Once again the narrative viewpoint is an "innocent" one: the story is told by an intelligent, sensitive, and awkwardly adolescent boy named Yurka. A man and a woman from "the city" turn up in the southern community where he lives and rent a plot of ground on which to pitch their tent. Yurka promptly falls in love with Vitaly and Yulivanna. Unlike his own family, they are cultivated, gentle, kind. At first their identity and purposes are a mystery, but gradually and deftly the author reveals that Vitaly is an architect who abandoned his work to escape the philistines in the profession who regularly canceled out anything original and creative in his projects. When

tragedy strikes with Vitaly's death by drowning, it turns out
that Yulivanna is his mistress, that indeed he had abandoned
a living and legal wife. Immediately the attitude of Yurka's
family toward Yulivanna changes and he is honestly repelled
when they abuse her, cheat her, and drive her away. There
are "good" and "bad" people in the story. The good people
are unconventional in taste and behavior. They are runaways
from respectable family life, from the ponderous "art" world
of socialist-realist canvases and monumental structures, from
established social values. The "bad" ones are legal wives, de-
manding mothers, and honored artists of the republic. Dubov
attempts in this story to examine the experience of growing
up in a given milieu and to realize as moral problems the
difficulties an adolescent faces.

An exhilarating bit of evidence that good satire is not dead
in the Soviet Union and that it may even be published is the
work of a young poet and writer of fiction, Fazil Iskander.
He is a specialist in humorous, innocent-seeming satire that
hits squarely upon its social target without arousing offense
or anger. Each of his stories delivers a sharp point, but
delivers it with a smile. He manages this by presenting situations—and we have seen that in general this device is very
common in contemporary fiction—from the viewpoint of
simple-minded, faintly ridiculous characters or of children.
He has been published in various journals and in the *Literary
Gazette*, and in 1966 two collections of his stories were published in book form. A story that demonstrates his method
in its purest form is one called "My Uncle Had the Highest
Principles," in which an absurd little boy of approximately
cub-scout age, his patriotic head full of journalistic warnings
about the need for vigilance against spies, is suddenly visited
by the idea that his crazy uncle is neither crazy nor an uncle
but a foreign spy. Once the idea has taken firm root, uncle's
innocent but daft actions all take on an aura of suspicion. So
much evidence accumulates that the boy is soon ready to
make a formal accusation, which he does in an exquisitely
amusing scene. Iskander, in this story about an unhinged old
man and his silly nephew, thus treats very lightly a situation
that contains essential ingredients of the terror and the purge.

Perhaps Iskander's best story is one entitled "Sozvesdie Kozlotura," which may be rendered "The Constellation of the Goat-Buffalo." It relates the misadventures of a dogmatic bureaucrat who devises a project of crossing goats with buffalo in order to produce a new animal that will give more milk, be more lively, and grow a new kind of wool. With Party support this weird project is adopted, in spite of the serious doubts raised by qualified geneticists and agrobiologists. Iskander's style in the story is freshly ironical, and at times it is a parody of the somber and solemn cant to be found in much Soviet journalism and other writing. He pointedly mimics the elaborately vacuous Byzantine statement, the worn political cliché, the empty phrase. Both satire and parody are specifically aimed at the so-called Michurinist school of agrobiology, the group led by Trofim Lysenko, whose theories in recent years did great harm to Russian science. Iskander has mastered, no doubt by taking great pains, a very casual narrative style. Ordinary joys and frustrations—the loss of a watch, a momentarily attractive girl, a conversation in a café, an effort to catch a bus—are all presented as at least on an equal level of importance with such world-shaking projects as the discovery of the Goat-Buffalo. What happens to ordinary people in the struggle to live decently is in the forefront of Iskander's attention.

An important contemporary theme often skillfully handled is the life of the Russian backwoods. We have already seen that Tendryakov often favors that locale. Some writers, Valentin Ovechkin and Yefim Dorosh for example, have produced important and apparently objective sketches and diaries containing observations of peasant life. Dorosh's *A Dry Summer* (1964) provides vivid pictures of life on the collective farms. Vladimir Soloukhin's *Lyrical Stories* (1962) contains his "Back Roads of Vladimir District," a poetic account of a journey into the deep interior of central Russia, and of the peasant life he found there.

A persistent and deep concern of Soviet literature since 1945 has been the Second World War and Russia's part in it. Much of what has been written on the subject has fallen obediently into the well-worn ruts of the patriotic cliché, but after 1956 a number of works appeared whose conscious purpose was to provide a frank and, as the Soviet critics put it, "truthful" literary treatment of that catastrophic experience. This development, like the current popularity of "memoir" literature, reveals the passionate interest of the Soviet reader in books that purport to correct particular items in the general falsehood that enveloped the years of Stalin. Some excellent and important novels about World War II have just this purpose. Grigory Baklanov's *July 1941* relates the experiences of a front-line commander who is in charge of a unit at the border in the early stages of the war. The novel is written in a lean and vigorous prose, and in one dramatic scene after another it depicts the military collapse in the summer of 1941 and the deep retreats that took place. The central concern of the novel is a subject until recently taboo: the dreadful failures of the first months of the war.

Vasily Bykov's *The Dead Feel No Pain* describes the Stalinist methods used at the front lines during the war and their survival into the present. Sakhno is a Stalinist commissar who was responsible for the deaths by execution of many soldiers; his double, Gorbiotok, survived the war and the de-Stalinization period and still stands ready to apply brutal measures if given a chance. Bykov's novel opens questions that were closed but never answered by the official formulas— "cult of personality," for instance—offered to explain the purges. Who were the police officials that actually carried out the thousands of illegal sentences, and where are the ones who provided them with the denunciations upon which to act? How do they explain what they did? What deep sources of fear, suspicion, racial hatred, paranoia, or sheer brutality fed the purges? These questions take dramatic form in Bykov's novel.

Anatoly Kuznetsov's *Babi Yar*, in some ways one of the best of the Soviet war novels, graphically brings to light the Russian retreat in the Ukraine and the German capture of Kiev as seen through the eyes of a young boy. The novel has an explicit documentary flavor: together with eyewitness accounts by the youthful observer, it presents the brutal communiqués and proclamations of the Germans. From direct

and incredibly detailed accounts we learn of the mass murders
of Jews and gypsies. Very quietly and without emphasis the
book reveals widespread anti-Soviet attitudes among the local
populace.

Another important novelist whose subject is World War II
is Yury Bondarev, who wrote *Battalions Ask for Fire* and *The
Last Command*. His novel *Quietude* (1962) deals with the
aftermath of war and the search for civilian readjustment of
two demobilized officers who find the peaceful life of postwar
Moscow beset with difficulties, many of which stem from
government policies.

The prose writing we have so far examined is interesting,
skillfully done, and certainly honest, but it offers only a small
measure of formal or thematic excitement. By comparison
with the experimentation that dominates literary life in the
West, Soviet prose of the sixties is conventional in form and
thematically tame. Yet there is good reason to believe that
should the Party loosen its hold, there would be an immediate
search for a new kind of fiction and for a new accent in
poetry. New themes, hitherto taboo in the puritanical pages
of the Soviet press, would suddenly blossom forth, and Soviet
Russian literature might begin to resemble somewhat the
literature of the West. Many writers would eagerly take up
the search for the fantastic and the exaggerated, and would
explore the offbeat and the unusual. Some would abandon
traditional realistic narrative, the traditional story form, and
the traditional novel in favor of experimenting with the
perception and presentation of time, objects, or states of mind.
The work of Sinyavsky-Tertz is an indication that some
writers would like to embark on ventures into the grotesque
or to examine perversion, impotence, and paranoid states of
mind. For instance, in one story, "The Holy Well," published
in 1966, we find a conscious effort to abandon realistic narration and recover the experience of the author's long lifetime in the form of fantastic dream images framed in a
dimension that has nothing to do with common-sense notions
of time sequence. The work is quite frankly an experiment,
and with its appearance the rebels against traditional art

forms now include in their number not just a few young people who will some day grow up and be sensible, as Sholokhov would have it, but one of the oldest and most respected writers in the Soviet Union, Valentin Katayev.

The same author's "The Grass of Oblivion" (*New World*, 1967, No. 3) is another effort to recover the past, but one that uses arrangements and contrivances usually considered the property of fiction. Katayev makes no claim that his reminiscences are documentary; rather, they are an imaginative re-creation of an intricate set of relationships with certain people and events: with Bunin and Mayakovsky; with "Klavdia Zaremba," an invented character who symbolizes the women he knew who gave everything for Communism; with "Riurik Pchelkin," another invented character, who is the author's own shadow—a young man who wrote agitational articles for the Bolshevik press. The revolution itself figures as a mysterious and overwhelming event whose complex and unpredictable effects shaped all of their lives.

"The Grass of Oblivion" is an extraordinarily subtle experiment in the creation of a literature somewhere on the border between fact and fiction. It bestows upon certain real people a vividness of character and presence that history has so far denied them. The poets Bunin and Mayakovsky are presented from the viewpoint of a young man for whom poetry is a kind of faith. We are given significant but sparse details of their appearance, manner, and effect, but they are fully characterized by remembered lines of their poetry. It may very well be that Katayev is making an important point in his juxtaposition of Bunin and Mayakovsky—two mutually exclusive human beings who hated one another—as the most important influences in his own life. His work suggests that the "grass of time" may at last make possible a reconciliation between the two segments of modern Russian literature, Soviet and *émigré*, which have anathematized each other. The work also contains an implicit reflection on the irreality of time and the insubstantial quality of memory. Did the young Katayev, who figures as "Riurik Pchelkin," really exist, or is he just an episodic actor temporarily incarnated in the shifting forms of memory?

The works discussed here in detail have been selected because they offer some degree of interest or originality in theme or style. To maintain a true perspective we must bear in mind that the production of Soviet belles-lettres is a vast public enterprise, the major part of which consists of works that communicate approved attitudes and ideas. The catalog of novels that deal with agricultural production, exploration for minerals, Siberian enterprises, scientific developments, and the like is very long, and some of the more interesting examples should perhaps be mentioned. B. Mozhaev's *The Life of Fyodor Kuzkin* deals with the problems involved in organizing country life along collective lines. V. Kozhevnikov's *Meet Baluev!* features a Party activist as a positive hero and model of behavior. Y. Trifonov's *The Quenching of Thirst* describes the lives of workmen and engineers constructing a canal in Turkmenia. Daniil Granin's *Into the Storm* reveals the problems faced by Soviet scientific and technical workers. V. Popov's *The Broken Circle* treats the theme of innovation and rationalization in production. Natalya Ilina's *Return* tells of Russian *émigrés* in Harbin and Shanghai who feel the necessity of maintaining ties with the Soviet homeland. These are a few examples of the common run of purposeful and didactic fiction that pours from the Soviet presses at a fantastic rate. The total number of *titles* published in the Soviet Union in all genres reached 7,112 in 1967! Some of the "novels" produced are actually polemical tracts—for instance, Vsevolod Kochetov's *Secretary of the Provincial Committee* (1962), which sorts out in clear terms those characteristics that a good Party man should and should not have. But the work of Kochetov has no standing whatever among Soviet citizens who understand and value literature.

CONCLUSION

IN IVAN BUNIN'S fine novel *The Village* (1910) a disillusioned country poet, Kuzma Ilych, reflects on the barbarism of the Russian nation, revealed in their treatment of literary geniuses. One possible answer to the poet is that not the nation itself but the Czarist "regime" persecuted those writers; but an even more devastating indictment could be brought against the people and the "regime" in the twentieth century by many a disconsolate Kuzma Ilych: "What a savage nation! Poets they drive to suicide: Mayakovsky, Yesenin, Tsvetaeva; their best writers of prose they sent to prison or into exile: Pilnyak, Babel, Zamyatin; sensitive critics they hounded to death: Voronsky, Lezhnev; satirists they treated as traitors: Bulkagov; theater directors with an original touch they deprived of liberty: Meyerhold." And the list could be expanded for several pages. Barbarism in the waste of literary talent has characterized the nation in modern times, too.

And yet Kuzma Ilych is omitting something. What he neglects to say is that the reason writers have been treated so abominably in Russia is that in Russia they are important. This paradox conceals the key to the Russian literary riddle. Literature in the nineteenth century was a source of knowledge and a well of hope. Russian writers satisfied a demand not only for aesthetic experience but for ideas. In the great majority they accepted the role of educator and uplifter. Gogol sought to improve morals, Turgenev to instill respect for the enserfed folk, writers of the so-called "Natural School" to expose social injustice, Dostoevsky and Tolstoy to find and preach a firm faith. Because their work and their message was taken seriously by the people the attention of the autocratic government was frequently drawn to these writers. Sometimes they suffered from this. The literary history of Western Europe in the nineteenth century offers no clear parallels.

In Soviet times, too, literature has been important—in fact a matter of life and death. Consider the literary disputes and the interest in them of highly placed personages. Lenin himself took a hand in the discussion of the Proletcult. Probably the most stimulating comments on Mayakovsky and Pilnyak came from the pen of Trotsky. Bukharin had a sophisticated understanding of modern poetry. Lunacharsky was a man of broad culture and tolerant taste who took an active part in literary work. To read and to argue about literature was an important part of the work of government leaders. Their successors of the Stalin era shared the conviction that literature is important, though they knew little or nothing about it. The distance from Bukharin to Zhdanov is polar: Bukharin knew literature, whereas Zhdanov did not; Bukharin did not represent himself as an authority, Zhdanov did; Bukharin's intervention tended to increase variety in literature, Zhdanov's intervention narrowed the range. And because Zhdanov knew that literature is important he periodically scrutinized and purged the ranks of its producers.

There was one important difference between Zhdanov and his successor, Khrushchev. The latter was also ignorant of literature, but he seemed to be cheerfully aware of his ignorance and reluctant to make authoritative judgments. His important speech to the Union of Writers in 1959 was crudely jocose and casual. "You cannot control the unknown," said Shklovsky in 1920; and the ironic realization of that idea in contemporary Russian life was Khrushchev's frank expression of interested ignorance. He modified this eminently sane viewpoint in 1963 when he spoke out scornfully on "modernism." And yet, after Khrushchev's fall, no clearly appointed lawgiver appeared. This may be the result of profound changes in the cultural level of those "masses" of whom the state must take some account. The unstilled voice of liberalism in the sixties is evidence that education may be having its effect on the Party itself, and a return to the simple precepts of Stalinism is probably out of the question.

But literature is still regarded as important and as vitally bound to life. The crowds that gather in Moscow to hear the poet Yevtushenko are evidence that the tradition of literature as social commentary continues in Russia, and that the writer will not be without honor. The whole tendency of the recent period has been toward recognizing that the literary artist, though his work be firmly anchored in the soil of a particular social group, must fashion for himself his own view of reality and find his own means for expressing it. This is the meaning of the quiet exploration of individual experience in so much contemporary writing. Writers tend to reject formulaic statement in favor of simple, tentative thought processes. After nearly a generation of clearly stated socialist tendency in literature, the new men, in the words of a character in a proletarian novel of 1929, refuse to "reduce this magnificent tongue-tied life to the terms of a poor Marxist dialect."

That the demand for freedom from censorship so cogently expressed in Solzhenitsyn's letter has widespread support was made evident in the appearance during the summer of 1968 of an essay written by a leading Soviet physicist, Professor A. D. Sakharov. In this unpublished but widely circulated essay he said that "the salvation of mankind requires intellectual freedom, freedom to obtain and distribute information, and freedom from intimidation by officialdom." Censorship, he said, has killed the "living soul" of Soviet literature. Sakharov's intelligent and courageous statement offers strong support to Solzhenitsyn and others who oppose ignorant and wasteful official policies. One can hope that the general liberalization attempted in Czechoslovakia and other countries of eastern Europe will, in the end, prove irresistible to Moscow.

A NOTE ON ÉMIGRÉ LITERATURE:
NABOKOV AS A RUSSIAN WRITER

MODERN RUSSIAN LITERATURE includes a variegated and substantial body of writing published outside the Soviet Union. The stream of Russian literature bifurcated in 1917 into two currents: *émigré* literature, or what the *émigrés* call "Russian literature abroad," and the domestic—and in some periods safely domiciled—literature produced in the Russian homeland. If we are eventually to place modern Russian literature in proper perspective, it will be necessary for future historians to trace and follow the two currents as part of a single stream. Those writers who produced their books in the lonely freedom of Russian *émigré* colonies dispersed through the cities of western Europe and the United States have never received their full due of critical attention, even though one of them, Ivan Bunin, received the Nobel Prize in 1933, and another, Vladimir Nabokov, has recently been discovered as one of the great novelists of the twentieth century.

Even the official Soviet attitude toward *émigré* literature and culture is softening. A number of *émigré* writers have recently been republished in the Soviet Union. Ivan Bunin has reappeared in a handsome nine-volume set. Indeed, a tentative *rapprochement* between Russian writers and artists at home and those abroad is a prospect not totally dark. The music of Stravinsky has been revived with enormous public success. The latest editions of the *Concise Literary Encyclopedia* and the *Theatrical Encyclopedia* have restored to their place in cultural history a number of writers who had been forgotten, among them Mark Aldanov, Boris Zaitsev, and Konstantin Balmont. And the poetic genius of Ivan Bunin, as we have seen, is one of the chief themes of Valentin Katayev's "The Grass of Oblivion."

It is of course too early to speak of the possibility of a dialogue between the *émigré* writers and those still in the

Soviet Union, but many things point to the beginning of a historical development that would seem to be inevitable. As time moves on and the embittered political issues of the century fade into the past, *émigré* writers will eventually take their place as a component of Russian literature, just as Alexander Herzen, who wrote most of his work in exile, is now firmly established in the history of Russian nineteenth-century literature.

The vitality and importance of *émigré* Russian literature have been highlighted by the attention bestowed during the sixties upon a Russian writer of the emigration whose first work appeared in Berlin in the twenties under the pseudonym V. Sirin—Vladimir Nabokov. The inclusion of Nabokov in a discussion of modern Russian literature is just and proper, since the roots of his style are in the Russian tradition, even though he has been formed by a variety of Western literary experiences. This can be demonstrated in a number of ways. Nabokov's own testimony as to his first, dearest, and most native language is to the point: "I had to abandon my natural idiom, my untrammelled, rich, and infinitely docile Russian tongue for a second-rate brand of English. . . ." There is a perhaps intentional and almost frivolous revelation contained in the novel *Lolita* that the language organic to Nabokov is not English but Russian. At one point the main character and great lover of little girls, Humbert Humbert, intones a prose poem, a kind of hymn to his girl: "Lolita, light of my life, fire of my loins. My sin, my soul, Lolita: the tip of the tongue taking a trip of three steps down the palate, to tap at three, on the teeth." This is beautifully instrumented prose, but let us examine what it says. In an English pronunciation of the name "Lolita" the tongue does not take that enchanted journey ending with a tap on the front teeth. That tap on the teeth happens in a Russian pronunciation. In an English pronunciation of the *t* sound the tongue does not reach the teeth but taps on the alveolar ridge above them. It is clear, then, that Humbert pronounced his girl with a Russian accent.

Another evidence of Nabokov's essential Russianness even when he writes in English is the nature of his vocabulary and phrasing, and this is especially true of the English he uses in

Lolita. Nabokov exhibits in his dealings with language a tender curiosity about it which is, I think, in the Russian rather than in the English or American tradition. When he writes English he discovers a new felicity in archaic, dialectal, technical, scientific, or even slang words that a native writer would tend to avoid. Critics of his translation of *Eugene Onegin* have been unduly shocked by the appearance in it of words that have for many generations lain dormant between the thick covers of Webster's Unabridged, the Oxford English Dictionary, or Roget's Thesaurus. Nabokov, untroubled by a native speaker's rigid psychological blocks, uses such curious items of dictionary English as *sapajous, carrick, levin, penates, coulisses,* and the like when he needs them for precision of meaning or special nuance. He is able to mimic the professional idiom of motel-keepers, school-mistresses, moviemakers, town-namers, sexual perverts, professors, and garage mechanics. At first sight Nabokov seems purely and perversely individual—a writer without antecedents or relatives—but Professor Gleb Struve has noted his affinity with Russian literature of the early twentieth century, especially with Andrey Bely. Nabokov's interest in revealing rich new veins of linguistic ore at various levels of speech also betrays an affinity with Alexey Remizov and Eugene Zamyatin, both of whom, like Nabokov, began as Russian writers, then joined the emigration. The character of his virtuosity in the use of English is distinctly foreign: the English language for Nabokov is an exotic game that he has learned to play with masterful ease.

Of course the best argument for treating Nabokov as a part of modern Russian literature is the historical fact that his first nine novels, his short stories, and all his poetry were written in Russian; indeed, three of the novels are practically unknown to readers of English. Nabokov is a Russian writer; he is original and idiosyncratic; he has no official sponsors; he renders no homilies in literary form; and he is fascinating. Future historians of Russian literature will surely claim him as their own.

Our experience of Russian literature in the modern period will one day be enriched by a reawakened appreciation of the novels of Mark Aldanov and Boris Zaitsev, the humorous stories of N. A. Teffi, the poetry of Boris Poplavsky, Vladislav Khodasevich, and Georgy Adamovich, the literary criticism of Konstantin Mochulsky and P. M. Bitsilli, the latter of whom is little read even among *émigré* Russians. These are only a few names out of many that might be mentioned, and in their sum they comprise a segment of Russian literature which developed unsponsored and free, maintaining vital contacts both with Russian literary tradition and with contemporary movements of thought and art in the Western world. The liberalization in the Soviet Union that everyone hopes for will surely lead to at least a partial reassimilation of the Russian literature that was produced "abroad."

NOTES

Chapter 2

1. L. Kassil', *Mayakovsky sam*, Moscow, 1960, p. 146.
2. The full text of the note, together with a photographic reproduction, is given in *Literaturnoye nasledstvo*, No. 65, Moscow, 1958, p. 199.
3. Ilya Ehrenburg, *Liudi, gody, zhizn'*, Moscow, 1961, p. 399.
4. Vladimir Mayakovsky, *Polnoye sobraniye sochinenii* (1955–58), Vol. I, p. 19.
5. *Ibid.*, p. 21.
6. *Ibid.*, p. 27.
7. Lawrence Stahlberger in *The Symbolic System of Mayakovsky* (unpublished doctoral dissertation, Harvard, 1957) sees in the central character of this poem the "archetypal" image of the poet as scapegoat, who must suffer for all.
8. V. Katanyan, *Mayakovsky, Literaturnaya khronika*, Moscow, 1961, p. 77.
9. *Ibid.*, p. 495.
10. Mayakovsky, *op. cit.*, Vol. II, p. 506.
11. Quoted in I. Mashbitz-Verov, *Poemy Mayakovskogo*, Kuibyshev, 1960, p. 106.
12. L. Trotsky, *Literatura i revolyutsiya*, Moscow, 1924, p. 73.
13. Mayakovsky, *op. cit.*, Vol. I, p. 26.
14. Katanyan, *op. cit.*, p. 365.
15. See R. Jakobson, "O pokolenii, rastrativshem svoikh poetov," *Smert' Vladimira Mayakovskogo*, Berlin, 1931, and also by the same author, "Unpublished Verses by Vladimir Mayakovsky," *Russkii literaturny arkhiv*, New York, 1956. See also the Introduction by Patricia Blake to *The Bedbug and Selected Poetry*, New York, 1960.

Chapter 3

1. E. Zamyatin, *We*, tr. by Gregory Zilboorg, New York: E. P. Dutton, 1959, p. 115.
2. Translations of passages from *Envy* and *Liompa* are from Yury Olesha, *The Wayward Comrade and the Commissars*, tr. by Andrew R. MacAndrew, New York, 1960.

Chapter 4

1. The contribution of Gorky, a writer of an older generation, in preserving literary life during the years of hunger and oppres-

sion should not be forgotten. Both Fedin in *Gorky among Us,*
Moscow, 1943, and Zamyatin in his essay on Gorky in the collection *Litsa,* New York, 1955, attest to his influence and authority
in their movement.

2. The best study of the Serapions in English is William Edger-
ton, "The Serapion Brothers, an Early Soviet Controversy,"
American Slavic and East European Review, Vol. VIII, No. 1,
1948.

3. Yury Libedinsky, *Sovremenniki,* Moscow, 1958, p. 165.

4. For a treatment of Shklovsky and the formalists, see Victor
Erlich, *Russian Formalism—History, Doctrine,* The Hague, 1955.

5. For a detailed account of these events see Max Hayward,
"Pilnyak and Zamyatin—Two Tragedies of the Twenties," *Survey,*
April–June, 1961.

Chapter 5

1. Babel's work has attracted the attention of some of the most
acute critics, both in Russia and elsewhere. Shklovsky's article in
Lef, No. 5, 1924, "Isaac Babel: a Critical Romance," ironic and
impressionistic in style, stresses the anecdotal form of Babel's
tales. Lionel Trilling in the Introduction to Babel's *Collected
Stories,* New York, Criterion Books, 1955, has a number of interesting insights, and Renato Poggioli's "Isaac Babel in Retrospect"
in *The Phoenix and the Spider,* Cambridge, 1957, contains both
information and ideas. Marc Slonim's *Portrety sovetskikh pisatelei*
(Berlin, 1933) contains stimulating commentary on Babel and
others. Other articles could be added to the list.

2. Ernest J. Simmons in *Russian Fiction and Soviet Ideology,*
New York, 1958, has contributed a detailed and perceptive study
of Fedin's work.

Chapter 6

1. A full account of this and other proletarian movements is
to be found in E. J. Brown, *The Proletarian Episode in Russian
Literature,* New York, 1953.

Chapter 7

1. A fascinating and well-documented account of this process
is Maurice Friedberg, "New Editions of Soviet Belles-Lettres: A
Study in Politics and Palimpsests," *American Slavic and East
European Review,* Vol. XIII (1954), pp. 72–88.

2. Some interesting ideas on Sholokhov are to be found in
Helen Muchnic, *From Gorky to Pasternak: Six Writers in Soviet
Russia,* New York, 1961. A penetrating study of the role of the
hero in certain proletarian novels is provided by Rufus Mathewson, *The Positive Hero in Russian Literature,* New York, 1958.

Chapter 8

1. V. Ivanov, in *Znamya*, Nos. 5 and 6, 1958.

2. The facts concerning Voronsky are contained in the article noted above, as well as in G. Glinka, *Na perevale, sbornik proizvedenii pisatelei gruppy Pereval*, New York, 1954.

3. Voronsky's views were presented in a series of articles in the magazine *Krasnaya nov'*, most of which were later published in book form. The following volumes are most important: *Iskusstvo i zhizn'; sbornik statei*, Moscow, 1924; *Na styke, sbornik statei*, Moscow, 1923; *Literaturnye zapiski*, Moscow, 1926; *Literaturnye tipi*, Moscow, 1927; *Iskusstvo videt' mir*, Moscow, 1927.

4. Raissa Messer, "Estetika Bergsona i shkola Voronskogo," *Literatura i iskusstvo*, No. 1, January, 1930.

5. Ivan Katayev, *Izbrannoye; povesti i rasskazy, ocherki*, Moscow, 1957.

6. N. L. Brodskii, *Literaturnye manifesty ot simvolistov k oktiabryu*, Federatsiya, 1929, p. 272.

7. A. K. Voronskii, "Po povodu odnoi vstrechi," *Iskusstvo i zhizn*, p. 219.

8. Sborniki *Pereval*, Nos. 1–6, Moscow, 1922–28; *Rovesniki*, No. 7, Moscow, 1930; *Rovesniki*, No. 8, Moscow, 1932.

9. As quoted in G. Glinka, *op. cit.*, p. 26.

10. *Na literaturnom postu*, No. 9, May, 1930, p. 103.

11. *Literaturnaya gazeta*, May 19, 1930.

12. A part of this chapter was first published in *Survey*, April, 1961.

Chapter 9

1. The period of the first Five-Year Plan is treated in detail in E. J. Brown, *The Proletarian Episode in Russian Literature*, New York, 1953. For an excellent treatment of the theory and practice of literary control, see E. J. Simmons, "The Origins of Literary Control," *Survey*, April–June, 1961, pp. 78–85.

2. A. Afinogenov, *Dnevniki i zapisnye knizhki*, Moscow, 1960.

3. Three articles published in 1956 in the collection *Literary Moscow* (II) revealed much about the "system" of administration in literature: A. Kron, "Zametki pisatelya," M. Shcheglov, "Realizm sovremennoi dramy," and L. Chukovskaya, "Rabochii razgovor."

4. As quoted in Alexander Werth, *Musical Uproar in Moscow*, London, 1949.

Chapter 11

1. The period under discussion is treated in detail in George Gibian, *The Interval of Freedom*, Minneapolis, 1960. A selection of translated articles and literary works characteristic of the

period, introduced by an excellent brief survey, is in Hugh McLean and Walter Vickery, *The Year of Protest: 1956,* New York, 1961. This work must be credited with pointing out clearly that there were two distinct periods of "thawing out" after Stalin's death. The excerpt on "the Drozdovs" is quoted from this collection.

Chapter 12

1. *Literaturnaya gazeta,* February 21, 1956.

2. Four interesting articles on new trends in literature were published in *Survey,* April–June, 1961: Barbara Bode, "1960: The Literary Harvest"; Vera Alexandrova, "Voices of Youth"; George Gibian, "New Trends in the Novel"; and Tibor Meray, "Three, Seven, Ace."

TITLES OF JOURNALS AND MAGAZINES

English	Transliterated Russian
English	*Transliterated Russian*
Art of the Commune	Iskusstvo kommuny
The Banner	Znamya
Day of Poetry	Den' poezii
Foreign Literature	Inostrannaya literatura
Izvestia	Izvestia
Lef	Lef
Leningrad	Leningrad
Literary Gazette	Literaturnaya gazeta
Literary Moscow	Literaturnaya Moskva
Literature and Art	Literatura i iskusstvo
Moscow	Moskva
Neva	Neva
New Lef	Novy Lef
New World	Novy Mir
October	Oktiabr'
Pravda	Pravda
Red Virgin Soil	Krasnaya nov'
Soviet Music	Sovetskaya musika
Star	Zvezda
Theater	Teatr
Young Communist Truth	Komsomolskaya pravda
Young Guard	Molodaya gvardiya
Youth	Yunost'

SELECTED BIBLIOGRAPHY

Books on Soviet Literature

Aragon, Louis, *Littératures soviétiques*. Paris: Donoël, 1955.

Blake, Patricia, and Hayward, Max, eds., "Dissonant Voices in Soviet Literature," *Partisan Review*, Nos. 3–4, 1961.

———— eds., *Halfway to the Moon: New Writing from Russia*. New York: Holt, Rinehart & Winston, 1965.

Borland, Harriet, *Soviet Literary Theory and Practice during the First Five-Year Plan, 1928–1932*. New York: King's Crown Press, 1950. (Bibliography.)

Brown, Edward J., *The Proletarian Episode in Russian Literature, 1928–1932*. New York: Columbia University Press, 1953. (Bibliography.)

Crowley, Edward L., and Hayward, Max, eds., *Soviet Literature in the 1960's*. New York: Praeger, 1964.

Eastman, Max, *Artists in Uniform; a Study of Literature and Bureaucratism*. New York: Alfred A. Knopf, 1934.

Eng-Liedmeier, A., *Soviet Literary Characters; an Investigation into the Portrayal of Soviet Men in Russian Prose, 1917–1953*. The Hague: Mouton, 1959.

Erlich, Victor, *Russian Formalism; History—Doctrine*. The Hague: Mouton, 1955. (Bibliography.)

Forgues, Pierre, *Ecrivains soviétiques d'aujourd'hui*. (Les lettres nouvelles, No. 25.) Paris: Juillard, 1962.

Friedberg, Maurice, *Russian Classics in Soviet Jackets*. New York: Columbia University Press, 1962.

Gibian, George, *Interval of Freedom; Soviet Literature during the Thaw, 1954–1957*. Minneapolis: University of Minnesota Press, 1960. (Bibliography.)

Goriely, Benjamin, *Science des lettres soviétiques*. Paris: Editions des Portes de France, 1947.

Harper, Kenneth Eugene, *Controversy in Soviet Literary Criticism on the Doctrine of Socialist Realism*. Ann Arbor: University Microfilms, 1950, i.e., 1951. (Bibliography.)

Hayward, Max, ed. and trans., *On Trial: The Soviet State vs. "Abram Tertz" and "Nikolai Arzhak."* New York: Harper & Row, 1966.

Ielita-Wilczkowski, Cyril, *Ecrivains soviétiques*. Paris: Revue des Jeunes, 1949. (Initiations.)

Kaun, Alexander, *Soviet Poets and Poetry*. Berkeley: University of California Press, 1943.

Lettenbauer, W., *Russische Literaturgeschichte,* 2nd ed. Wiesbaden: Otto Harrassowitz, 1958.

Lo Gatto, Ettore, *Storia della letteratura russa contemporanea.* Milano: Nuova Accademia, 1958. (Bibliography.)

Lukacz, György, *Der russische Realismus in der Weltliteratur.* Berlin: Aufbau-Verlag, 1949.

Maguire, Robert A., *Red Virgin Soil: Soviet Literature in the 1920's.* Princeton, N.J.: Princeton University Press, 1968.

Mathewson, Rufus W., *The Positive Hero in Russian Literature.* New York: Columbia University Press, 1958. (Bibliography.)

McLean, Hugh, and Vickery, W. N., eds. & trs., *The Year of Protest: 1956.* New York: Random House, 1961.

Mirsky, D. S., *Contemporary Russian Literature, 1881–1925.* New York: A. A. Knopf, 1926.

Muchnic, Helen, *From Gorky to Pasternak.* New York: Random House, 1961.

Perus, Jean, *Introduction à la littérature soviétique.* Paris: Editions Sociales, 1949.

Poggioli, Renato, *The Phoenix and the Spider.* Cambridge: Harvard University Press, 1957.

———— *The Poets of Russia, 1890–1930.* Cambridge: Harvard University Press, 1960. (Bibliography.)

Pozner, Vladimir, *Panorama de la littérature russe contemporaine.* Paris: Kra, 1929.

Reavey, George, *Soviet Literature Today.* New Haven: Yale University Press, 1947.

Rühle, Jurgen, *Literatur und Revolution.* Köln, 1960. (Bibliography.)

Simmons, Ernest J., ed., *Continuity and Change in Russian and Soviet Thought.* Cambridge: Harvard University Press, 1955.

———— *Russian Fiction and Soviet Ideology: Introduction to Fedin, Leonov, and Sholokhov.* New York: Columbia University Press, 1958.

———— ed., *Through the Glass of Soviet Literature; Views of Russian Society.* New York: Columbia University Press, 1953.

Slonim, Marc L., *Modern Russian Literature from Chekhov to the Present.* New York: Oxford University Press, 1953. (Bibliography.)

Stahlberger, Lawrence L., *The Symbolic System of Mayakovsky.* The Hague: Mouton, 1964.

Struve, Gleb, *Soviet Russian Literature, 1917–50.* Norman, Oklahoma: University of Oklahoma Press, 1951. (Extensive bibliography.)

———— *Geschichte der Sowjetliteratur.* Munchen: Isarverlag, 1957.

Swayze, Harold, *Political Control of Literature in the USSR, 1946–1959.* Cambridge: Harvard University Press, 1962.

Tertz, Abram, *On Socialist Realism.* New York: Pantheon, 1960.

Trotsky, Leon, *Literature and Revolution.* New York: Russell & Russell, 1957.

Vickery, Walter N., *The Cult of Optimism.* Bloomington, Indiana: Indiana University Press, 1963.

Whitney, Thomas P., ed. and trans., *The New Writing in Russia.* Ann Arbor: University of Michigan Press, 1964.

Yarmolinsky, Avrahm, *Literature under Communism.* Bloomington, Indiana: Indiana University Russian and East European Institute, 1960.

Zavalishin, Viacheslav, *Early Soviet Writers.* New York: Praeger, 1958.

Translations into English of Authors Discussed in the Text

Babel, Isaac E., *Benya Krik, the Gangster, and Other Stories,* ed. by Avrahm Yarmolinsky. New York: Schocken, 1948. (Schocken Library, No. 15.)

—— *Collected Stories,* ed. and trans. by Walter Morison; Introd. by Lionel Trilling. New York: Criterion, 1955.

—— *The Lonely Years, 1925–1939: Unpublished Stories and Private Correspondence,* ed. by Natasha Babel. New York: Farrar, Straus & Giroux, 1964.

—— *Sunset.* New York: Noonday, 1961.

Bulgakov, Mikhail, *Black Snow,* trans. by Michael Glenny. New York: Simon and Schuster, 1967.

—— *The Heart of a Dog,* trans. by Michael Glenny. New York: Harcourt, Brace & World, 1968.

—— *The Master and Margarita,* trans. by Michael Glenny. New York: Harper & Row, 1967.

Chukovskaya, Lidiya, *The Deserted House.* New York: Dutton, 1968.

Dudintsev, Vladimir, *A New Year's Tale,* trans. by Gabriella Azrael. New York: Dutton, 1960.

—— —— Trans. by Max Hayward. London: Hutchinson, 1960.

—— *Not by Bread Alone,* trans. by Edith Bone. New York: Dutton, 1957.

Ehrenburg, Ilya G., *A Change of Season* (*The Thaw* and its sequel, *The Spring*), trans. by Manya Harari and Humphrey Higgins. New York: Knopf, 1962.

—— *Julio Jurenito,* trans. by Anna Bostock and Yvonne Kapp. London: MacGibbon, 1958.

—— *Ninth Wave,* ed. by Yvonne Kapp; trans. by Tatiana Shebunina and Joseph Castle. London: Lawrence, 1955.

—— *Out of Chaos* (*The Second Day*), trans. by Alexander Bakshy. New York: Holt, 1934.

―――― *People and Life: Memoirs of 1891–1917*, trans. by Anna Bostock and Yvonne Kapp. London: MacGibbon, 1961.

―――― *Storm*, trans. by J. Fineberg; ed. by Isador Schneider and Anne Terry White. New York: Gaer, 1949.

―――― *Stormy Life of Lasik Roitschwantz*, trans. by Leonid Borochowicz and Gertrude Flor. New York: Polyglot, 1960.

―――― *The Thaw*, trans. by Manya Harari. London: MacGibbon, 1961.

Fadeyev, Aleksandr A., *Leningrad in the Days of the Blockade*, trans. by R. D. Charques. London: Hutchinson, 1946.

―――― *The Nineteen*, trans. by R. D. Charques. New York: International Publishers, 1929.

―――― *Young Guard*, trans. by Violet Dutt; ed. by D. Skvirsky. London: Universal Distributors, 1959.

Fedin, Konstantin A., *Early Joys*, trans. by Hilda Kazanina; Introd. by Ernest J. Simmons. New York: Random House (Vintage), 1960.

―――― *No Ordinary Summer*, 2 vols., trans. by Margaret Wettlin. Moscow: Foreign Language Publishing House, 1950.

Furmanov, Dmitry A., *Chapayev*, trans. by George Kittell and J. Kittell. Moscow: Foreign Language Publishing House, 1959.

Gladkov, Fyodor V., *Cement*, trans. by A. S. Arthur and C. Ashleigh. New York: International Publishers, 1929; New York: Ungar (paperback), 1960.

Ilf, Ilya A., and Petrov, Evgeny, *Diamonds to Sit On: A Russian Comedy of Errors*, trans. by Elizabeth Hill and Doris Mudie. New York: Harper, 1930.

―――― *Little Golden America*, trans. by Charles Malamuth; illus. by Georg Hartmann. New York: Farrar, 1937.

―――― *Little Golden Calf*, trans. by Charles Malamuth; Introd. by Anatole Lunacharsky. New York: Farrar, 1932; New York: Ungar (paperback), 1961.

―――― *The Twelve Chairs*, trans. by John H. C. Richardson; Introd. by Maurice Friedberg. New York: Random House (Vintage), 1961.

Ivanov, Vsevolod V., *Adventures of a Fakir*, abridged trans. New York: Vanguard, 1935.

―――― *Armoured Train 14–69*, trans. by Gibson-Cowan and A. T. K. Grant. New York: International Publishers, 1933.

Kassil, Lev Abramovich, *Land of Shvambrania*, trans. by Sylvia Glass and Norbert Guterman. New York: Viking, 1935.

―――― *Story of Alesha Ryazan and Uncle White Sea* (story for children), illus. by Fred Ellis. Moscow: Cooperative Publishing Society, 1950.

Katayev, Valentin P., *The Embezzlers*, trans. by L. Zarine; Introd. by Stephen Graham. New York: Dial Press, 1929.

―――― *The Holy Well*, trans. by Max Hayward and Harold Shukman. New York: Walker, 1967.

—— *Peace Is Where the Tempests Blow,* trans. by Charles Malamuth. New York: Farrar, 1937.

—— *Small Farm in the Steppe,* trans. by Anna Bostock. London: Lawrence, 1958.

—— *Squaring the Circle,* trans. and adap. by Charles Malamuth and Eugene Lyons. New York: French, 1936.

—— *Time, Forward!,* trans. by Charles Malamuth. New York: Farrar, 1933.

Kaverin, Venyamin A., *The Larger View,* trans. by E. Leda Swan. London: Stackpole Sons, 1938.

—— *An Open Book,* trans. by Brian Pearce. London: Lawrence, 1955.

—— *Two Captains,* trans. by Brian Pearce. London: Lawrence, 1957.

—— —— Trans. by E. Leda Swan. New York: Modern Age, 1942.

—— *Unknown Artist* (with Y. K. Olesha, *Envy*), trans. by P. Ross. London: Westhouse, 1947.

Kirshon, Vladimir M., and Uspensky, A. V., *Red Rust,* adap. by Virginia and Frank Vernon. (Theatre Guild Plays.) New York: Brentano's, 1930.

Krymov, Yury S., *Tanker Derbent,* trans. by B. Kagan. Kuibyshev: Mezhdunarodnaya Kniga, 1940.

Leonov, Leonid M., *The Badgers,* trans. by Hilda Kazanina. London: Hutchinson, 1946.

—— *Chariot of Wrath,* trans. by Norbert Guterman. New York: Fischer, 1946.

—— *Road to the Ocean,* trans. by Norbert Guterman. New York: Fischer, 1944.

—— *Skutarevsky,* trans. by Alec Brown. New York: Harcourt, 1936.

—— *Soviet River,* trans. by Ivor Montagu and Sergey Nolbandov; Foreword by Maxim Gorky. New York: Dial Press, 1932.

—— *The Thief,* trans. by Hubert Butler. New York: Dial Press, 1931.

—— —— Introd. by Rufus W. Mathewson, Jr. New York: Random House (Vintage), 1960.

Libedinsky, Yury, *A Week.* New York: Huebsch, 1923.

Lunts, Lev N., *City of Truth,* trans. by John Silver. London: O'Dempsey, 1929.

Mayakovsky, Vladimir V., *The Bedbug and Selected Poetry,* ed. by Patricia Blake; trans. by Max Hayward and George Reavey. New York: Meridian Books, 1960.

—— *Mayakovsky and His Poetry,* 3d ed., comp. & trans. by Herbert Marshall. Bombay: Current Book House, 1955.

Makarenko, Anton S., *Road to Life,* 3 vols., trans. by Iva and Tatiana Litvinov. London: Collet, 1952.

Nagibin, Yury, *Each for All.* London: Hutchinson, 1945.

Nekrasov, Victor, *Kira Georgievna,* trans. by Walter Vickery. New York: Pantheon, 1962.

Neverov, Alexander (pseud.), *City of Bread (Tashkent),* trans. by Reginald Merton and W. G. Walton; illus. by Theodore Nadejen. New York: Doubleday, 1927.

Nilin, Pavel F., *Comrade Venka,* trans. by Joseph Barnes. New York: Simon & Schuster, 1959.

Olesha, Yury K., *Envy* (with V. Kaverin, *The Unknown Artist*), trans. by P. Ross; Introd. by Gleb Struve. London: Westhouse, 1947.

———— *The Wayward Comrade and the Commissars (Envy,* etc.*),* trans. by Andrew R. MacAndrew. New York: Signet, 1960.

Ostrovsky, Nikolai A., *Born of the Storm,* trans. by Louise Luke Hiler. New York: Critics Group, 1939.

———— *The Making of a Hero,* trans. by Alec Brown. New York: Dutton, 1937.

Panfyorov, Fyodor I., *And Then the Harvest,* trans. by Stephen Garry. Toronto: McClelland, 1939.

Panova, Vera F., *Factory,* trans. by Marie Budberg. Toronto: McClelland, 1950.

———— *Span of the Year (Four Seasons),* trans. by Vera Traill. London: Harvill, 1957.

———— *The Train,* trans. by Marie Budberg. New York: Knopf, 1949.

———— *Time Walked (A Summer to Remember).* Cambridge, Mass.: Arlington Books, 1959.

Pasternak, Boris, *The Adolescence of Zhenya Luvers,* trans. by I. Langnas. New York: Citadel, 1961.

———— *Collected Prose Works,* Introd. by Stefan Schimanski. London: Drummond, 1945.

———— *Doctor Zhivago,* trans. by Max Hayward and Manya Harari. New York: Pantheon, 1958.

———— *Essay in Autobiography,* trans. by Manya Harari; Introd. by Edward Crankshaw. Toronto: Collins, 1959.

———— *I Remember: Sketch for an Autobiography,* trans. by David Magarshack. "Essay on Translating Shakespeare," trans. by Manya Harari. New York: Pantheon, 1959; New York: Meridian Books, 1960.

———— *Last Summer,* trans. by George Reavey. Toronto: Copp, 1959.

———— *Poems, 1955–1959 (Kogda razgulyaetsa).* Parallel Russian and English texts; English trans. by Michael Harari. Ontario: Collins, 1960.

————— *Poetry 1917–1959,* ed. and trans. by George Reavey. New York: Putnam, 1959.

————— *Prose and Poems,* ed. by Stefan Schimanski; Introd. by J. M. Cohen. London: Benn, 1959.

————— *Safe Conduct.* New York: Signet, 1959.

————— *Safe Conduct; an Autobiography, and Other Writings.* New York: New Directions, 1958. (Reprint of *Selected Writings.*)

————— *Safe Conduct; an Early Autobiography and Other Works,* trans. by Alec Brown and Lydia Pasternak-Slater. London: Elek, 1959.

————— *Selected Poems,* trans. by J. M. Cohen. Toronto: McClelland, 1958.

————— *Selected Writings (Safe Conduct,* trans. by Beatrice Scott, and other selections). New York: New Directions, 1958.

Paustovsky, Konstantin G., *Black Gulf,* trans. by Evgenia Schemanskaya. London: Hutchinson, 1946.

————— *The Golden Rose,* trans. by Suzanna Rosenberg; ed. by Denis Ogden. Moscow: Foreign Languages Publishing House, 1961.

Pilnyak, Boris (pseud.), *Ivan Moscow,* trans. by A. Schwartzman. New York: Christopher, 1935.

————— *The Naked Year,* trans. by Alec Brown. New York: Brewer, 1928.

————— *Tales of the Wilderness,* trans. by F. O'Dempsey; Introd. by Prince D. S. Mirsky. New York: Knopf, 1925.

————— *The Volga Falls to the Caspian Sea,* trans. by Charles Malamuth. New York: Farrar, 1931.

Polevoy, Boris N., *Story about a Real Man.* Moscow: Peoples Publishing House, n.d.

————— *To the Last Breath.* London: Hutchinson, 1945.

Prishvin, Mikhail M., *Jen Shing, the Root of Life,* trans. by George Walton and Philip Gibbons; Foreword by Julian S. Huxley. New York: Putnam, 1936.

————— *The Lake and the Woods; or Nature's Calendar,* trans. by W. L. Goodman; illus. by Brian Hope-Tayler. New York: Pantheon, 1952.

————— *Shiptimber Grove,* trans. by David Fry. London: Lawrence, 1957.

————— *Treasure Trove of the Sun,* trans. by Tatiana Balkoff-Drowne; illus. by Feodor Rojankovsky. New York: Viking, 1952.

Romanov, Pantaleimon S., *Three Pairs of Silk Stockings (Comrade Kislyakov),* trans. by Leonide Zarine; ed. by Stephen Graham. New York: Scribner, 1931.

————— *Without Cherry Blossom,* trans. by L. Zarine; ed. by Stephen Graham. New York: Scribner, 1932.

Serafimovich, A. S. (pseud.), *The Iron Flood.* New York: International Publishers, 1935.

Sholokhov, Mikhail A., *And Quiet Flows the Don,* with *The Don Flows Home to the Sea, Parts I and II (The Silent Don),* trans. by Stephen Garry. New York: Knopf, 1941.

——— *Harvest on the Don* (Vol. II of *Virgin Soil Upturned*), trans. by H. C. Stevens. New York: Knopf, 1960.

——— *Seeds of Tomorrow* (Vol. I of *Virgin Soil Upturned*), trans. by Stephen Garry. New York: Knopf, 1935.

——— *Tales of the Don,* trans. by H. C. Stevens. New York: Knopf, 1962.

Solzhenitsyn, Alexander, *The Cancer Ward,* trans. by Rebecca Frank. New York: The Dial Press, 1968.

——— *The First Circle,* trans. by Thomas P. Whitney. New York: Harper & Row, 1968.

——— *One Day in the Life of Ivan Denisovich,* trans. by Max Hayward and Ronald Hingley. New York: Praeger, 1963.

Tarasov-Rodionov, Aleksandr I., *Chocolate,* trans. by Charles Malamuth. New York: Doubleday, 1932.

——— *February, 1917,* trans. by William A. Drake. New York: Covici, 1931.

Tertz, Abram (Andrey Sinyavsky), *Fantastic Stories.* New York: Pantheon, 1963.

——— *The Makepeace Experiment,* trans. by Manya Harari. New York: Pantheon, 1965.

Tolstoy, Aleksey N., *Bread,* trans. by Stephen Garry. New York: Ryerson Press, 1938.

——— *Darkness and Dawn,* trans. by Edith Bone and Emile Burns. New York: Longmans, 1936.

——— *Death Box,* trans. by B. G. Guerney. London: Methuen, 1937.

——— *The Garin Death Ray,* trans. by Yevgeny Rakuzin. Moscow: Foreign Languages Publishing House, 1961.

——— *Nikita's Childhood,* trans. by Violet Lansbury Dutt. London: Hutchinson, 1945.

——— *Peter the Great,* trans. by Edith Bone and Emile Burns. New York: Ryerson Press, 1936.

——— *Peter the First,* trans. by Tatiana Shebunia. New York: Macmillan, 1959.

——— *The Road to Calvary,* trans. by Edith Bone. New York: Knopf, 1946.

Tretyakov, Sergey M., *Chinese Testament; an Autobiography as Told to S. Tretiakov.* New York: Simon and Schuster, 1934.

——— *Roar China!,* trans. by F. Polianovska and Barbara Nixon. New York: International Publishers, 1932.

Voronsky, Aleksandr K., *Waters of Life and Death,* trans. by L. Zarine. London: G. Allen, 1936.

Voznesensky, Andrey, *Antiworlds and the "Fifth Ace."* New York: Doubleday (Anchor Books), 1967.

Zamyatin, Evgeny I., *We,* trans. by Gregory Zilboorg. New York: Dutton, 1924; Everyman paperback, 1959.

Zoshchenko, Mikhail M., *Russia Laughs,* trans. by Helena Clayton; Foreword by Whit Burnett. Toronto: Longmans, 1935.

―――― *The Woman Who Could Not Read, and Other Tales,* trans. by Elizaveta Fen. London: Methuen, 1940.

―――― *Wonderful Dog, and Other Tales,* trans. by Elizaveta Fen. London: Methuen, 1942.

―――― *Scenes from the Bathhouse, and Other Stories of Communist Russia,* trans. with Introd. by Sidney Monas. Ann Arbor: University of Michigan Press, 1961.

Index

Litvinov, Maxim, 300
Litvinov, Pavel, 300, 301
Lolita (Nabokov), 340–41
Lomonosov, Mikhail, 106
Lowell, Robert, 321
Luminists, 29
Lunacharsky, Anatol V., 23, 55, 137, 157, 199, 336
Lunts, Lev, 98, 99, 102, 124, 135
Luzhniki Sports Stadium, 318
Lyashchenko, N. N. (N. Lyashko), 140, 189–90
Lyrical Stories (Soloukhin), 329
Lysenko, Trofim, 329
Lyubimov, see Makepeace Experiment, The

Machines and Wolves (Pilnyak), 109
Mad Haberdasher, The (Surov), 229
Mahogany (Pilnyak), 110–11, 113
Makarenko, Anton, 31
Makepeace Experiment, The (Sinyavsky), 308, 309
Making of a Hero, The (N. Ostrovsky), 31
Malevich, 294
Malinovsky, *see* Bogdanov
Malyshkin, A. G., 162
"Man from MINAP, The" (Daniel), 310–11
Mandelshtam, Osip, 294, 312, 313
Markov, Georgy, 295
Martynov, Leonid, 324
Marx, Karl, 40, 103, 172, 200, 235, 311
MAPP (Moscow Proletarian Association), 97
Master and Margarita, The (Bulgakov), 315–17
Matveeva, Novella, 323
Mayakovsky, Vladimir, 28, 37–42, 60, 69, 73, 97, 133, 233, 263, 320, 321, 332, 335, 336
Meet Baluev! (Kozhnevnikov), 333
Mekhlis, L., 30
Memory (Slutsky), 323
Myerhold, V. E., 294, 335

Mirsky, Prince Dmitry, 220, 269
Mitrofanov, A., 191, 209
Mochulsky, Konstantin, 342
Mosaic (Voznesensky), 320
Moscow, 278, 313, 315
Moscow Art Theatre, 314
Mozhaev, B., 333
My Brother My Enemy (Wilson), 261
Mystery Bouffe (Mayakovsky), 52–54, 55, 56, 59
"My Uncle Had the Highest Principles" (Iskander), 328

Nabokov, Vladimir, 339, 340–41
Nagibin, Yury, 286–88
Naked Year, The (Pilnyak), 104, 105–109, 111, 114
Natalya Tarpova (Semyonov), 27, 191
Neizvestny, Ernest, 294
Nekrasov, Victor, 52, 65, 163, 283
Neva, 278
Neverov, Alexander, 190
New Lef, 57–61, 153, 194
New Review, The, 307
New World, 109, 110, 130, 131, 241, 249, 256–57, 258, 259, 264, 272, 278, 282, 283, 284, 287, 290, 291, 294, 295, 304, 314, 323, 326, 327, 332
"New Year's Tale, A" (Dudintsev), 284
"New York Airport at Night" (Voznesensky), 321
New York Times, The, 300
Nihilists, 29
Nikitin, Nikolai N., 99, 101
Nikonov, 293
Nilin, Pavel, 267
Nineteen, The (Fadeyev), 26–27, 163, 172–76, 178
1984 (Orwell), 24, 75, 76–77, 79
NKVD, 314
Nobel Prize, 296
Not by Bread Alone (Dudintsev), 34–35, 259, 261–64, 267, 268, 273, 277, 284, 292
Novichenko, Leonid, 295